Religious Authority in
the Spanish Renaissance

The Johns Hopkins University Studies in
Historical and Political Science

118TH SERIES (2000)

I.

Religious Authority in the Spanish Renaissance
Lu Ann Homza

Religious Authority in the Spanish Renaissance

◆ ◆ ◆ ◆

LU ANN HOMZA

The Johns Hopkins University Press

BALTIMORE AND LONDON

This book has been brought to publication with the
generous assistance of the Program for Cultural Cooperation
between Spain's Ministry of Education and Culture and
United States' Universities.

The Johns Hopkins University Press
2715 North Charles Street
Baltimore, Maryland 21218-4363
www.press.jhu.edu

Library of Congress Cataloging-in-Publication Data will be found
at the end of this book.
A catalog record for this book is available from the British Library.

ISBN 0-8018-6243-4

To Thomas B. Payne

Contents

Acknowledgments

Every publication, like every picture, tells a story about its author as well as its subject, and although the creative process is hidden from the public at large, my family, friends, and colleagues know what this project has required of me. I salute them here for their appraisals and sustenance, whether past or present. At the University of Chicago, the late Eric Cochrane fostered my interest in Renaissance humanism and early modern Catholicism, and refined my prose: his memory endures for those of us who were fortunate enough to study under him. My other mentor, Julius Kirshner, instructed me in the nuances of primary sources as a graduate student, and several years later stopped this book from going in the wrong direction at an early stage: his evaluations of my work always have been a blessing. Thomas Mayer and Sara T. Nalle have extended support, sources, and keen critiques for almost a decade. Diana Robin assessed the opening and closing material, Alison Weber read an early version of the Introduction, and James Amelang commented on Chapter 6; all three helped me improve my arguments. Bethany Aram, Benjamin Ehlers, and Elizabeth Wright offered enthusiasm just when I needed it. Richard L. Kagan brought the project to the attention of the Johns Hopkins University Press; he knows how grateful I am for his intercession. I am indebted as well to Carlos Eire, who read the manuscript for the Press; the result owes much to his astute suggestions.

At the College of William and Mary, colleagues in the History Department—especially Dale Hoak, Leisa Meyer, and Carol Sheriff—applied their sharp eyes to drafts of chapters and prospectuses for publishers. In the English Department, Monica Potkay shared her expertise on literacy and Catholicism in late medieval England, while George Greenia in Modern Languages vetted my translation of one particularly salacious expression from Juan de Vergara's trial. One of our department's excellent graduate students, Lauri Bauer Coleman, deftly proofread the first half of the book; a highly gifted history concentrator, Will Hulcher, found infelicities that I did not see.

In Spain, staff at the Archivo Histórico Nacional and the Biblioteca Nacional eased the filming of manuscripts and printed books; archivists at El Escorial, the University Library in Salamanca, and the Cathedral in Segovia helped me locate crucial materials. Without the help of such experts, this study never would have appeared. Since 1985 Fernando García and Remedios Almagro Pérez have offered me a home at the Hostal Residencia Jamyc in the Plaza de las Cortes, and have made landing in Madrid a joy. Finally, I deeply appreciate the expertise of my copyeditor, Maria E. denBoer, and the assistance of Executive Editor Henry Tom at the Johns Hopkins University Press in guiding this book to publication.

I thank Lisa Esposito for her esprit de corps. I thank my parents, Daniel and Marjorie Homza, and my brother, Christopher Daniel Homza, for their unwavering love, conviction, and sense of humor. I dedicate the book to Tom Payne, who has lived with Ciruelo, Vergara, and the rest of these ecclesiastics for a long time, and who remains the human authority I cherish most.

Note on Translations

Unless stated otherwise, the translations are my own. I have resolved abbreviations, added diacritics, and allotted punctuation in the interest of clarity. I have left the primary sources in their original spelling and syntax, except when extreme ambiguity could ensue. All biblical quotations are taken from the *Biblia sacra iuxta vulgatam versionem,* ed. Robert Weber, 2nd ed., 2 vols. (Stuttgart: Württembergische Bibelanstalt, 1969).

Introduction

etween 1520 and 1521, the Spanish towns of Castile revolted against the financial demands of Charles V, their king and the new Holy Roman Emperor. That rebellion provoked Bernardino Flores, the parish priest of Pinto, into giving a sermon in the city of Toledo. In his homily, Flores exhorted his audience to storm a local castle that had sided with royal forces; to that end, he quoted a New Testament verse, Matthew 21:2, which purportedly said, "Go into the castle that is against you" ("Ite in castellum quod contra vos est").[1] There was nothing odd about Flores's reliance on the Bible, since clerics in the sixteenth century routinely plucked moral lessons from Scripture.[2] Nor did Flores's reading seem to violate the New Testament's language, since the Latin noun *castellum* looked like the Spanish one for castle—*castillo*—and the preposition *contra* could have identical meanings in both idioms. All the same, sixteenth-century castles did not exist in the Roman Empire, early Christians did not assault imperial fortifications, and translating by cognates could lead to spurious results. For Flores employed Matthew 21:2 in a creative but false way: the verse literally quoted what Jesus said to his disciples before he rode into Jerusalem. Consequently, *castellum* signified "village," *contra* meant "across," and the line read "Go into the village which is opposite you," where the disciples would find an ass for Jesus' transportation.[3]

Flores's sermon passed into the historical record after he had quarreled with a much more famous contemporary, Juan de Vergara, and testified before the Spanish Inquisition about the altercation. Flores then was maligned by Vergara himself after the latter was arrested by inquisitors in Toledo.[4] And because Vergara read Greek, served as secretary to three archbishops of

Toledo, and acted as a prominent correspondent of Desiderius Erasmus, his confrontation with Flores tells us something about the Spanish Renaissance—although not, perhaps, what we expected to hear.

When Flores was deposed before the Inquisition in 1530, he recounted a conflict over the proper languages, translations, and interpreters of the Bible. His interchange with Vergara had escalated into an argument. Flores recalled that he had personally spurned recent renditions of the Hebrew and Greek Bible into Latin: he preferred the conventional translation, the Vulgate, which was accepted as the work of St. Jerome. He had told Vergara that new versions of the Bible threatened Christianity, since they encouraged the emendation of the Vulgate through different readings found in different languages. When Vergara had retorted that faulty Greek made St. Augustine's writings less reliable, Flores had fiercely objected:

This witness, being in this town of Madrid in the residence of the Lord Archbishop of Toledo, and in his presence having a conversation about these translations of sacred Scripture that have been made recently from Hebrew and Greek into Latin, this witness said he held the one that the holy mother Church uses now as much better and more certain than any other translation that might be newly brought out; because it is like opening a door, so that holding something as uncertain about the translation that we use, each person may judge that substantial matters of sacred Scripture are not translated well. . . . And being present there, doctor Vergara . . . said that saint Augustine, on account of not knowing Greek, didn't know what he was saying in the exposition that he made on the Psalms of David, in the book called the *Quinquagenas* [the *Enarrationes in Psalmos*]; and this witness said that assertion seemed very wicked and very disrespectful, on account of that being a book by someone whom the whole universal Church holds in very great esteem.[5]

Flores then declared that Augustine had written under the influence of the Holy Spirit; Vergara replied that Flores did not know what the Holy Spirit was, and the archbishop told them both to shut up.[6] The Inquisition found their dispute of great interest. By the time its prosecutor presented his formal indictment, he charged Vergara with favoring the Greek over the Latin version of Scripture, impugning things approved by the Church, and audaciously criticizing the saints, among other accusations.

Inquisitors never revealed the identity of witnesses, but they transcribed their testimony for defendants. Vergara recognized Flores as one of the deponents against him; in his defense, he presented himself as the opposite of his accuser. He proclaimed his own skills as a theologian and a textual critic. He contended that St. Jerome himself based his biblical scholarship on Greek and Hebrew.[7] He declared that anyone who knew anything realized that scribes commonly erred in the translation and transmission of Scripture because they were ignorant about its languages. And Vergara raised Flores's behavior during the earlier revolt, cited the sermon on storming the castle, and warned that anyone who could use scriptural words so falsely could produce a fraudulent deposition.[8]

Vergara's and Flores's statements seem to make them polar opposites: we could read their encounter as a skirmish between the critical, classicizing impulses we think we find in Renaissance humanism, and the agglomerative, universalizing preferences we label scholasticism.[9] Certainly Vergara's intellectual credentials verify his status as a Renaissance humanist, according to the most astute construction of that term. In the nineteenth century, Jacob Burckhardt contended that the importance of the Renaissance lay in its secular ethos and embryonic modernism; in the twentieth, leading historians tie the meaning of the Renaissance to a movement called humanism, which involved the recovery and application of ancient literature. In current scholarship, Renaissance humanism signals the deliberate employment and elevation, from the fourteenth through the sixteenth centuries, of what Cicero called the humanities—the grammar, rhetoric, poetry, history, and moral philosophy of classical Latin and Greek authors.[10] Renaissance humanists preferred these subjects and sources to the seven liberal arts—grammar, rhetoric, logic, arithmetic, geometry, astronomy, and music—which had constituted an elite education for generations. Humanists extolled the same disciplines as their classical predecessors. They borrowed their ancient structures and much ancient content. In their desire to emulate antiquity, Renaissance humanists discovered and preserved more of it to employ.

Still, if scholars at the end of the twentieth century explain the Renaissance as humanism, and then define humanism as the invocation of classical culture, they differ on what Renaissance humanism finally implies, for its importance can vary. Some historians simply describe it as a more fulsome revival of the *studia humanitatis* than what the ninth or twelfth centuries had offered. They limit the value of Renaissance humanists to the discovery and transmission of classical sources; thus these historical figures matter because they rescued the works of Greek and Latin antiquity. And yet the impact of their ancient materials could be limited. Greek and Latin texts may have prompted Renaissance humanists to duplicate certain literary forms and absorb some values, but few followed classical models and systematically tackled philosophy: instead, celebrated individuals such as Francesco Petrarca and Poggio Bracciolini circulated letters and collected marble busts, but never expressed a consistent point of view.[11] This reading of the Renaissance credits it with having preserved the literary canon of Greece and Rome but hesitates to grant substantial intellectual weight to most of the humanists themselves.

A more dramatic interpretation finds that the Renaissance differed in quality as well as quantity from earlier "rebirths" of Latin and Greek antiquity. In this scholarly version, a conceptual shift accompanied the humanists' resurrection of the ancient: they began to regard the historical setting of their materials, worry about the accuracy of manuscripts, and quote classical counsel with a discriminating eye.[12] Renaissance humanists consequently engaged in more than the preservation of literature or slavish aping. They noticed distinctions between themselves and their sources; they recognized how manuscripts could differ. They perceived what Petrarca called the "gap of time," and gauged what classical elements they could emulate appropriately. For example, Petrarca discovered Cicero's letters to Atticus in the Verona cathedral in 1345, whereupon he decided to edit and circulate his own; but the same find also prompted him to face Cicero's political career and the contrast between his ethics and his model's. Leonardo Bruni, chancellor of Florence between 1427 and 1444, translated Aristotle's *Politics*. Robert Grosseteste did the same in the thirteenth century, but Bruni could spot his predecessor's errors because he handled the Aristotelian text within a larger framework of Greek history.[13] Renaissance humanism thus entailed ways of reading classical works as well as a preference for them. And Renaissance humanists' historical outlook gave their endeavors philosophical implications, though they seldom practiced formal philosophical inquiry.[14]

The most profound vision of the Renaissance focuses on historical distance, textual criticism, and shrewd imitation vis-à-vis ancient culture. Given such criteria, Flores would not be included in the humanist camp.[15] He did not regard Matthew 21:2 as part of a larger document recorded by a specific person; he ignored the language that surrounded that particular line. Instead Flores viewed sacred literature with an ahistorical but analogical eye, which allowed him to equate the Spanish *castillo* with the Latin *castellum*; he worked from his sermon's overarching point to the scriptural evidence that would support it, and not the other way around. Flores refused to consider potential discrepancies between the various renditions of the Bible: he revered the Latin Vulgate because it was customary, not because it was textually superior to the original idioms and manuscripts of Scripture. The same tendency to treat the established as the eternal and exalt the celestial over the natural governed his idea of sanctity.[16] Flores relied upon Jerome's and Augustine's current position as Catholic saints rather than their initial one as inhabitants of the late Roman Empire: he depicted them as if they had existed in a state of eternal canonization. He also viewed early Christian writings as emanations of the Holy Spirit rather than as products of earthly individuals. Ultimately he ranked the universal Church, which he read as the current institution, over its appearance in history. He interpreted Christianity in terms of permanence rather than process.

Vergara, on the other hand, looks like a humanist. He scorned Flores's reading of "Ite in castellum quod contra vos est." He entertained comparisons between the Latin Vulgate and its Hebrew and Greek counterparts, even if the latter contradicted St. Jerome. He understood that copyists of sacred literature could err and that saints were human before they were holy; as a result, St. Augustine could botch his Greek despite his status as a Father of the Church. Vergara's historical consciousness was marked, his awareness of language sharp, and his critical faculties acute. He fits our notions of the Renaissance, while Flores does not.

Yet this interpretation is so tidy that it ought to provoke our suspicions, given the difficulties of the sources and the fickleness of intellectual practice in the European past. To a certain degree the record of Vergara's and Flores's conflict is opaque, because inquisitorial procedure revolved around coercion and intermediaries.[17] Witnesses were often summoned to the Inquisition's courtrooms, and testimony was almost always prompted by direct questions. Evidence was filtered as the notaries wrote it down, and interlocutors, especially defendants, were placed under extraordinary pressure and could attempt to manipulate the situation. Vergara had everything to gain by exaggerating Flores's ineptitude; Flores's treatment of "Ite in castellum" may not have been typical of his preaching. Most important, even if Flores's homily and subsequent testimony exemplified his approach to the Bible, we cannot use his case to color scholasticism as a whole, for St. Augustine himself explicitly sanctioned the emendation of Scripture in his *De doctrina christiana,* and corrections to the biblical text occurred sporadically from the ninth century on.[18]

Renaissance humanists also ignored the very priorities we have ascribed to them. They could neglect chronology in pursuit of a larger point, advocate allegorical readings as well as historical ones, and rely on Latin translations when Greek originals ought to have governed their work. In *Praise of Folly,* Erasmus mocked theologians who disregarded language and context and turned the prophet Habakkuk's tents into St. Bartholemew's skin; but he also instructed his readers to follow Plato, pursue the essential, and contemplate the invisible.[19] In his 1516 edition of the New Testament, Erasmus derived the final Greek verses of the Book of Revelation from the Latin, instead of transcribing what his Greek manuscript actually contained.[20]

As for their awareness of historical distance, the humanists' very desire to imitate the ancients undermined their perception of anachronism, at least theoretically: after all, they drew models and lessons from sources that were removed in time, and less than relevant to their own situations.[21] We even can turn humanistic achievements upside down, for scholastic glosses, commentaries, and allegories may have "socialized" texts by fitting them to different needs and locales. Flores thus adapted source to community, while Vergara favored a "textual fundamentalism" that esteemed sources over inter-pretations. In this scheme, Renaissance humanists promoted nothing more than antiquarianism.[22]

Such scholarly misgivings have complicated our perception of what Re-naissance humanism was and why it counted. We must acknowledge medi-eval precedents to humanist criticism and recognize the erraticism of the humanists' methods. Nevertheless, many historians continue to see valid distinctions between scholasticism and humanism, and to discriminate be-tween the textual criticism of the twelfth century and what could take place in the fifteenth and sixteenth.[23] The challenge, then, is to recognize inconsis-tencies and forerunners within Renaissance humanism, but preserve the con-trasts with scholasticism that possess heuristic value. Once we admit that early modern individuals had a variety of literary sources and styles at their disposal, we can begin to measure their preference for scholastic or humanist elements, uphold their right to contradict themselves, and expound their emphases with all the nuances intact. This approach has significant advantages. It allows us to pursue continuity and change at the same time. It lessens the temptation to fit the evidence to the pattern instead of the reverse. It diminishes our tendency to create "mythologies of coherence," whereby we delete items that do not seem to fit our paradigms, or stamp the subjects we are studying as "impostors" when they contravene our categories. This angle gives us a more historical, rather than metaphysical, account of Renaissance humanism, one in which Petrarca's own admission of inconsistency, for instance, could play a conspicuous rather than trivial role.[24]

But when it comes to the Renaissance in Spain, assessments that depend upon history and philology are recent, and ones that highlight ambiguity are missing altogether.[25] The dominant portrait of the Spanish Renaissance is governed by religious and moral messages. In 1937, Marcel Bataillon en-dorsed what had become a traditional link between the Spanish Renaissance and spirituality when he identified Erasmus as the critical influence on Spain's intellectual and religious culture in the sixteenth century.[26] Although Erasmus refused to visit the Peninsula, Bataillon proposed that his counsel about Christianity swiftly infiltrated Castile: its transmission was purportedly facilitated by the return of Charles V and his court in 1522, promoted by printers and professors at the University of Alcalá, and finally animated by mass enthusiasm. The result was a religious revolution.

Still, not all Spaniards appreciated Erasmus's ideas. By the mid-1530s, the Inquisition's prosecutions and natural deaths had diminished the number of Erasmus's supporters; some twenty years later, indices of prohibited books, a ban on foreign study for university students, and the burning of suspected Protestants in Seville and Valladolid summarized the formal rejection of his influence.[27] For Bataillon, the story of Erasmus and Spain was a lost opportunity, and hence a pivotal moment in Spanish history: it was Spain's chance to absorb the religious toleration and spiritual interiority that Erasmus personified and that much of the European community embraced.[28] Affected by his observation of Spanish politics in the twentieth century, Bataillon plotted his narrative of the sixteenth along a dialectic of advancement and reaction, in which he identified the progressive forces as Erasmian and labeled them as humanist.[29] His vision was powerful and poignant, given what Spanish humanists signified and what their defeat might explain.

Even though Bataillon's diagram for early modern Spain was not unassailable, no other has proven as important for interpreting the intellectual and religious history of the Peninsula in the early modern epoch.[30] Its vocabulary has been absorbed by scholars in every language; learned and influential syntheses, especially in English, have presented it nearly unscathed. Historians have examined connections between Ignatius of Loyola and Erasmus, pondered the Erasmian heritage of Juan de Valdés, and provided Teresa de Jesús with a religious lineage that includes Erasmus via Juan de Avila.[31] Decades after its publication, *Érasme et l'Espagne* remains the "indispensable point of reference" for the study of the peninsular Renaissance.[32]

Of course, exploring the Renaissance through religion or positing Erasmus as a gauge of humanist practice is not inappropriate for Spain or any other country, because humanists exercised their criticism on sacred as well as classical sources.[33] Modern research has abolished the notion that the Renaissance produced a secular society, and some Italian intellectuals addressed problems in New Testament manuscripts, although their northern successors eclipsed them in what is commonly called Christian humanism. Erasmus himself practiced humanist methods on ancient pagan sources, but reserved his most extensive efforts for sacred literature. He supervised one of the earliest printed editions of the Greek New Testament in 1516, provided it with a new Latin translation in 1519, and revised the collected works of Latin and Greek Fathers of the Church, including Cyprian, Jerome, and Chrysostom.[34]

Meaningfully, Erasmus derived the most profound features of his spiritual counsel from his critical interest in sacred texts and his historical perception that early Christianity differed from the religion of his own epoch. He endorsed the *Our Father* above all other prayers because it appeared in the New Testament; he criticized pilgrimages and relics because they were absent in the primitive church.[35] His emphases were humanistic *because* they relied upon a philological and historical approach to the earliest Christian sources. There was nothing particular to the Renaissance about a call to imitate Jesus, or a demand to eradicate clerical abuses, unless the entreaty arose from the recognition of difference between current religious priorities, and those of biblical and patristic literature.[36]

But when scholars summon Erasmus as a touchstone for the Spanish Renaissance, all too often they proceed through messages and influence instead of a manner of reading. They thereby demonstrate their lingering debt to Bataillon, who, like other historians between the World Wars, preferred to define humanism and humanist according to the cognates of *human*-ness and *humane*-ness, and fashioned a portrait of Erasmus that extolled Christocentrism, spiritual interiority, and tolerance as the most important aspects of his thought. Bataillon identified these qualities as "humanist" without any other stipulation; he then tied Erasmus's pious recommendations to analogous expressions in Spain. By default, Spaniards who voiced similar sentiments to Erasmus's became Erasmians and Renaissance humanists. There are notable difficulties with this line of reasoning. Bataillon and his successors often deciphered an endorsement or echo of Erasmus as connoting the acceptance of all of his ideas.[37] Their methodology read pious phrases as hermeneutical signs, but they frequently neglected to investigate whether humanist methods were really in play.

Ultimately these interpretative leaps reduce the intellectual autonomy of Spaniards by erasing their preferences and choices. They render sixteenth-century men and women passive in the face of Erasmian ideas; they overlook the range of materials and approaches that early modern intellectuals could pursue. I would prefer to submit a different story, one that substitutes stylistic fluctuation and relative propensities for a series of oppositional camps. Significantly, when we examine the Spanish Renaissance from the angle of religious authority, the premises usually applied to it begin to splinter.

Early modern ecclesiastics understood "religious authority" in two inter-related ways, both of which arose from the Latin noun *auctoritas*: as opinions, judgments, and advice; and as power, influence, and dignity. When clerics provided references for their arguments, or evaluated one written source against another, they were preferring and weighing authorities. The citations and texts they favored could be more or less ancient. Their references could be more or less sensitive to philology and history. Their choices elucidate in turn their relative inclinations toward humanist or scholastic conventions.

The notion of religious authority also raises the issue of practical power, for the Latin noun auctoritas reverberates in the Latin verbs *agere,* to manage or administer, and *augere,* to increase and magnify. When we consider the ends to which Spanish ecclesiastics employed their sources, we may discover that they cited literary authorities to oversee, augment, or even alter the practical hierarchies around them. The materials they brandished, the way they invoked them, and the stances they promoted often raze the usual conclusions of the historiography.

Spanish clerics used "scholastic" to connote a man with a university education; they neglected to create a Spanish equivalent for the Italian *umanista*. But they understood the different structures and procedures that resided in humanism and scholasticism, and their self-consciousness about the two modes could be palpable. In debates over Erasmus's orthodoxy, royal secretary Luís Coronel noted when he was about to speak like a dialectician ("ut more dialecticorum loquar"); in contrast, Juan de Vergara created a humanist self-portrait by calling up distinctions in formal education, intellectual activities, and social class. Vergara persistently called himself erudite (*letrado*) over and against his enemies, who were idiots (*idiotas*); he explicitly tied his erudition to Latin and Greek scholarship, to translations, correspondence, and conversation, and finally to his place in the episcopal household.[38] Calling him a humanist is not anachronistic, although he never referred to himself as one.

What Coronel and Vergara were doing in such instances—defining their intellectual and rhetorical voices through contrasts—may suggest an ability to cross over to a different style and method of exposition, if only because of their sensitivity to what the "other" involved. In fact, they and their peers betray endless paradoxes once we start to appraise their relative intellectual emphases: few individuals in this book followed scholastic or humanist practice in a wholly consistent way. My findings reveal discrepancies in every area we have supposed congruent, from the staunch antagonism between humanism and scholasticism, to the connections between devotional preferences and ways of reading texts. Purported humanists argued dialectically;

reputed scholastics summoned historically perceptive and linguistically care-ful citations. Spanish intellectuals could fluctuate between and even combine humanist and scholastic modes of presentation and interpretation.

Moreover, clerics might arrive at the same directive by divergent routes: no longer may we assume that a particular outlook arose from a particular method of reading, or even from a predilection for a specific source. Christo-centric piety did not have to rest on textual criticism, the early church, or the New Testament, and recommendations to censor were voiced by individuals who trumpeted their Erasmian credentials. Although a recent argument stip-ulates that humanists and scholastics in Northern Europe made up "two rival cultures," Spanish ecclesiastics routinely intersected both. Although human-ism and scholasticism involved "two antithetical conceptions of proper intel-lectual method," that incompatibility obviously had its limits for these early modern individuals.[39] Sixteenth-century Spaniards, even clerics, were not passive adherents to intellectual styles or religious themes, although we have omitted their flexibility as well as their inventiveness from our histories.

This project looks for the Renaissance in modes of reading as well as pious messages. It notices eclecticism; it hypothesizes that inquiry into religious authority as citation and religious authority as power will deepen our percep-tion of humanism and religion in early modern Spain. I chose this approach because it allowed me to include new figures and new sources in the Spanish Renaissance, while redressing the argument that dominates its interpretation. My perspective on the subject is not eccentric: the notion of authority is thoroughly entangled in our theoretical understanding of Renaissance hu-manism and these clerics' practice of the same. When humanists exalted antique materials, they tried to make them more prestigious. When they evaluated history, they often labeled certain moments as especially worthy of imitation, and went on to underscore contingency and human beings over providence and God in the construction of the past. The Renaissance in-volved authority because humanists made hierarchies. And their rankings became that much riskier, and raised practical authority on a grander scale, when they classified and preferred materials that concerned Christianity. The Renaissance in Spain always has been assessed through a filter of dogma and spirituality; its partisans and enemies always have been construed mono-lithically. It thus seemed both appropriate and galvanizing to investigate the Spanish Renaissance through its clergy, as a familiar but most difficult test case; and to pose questions *about* hierarchies that end up amending the very stratifications of the scholarly literature.

The quantity of material that could be treated here is immense, for every ecclesiastical writer in the sixteenth century had something to say about religious authority, whether directly or implicitly. My interest lies in studying expressed and tacit sentiments from higher and lower tiers of the Catholic establishment. The clerical writings in this book range from Latin biblical prologues to vernacular moral tracts. A great many of them have been neglected by the academic community; the rest have never been approached from this perspective, or considered with sufficient attention to their literary and practical contexts. The two parts of this book are complementary. They also evince two internal arches, as each proceeds from easier to more difficult cases to prove.

Accordingly, the first three chapters handle explicit statements on hermeneutics that occurred in more polemical environments. Juan de Vergara's Inquisition trial, the Valladolid conference of 1527, and Pedro Ciruelo's promotion of the "literal" sense of Scripture directly raise arguments about the correction of sacred texts, the fallibility of church fathers, and the historical development of the Church itself. These sources illustrate unforeseen combinations of custom and innovation, and scholastic and humanist rhetoric. They also reveal an unexpected breadth and nuance of opinion on ecclesiastical power. Their subtleties confute the blunt distinctions of previous studies.

Pastoral materials offer similar findings, albeit more quietly. Through close readings of primarily vernacular treatises, the last three chapters examine the relationship between the priesthood and the laity; the process of confession; and the detection of witchcraft, as promoted by prescriptive sources. These works speak directly to religious authority as practical hierarchy, but also engage problems of modeling that pertain to humanism. Their authors deliberately aimed their books at a lay and a clerical audience; they invariably mixed tradition with history, and medieval models with patristic and biblical sources. The irony is that such treatises may divulge humanist methods for all their scholastic antecedents, and a relatively flexible pastoral ethos despite their premise of clerical privilege. Like the other texts in this book, they link elements we tend to separate, and thereby deepen relationships we too often portray as elementary.

Religious Authority in
the Spanish Renaissance

Chapter One

The Trial of
Juan de Vergara

It is good to have friends even in hell.
SPANISH PROVERB

I t was Juan de Vergara's singular misfortune to have a brother who dabbled in the more experimental currents in Spanish Catholicism. Vergara was born in 1492 and died in 1557. In the course of his career, he was secretary to the most prominent Spanish ecclesiastics, the archbishops of Toledo; he moved in rarified circles. He was and is celebrated as one of Iberia's outstanding intellects, if only for his position as the steadiest correspondent in Spain of the most famous scholar in Europe, Desiderius Erasmus. And he might have expected to continue in steady promotions, ample reputation, and relative peace had his sibling not tumbled into the hands of inquisitors.

Vergara's talents and position were exceptional when compared to his peers', but the formal aspects of his life were echoed in the careers of numerous individuals in this book. Like the entire company from Alcalá (Chapter 2) and Pedro Ciruelo (Chapter 3), Vergara's intellectual endeavors were associated with a deliberately innovative institution, the College of San Ildefonso at the University of Alcalá. San Ildefonso was a *colegio mayor,* one of six "major colleges" created in Spain between 1401 and 1521. In contrast to Spain's other colleges, which admitted poor undergraduates, the major ones received only mature scholars who had already attained their first degrees; they then supported those individuals for a fixed length of time, which enabled the scholars to read in advanced subjects. The original goal of every major college was to cultivate an academic aristocracy.

If the colegios mayores were distinctive as a whole, San Ildefonso was particularly unusual: founded about 1508 by Francisco Jiménez de Cisneros, archbishop of Toledo, inquisitor general, and eventually co-regent of Spain, it did not admit jurists in canon or civil law. It possessed thirty-three places for *colegiales,* the largest number of any colegio mayor. And its identity was thoroughly mingled with that of the University of Alcalá as a whole, since Cisneros made sure that the officers of his college became the administrators of his university, to the point that the rector of one directed the other.[1] Such structural peculiarities, in combination with the college's sheer size, meant that for all intents and purposes San Ildefonso *was* the University of Alcalá, at least in its first two decades. The faculty of that college could express different intellectual priorities, as Chapter 2 makes clear. They also displayed a wide range of income, from renewable professorships to multiple prebends, the latter being revenues derived from a cathedral or collegiate church's endowment. Whatever their critical perspectives and degrees of wealth, though, their link to San Ildefonso would have given them at least a modicum of religious authority.

The most important reason for their prestige was that Cisneros explicitly created San Ildefonso and the University of Alcalá to resuscitate theological studies, and from there to cultivate better-educated secular clerics, that is, priests who did not belong to religious orders. To that end, San Ildefonso's members were supposed to direct their time and attention to theology: Cisneros sponsored chairs in Thomism, or the writings of Thomas Aquinas; Scotism, from the works of the thirteenth-century Franciscan Duns Scotus; and nominalism. These professorships were prescient as well as personal, since they foreshadowed the elevation of Aquinas as a Doctor of the Catholic Church in 1567, and Cisneros's own insistence that the Franciscan order in Spain move toward greater observance of St. Francis's Rule. Scholars have found the chair in nominalist theology particularly provocative, since nominalism—from the Latin noun *nomen* (name)—was a philosophical stance with extensive and ambiguous ramifications for thought about God.

Cisneros promoted a range of theological angles in his university, from Thomistic knowledge and reason to Scotist love and will to nominalist mercy and trust. At the same time, he provided the means to study Scripture as well as medieval authorities, for he explicitly sponsored chairs in Hebrew and Greek.[2] These professorships in biblical languages, which were filled sporadically, went along with an even more ambitious enterprise that Cisneros began to advance seriously around 1510: a plan to print a multilingual edition of the Old and New Testaments. The proposed publication drew Hebrew and Greek scholars to Alcalá, and eventually resulted in the work known as the Complutensian Polyglot Bible, a six-volume behemoth in parallel columns of Hebrew, Aramaic, Greek, and Latin.[3] The men who came to San Ildefonso between its foundation in 1508 and Cisneros's death in 1517 thus found themselves in a climate of theological exposition, textual criticism, and linguistic fluency.[4] They and their successors were true to their benefactor's aims: throughout the sixteenth century, all the members of San Ildefonso found success in the Church.[5]

It is no wonder, then, that scholars consistently describe the men connected with San Ildefonso as a sort of religious vanguard; they often go on to pick Juan de Vergara as one of that cadre's stars. Vergara entered San Ildefonso as a clerical servant or *familiar* in 1509, when he was seventeen, and he remained there in that capacity for three years. In 1514, after reading for the master's in arts, he returned to San Ildefonso as a full-fledged associate or colegial; by 1517 he had attained a doctorate in theology. In some respects his relationship with his colegio mayor was typical. San Ildefonso's constitutions reflected a preference for members from Toledo, as befit its founder, and Vergara was born in that city. The college only accepted mature scholars, and Vergara had achieved a master's before he entered; at twenty-two, he fit the age requirements for admission to a colegio mayor.[6] He also fulfilled the larger objectives of San Ildefonso when he spent the three years from 1514 to 1517 in theological study. Yet his time at Alcalá's most prestigious college involved him in even more erudite tasks than the tenures of most of his peers, for Vergara read Greek and helped render the Old and New Testaments for the Complutensian Polyglot, as well as translating the *Physics, Metaphysics,* and *De anima* of Aristotle.[7]

Vergara carried out this scholarship under the sponsorship of Cisneros, and his abilities obviously garnered the archbishop's favor: in 1516, he joined Cisneros's household as his secretary. The advancement raised his status and eased his assumption of similar responsibilities under subsequent prelates. One year after Cisneros's death, he became the secretary of the new archbishop, the nineteen-year-old Guillaume de Croy; in 1524, he continued the same position under Alonso de Fonseca. His employers required him to travel. As part of Croy's retinue, Vergara went to Brussels in 1520, where he met Erasmus; after Croy's accidental death in January 1521, he remained as a chaplain in the court of Charles V. His place in the emperor's retinue meant that he witnessed the famous Diet of Worms and its condemnation of Martin Luther.

As of 1524, then, Vergara had served three archbishops of Toledo and a Holy Roman Emperor. Over the course of his life, he also would amass at least eight benefices, which sometimes carried pastoral responsibilities: he was the parish priest of Torrelaguna and archpriest of Santa Olalla, as well as the recipient of church funds from Alcabón, La Puebla, Noves, and Tortuero.[8] In 1519, his prebend in Alcalá—which originally was linked to San Ildefonso itself—was transferred to that city's collegiate church, San Justo y Pastor, after San Ildefonso passed a purity of blood statute that forbade canons who were *conversos,* that is, Catholics of Jewish ancestry. Vergara had descended from such converts, but his genealogy appears to have had little effect on his career, or his intellectual and spiritual proclivities.[9]

The large number of prebends that Vergara enjoyed made him wealthier than most of his colleagues in San Ildefonso, especially when added to his salary and perquisites as secretary to Toledo's archbishops. It is equally certain that the most prestigious and lucrative of his benefices was the one that made him part of the governing body—called the chapter, or *capítulo*—of the Toledo cathedral. In 1522, the Toledan archbishopric as a whole brought in 80,000 ducats, the cathedral chapter as a body supported more than four hundred orphans within the city, and the canons individually possessed yearly rents of not less than 700 ducats. Small wonder that a visitor to the metropolis in the 1520s pronounced the Toledan church the richest in Christendom.[10]

It is safe to say that Juan de Vergara belonged to the ecclesiastical elite. His status as a Renaissance humanist looks equally secure, whether we pull clues from his correspondence, his library, or even his prosecution by the Inquisition between 1533 and 1535. Vergara was the Spaniard who wrote the most letters to Erasmus and received the most replies from the same. An inventory of Vergara's books after his death reveals his fondness for Cicero, Suetonius, Plautus, and Terence; he also owned works by Pietro Bembo, Lorenzo Valla, and, notably, Angelo Poliziano, the individual who practiced the most astute philological and historical criticism in fifteenth-century Italy.[11] Even Vergara's position as archepiscopal secretary fits the typical employment profile of Italian Renaissance humanists, who routinely acted as chancellors and secretaries, and therein used the skills they had gained from classical rhetoric. Vergara's arrest by the Inquisition in 1533 has only sealed his modern reputation as a humanist, because scholars believe the prosecution was dominated by dislike for Erasmus.[12] For most historians, Vergara's indictment thus seems to signal a trend toward intellectual and religious backwardness, a track that Spain purportedly followed with mounting speed over the sixteenth century as it repulsed Erasmianism with increasingly firm measures.

Nonetheless, there is evidence to undermine Juan de Vergara's portrait as a humanist. He focused on Aristotle's logical corpus in his translations instead of the *Politics* or *Ethics*; he owned extracts of classical authors as well as their complete works; he received the dedication of an anti-Erasmian polemic in 1522.[13] Such intellectual complications are predictable, given the erraticism of humanist practice. The more important question, though, is whether similar ambiguities occurred in Vergara's Inquisition trial, which modern academics have turned into a symbolic event that justifies the separation of Spanish culture into progressive and regressive factions. Originally collected by the Inquisition tribunal of Toledo, and now located in the Archivo Histórico Nacional, the manuscript of Vergara's trial comprises more than 385 folios. The trial corrects the usual version of Spanish intellectual and religious history by tempering the typical divisions between humanists and scholastics, the broad-minded and the fanatical, or rational and traditional Catholics. It also weakens any presumptions about Renaissance humanists and religious tolerance.

Despite its utility for the study of the Spanish Renaissance, Vergara's prosecution offers substantial obstacles to researchers who attempt to mine it for a story or even a straightforward sequence of events. Its paleography occasionally remains illegible to me despite my best efforts. It deserves an entire monograph, given its intricacy, but prosecutions that would abet our study of it have not survived. Other methodological obstacles include the fact that all legal proceedings feature rote expressions, and Inquisition trials entailed leading questions and ellipses in the notaries' transcriptions. These elements mean that the historian's leap from source to event is relatively compromised, since the engineers and record-keepers of Inquisition trials—the inquisitors and notaries—always attempted to squeeze circumstances into formulas, to elicit what they wanted to hear, and to discard what struck them, but not necessarily us, as irrelevant.[14]

Such difficulties prevent us from treating the records of the Spanish Inquisition as transparent or complete reflections of events or personalities. When a tribunal prescribed "perpetual imprisonment," for example, the phrase did not necessarily mean jail for life; when a notary wrote "among other things, he said . . . ," the historian confronts lacunae that are as vexing as they are common. Perhaps the thorniest issue is the matter of the deponents' sincerity. Because the Inquisition engaged in a dialogue with witnesses and defendants—with inquisitors putting the questions, and their objects often frantically trying to supply the right answers—the trials present us with endless dilemmas as to whether witnesses and the accused "really meant" what they said. The question is impossible to answer; the only way around the problem, it seems to me, is to assume that persons under interrogation uttered what they *thought* would persuade in a moment of life or death, although that "death" might involve only a loss of reputation. (Despite our current understanding of the Spanish Inquisition as a relatively benign institution, I never have seen evidence that an appearance before it was a casual event.) I would submit, then, that we can use Inquisition testimony to reveal what individuals thought was rhetorically effective, which in turn illuminates the range of their voices, their sources, and their reasoning.

What comes next is not a microhistory in the most replete sense of the genre, because space and sources would not allow it. It is not the only story that we can pull from the record, or even the one that some readers might find most compelling: students of the law or Juan de Valdés, for example, would ask other questions and elevate different details. I also have no doubt that the ensuing account will be amplified and altered with further research. Nevertheless, I have constructed the following narrative from a rather deeper reading of the Vergara trial than we have previously possessed; as we shall see, it presents us with a number of revelations about sixteenth-century Spain. A guide to its actors can be found at the end of this chapter.

Accordingly, Juan de Vergara saw his life materially affected by a brother, Bernardino de Tovar, who played on the edge of Catholic orthodoxy. Tovar was Vergara's older half brother from their mother's first marriage; Vergara's full siblings included Francisco and Isabella, who were highly educated as well. Out of the three men, Vergara was the most successful in terms of wealth, although Francisco worked as a Greek scholar and translator in Alcalá, and Tovar became a beneficed priest.[15] The reason everything went terribly wrong—at least, from Vergara's point of view—was that Tovar was persistently attracted to *beatas.*

Beatas were women who pursued a holy life by taking vows of chastity and often of poverty. Frequently they were tertiaries, or members of the Franciscan third order, which was specifically designed to allow laymen and women to live in the world but simultaneously follow a rule. Such women were plentiful and sometimes quite powerful in sixteenth-century Spain; between 1500 and 1530, for instance, their prophetic visions could draw the moral and financial support of kings, archbishops, and nobles.[16] The beatas who befriended Tovar enjoyed forceful patrons; occasionally neglected to practice poverty, chastity, and obedience; and shared a single, critical characteristic: they all were connected to a religious outlook called *alumbradismo* (illuminism), a phenomenon that modern historians have spent decades trying to interpret and codify, with only limited success.

What we know about the *alumbrados* (the illuminated ones), whether male or female, can be stated succinctly for the period 1500–35. They were commonly of converso ancestry. Their first practitioners emerged about 1512 from the context of the reformed Franciscan order, but spurned the physical manifestations of divine ecstasy—the trembling limbs, fainting spells, and oral exclamations—that were the rage in many Franciscan houses.[17] All alumbrados disowned the external rituals of Catholicism, from meditation on Jesus' crucifixion to physical gestures in church; they also demonstrated a certain anticlericalism, because they rejected priestly intermediaries between God and human beings. They stressed instead a spiritual, interiorized relationship with the divine, which ensued from *dejamiento* (abandonment) to the love of God and to the direction of the Holy Spirit. In practical terms, their abandonment meant that they identified internal impulses with holy cues, and reacted accordingly. If their spirit prompted them to act, they had to obey, even if the result went against the Ten Commandments and Church tradition; on the other hand, if that stimulus were absent, then they could not be moved, even toward good works.[18]

Significantly, the alumbrados of Castile were led by women in the first three decades of the sixteenth century. Isabel de la Cruz, a Franciscan tertiary, began to preach in the area around Guadalajara about 1512, thereby disrupting the leadership of Marí Núñez, who had her own claims to sanctity. Núñez eventually competed with Isabel for noble patronage. Isabel finally ran Núñez out of Guadalajara, and Núñez in turn denounced Isabel to the Inquisition in 1519, although her accusation went nowhere and her own career as a beata ended ignominiously. In the meantime, Isabel's entourage quickly grew to include Pedro Ruiz de Alcaraz, an accountant and lay preacher for the marquess of Villena in Escalona; and María de Cazalla, who took over as the reigning alumbrada of Guadalajara after Isabel was arrested in 1524. Finally, Francisca Hernández—who had grasped the mystery of the Trinity at the age of three, or so her disciples claimed—practiced a mixture of dejamiento, forecasting, and miraculous cures in Salamanca and Valladolid. Her followers seem to have been exclusively male, and featured a large number of Franciscans; they also included Bernardino de Tovar.

These women and their companions knew one another. María de Cazalla listened to Isabel, but also talked to Francisca; after a bout with the Inquisition in 1519, Francisca moved into the house of Pedro de Cazalla, María's cousin, in Valladolid.[19] Their disciples, too, could move from one beata to another, as Tovar's example vividly demonstrates: he counted himself a devotee of Francisca from some undetermined date until the end of 1522, although he continued to send her neophytes afterward. In 1525, he fell in with a plan to evangelize territory at Medina del Ríoseco, located north of Valladolid; the project involved acquaintances of Francisca, Isabel de la Cruz, *and* María de Cazalla. By the end of the 1520s, Tovar had transferred his spiritual regard to María alone.

Despite such fluidity among their followers, though, it looks as if differences existed among the three beatas themselves. Isabel apparently developed her dejamiento out of a Franciscan environment and medieval sources, while María combined dejamiento with writings by Erasmus. As for Francisca, she turned her visions to material gain, for she knew who was in heaven and in hell; with the help of magical belts, she rehabilitated friars addicted to masturbation. She also bilked clerics out of their savings, and allowed her adherents to call her holier than the saints: one of her disciples, Antonio de Medrano, announced that God would have chosen Francisca for His Incarnation, had He not picked Jesus first.[20]

Over the course of the 1520s, Bernardino de Tovar looks as firmly enmeshed in alumbrado circles as his brother Juan was in more formal ones of ecclesiastical authority. In fact, there is an odd and delightful sort of complementarity between the older brother obeying beatas, planning to reform Medina del Ríoseco, and deprecating external rites; and the younger one minding archbishops, translating Aristotle, and thriving on multiple benefices. Indeed, we might presume that Tovar and Vergara had nothing in common and little association, but that inference would be wrong. Their bond to each other was deep enough to prove disastrous.

Vergara would insist that he and Tovar had hardly seen each other once the latter had started to attend the University of Salamanca, but his attempts to rescue his brother from Francisca Hernández initiated his acquaintance with persons who eventually would be charged with heresy. In 1519, Tovar was thoroughly ensconced in Francisca's group in Valladolid; at the end of the same year, he and two other devotees were ordered by the Inquisition to cease direct contact with Francisca under suspicion of having committed lewd acts with her.[21] Vergara was simultaneously preparing to leave with Archbishop Guillaume de Croy and the royal court for Flanders, which entailed a northern embarkation from the Asturian shore. As Vergara would relate fourteen years later, he had cut off his brother from his customary financial support "as soon as Tovar left his studies" for Francisca. But in 1519 Vergara's route to the coast took him through Valladolid. He consequently decided to see Tovar and try to persuade him to leave Francisca's company, offering him two benefices in the process; he even implored the future bishop of Zamora, Francisco de Mendoza, "to talk to Tovar himself and make him leave that woman." Mendoza did his best—either to shame him or to sympathize with the attachment, he asked Tovar if he had managed to get Francisca into bed—but failed to change his mind. Vergara then proceeded to Flanders.[22]

When Vergara returned three years later, he attempted to intervene again, finding that Tovar was "living in a hamlet, as close as he could get" to Francisca, and "obeying and authorizing" her; this time, he offered his sibling a place in his own home in Alcalá. Tovar yielded, but also insisted, for the sake of courtesy, that his brother see Francisca and Antonio de Medrano "so that they would not be left discontent." Vergara acquiesced, but found no satisfaction in the meeting; he finally told his brother to move on to Alcalá, and Tovar was living there by 1523.[23] Over the next two years Vergara weighed and accepted another secretarial position, this time under the new archbishop of Toledo, Alonso de Fonseca, while Tovar disregarded official pronouncements of Church and State.

In 1524, the Inquisition arrested two prominent alumbrados, Isabel de la Cruz and Pedro Ruiz de Alcaraz. The reasons for their seizure were complex, and ran from conflicts among Alcaraz, two Franciscans in Escalona, and the vicar general of the Franciscan order, to the heresy of Lutheranism.[24] In the wake of Martin Luther's condemnation by both emperor and pope in 1521, the Spanish Inquisition ordered its officials to confiscate Lutheran books, and prohibited Castilians from selling, reading, or preaching Lutheran works and ideas. Aragonese inquisitors consequently intercepted Lutheran books in September 1521, Valencian officials seized them at approximately the same time, and the Navarrese found Lutheran contraband as soon as they were ordered to look for it. Suspicions about any and all of the alumbrados, including Alcaraz and Isabel, probably deepened in the wake of the Lutheran panic, however unfounded that panic was: it is very clear that inquisitors and prosecutors in the 1520s had few solid notions of what Luther promoted, but the alumbrados were sufficiently disrespectful of religious intermediaries and external rituals to fit the Inquisition's general impression of what Lutheranism involved.[25] The apparent justice of Isabel's and Alcaraz's arrests was only confirmed after a conference of theologians, convened by the Inquisition in 1525, determined that these two individuals were indebted to Luther for their disparagement of confession and the saints.[26]

In turn, Inquisitor General Alonso de Manrique—the nominal director of the entire inquisitorial apparatus, who acted in conjunction with the Suprema, the General Council of the Inquisition—quickly issued an edict of the faith on the alumbrado heresy. Consisting of forty-eight propositions culled from Isabel's and Alcaraz's trials, the edict was read in Castilian churches on Sundays and feast days: like all such documents, its explicit object was to prompt confessions about making similar statements and knowing other suspects.[27] Like other such edicts in previous years, the 1525 pronouncement worked. It prompted María de Cazalla, for instance, to denounce herself to the Toledo tribunal, for which she received a penance and, unbeknownst to her, a transcript was generated that could be used in the future.[28]

As of 1524 and especially 1525, then, it looks as if alumbradismo carried a manifest risk of attracting inquisitorial attention. Anyone even vaguely connected with the beatas or their followers should have recognized the danger, since news about the Inquisition's arrests always circulated despite that institution's official policy of secrecy. But amusingly enough, Isabel's and Alcaraz's indictments, Manrique's edict, and what must have been substantial public rumor did not dissuade Bernardino de Tovar from playing a role, if only a mediatory one, in the project at Medina del Ríoseco. Relatively little is known about the scheme to bring that site back "to true Christianity"; the project started with Juan López de Celaín, a priest formerly in the service of the noble Mendoza family at Guadalajara. About 1525, Celaín promoted the idea of recruiting twelve men to imitate Jesus' apostles, then sending them out to preach to the inhabitants of the estates owned by the admiral of Castile, Fadrique Enríquez.[29] In return, Enríquez was supposed to provide Celaín and his entourage with 20,000 marevedís a year and lodging. The plan never came off because Enríquez never supplied the money or the housing, but between 1525 and 1526 at least two groups of potential apostles reached and left Medina del Ríoseco. Tovar himself did not travel to the site, but one of the prospective missionaries was Juan del Castillo, who taught Greek in Toledo, knew Tovar, and had sought out Francisca Hernández on Tovar's advice.[30] Francisca later testified that Tovar was supposed to be the principal apostle in Medina del Ríoseco; she also insisted that in the mid-1520s he sent her more apprentices than just Castillo, including Bachiller Olivares from Pastrana, and Fernando de Santo Domingo and Cristobal de Gumiel from Toledo.[31] Santo Domingo, at least, was characterized by Francisca as a disciple of Tovar himself.

No matter what role Tovar actually played in the Medina scheme, the evidence implies that he was still connected to Francisca, however distantly, in 1525. It also looks as if Tovar's own status had climbed to the point that he could be described as possessing followers of his own, a reputation that a stable residence in Alcalá, not to mention his brother's wealth and position, probably helped secure. But whether or not Francisca exaggerated, the larger point is that Tovar and numerous others felt sufficiently secure to continue hatching plans and sending each other devotees even *after* the arrests of Isabel and Alcaraz, and an inquisitorial edict that was at once imprecise about alumbradismo, but persistent in connecting the alumbrados themselves to Luther. In fact, the very vagueness of that 1525 decree should have made the label of alumbrado more rather than less perilous, for its ambiguities permitted its application to a wide range of practices while simultaneously linking potential suspects to the most famous heresiarch in Western Europe.

Given such risks, it is tempting to draw Tovar and his acquaintances as if they inhabited a sort of religious underground, except that the players themselves hardly kept their activities a secret. Tovar and Castillo conversed regularly in Vergara's house and in front of Tovar and Vergara's sister, Isabella; the plan to recruit apostles for Medina del Ríoseco swept through the University of Alcalá. One way to make sense of such openness is to envision everyone in the environment, from Tovar to Vergara to the whole faculty at Alcalá, as part of the same spiritual vanguard. Another solution is provocative and intriguing: the possibility that Spanish religious culture was so flexible and equivocal in the 1520s that ritual and hierarchy and belief could be debated and tested. If such were the case, then Tovar and his peers may have believed they had nothing to hide.

Spain had its own printing boom in the early sixteenth century, and a prominent part of that torrent was vernacular literature on Christian subjects, aimed at both laity and clergy. Literacy rates turn out to have been higher for sixteenth-century Spain than modern scholars ever expected; contact with Christian dogma was bolstered further by the oral recitation and instruction of prayers and creeds.[32] There is no question that the Spanish population as a whole had greater access to more written religious doctrine between 1500 and 1536 than in any previous period. At the same time, that religious doctrine was highly eclectic, since it could encompass meditations on Jesus' Passion or dialectical treatises on the Decalogue, tracts on saints' lives or condemnations of gambling. Furthermore, until the proclamation of the Tridentine decrees—the Council of Trent convened intermittently from 1545 to 1563—there were no Catholic seminaries to educate secular priests, no conclusive explanation of the Catholic doctrine of salvation, no description of the standard Catholic Bible, and no official demarcation of Church tradition. Of course, the religious elite had multiple, recognized authorities who treated the episcopate and the sacraments, justification and exegesis. But without the imprimatur of the pope, one Catholic's source might easily conflict with another's.

Such findings mean that Catholic orthodoxy in Spain, as in Western Europe as a whole, was a polysemous phenomenon in the first half of the sixteenth century. Spanish Catholics could embrace a variety of doctrinal priorities and depend upon an assortment of customary references. None of these emphases and texts had to mesh with each other in every detail; all of them could be uttered by a clergy whose theological training ranged from the thorough to the vacuous; many of them might be promoted by laypersons who could read and write.

Contact with doctrine and a concomitant lack of authoritative definitions may well have produced a situation in which clergy and laity actually moved closer together instead of farther apart. If such were the case in Spain in the 1520s, it would help explain how Pedro Ruiz de Alcaraz, María de Cazalla, and Francisca Hernández, all of whom were laypersons, became spiritual advisers to nobles, friars, and priests, and remained in such roles for years.[33] Even new impulses to describe and restrict in the wake of Martin Luther may not have taken the toll we frequently imagine: after 1521, the Spanish Inquisition issued confiscation orders against Lutheran books, but inquisitors prosecuted suspected Lutherans with relative restraint in this early period. Even the 1524 arrest of Isabel de la Cruz and Pedro Ruiz de Alcaraz looks as if it were prompted as much by Franciscan encouragement as by fear of a Lutheran presence.

There was nothing inevitable about Bernardino de Tovar's own detention by the Inquisition tribunal in Toledo in September 1530: his arrest resulted from the Inquisition's indictment of Francisca Hernández and her servant, Marí Ramírez, in March 1529, and their subsequent naming of accomplices. In the course of her trial Francisca identified a large number of suspects, and modern historians have abused her for it. It is easy to see why: her testimony resulted in the seizure of numerous individuals, including Tovar, María de Cazalla, and Vergara himself. Nevertheless, in light of the Inquisition's procedures and goals, Francisca was only doing what was expected of her, for defendants were required to identify their cohorts as part of a complete admission of guilt.

A full disclosure of culpability was the veritable crux of inquisitorial technique, since it was the surest possible sign that the inquiry (the *inquisitio*) had succeeded.[34] Just as a confession to a priest had to be thorough in all its details as part of the sacrament of penance, so a statement to inquisitors had to include dates and locations, circumstances and accomplices, to ensure that an honest acknowledgment of heresy had taken place. Spanish inquisitors in the sixteenth century could be secular priests as well as jurists, which conflated the sacramental and judicial processes even further.[35] And so Francisca might have whipped off as many names as she could think of to satisfy her conscience and her examiners all at once. By listing offenders and offenses she had witnessed seven years' hence, she also attested her own sagacity, because she had identified the errors in the first place. She may have been pursuing a rather delayed sort of vengeance as well.[36]

Francisca was seized in March 1529; Tovar was interrogated in December of the same year and arrested in 1530. Records of both their trials have been lost: we do not know exactly why the Toledo tribunal seized Francisca or what charges were lodged against Tovar.[37] Still, their trials undoubtedly adhered to the pattern of inquisitorial practice that basically was set by the early sixteenth century. A case in the Inquisition proceeded through formal *audiencias* (hearings) in front of the inquisitors themselves and the tribunal's notaries, who transcribed the proceedings. An arrest was initiated by the *fiscal's* (prosecutor's) formal allegation against the supposed heretic, which he delivered in front of the two inquisitors who ran the particular tribunal. The indictment could be constructed from testimony given in other trials, and from depositions made by individuals who voluntarily appeared to denounce suspects. In his statement, the fiscal, who was an employee of the Inquisition and attached to a specific tribunal, listed the charges and demanded the accused's arrest. The potential offender was subsequently picked up by the constable for the inquisitorial district, deposited in the tribunal, and confronted with the fiscal's recitation of the charges. The defendant had to answer the allegations orally and at once; the inquisitors then received both sides "for proof," or the presentation of witnesses.

During the stage of proof, the fiscal gave his evidence to both the inquisitors and the accused, although he could continue to collect and present damning testimony in the course of the trial. Defendants were expected to respond in writing to the documentation against them, and to call individuals who might offer exculpatory statements. Particularly after 1521—as the Inquisition began to target heresies that initially, at least, were ill-defined— inquisitors routinely asked for help from theological consultants (*calificadores*), who evaluated the degree of heresy in the defendant's alleged missteps. As the inquisitors assessed the evidence from both parties, they took the calificadores' opinions into account. They also might confer with other inquisitors and theologians (*consultadores*) on the penalty to inflict once guilt was established. But neither the counsel of calificadores nor consultadores bound tribunals or prosecutors.

Because guilt was presumed and repentance desired, the Inquisition could resort to torture when the accused remained defiant and refused to admit their guilt or name their accomplices: the purpose of water being poured down the nose or straps tightened around the arm was to elicit a confession, which was the best proof imaginable in the epoch's legal culture, and the centerpiece of one of the era's most publicized sacraments. Because inquisitors ultimately pursued reconciliation to the Christian community, their sentences consistently exacted a penance instead of outright acquittal or "relaxation to the secular arm," a phrase that meant defendants were released to civil justices and put to death. It warrants emphasis that not every heretic was executed: the Spanish and Roman Inquisitions very frequently demanded that the guilty expiate their sins in the midst of their communities. Nevertheless, the penances imposed very often carried physical punishments, which could range from imprisonment to flogging to wearing a *sanbenito* (the yellow and red penitential garment) whenever the culpable left the house.[38]

A rule of secrecy was supposed to buttress the Inquisition's procedures and enhance its power to coerce. The seizure of suspected heretics was public knowledge, either through kinship or geographical proximity or gossip; but once defendants disappeared into a particular tribunal, their isolation should have been complete. They depended upon their families for their food, assuming their households could provide it, but the warden of the secret prison, which lay within the tribunal itself, oversaw those provisions. They might keep a servant with them if they were sufficiently wealthy, but they were prohibited from communicating with their fellow-prisoners; in theory, at least, defendants could not stay in cells with alleged accomplices. And although the fiscal handed the accused a transcript of the incriminating evidence (the *publicación de testigos*), he and the notaries had already excised the details that would allow defendants to match testimony to particular individuals: Tovar never should have been told the identity of the witnesses against him. Finally, before penanced heretics left the tribunal, they swore to preserve as secret whatever had happened to them inside. Historians formerly imagined that the Inquisition's practice of concealment just heightened its authority and furthered a pedagogy of fear. Given the sophistication of its methods, the apparent consistency of its procedures, and its awareness of the impact of a terrifying example, academics once felt secure in pointing out the Inquisition's quasi-modern sensibilities; indeed, they often described it as a "well-oiled machine."[39]

Thanks to scholars who have placed tribunals in specific geographical and social contexts, and tracked changes in indictments over time, we now recognize that the Spanish Inquisition did not function mechanically or even consistently across the Iberian Peninsula or during the early modern period.[40] What happened after Tovar's arrest just adds to our appreciation of the contingent in Inquisition history. If, on one level, Tovar's capture by inquisitors was routine once he was named as an accessory, what ensued with his detention was not, for he and his half brother worked to disable the Inquisition through wealth, patronage, and not a little audacity. In sum, they tried to fracture the system from the inside out, and the extent to which Juan de Vergara in particular succeeded in the sedition is at least as interesting as the fact that he ultimately failed.

Because Vergara was a secretary to the most prominent ecclesiastic in Spain, he was ideally placed to be a patron. As someone who listened to archbishops, handled episcopal correspondence, and possessed multiple sources of income, he enjoyed the sort of power that allowed him to ease or block the well-being of his contemporaries. His connections and his money meant that his kindnesses could have highly practical applications; conversely, his refusal to extend his rhetorical skills and favor could produce decidedly negative effects. With a word to Archbishop Fonseca, a letter delivered, or bread supplied, Juan de Vergara could materially affect the people around him. He did not hesitate to use his authority after his brother's arrest.

From 1530 until his own indictment on June 23, 1533, Vergara attempted to overturn or mitigate the evidence against his sibling by every means at his disposal. He questioned and threatened inquisitors.[41] He probably tried to influence men on the Suprema. At one point he even thought of interviewing the fiscal for the Toledo tribunal, and directed an associate to search for his house, although the attempt was unsuccessful.

His efforts were more fruitful when he brought his influence to bear on subordinates. Although historians have overlooked the incident, Vergara probably tried to wreck the career of one Gerónimo Ruiz, who had collected depositions against Tovar in Alcalá, and then searched Tovar's residence—which was Vergara's as well—in the same city. Ruiz later insisted, rightly enough, that Vergara had interfered with witnesses. What he could not have known was what Vergara would do with *him* after he found suspicious books in Vergara and Tovar's home. Significantly, Ruiz did not carry out the inventory of that house by himself: he had the help of Miguel Carrasco, one of Vergara's intimate friends, who jostled his way into the process after Ruiz already had received his instructions. As Ruiz recounted it, once he and

Carrasco located questionable volumes, Carrasco contended that they did not have to turn them over, Ruiz replied that they did, and Carrasco retorted that the inquisitors would be satisfied if he and Ruiz were. Carrasco ended up carrying the books to Toledo, but remained "viciously disposed" toward Ruiz. The rumors started afterward: Ruiz's friends and relations heard he had been whipped at Segovia and possessed secret Jews as ancestors. He would assert that Vergara had engineered such reports at the expense of his family's reputation.[42]

If Vergara really spurred the slander against Ruiz, then that effort formed only part of a much more daring strategy. We know that Vergara did his best to obstruct the Inquisition's collection of evidence against his brother; one of the ways he undermined that process was by managing the witnesses. In late September or early October 1530, a cleric named Francisco Gutiérrez deposed against Tovar and then went to Vergara's house in Madrid to tell him so. A month later, when he was the Inquisition's prisoner, Gutiérrez contended that Vergara never had solicited, and he had not volunteered, the gist of his testimony—although he conceded that he had spoken to Vergara *before* deposing as well. As for his motives in going to Madrid and informing Vergara about the interview, Gutiérrez knew that a prebend was vacant, and wanted Vergara to help him get it.[43]

Vergara's leverage clearly could inspire those around him, to the point that even employees of the Inquisition were anxious to please this potential benefactor: a notary attached to the Toledo tribunal, named Hermosilla, took money and food from Vergara in exchange for the names of prosecution witnesses, and even met with him over Francisca Hernández's testimony.[44] Vergara's longest act of subversion, though, involved at least two men who resided inside the tribunal itself: Juan de Ortega, the warden (*alcaide*) of the inquisitors' secret prison; and Ortega's servant, Juan Sánchez, who commonly was referred to as the "prison boy" (*mozo del carcel*).[45]

The secret prisons of the Inquisition were the holding pens where defendants remained during their trials: they were always located inside tribunals, which in turn were established in or near the center of urban areas. The Toledo tribunal was in the northwest section of the city, located in houses adjacent to the Church of St. Vincent; by the middle of the sixteenth century, it possessed about twenty-three cells, divided between upper and lower levels; its building also entailed a courtyard and a corral.[46] The site's staff included two inquisitors, a string of notaries, the fiscal, a receiver who tracked the tribunal's receipts and expenditures, a porter who conveyed prisoners to and from the hearings, a *despensero* (quartermaster) who dispensed food to the prisoners, and the warden of the secret prison. The warden, Juan de Ortega, registered entrances and exits, and thereby controlled access to the prisoners; he was in charge of security. He lived in the tribunal itself, and his assistant— Juan Sánchez, the mozo del carcel—helped him with his responsibilities.[47]

Juan de Vergara probably began to probe the inquisitorial network for weaknesses as soon as Tovar was arrested; the issue was how to best manipulate the system. No matter who his contacts were, Vergara bent them toward the same goal, which was to recover information about the incriminating witnesses and testimony in his brother's trial. Tovar had a great deal to gain from infractions of confidentiality: if he could identify the prosecution's deponents, he could recuse them more easily.

On April 11, 1533, Hernán Rodríguez arrived at the tribunal with a packet of raisins. Rodríguez was the chaplain for both Vergara and the choir of the Toledo cathedral. In the inquisitorial system, families routinely were responsible for their relatives' upkeep; for wealthy defendants like Tovar, there were no restrictions on the food they could receive unless the inquisitors decreed otherwise. Rodríguez was the person who typically transmitted provisions between Vergara's household and Tovar's cell; Vergara apparently had asked him to check on Tovar's needs on a daily basis, which meant that Rodríguez had visited the tribunal hundreds of times during Tovar's three years of imprisonment.[48] Under normal circumstances, Rodríguez would have passed the raisins to the alcaide, who would have transferred them to the despensero, who then would have handed them to Tovar. But on April 11 something went wrong: the despensero, Diego Gaspar Martínez, noticed that the raisins lay in a paper that was very white, very new, and not typical of wrappers for foodstuffs.[49] Martínez had been told to scrutinize the deliveries for Tovar; he believed he was holding something suspicious. He switched the raisins from one paper into another, and then examined the original in front of some live coals. He watched in amazement as the paper gradually betrayed "golden letters that could be read."[50] Eight days later, on April 19, Martínez found another message, this time in drink transported by Hernán Rodríguez: the paper acted as a bottle stopper for a little white pitcher of rose-water syrup.

The despensero reported his discoveries to the inquisitors; the latter then wrote to the Suprema, which told them to investigate at once. On April 21, the inquisitors debated an arrest order for Hernán Rodríguez and an interrogation request for Juan de Vergara, but delayed implementing either. Instead, they turned Tovar's lodgings upside down: on April 23, the inquisitors removed Tovar and his servant from their room, put them into separate chambers, and began to inspect their cell. They found a twig and some chicken feathers, as well as a lemon suspended from a string, in a hole in the wall. They also uncovered a Greek New Testament, a commentary by Thomas Aquinas, and a quantity of blank paper that had been lined by a notary and apparently stolen.[51]

On May 3, the evidence multiplied: as the inquisitors left an audiencia,

a cleric was there, called Hernán Rodríguez, chaplain of the choir of the holy church of Toledo, who is in charge of supplying Bernardino Tovar, brother of Juan de Vergara, with things he requests and needs. Hernán Rodríguez carried a glass cup of olives in his hand, which was covered by a paper. He showed it to the inquisitors, and requested that their reverences order it taken into the prison and given to Tovar. Their reverences immediately saw the cup with the olives, covered with the paper.[52]

The inquisitors reacted quickly. They told Rodríguez to hand the cup to the despensero, and commanded the latter to give it to Tovar; in the meantime, they secretly removed the paper cover, just as the despensero had snatched the ones from the raisins and rose-water. When they held the third paper in front of burning coals, it, too, revealed writing. They called Rodríguez for questioning the following day.

What the despensero and the inquisitors uncovered between April 11 and May 4, 1533, was a secret correspondence between Vergara and Tovar that had been going on for approximately three years. The two brothers wrote to each other in lemon or orange juice in the summer, pomegranate juice in the winter; once dry, their communications were nearly imperceptible, but when held before a source of heat, the citric acid in the juice burned and the words became visible. This writing technique was hard to detect and equally laborious to complete: when Vergara composed one of these epistles, he asked for an orange, locked himself in his bedroom, and only emerged the following morning. The messages traveled in food or containers for the same. Vergara funneled his bulletins as wrappings or stoppers or covers, while Tovar shipped his as corks or tops for empty pitchers or bottles.[53]

Vergara's ability to move these letters in and out of the Toledo tribunal without ever appearing himself was the secret to three years of subterfuge. Hernán Rodríguez was a crucial element in the process: when Vergara was at court, Rodríguez ferried his letters into the food and then into the prison; he even forwarded Tovar's messages when Vergara was out of town. On Vergara's instructions, Rodríguez also muzzled the Inquisition's own officials, specifically the warden and his servant. When the warden complained about the frequency of his visits, Rodríguez showed up with six pairs of hens "for

Tovar": he would claim not to know where those chickens ended up. On another occasion, Rodríguez handed twelve bushels of wheat to the warden, who took it home and parceled it out to his poorer relatives; once he publicly sent the warden bread, which he expected him to use for the same purpose. Rodríguez tried to help the mozo's sister enter a convent, and gave the mozo himself a clerical cap, a gift that implies a great deal about the status of ecclesiastics in Toledo.[54] As for the presents to the warden, food was meaningful in a city wracked by periodic subsistence crises; even more important, such gestures looked like acts of charity, as Vergara and Rodríguez well knew. These measures were quite effective. The warden and his servant kept their mouths shut, as did the despensero, who undoubtedly took part in the game, given his position in the chain of command.[55]

Vergara did not rely on Hernán Rodríguez alone in his efforts to abrogate the inquisitorial system; his connections with his subordinates amount to a spider's web of personal, professional, and always profitable links. One of the best ways to grasp this matrix is to view it from the perspective of patron-client relations. In the largest sense, patronage is a relationship between more and less powerful individuals who are bound to each other for mutual benefit: the links between patrons and clients are unequal, personal, and reciprocal. Their connection could be flexible and intricate; their bonds might hinge on friendship as well as constraint. The extent of the reciprocity could be substantial, since every individual in the fifteenth and sixteenth centuries was part of an extensive kinship network; hence whole families were affected by bonds of clientage, although the clients themselves tended to be linked vertically to a common patron, instead of horizontally to each other.[56]

Finally, and perhaps most notably, the type of assistance rendered within clientage could be oblique and peaceful as well as explicit and violent. A client could just accompany his patron to the forum, as Quintus and Marcus Tullius Cicero well knew in the last century of the Roman Republic; a patron might help his client in person, or simply expedite a request. For instance, Cosimo de'Medici, the unofficial ruler of the Florentine Republic between 1434 and 1464, became the "father of his country" because he acted as a *padrino*. He won the allegiance of so many clients by securing so many favors: out of more than 1,230 extant letters to him, most sought courtesies that he in particular could expedite, such as dowries, papal audiences, and access to certain manuscripts. Cosimo's connections in distant places only heightened his ability to accomplish what was troublesome, while the money that he and his family enjoyed gave him those connections in the first place.[57]

Juan de Vergara handled his tangle of helpers in similar ways and with multifarious motives and results. He and Tovar asked their respective servants, Francisco and Diego de Aguilar—another pair of brothers—to act as go-betweens both outside and inside prison. Francisco smuggled one of Vergara's letters to Tovar as the latter was being transported to the Toledo tribunal; as we shall see, Diego helped Tovar correspond with other inmates. In such instances the Aguilar brothers were acting under constraint, because they were performing under the direct orders of their employers; and yet the same masters tried to deflect attention away from their servants when they were interrogated by the Inquisition. Obviously, Vergara and Tovar could look on their domestics as persons to be manipulated and protected all at once, and the evidence suggests that Diego de Aguilar shared the same outlook vis-à-vis his employer: he complained to other prisoners that Tovar beat him, but begged to be returned to him once the inquisitors put them into separate cells.[58]

Such complex alliances surface repeatedly in Vergara's trial. For instance, Vergara persuaded Cristobal de Gumiel to act on his behalf with a forged ecclesiastical prebend, while Gumiel explicitly hoped to gain some church offices from this potential sponsor. Still, personal loyalty entered the scenario as well: when Gumiel thought he was dying, he asked that his papers go to Vergara alone.[59] Vergara's simultaneous interactions with Gaspar de Lucena demonstrate coercion as well as beneficence. Lucena had a brother, Juan del Castillo, who was a friend of Tovar's. When Tovar was arrested, Castillo fled Spain and became a fugitive from the Inquisition. Vergara knew that Castillo most likely had damaging things to say about Tovar; he accordingly tried to control the situation by handing off messages to and from the outlaw. He passed two letters from Castillo in Paris to Lucena in Castile; he told Lucena about a Latin order for Castillo's arrest, and warned him the decree would arrive in Paris first.[60]

It would be easy to conclude that Lucena and Vergara were working in tandem to guard their siblings: certainly they had good reason to be acquainted and to seek each other's help, given their relatives' familiarity. But that cooperative gloss would tell only half the story, because here the relationship may have turned on intimidation as much as acquaintance. Lucena was tortured by the Inquisition in late January 1535, and although he uttered his remarks under duress, his comments illustrate the menace that could inhere in Vergara's authority.

Under torture, Lucena portrayed his relationship with Vergara in perilous terms. Vergara had told him about the arrest order, and had directed him to pass the news to Castillo; in the process, Vergara also attempted to warn

Castillo, long-distance and through Lucena, about the inquisitors' tactics if he were caught. Vergara said the inquisitors would try to play Castillo and Tovar against each other, by warning one that the other had already deposed. Clearly Vergara feared that Castillo would not remain silent in such circumstances, and hoped that Lucena would apprise his brother of the potential danger and thereby silence him. Unfortunately, Lucena himself was unable to keep Vergara's counsel a secret, or so Vergara believed: two days before Lucena was seized by the Inquisition, Vergara cornered him and demanded to know whom he had told about Castillo's arrest order. As Lucena faced the torture instruments in 1535, he confessed that he had been telling the general truth, but had curtailed the details because Vergara was *poderoso*—a powerful man who controlled everything in Alcalá, including the magistrates. Lucena had been terrified that if he relayed all he knew to the inquisitors, Vergara would destroy him, his house, and his relatives, "as he very well has the authority to do."[61]

Nevertheless, Vergara seems to have secured his clients' fidelity mostly through favors instead of threats. His own benefices gave him wealth, and that substance could translate into the distribution of hens and wheat to the "deserving poor": if the indigent happened to include a prison warden with a blind eye, so much the better. Vergara's activities as an episcopal secretary also gave him a way to express his approbation: he intervened with Archbishop Fonseca when it came to passing out ecclesiastical offices and promoting particular candidates for them.[62] In sum, Vergara's ties to royal and ecclesiastical circles meant that his conversation and his letter-writing could assume a critical importance for his less fortunate contemporaries, as they recognized only too well. To suggest that he might have achieved a kindness by simply opening his mouth or applying his pen would be an exaggeration. But he could exploit substantial personal contacts.

Yet Vergara's clients and patrons could not prevent his seizure by the Inquisition. After the discovery of the secret epistles on April 11 and 19, the search of Tovar's cell on April 23, the discovery of Hernán Rodríguez and the third letter on May 3, and the questioning of Rodríguez himself on May 4, two more covert letters arrived for Tovar, on May 11 and 17.[63] On May 17 the fiscal presented a writ against Vergara. Three days later the warden and the mozo del carcel were detained, and Vergara interrogated; he was arrested in the course of a second audiencia on June 23.

There is no doubt that Vergara was interrogated and indicted because of the secret correspondence with his brother, although the tribunal had solicited depositions against him for nearly three years. The inquisitors had listened to sixteen witnesses between 1529 and the end of 1532, all of whom had damaging things to report. Francisca Hernández and Marí Ramírez called Vergara a Lutheran and an alumbrado; Diego Hernández and Gil López de Bejar confirmed, more or less willingly, Vergara's approval of Lutheran doctrine. Tovar relayed that Vergara owned a work by Oecolampadius, a supporter of Luther. Bernardino Flores argued that the culprit had insulted Augustine, while Francisco de Silva recalled that the suspect had neglected to hear Mass seven years hence, and Juan de Medina remembered that Vergara had urged the printing of Juan de Valdés's *De doctrina cristiana* in 1529.[64] Six of the witnesses who testified against Vergara were already being tried for Lutheran and alumbrado sentiments, or as promoters of those heresies.[65] But the other ten enjoyed decent reputations and profitable occupations, and their statements should have counted: by and large, they were canons of cathedrals, professors of theology, and royal preachers. Furthermore, two groups of calificadores, which met a year apart and comprised different persons, found heresy in nearly all the allegations they perused.[66]

Yet the inquisitors moved only after the discovery of the letters, as demonstrated by the sequence of events and the prosecutor's own language. The tribunal never attempted to interview Vergara until the secret correspondence was unearthed. The fiscal's writ of May 17 called Vergara an abettor of heretics and a suborner of Inquisition personnel, and never raised the question of sympathy for Luther and Erasmus; the same prosecutor's formal indictment on July 12 made Vergara's subversion of the Holy Office the introduction to charges of heresy.[67] In truth, I suspect that the Toledo inquisitors literally could not arrest Juan de Vergara on the basis of the testimony collected between 1529 and the end of 1532, because their sixteen witnesses were almost entirely singular: these deponents recounted discrete instances in which Vergara purportedly erred.

In the Inquisition's legal system, a lone eyewitness to an event could only constitute a partial proof of heresy, and a string of unique informants would only result in a series of partial proofs; no combination of partial proofs ever amounted to a full demonstration of culpability. Instead, a replete determination of heresy depended upon multiple witnesses to the same event or a confession, and although the inquisitors had corroborative testimony from Francisca Hernández and her servant, Marí Ramírez, they either viewed that evidence as too shaky to act upon, or they faltered in the wake of Vergara's connections. But once the despensero caught Hernán Rodríguez with the secret messages on April 11 and 19, 1533, the tribunal could pursue an affront to its procedures; when inquisitors Vaguer and Yáñes intercepted the same

Rodríguez with a letter on May 3, they could corroborate the offense that the despensero had attested. To further validate Vergara's part in the correspondence, they stopped the messages from reaching Tovar but disclosed nothing to Vergara himself. He continued to send the letters; he thereby gave the Inquisition a reason to indict him.

In all fairness, inquisitors Yáñes and Vaguer found themselves pushed to the wall by May 1533. As they investigated Vergara and Tovar's correspondence, they also uncovered Tovar's habit of scribbling to other inmates: just as Vergara acted as a *patrón* outside their prison, so Tovar seems to have fulfilled the same role within it. When the inquisitors learned of Vergara's letter of April 19, they began to explore what had been happening behind their backs in their own tribunal. What they found was explosive. Tovar was not lodged with any of his supposed contacts among the alumbrados, but their cells were in the same general location within the tribunal, although split between upper and lower floors. On April 23, when the inquisitors interrogated Tovar and his servant Diego, they found that messages had traveled from Tovar to fellow-prisoners Gaspar de Lucena and María de Cazalla; Lucena was the sibling of Juan de Castillo, Tovar's close friend and fugitive, while María was the beata whom Tovar had followed since the mid-1520s. To make matters worse—from the inquisitors' point of view—Tovar tried to advise another female prisoner about the compurgatory oath, which entailed reputable persons swearing to the innocence of the accused. He also distributed sweets to his fellow-inmates. The agent in these machinations was Tovar's servant, Diego de Aguilar, who escaped his confinement through the excuses of exercise and even assistance to the mozo del carcel, and then conveyed notes between the prisoners' cells. María de Cazalla's domestic acted in similar ways, but with less success: at one point, she mistook one location for another and ended up throwing missives for Tovar into someone else's chamber. The unintended recipient subsequently extorted better treatment, in the form of partridges and garbanzo beans, from the warden and the mozo, since he correctly deduced that they must be involved in what amounted to a prison-wide flow of memoranda.[68]

Such antics were not new to the workings of the Spanish Inquisition. After Juan López de Celaín was arrested as a Lutheran, he escaped from the Granada tribunal not once but twice before being released to the secular arm and burned at the stake in 1530: bribery of the prison warden facilitated his breakouts. It was alleged that Francisca Hernández met with two prisoner-disciples through holes in the wall during her stay in the Toledo tribunal; the evidence also suggests that the warden, at least, spent hours in her cell, and the mozo turned into her fervent partisan.[69] In 1560, the warden at Valladolid was caught passing news to some prisoners and forcing work upon others; in the early 1570s, the Granada alcaide got his family's clothing from an imprisoned tailor. During his sojourn in the Cuenca tribunal, Pedro de Orellana became one of that city's most popular poets: at first he proclaimed his verse from the windows of his cell, and then handed his letters and poetry to the despensero, who lowered sacks of those compositions to Orellana's admirers in the dead of night. A few decades later the prophetess Lucrecia de León and her compatriots would converse with each other, socialize with the inquisitors, and solicit favors from the warden and despensero after their incarceration in the Toledo tribunal.[70] When sedition occurred in the Inquisition's prisons, wardens and their entourage almost always had something to do with it. These officials' tendency to break the rules makes sense when we consider that they actually lived in the jails and managed security there: steady exposure to the defendants gave them ample opportunity to compel a favor or to accept one.

Schemes to upset the Inquisition's rules occurred everywhere in Spain throughout the sixteenth century; Vergara's and Tovar's efforts were not unique. Nonetheless, their intrigues were highly offensive to the Toledo inquisitors, who saw the letters as a violation of their secret environment by another clandestine circle.[71] Tovar had dared to create a veritable scriptorium inside the Toledo tribunal, and he and his brother had conducted privileged details in and out of the same building. The inquisitors knew that this correspondence was not innocuous, although Vergara and Tovar focused on the misery of their family's situation in their testimony and stressed the solace that one brother attempted to give the other. In fact, Vergara often wrote his epistles—the only ones that we possess—in code, as well as in a thoroughly macaronic mix of Latin and Spanish, which he may well have intended to obscure the letters' substance. His messages mentioned the recusation of Inquisition officials in his brother's case, warned Tovar about María de Cazalla, and shared rumors about Juan del Castillo's whereabouts.[72] Before and after Vergara's arrest, the brothers insisted that the younger had been acting as the elder's informal lawyer. But given the interception of Hernán Rodríguez, the content of the confiscated memos, and the correspondence that Tovar sustained within the prison itself, it is not surprising that the inquisitors treated such violations of secrecy very seriously indeed.

From the thrust of their queries to their prosecutor's formal accusation, in the spring and summer of 1533 the inquisitors plainly wanted Vergara to tell them how he had helped his brother and what he had learned in the process. Before his arrest, when he appeared before Yáñes and Vaguer on May 20, 1533, the interrogation concerned only his knowledge of Inquisition secrets. Inquiries about Luther or Erasmus or the alumbrados were simply absent. When examined about Tovar's confidential messages, Vergara admitted his reception of them, quickly mentioned Hernán Rodríguez's role in Tovar's provisioning, and thereby implied that the memoranda related to foodstuffs, clothing, and Tovar's general health. He was asked whether he had received details about Tovar's trial, and quizzed about what, if anything, Tovar had related of the other prisoners, especially the female ones: Vergara refused to comment on either possibility. He rejected the notion that *he* had suggested recusing inquisitors or members of the Suprema. He insisted that the idea to disqualify Jerónimo Suárez Maldonado, the bishop of Mondoñedo, was Tovar's.[73]

Vergara's abbreviated replies and outright denials on May 20 earned him an *amonestación,* a formal warning that inquisitors leveled against negatory defendants. Inquisitors Yáñes and Vaguer informed him that he would not be in an interrogation if they did not already possess evidence to his detriment; they also reminded him of the oath he had sworn to tell the truth. Vergara instantly backed down: he replied that his communication with Tovar had been so secret that he had believed it would defy discovery. He went on to depict himself as a solicitous family member who only had promoted his brother's welfare. He had counseled Tovar on any and every aspect of his defense, which amounted to so much advice that he could not remember exactly what he had written. He had told Tovar to quit meddling with the women prisoners; he had directed him to tell the truth about his conversations with Juan del Castillo. He had worried particularly about any talks between Tovar and Castillo that had taken place in Alcalá, since his younger sister Isabella might have been present, and he feared her inculpation. Throughout his testimony, Vergara insisted that his brother was blameless, which was why he had not hesitated to intervene in his case.[74] With such statements, he achieved three ends at once: he proclaimed his brother's innocence, linked Tovar's sincerity to his own honor, and managed to raise, implicitly, his personal animosity toward heretics.

Significantly, much of what Vergara told the inquisitors in the interview of May 20 was accurate: he had warned Tovar about beatas and telling the truth in the letters that were seized and transcribed. Perhaps there was just enough consensus between Vergara's statements during the first interrogation and the messages themselves to stall the inquisitors, at least temporarily: the exchange of May 20 ended inconclusively, since Yáñes and Vaguer pronounced Vergara free to depart—although they gave that liberty an ominous twist when they cautioned him to treat the city of Toledo as a prison, and not to leave it without their permission.[75] On June 23, they again called Vergara for questioning: this time, Yáñes and Vaguer asked him to identify the five recovered letters as his own, which he did; they then pressed him on his knowledge of other prisoners besides his brother, and his bribery of their officials.[76]

Vergara responded that he only knew whom the tribunal had seized, which was a matter of public rumor. He had not retained any messages from Tovar, because he was a very busy man who typically lost half his correspondence and scribbled the rest illegibly. He denied knowing the warden and his mozo; when he told Hernán Rodríguez to provide them with bread, he meant the gift as alms, which was why no one bothered to hide the transaction. His only motive was to secure the decent treatment of his brother; he believed the same impulse had prompted Rodríguez to give the mozo a hat. He had told Hernán that he was writing to Tovar, but had never divulged the content of the notes.[77] He thought it impertinent of the inquisitors to inquire which brother had initiated the correspondence. Finally, when Vaguer and Yáñes asked whether he believed he had done anything wrong, Vergara said he did not. "He does not grasp that he has committed any error in advising and writing to his brother what he in fact wrote, because he views his brother as a good Christian . . . and this witness is [Tovar's] brother and he has experienced an understandable pain over his brother's prison and ordeal. And besides all this, this witness is his lawyer."[78] The inquisitors asked Vergara to ratify his statements, which he did, and then sent him out of the room. During his absence, they discussed his guilt in the correspondence, wondered whether they had learned all he knew, and decided to punish and pressure him with a stay in their prison.

When Vergara returned to the hearing, the inquisitors ordered him to read their decision, and then turned him over to Diego Gaspar Martínez, who now was acting as both alcaide and despensero. I find it exacting to recapitulate this scene, which both repels and attracts the imagination; it is difficult not to inject drama into the transcription, which simply records: "immediately the said doctor [Vergara] said he appealed the wrongful imprisonment and demanded they give him the chance to name an attorney to prosecute said appeal before the lords of the Suprema. The inquisitors said that they will see about it, and the reply will be given to him at the appropriate moment."[79] I suspect that Vergara's overwhelming reaction was anger: for that reason, I have translated *pidió* as "demanded." But he might just as well have been frightened, and "begged," "supplicated," or "solicited" the inquisitors for the opportunity to designate a lawyer and pursue an appeal. Any of these emotions would have been appropriate to his situation, since he now entered the

Inquisition's system, such as it was, as a suspect. He would not leave the Toledo tribunal for two and a half years.

Vergara immediately deduced the reason for his arrest. When the inquisitors finally gave him paper, he submitted a petition, on June 26, in which he stated that his imprisonment occurred because he had not told the truth about his and Tovar's correspondence from the start, or because their letters revealed things about female prisoners, although such details were hardly his doing, since he had warned Tovar to mind his own business. Only afterward did he raise possible depositions about heresy that the Inquisition might possess: if the inquisitors had solicited such statements against him, he was no fool and could be examined about them, for he "could give reasons that might satisfy" any misgivings.[80] Vergara went on to claim that the Toledo inquisitors had moved too quickly in his case and possibly had contravened their own mandates. In his arrest they had insulted someone who had far more honor than their usual targets; moreover, they could not possibly have had the Suprema's permission to imprison him. If Vaguer and Yáñes cut off his appeal, he would protest the denial, and if they refused him paper and books, he would appeal that refusal as well.[81]

Vergara's initial petition and subsequent interviews, as well as the prosecutor's own statements, corroborate the notion that he was arraigned because of the clandestine correspondence with his brother.[82] It seems that the Inquisition pursued and Vergara answered two lines of accusation, one of which pertained to the secret letters, the other to his purportedly heretical comments. Throughout his incarceration, he was only interrogated about his sabotage of inquisitorial procedure; furthermore, in September 1533 the fiscal told Inquisitor Vaguer that he knew Vergara had principally been arrested because of the epistles.[83] Yet the publication of testimony concentrated on the depositions about heresy that the inquisitors collected between 1529 and 1532.[84] Obviously a trial in the Spanish Inquisition could entail multiple tracks of prosecution, but in this case modern scholars have neglected the more immediate causes of Vergara's arrest.

Finding Vergara's letters to Tovar motivated the trial in one particular respect: their discovery illuminated Gaspar de Lucena's testimony in May 1532. At that point, Lucena had relayed his foreknowledge of the Latin arrest decree for his own brother, Juan del Castillo, and had pinpointed Vergara as the source of his information. A year later, when the Toledo inquisitors exposed the messages flowing between Vergara and Tovar, and again between Tovar and the other prisoners, Lucena's statements took on a deeper significance, for the same officials now understood how news about their arrest order could have seeped out of their building. They grilled Vergara on June 27, 1533, four days after his incarceration: the entire interview revolved around his awareness of Castillo's whereabouts and his potential corruption of Toledo's inquisitorial staff. Yáñes and Vaguer then questioned him in December 1533, and again in January, March, and May 1534: in each session, they attempted to grasp how Vergara had learned about the arrest decree for Castillo and the extent to which he had suborned their officials. In the process, they unearthed more details about the sabotage.

On June 27, 1533, Vergara told the inquisitors that he would not divulge how he knew about the arrest order, because the transmission of that information had been a secret, "in the way a priest can know a secret that he cannot reveal, and it should be enough to believe his oath, that he had not heard it from anyone who worked in this Holy Office." Vergara insisted that he was charged with this trust "under the secret sign of the sacrament of penance and confession"; he noted that he had bothered about Castillo only because of that individual's potential impact on Tovar's case.[85] Three days later, on June 30, the inquisitors turned to the now imprisoned Hernán Rodríguez, in the hope that he had functioned as the intermediary and carried the information about Castillo to Vergara. But Rodríguez testified that he never had sworn an oath of secrecy to Vergara, or obtained one either.

The Toledo tribunal stalled in its quest for six months. But on December 15, 1533, Vergara asked for an *audiencia*, and the inquisitors turned his request into an interrogation. On that date they asked Vergara a leading question: whether he had told someone besides Hernán Rodríguez about the letters to Tovar, and used a *second* intermediary. Vergara took the hint and conceded that he had called upon Cristobal de Gumiel, an old acquaintance of Tovar's and a Greek pupil of Castillo's, to transfer messages too. He then refused to acknowledge anything else, to the point that he insisted he never even had conversed with Gumiel at length.

The inquisitors pushed harder: they produced Gumiel himself, and cross-examined him on December 20. To say that Gumiel was a devastating witness would be an understatement, for he betrayed countless details about Tovar's and Vergara's arrangements. It turned out that Vergara had promised one Hermosilla, a former notary for the Toledo tribunal, food and 15,000 maravedís a year in return for his assistance with Tovar's case; Gumiel had mediated the offer. Once Hermosilla accepted the bribe, he passed Gumiel the names of the prosecution's witnesses against Tovar, and the same names then found their way to Vergara. Gumiel talked to Hermosilla about Francisca Hernández's testimony, and conveyed the information to Vergara; he even arranged a private meeting between Hermosilla and Vergara in the cloister of the Toledo cathedral. Gumiel told the inquisitors that Archbishop Fonseca knew about Vergara's and Tovar's clandestine schemes. He also reported that Vergara wrote to Tovar *por puntos*, or through dots placed under the letters of books that one brother sent to the other.[86]

Gumiel confirmed that he and Vergara had sworn each other to secrecy, an oath that Vergara acknowledged when he was questioned several weeks later; Vergara also admitted having told Gumiel that secrets between friends could be preserved, even if those confidences occurred outside the sacrament of penance. But Vergara insisted he had spoken to Hermosilla merely once or twice in his life, maintained that he never had promised that notary anything, and declared that he actually had received the names of Tovar's accusers through Archbishop Fonseca and common gossip. When Vaguer and Yáñez pressed him, Vergara contended that he was obliged to try and discover the deponents against his brother, while the *manner* in which he learned their identity was unimportant.[87] He conceded that his and Tovar's aim was to learn about the witnesses in order to recuse them.

Although the inquisitors gleaned details about the corruption of their personnel from Gumiel's and Vergara's testimony in December and January 1533–34, they did not manage to crack the problem of Castillo and the arrest order until May 2 of the latter year. On that date, Vergara finally admitted what Gumiel had already implied: he conceded that Gumiel was his informant and Hermosilla the source of the news. Amazingly enough, given his attempts to manipulate his brother's case, Vergara learned about the warrant for Castillo by accident. As he spoke to Gumiel about Tovar's case, Gumiel told him that Hermosilla could not investigate Vergara's requests, because the same notary was very busy translating a Spanish document into Latin, which would be "sent outside the kingdom against a Master Castillo."[88] Once Vergara deduced that Castillo was about to be arrested, he wished to ensure the refugee's flight, and accordingly relayed the news of the decree to Castillo's brother. Considering that the authorities eventually found Castillo in Bologna, it looks as if Vergara's plan worked for a time.

Vergara's actions outside the Toledo tribunal and Tovar's within it illustrate the potential fragility of an institution—at least in the face of the well-connected—that all too often symbolizes religious authority in early modern Spain. But despite the threats that Vergara and his clients posed to the Inquisition's performance, its bureaucrats still managed to hold him for two and a half years, notwithstanding three letters from Archbishop Fonseca to the tribunal itself and at least one to the Suprema on his secretary's behalf; even the Suprema ordered the tribunal to speed up the trial, to absolutely no effect.[89] It truly appears as if neither the archbishop of Toledo nor the Suprema could influence or control the Toledo tribunal, whose inquisitors justified Vergara's detention with the depositions they had collected between 1529 and 1532.[90] The fiscal could not turn Vergara's subornation into the crux of the charges, because Vergara and his friends might easily have claimed that the prosecution arose from revenge, a motive that inquisitorial procedure absolutely proscribed. The fiscal and the inquisitors consequently draped their personal vengeance with depositions about Vergara's Lutheran and alumbrado sympathies, which were heresies of national importance. They arrested Vergara for local and practical reasons, but then tried him according to much larger priorities.

The prosecution testimony collected against Vergara alleged one affront after another to religious authority. Witnesses reported challenges to papal primacy and ecclesiastical rituals, the elevation of Erasmus over other experts, and the deprecation of the saints. Francisca Hernández and Marí Ramírez supplied the largest share of the charges: among other things, they recalled that Vergara favored Luther's opinions in general, laughed at papal bulls and indulgences, disputed the utility of oral prayer, and remarked that there were two superfluous "saints" in the world, the *sancta inquisición* and the *sancta cruzada*. Between April and May 1534, the fiscal added more accusations to the roster, which he culled from testimony by Miguel Ortíz and Alonso Ruiz de Virués.[91]

In the formal indictment and the publication of evidence, which occurred in July and November 1533, respectively, Vergara became a heretic as well as a supporter of suspected ones. According to a renowned definition from the thirteenth century, "Heresy is an opinion chosen by human faculties, contrary to Holy Scripture, openly taught, and pertinaciously defended."[92] True to intellectual tradition, the fiscal summarized Vergara's fault as the obstinate, persistent promotion of views attached to Lutherans, alumbrados, and Erasmus. That only two of these categories or individuals were formally classified as heretical by 1533, while all three contradicted each other, simply illustrates that the identification and prosecution of heresy was a pliable, even ambiguous process in the 1520s and 1530s. Although Erasmus had not been formally excommunicated, the Inquisition's prosecutor did not hesitate to adduce instead the Sorbonne's condemnation of him. If the Inquisition's victims occasionally outwitted its procedures, its prosecutors, too, could overlook some sanctions and elevate others.

Defendants as clever and resourceful as Vergara could also refuse to cooperate in their own trials. From his arrest in June 1533 until his final sentencing in December 1535, Vergara protested his incarceration and refused to submit witnesses: he attempted to block the tribunal by simultaneously calling on the Suprema and declining to mount a defense. Between June and September 1533, he petitioned the Suprema over the injustice of his imprisonment, and renewed or inquired after that motion repeatedly. On July 19, he submitted another appeal, this time over maltreatment: the inquisitors had nailed his windows shut because he was leaning out of them and conversing with people on the street.[93] In August 1533, when the Suprema responded to his original plea and upheld Toledo's authority to arrest him, Vergara found that reply irrelevant to the gist of his appeal, which primarily concerned his imprisonment; he insisted his petition was still in play. He even tried to control the inquisitorial process after formal charges were delivered in July, for he demanded the publication of incriminating testimony on September 15, October 3, October 16, October 24, and November 4: such petitions were absolutely legal, but they imply that he attempted to eclipse the system by suffusing the tribunal with as much paper as he could obtain. Meanwhile, he declined to present any defense witnesses: he renounced the formal period of proof in March 1534 and again in May 1535, declared his portion of the case concluded, and demanded a sentence. Provocatively, members of his cohort—Hernán Rodríguez and Diego de Aguilar—refused to call defense witnesses as well. The coincidence implies a joint legal strategy.[94]

Although Vergara repeatedly requested a speedy verdict, a decision on his heresy was not forthcoming, although the last and weightiest statement on the depositions against him was issued in November 1534: at that point, three calificadores found that thirteen out of twenty-two propositions attributed to him either were heretical or favored heresy.[95] Over the spring and summer of 1535, the Suprema and the tribunal tried to force Vergara to present witnesses, with no success. In June 1535, the Toledo cathedral chapter pleaded with the Suprema to pressure the tribunal over the case; in July, Vergara filed a statement of aggravation over the delay. On November 6, a member of the Suprema itself, Diego Girón de Loaysa, urged the inquisitors to put Vergara through a public or private auto-da-fé, and quickly, for Vergara was sure to file another appeal over the holdup in his sentencing: this time, the chances were good that the Suprema would uphold his petition, in which case the Toledo office would lose control over the trial and compensation for monies spent in its prosecution.[96] Nevertheless, the tribunal did not move. On November 29, 1535, when Vergara complained about the seemingly endless waiting, Yáñez and Vaguer replied that his time in prison was his own fault.

The Toledo tribunal did not oblige Vergara with a judgment until the following month, and given his status, it was a harsh one: the inquisitors decreed that he should go through a public auto-da-fé in Toledo's main square, where he would hold a wax candle in his hands and wear the robes that signified his penitential condition. Thus on December 21, 1535, Juan de Vergara stood on an open scaffold in Zocódover Plaza and heard that he had favored Luther and ridiculed papal bulls. He learned that he had deprecated purgatory and indulgences, and owned Lutheran books after their possession had been forbidden. He had spurned vocal prayer, dismissed fasts, and deprecated the saints. He had seconded statements of the alumbrados and favored Erasmus. The verdict only raised the subornation of the Holy Office at the very end of the list: it called Vegara an abettor of heresy and a corrupter of the Inquisition's employees through words, works, and promises. It pointed out that Vergara admitted only his bribery. It then sentenced him to a full year of irremissible seclusion in a monastery and administered a fine of 1,500 gold ducats.[97]

In January 1536, Vergara was taken to the monastery of St. Augustine. In March, Inquisitor General Manrique ordered him to serve out his sentence at the Toledo cathedral, to begin on the Feast of John the Baptist; the cathedral chapter had requested the transferal. Accordingly, on the eve of the feast day, June 23, 1536, Vergara was moved to the cathedral, where he continued as a prebendary, if not an archepiscopal secretary, until his death in 1557.[98] In his will, he left the bulk of his income to the insane asylum, the Casa del Nuncio, that he and his fellow-canons supported; he recorded that "on very many occasions, the crazy and demented are the ones who voice the great truths and excellent arguments."[99]

Juan de Vergara's ordeal has impressed twentieth-century historians, who have turned it into a critical piece of evidence in their constructions of sixteenth-century Spain. Certainly the trial attests a fission between the defendant and the inquisitors, whether in terms of intellectual independence or spiritual priorities: Vergara was not a typical ecclesiastic, but he can symbolize what his peers might have become under different conditions. He willfully mocked the Inquisition and vigorously supported Erasmus: from such fearlessness, it is but a short step to interiority, tolerance, and all the other progressive characteristics that might have altered Iberia had Spanish Erasmians not been cut down.[100]

Obviously Vergara defied the Inquisition with stunning regularity. He publicized his debauchment of it even before his arrest, since he told associates about his correspondence with Tovar; after his incarceration, he denied the same institution's right to judge him. He critiqued its methods by claiming that some witnesses had been prompted into their testimony. He implied that the Inquisition was fundamentally corrupt, because its officials could solicit hurtful rumors about anyone, given the fear and horror with which people regarded it, not to mention the secrecy that protected accusers from their victims' wrath.[101] He often ridiculed his judges: at one point, he remarked that his defense statement should be sent to Archbishop Fonseca, because it was only fitting for the archbishop to learn of his secretary's heresies, not having suspected them over the previous ten years.[102] But if Vergara repeatedly dismissed the Inquisition's prerogatives, the issue becomes what sort of religious authority he endorsed, for he was too thoroughly entrenched in Spain's ecclesiastical hierarchy to stand outside it in some essentially critical way. Notably, his promotion of caste was as frank as his attack on inquisitorial jurisdiction.

Although he refused to present witnesses in his defense, Vergara responded to the fiscal's publication of testimony. On November 8, 1533, the prosecutor finally handed him a summary of the incriminating depositions, in which all identifying markers of the witnesses had been erased. Vergara reacted immediately and verbally to the charges. He then spent perhaps four months writing up his rebuttal, which he presented to Vaguer and Yáñez on March 6, 1534; his reply extends over thirty-five folios and is in holograph. Vergara's oral and written defense immediately sparks the question of truthfulness, since he spoke and wrote under compulsion: in every instance, he presumably intended to lessen his purported faults and inculpate his enemies. Nonetheless, if he exaggerated his sentiments under the burden of self-defense, from a different perspective he also made the most extreme or moderate statements of which he was capable: his responses illustrate the limits to his intellectual and religious emphases, no matter what the direction. Vergara was attempting to persuade inquisitors, but he still had to put forward views that would be plausible for a man in his position. In that respect, the potential gap between his spoken and written utterances, and his private thoughts, becomes irrelevant.

In terms of status, Vergara hit the same notes so frequently that his various defense statements end up looking like a coherent piece of work.[103] We should not be fooled by his arrogance toward the Inquisition; he did not advocate an unfettered religious environment. Instead, he promoted a male ecclesiastical meritocracy, university trained with court connections. When he regarded the alumbrados—or specifically, the alumbradas Francisca Hernández and Marí Ramírez, whom he knew testified against him—Vergara turned their religiosity and class into the opposite of his own. He coated that inversion with gendered stereotypes and charges of villainy.

Francisca's and Marí's statements undoubtedly resulted from collusion, for mistress and servant were housed in the same cell in the tribunal. Their depositions centered on Vergara's affection for Lutheran and alumbrado opinions, and his corresponding ridicule of papal prerogatives. Theoretically, Francisca and Marí were alarming, for they corroborated the same offenses; Vergara could not immediately point to the singularity of their statements, as he did with every other witness, but instead had to demolish their potential persuasiveness. He accordingly turned to the legal implications of capital enmity and public reputation, and showered his discourse with negative clichés about the feminine.

In his version of events, Francisca had plotted her revenge against the two brothers since 1522, when Vergara removed Tovar from her company. She was a malevolent female who used the Inquisition for retribution against anyone who might have spurned her spiritual leadership. She was Tovar's mortal enemy and hence could offer only worthless testimony; she had simply transplanted incidents from one brother's case into the other's. She was a notoriously false witness, a perjurer, and a hypocrite. She and Marí pretended to be holy while they were not, they simulated miraculous acts, and if they faked works they would lie that much more easily. Finally, Vergara raised the subordinate relationship between Marí as a servant and Francisca as her employer: the former was in the latter's power, which meant that Marí's depositions could not be trusted, especially since she was only a child when she purportedly overheard incriminating conversations.[104] Although the two women confirmed each other's testimony, their affidavits meant little.

With such statements as these, Vergara tried to annul the probative value of two eyewitnesses to the same incriminating incidents. In the process he sketched a likeness of Francisca that could crush her character and nullify her depositions. By raising her (persistent) dissimulation and the public's widespread knowledge of her chicanery, Vergara deliberately linked her to infamy, a legal category that signaled a notorious reputation for wickedness and dishonor. As a factor in civil and canon law, infamy heightened the presumption of guilt.[105] Then Vergara went even further and summoned images that would tie Francisca and her circle to the demonic. He referred to her group as a sect, thereby summoning a standard term in Western descriptions of heretics and, by the sixteenth century, of witches. When he stipulated that Francisca and Marí deceived people, he furthered their connections to the diabolical because the Devil was the father of lies. As he tied Francisca's testimony to retribution, he summoned the equally resonant trope that women appealed to demons for their vengeful schemes because the usual routes to justice were barred to them. Paradoxically, Vergara also insisted upon the frailty of female memory, which undid some of his assertions: a woman who could not remember an insult could hardly plot to avenge it. Nevertheless, his remarks conjured up the absolutely gendered stereotype of the libidinous and deceitful, powerless and hence malevolent female. Provocatively, many of his comments duplicate both the sequence and the content of the sixth *quaestio* of the *Malleus maleficarum*'s first division: that inquiry addressed female propensities for witchcraft.[106]

As Vergara maligned Francisca and Marí, he turned himself into a champion of Christian tradition in the face of odd religious practices. *He* was not eccentric in his conversation or diversions; in contrast, the alumbradas specialized in *vanidades,* an epithet with gendered and demonic connotations. He called Francisca and Marí "inventors of new opinions [and] new forms of living against the common practice of the Church and of the Christian faithful." He labeled himself as perpetually hostile to "these beatas" and continuously skeptical of "their *beaterías.*"[107] He explicitly distinguished his life from the alumbradas' by contrasting their works, companions, and exercises with his own; in one inversion, Vergara contended that stamping him as an alumbrado would be akin to calling a black man Juan Blanco (John White).[108] As for conversing with Francisca about theological matters, Vergara exuded disdain over the very possibility: the idea that he, of all people, would talk about books with this alumbrada was absurd, as was the notion that he would share his opinions with her or suffer her criticism, for that matter. He deemed it most incongruous that such idiot [sic] women as these could be summoned against a man like himself.

In previous treatments of the trial, historians have neglected the formulas in Vergara's defense, and presumed instead that he was telling the truth when he charged Francisca with infamy, deceit, and rancor; of course, to some extent he probably believed she possessed such qualities. The larger point, though, is that he regarded Francisca and Marí as dangerous, and consequently turned to a series of stereotypes in his defense. Even his charge about the alumbrados' novelty transmitted heretical and diabolical clichés about *curiositas* (untoward curiosity) and women's proclivity to indulge in it.[109] Vergara used such truisms both because they were options within his cultural matrix, and because he intended the conventions to move his audience and temper his guilt. His arguments against the alumbradas place him in a specific historical environment, rather than outside it; they should mitigate any tendency to see him as protomodern.

When it came to his responses to male deponents, Vergara preserved his elevated claims to social status, whether in the duties he performed, the conversations he sustained, or the behavior he could chastise. As an episcopal secretary, he typically received stacks of correspondence from Rome and other distant places, and handed them off to whoever claimed them, including Gaspar de Lucena.[110] When he was at the archbishop's residence in Valladolid, his responsibilities were so heavy that he went to bed at one, two, or even three in the morning; he did not feel obliged to hear Mass every day, "especially being as busy as he was."[111] His quarrel with Bernardino Flores should not have scandalized anyone, "especially not being in public or before the masses, but before an archbishop of Toledo and two other gentlemen, one of whom was an educated man and an ecclesiastic."[112] Vergara further underscored such social and intellectual distinctions when he relayed how Juan de Valdés had "meddled in matters he had not studied" in the course of writing the *Doctrina cristiana*. And after he was confronted with a story of having scolded a preacher in Alcalá, in 1525, Vergara replied that if he had rebuked the cleric, the victim undoubtedly deserved it. Significantly, the homilist in question had been imploring priests to reside in their benefices and to supply sermons to their congregations.[113]

In each of these instances, Vergara mentioned his position and his education to justify his actions: he saw himself as part of the religious and academic elite, and possessed a sharp sense of his place over and against the rest of Spanish society. His status freed him from certain restrictions, but his perception of his own independence did not lead him to extend that liberty to others. Instead, he summoned a hierarchy that had as many practical implications as the Inquisition's, given his standing, and his resulting financial and even human capital. Inquisitors were his inferiors, and he could move around them. He could critique books written by amateurs. He might flatten a friar who did not know Greek or a preacher who presumed to tell his betters to take care of their parishioners. Vergara had a finely tuned sense of privilege, although his usual portrait—and that of Spanish Erasmians as a whole—conditions us to imagine something very different.

Vergara's claims to entitlement did not jolt his peers. During the final debate over the verdict, when the inquisitors called in both theological and legal consultants, Juan de Medina agreed with Vergara's assessment of Francisca Hernández and Marí Ramírez, and argued that the weight of their testimony should be diminished. Another adviser cited Vergara's lengthy prison stay, expenses, and afflictions, and requested compensation; the same individual maintained that Vergara should not be put on the public scaffold, but simply abjure his faults in the Church of San Juan de los Reyes or some other private setting. Recommendations for leniency did not succeed in this instance; the sentence ultimately cast Vergara as a warning to others who might try to pitch their own authority against the Holy Office's. Nevertheless, the fact that the consultadores attempted to balance culpability with rank illustrates the extent to which Vergara had expressed a familiar language of law, sex, and status.

He could speak for tradition in other ways as well. His trial may demonstrate his awareness and practice of Renaissance humanism, but it also illuminates his indebtedness to the trivium and quadrivium, as well as Aristotle. Vergara was not a stranger to the theological authorities of the thirteenth and fourteenth centuries. He was not aloof from the intellectual culture that he and his peers inherited, but moved smoothly from humanism to scholasticism and back again.

When surveyed as a whole, the prosecution's case reflected a minor interest in manuscript transmission, saints' errors, and the historical development of the Catholic Church; furthermore, the calificadores' evaluation in 1534 tended to pardon Vergara's comments on such matters. The defendant himself found the subjects of greater import: he not only highlighted his relationship with Erasmus, but wrote a reply to Bernardino Flores whose length was out of all proportion to the published charge.

Vergara attested repeatedly that he trusted Erasmus's orthodoxy and implied, at least, that he extolled his authority above other, more institutional, voices. He was Erasmus's friend. Erasmus could relinquish Mass in order to study, even if that choice were questionable. Erasmus rightly noted the Church's failure to pronounce confession as divine law—which was rather different from arguing *whether* confession were divinely ordained.[114] The Sorbonne had condemned Erasmus over the same issue, but that censure was illegitimate, for no one could proceed against anyone else without a conclusion by the Church; not even the Inquisition had the authority to determine such questions, since they must be referred to Rome.[115] As for the purported errors in Erasmus's *De esu carnium*, Vergara spat back that when misjudgments occurred in that author's *opera* or anyone else's, he would not discard the work in question.[116]

Although Vergara also would concede that the Sorbonne had some valid criticisms of Erasmus—and admit that he himself had spoken to Erasmus only three or four times in his life, and then very summarily—the mass of the transcript suggests that he deserves his modern reputation as an Erasmian, insofar as he read that individual's works and agreed with many of his emphases. The more profound issue, though, is whether he shared Erasmus's critical outlook on sacred texts and Church history. Evidence that he did lies in his reaction to Bernardino Flores.

The prosecutor turned Flores's deposition into the following charges. Vergara had challenged the accuracy of the Latin Vulgate, the Church's common translation of the Bible. He had deprecated St. Augustine's knowledge of Greek, and from there that saint's exposition of the psalms in the *Quinquagenas*. In the wake of Flores's defense of Augustine, Vergara made rude remarks about Flores's understanding of the Holy Spirit, and contended that Augustine did not know what he was doing. Finally, he had mentioned discrepancies between the Latin and Greek versions of the Psalms, explicitly favored the latter, and noted that monks in general were fools.[117]

Vergara's response to Flores's testimony was detailed and intricate. He instantly recognized his accuser; he first turned to the law to weaken the deposition, and summoned hearsay and anecdotes to lessen Flores's credibility. Flores was an "infamous person, and guilty of treason; he incited the people to robberies, murders, fires, sacrilege, and other classes of serious and enormous crimes."[118] Flores's role in the *comunero* revolt was notorious, and he was a perjurer who was known to have broken two or three solemn vows in a week, one of which was made on a missal. Just like Francisca Hernández, Flores testified out of hatred, for he believed that Vergara had delayed his acquisition of the Pinto benefice.[119] Meaningfully, Vergara jammed the story of Flores and "ite in castellum" into a diatribe about his accuser's sedition: the thrust of the narrative pertained to treason, not intellectual incompetence.[120]

Vergara chose his words carefully. Linking Flores's crimes to both notoriety and treason was a twofold punch, for infamy reduced the weight of the testimony and treason was the heretic's ultimate offense: from the late twelfth century on, canon and civil lawyers had conceived of heresy as sedition against God. But Vergara did not try to escape the charges through recusation alone: he spent far more time on the intellectual issues that prompted his and Flores's original argument. As he enumerated his thoughts on language, error, and ecclesiastical authority, he did not lay out his message in any sort of order; as he entertained objections or multiplied examples, he raised, discarded, and summoned again relevant points. What follows steadies and compresses his statements.

Vergara immediately tried to distance himself from the charge of disrespect toward Augustine and, by extension, toward sacred authorities as a whole. He never said that Augustine did not know what he was doing in the *Quinquagenas*; everyone, educated or not, owed complete veneration and respect to the writings of the church fathers; the comment in play was contemptuous and not his, although it also was far from heretical.[121] The real issue in Flores's deposition was whether anyone was allowed to point out flaws in works utilized by the Church. Flores's stupidity lay in not understanding the sort of authority that the Church extended to different sacred writings: for instance, no one was allowed to disagree with the substance of Holy Scripture. But the Church's approval of particular doctors did not explicitly confirm everything those individuals wrote, to the point that their words became irrefutable and no one was permitted to dissent from them; not even canonization conferred such prestige. Poor Flores thought that by "singing something in Church, that is, within the very walls of the sanctuary, then the Church—that is, the congregation of the faithful or the council or the pope—approved that something letter-by-letter like the Gospel itself."[122] Saints composed out of their own intelligence as well as through the inspiration of the Holy Spirit, and could be misled. Disagreements and mistakes littered patristic texts: Augustine and Jerome differed over the end of the Law, Paul rebuked Peter over the need for Jewish rituals, and Cyprian erred on the baptism of heretics.

The possibility of mistakes extended to the saints' linguistic skills and even the languages of the Bible. A gloss might rationalize other sorts of statements, but not a translation: no commentary could straighten out Isidore of Seville's claim that "acolyte" in Greek meant *ceroferarius* (wax-bearer) in Latin.[123] Anyone could see the corruption in Augustine's version of the Psalms by collating it with what was used in 1534; Jerome certainly should receive more credit in matters of idioms and translations. Moreover, the Latin Psalms contained numerous differences from their Hebrew originals: Augustine himself had discovered an error in Wisdom 4:3, which the Latin translator had rendered as *vitulamina* (sprigs) instead of *plantationes* (transplantings).

Vergara's sense of change over time was as sophisticated as his outlook on philology. He rejected outright the notion that the Church's current usage should dictate its scholars' intellectual hierarchies. Christianity's very history and holiest authorities prevented the sanctification of Latin. If recurring to the original languages of Scripture were wrong, then why did Augustine and Jerome tell us to do it? Augustine frequently followed the Greek, and instructed us to follow his example in *De doctrina christiana*. Jerome acted similarly; so did Nicholas de Lyra, the fourteenth-century Franciscan exegete who used Hebrew to annotate the Old Testament. The late Cardinal Cisneros preserved Lyra's annotations by printing them in the Complutensian Polyglot Bible. Even Cajetan, the current head of the Dominican order, recently had expounded the New Testament in accordance with the Greek, and in the process changed words and opinions that the Church routinely used. Vergara concluded that he personally would be pleased to join such heretics.[124] He added that anyone who maintained that *all* monks were fools would be foolish himself: there were thoughtful friars as well as secular clerics, and monastic garb could dress men in wisdom as well as stupidity.[125]

More material on language and history lies in Vergara's responses to other witnesses. When the prosecutor denounced him for owning a book by Oecolampadius, he noted that the text in question was written by Theophylactus, the eleventh-century commentator: Oecolampadius only translated Theophylactus's work, and did so when he was still a Catholic. When told he favored Luther, Vergara replied that there were neither reports about nor books by Luther in Spain at the time of his supposed conversations with Francisca Hernández and Marí Ramírez.[126] When charged with ridiculing external religious acts, such as fasts and oral prayer, Vergara noted that he could not ignore the fasts and prayers of Jesus and the apostles; he could scarcely find a single learned man in the early church who did *not* fast.[127]

Vergara's responses reveal all the hallmarks of Renaissance humanism. He had not only read Erasmus's works, but discerned how Erasmus himself approached Christianity; he occasionally quoted or paraphrased his ideas. He openly grasped the contradictions in ecclesiastical authorities, and implicitly attested the importance of linguistic preparation for biblical scholarship. He personally followed Augustine's and Jerome's advice to turn to Scripture's original languages, but he also knew that saints, as human beings, were liable to err. He discerned the differences between the Latin Old and New Testaments, and their Hebrew and Greek archetypes; he evinced little patience with Isidore's wrongheaded etymologies. Moreover, his historical sensitivity was conspicuous: he understood the difference between the primitive church and his own, and seemed to elevate the former; he also possessed an exquisite perception of when, exactly, Luther and his followers became heretics. Vergara apparently saw religious authority as a shifting entity that developed over centuries: its parameters in many respects were dictated by human beings, and thus were subject to challenge and correction.

Yet the testimony of this intellectual also presents us with a conundrum, for Vergara was an Erasmian and a humanist who wielded scholastic vocabulary and authorities. If his endorsement of philological and historical criticism was marked, so was his reliance on medieval commonplaces. That dependence in turn should prompt us to lower or at least soften the barrier we have erected between humanists and scholastics in sixteenth-century Spain.

Vergara did not hesitate to portray himself as a partisan of custom. He noted with approval that the Church, not "individual idiots," fixed the traditions behind prayer and fasts. His references to Jerome were double-edged: they allowed him to elevate Hebrew, but also to exalt the traditional author of the Vulgate Bible, who was nothing if not a conventional authority. When he contrasted Augustine's corrupt version of the Psalms with "what we use today," he looked as if he were glorifying the Vulgate. He asserted that Augustine's *Quinquagenas* was an "excellent and singular" book. He judged the saints' errors in language as less serious than ones they made over the sacraments. He reported that it "must not be held as good to speak disrespectfully, in displeasure, about the saints and their books, but rather to excuse them and gloss their statements with reverence." And he stressed his philological expertise in translations of Aristotle instead of the Bible.[128]

If we scrutinize the transcript as a whole, Vergara's references to standard techniques and authorities are as plentiful as his critical remarks on the same. He cited etymologies of his own, despite his disparagement of Isidore of Seville.[129] He frequently employed words with distinguished and suggestive genealogies from the twelfth and thirteenth centuries, such as infamy, curiosity, and sect. He also invoked quintessentially medieval authorities like Bonaventura. But the best evidence for Vergara's employment of scholasticism lies in the middle of the trial transcript. Between January 13 and January 18, 1534, as he was quizzed about Latin arrest orders and lists of witnesses, Vergara wrote a Latin defense of his silence, which he deliberately cast in the form of a dialectical *quaestio* (inquiry), "after the style of theologians."[130]

Running for approximately five folios, and in holograph, the significance or even presence of Vergara's apologia has never been raised by scholars. It is prefaced by a substantial vernacular letter to the inquisitors and the Suprema, also in Vergara's hand. In his preamble, Vergara explained that he had been grilled about the prosecution witnesses against Tovar on January 13, 1534, and commanded to reveal what he knew and how he had learned it. The inquisitors had known for a month that an Inquisition notary had passed prosecution testimony to Cristobal de Gumiel, who in turn conveyed it to Vergara. But the tribunal had not yet succeeded in getting Vergara to verify Gumiel's statement, and since a confession was the "queen of proofs" in the Inquisition's legal culture, in January 1534 Vaguer and Yáñez increased the pressure.

Vergara reacted by composing this Latin apologia, which he handed to his interrogators on January 18. He remarked that the inquisitors' insistence provoked his scruples, because his acquisition of the witnesses' names was a secret, a promise sealed "under the sign of confession, although not sacramental." If that promise had been his own—if he had exacted it for self-protection—then he would have obeyed the inquisitors' mandate and told what he knew. But since the vow was principally to protect another, and Vergara had given his word, he would commit a very base act if he divulged what he should not and the person were ruined in the process; furthermore, such a revelation would make it difficult to trust him in something more substantial.[131] Accordingly, he had written a tract that explained why he could not legitimately declare what he was ordered to say. He had built his case from the best opinions of the best doctors of the Church; he believed he would secure his conscience with their authority.[132]

Vergara then delivered a scholastic treatment of secrets, promises, and the relative obligation of disclosure. The opening stated that secrets about witnesses in an Inquisition trial had been revealed to John, that is, to Vergara himself. The ensuing question asked "Whether John, who accepted not only the person but also the secrets themselves under the sign of confession, although outside true confession by contract, may be held to reveal those secrets according to a superior's order."[133] What followed were yes-and-no arguments as the apologia moved through affirmative and then negative points; it was devised in classic dialectical fashion. Assumptions were numbered, such as "first it is supposed" and "second it is supposed"; conclusions were broken down and summarized; objections to those conclusions were grouped at the end of the tract.[134] All these features were standard ones in scholastic discourse, and Vergara clearly knew how to employ them in his own writing.

When it came to his authorities, Vergara relied upon theology over canon law because he placed secrecy and fidelity in the realm of natural law, and natural law in turn was the special province of the theologian.[135] He invoked Aquinas's quodlibets and *Summa theologica* more than any other literature, because St. Thomas "usually is celebrated above the rest in moral issues respecting man."[136] Vergara was perfectly correct: the *secunda secundae* of Aquinas's *Summa* was recognized as the zenith of moral theology. Some of his other sources, though, look somewhat unusual: Jean Gerson conceivably, and Pope Adrian VI certainly, were rather contemporary to serve as authorities, since the one had died in 1429, the other in 1523. Nevertheless, Gerson's works were very popular in Spain in the early sixteenth century, and the ones Vergara cited—the *Regulis moralibus* and *Opus tripartito*—were relevant to his argument. The *Regulis* addressed charity, which related to injury to neighbors. The *Opus* included a work on confession, and all treatises on confession and the sacrament of penance adjured clerics and monks to secrecy when it came to penitents' revelations.[137] Vergara could have thought Adrian VI's four-part work on confession was germane for similar reasons, although his reference to that pope undoubtedly was supposed to convey political vibrations, since the same individual had tutored Charles V as Adrian of Utrecht.

It would be easy to dismiss Vergara's scholastic tract as an exercise designed to impress both the Toledo tribunal and the Suprema; according to a recent pronouncement on the subject, when Renaissance humanists attempted to imitate a scholastic voice, they generally did so very badly.[138] Still, expertise is a comparative concept, and Vergara argued very well indeed. He developed his points and arranged them sequentially. His reasoning appears deliberate instead of random.

Vergara contended that secrets between men related to fidelity, which in turn fell under the topic of natural law; conversely, infidelity violated natural law, and such infractions occurred when a confidence was broken.[139] Nothing could be demanded of a human being that contravened natural law, and thus neither could the narration of a secret. Moreover, a priest acted not as a man but as God during the sacrament of penance; an ecclesiastical sacrament dictated greater obedience than a human precept; in no way should the priest make known the confession. The sacramental environment exempted the cleric from conveying a secret to his prelate. By extension, a secret committed to another by means of an agreement could not be divulged either, at least not without breaking the faith that the one party had handed over to the other.[140]

Vergara provided the following conclusions. A subject was only obliged to unveil a secret according to a superior's order, when the subject also was charged to reveal that secret spontaneously and *without* the order, namely, by testifying or denouncing. A subject was only required to divulge a secret spontaneously when the matter entailed a public or private, spiritual or corporal danger that anyone was bound to avoid.[141] Thus a secret could be revealed in the event of authentic spiritual or corporal necessity—but *not* in a case that turned on the advantage of the majority. Hence, Juan de Vergara was not obliged to disclose what he knew. The secret he possessed had entailed a passing, one-time danger, not a continuous one; it consequently did not carry the burden to reveal or denounce. If the bearer of the information posed a risk to the functioning of the Holy Office, then disclosure would be warranted, especially if the situation could not be repaired through a private interchange. But Vergara could reassure the Inquisition that the confidence had not come from an inquisitor. He finally concluded that because the revelation would injure someone, he would sin mortally against the precept of charity if the inquisitors forced him to say what he knew. He ended with a scriptural reference: Romans 3 stipulated that evil things should not be done so that good ones might ensue.[142]

The details of Vergara's argument echo in events and circumstances: he and Gumiel had sworn an oath of secrecy; Gumiel was not an inquisitor, and strictly speaking, neither was *Gumiel's* informant, the notary Hermosilla. Provocatively, it was Gumiel who suggested that Vergara find some legal and theological justification for his silence vis-à-vis the Inquisition. After his initial interview in the Toledo tribunal, Vergara told Gumiel that he was troubled by his own taciturnity in the exchange. Gumiel in turn recommended that Vergara

study the problem, [to see if] he were obliged or not [to talk], to give some reason for what he had denied. . . . Vergara might write down the doctors who address the matter, and when the inquisitors call him, he might tell them everything that occurred, and carry with him, written down, the principle that caused him not to speak the truth immediately.[143]

Vergara liked Gumiel's idea: he told him to look in Cajetan's commentary on Aquinas's *Summa theologica,* as well as in the *Summa* itself, for material on oaths, silence, and disclosure. When Gumiel testified before the inquisitors in December 1533, he reported that he had given Vergara the Cajetan, but since he was no theologian, he had no idea what the material actually relayed.

Given this evidence, we could discount the Latin apologia as a long-standing, deliberately conceived maneuver that cannot illuminate Vergara's intellectual priorities. Yet the more important matter is not whether Vergara experimented in his Latin tract, or even believed his own arguments, which would be impossible to measure in any case. What counts is that he could and did write according to scholastic norms, with the expectation that such a composition would be both appropriate and convincing. He knew how to arrange a dialectical exposition. He also knew where to look for the relevant material—namely, in Aquinas's *Summa theologica* (II.II., qu. 70)—and he was smart enough to cite the *Summa* itself instead of Cajetan's gloss of it.

A relatively longer view of historical change renders Vergara's chameleon-like qualities perfectly predictable, since the trivium and quadrivium co-existed with the humanities and Aquinas circulated throughout the sixteenth century. But the nuances of Vergara's ordeal and the prismatic features of his intellect do not fit modern scholarship on early modern Spain. The fact is, we have expected so much consistency from Vergara and his contemporaries that we have turned them into parodies; we then have used those caricatures to sustain categories of the backward and the progressive in Spanish religious and intellectual life. Unfortunately, such dichotomies often block our scholarly investigations because they deflect our attention from the ambiguities in the historical record. Vergara was a humanist who invoked Aquinas and an Erasmian who cherished his own rank. At one time he read and admired Luther, but he also mocked beatas and disparaged alumbrados, not least because they were laypersons who presumed an expertise their station did not permit. He routinely lied to inquisitors, but esteemed the power of oaths; legal expertise and consolatory aims run side by side in his depositions. As for Vergara's enemies, his accusers had to be summoned before they deposed, the calificadores excused his statements about St. Augustine's Greek, and his verdict so neglected his Erasmianism as to make it moot. All these shadings amplify our grasp of the Spanish clerical elite; they clarify the finer details of that cadre's intelligence, and the myriad powers they might promote, in the first half of the sixteenth century.

Appendix: Principal Figures in the Vergara Trial

Aguilar, Diego de. Tovar's servant, who ferried Tovar's messages, whether written or oral, to other prisoners. Diego was separated from his master and placed in a separate cell on April 23, 1533, the date the inquisitors began to probe their officials' and prisoners' machinations; he was prosecuted on charges of assisting heretics. Sentenced in 1535 to one hundred lashes in a public auto-da-fé, Diego found his sentence commuted to two dozen lashes within the prison and the payment of 80 gold ducats, thanks to the intervention and deep pockets of Miguel Ortíz, a member of Vergara's circle. On Ortíz, see below.

Aguilar, Francisco de. Brother to Diego, servant to Vergara, Francisco transferred at least one message to Tovar as the latter was being transported to the Toledo tribunal.

Castillo, Juan del. Teacher of Greek, friend of Tovar and Francisca Hernández, and the brother of Gaspar de Lucena. Castillo fled Spain after Tovar's and Francisca's arrests, and was finally captured in Bologna; he was burned at the stake for Lutheranism in 1537. While a fugitive, he was able to communicate with his brother through Vergara's mediation.

Cazalla, María de. Follower of Isabel de la Cruz, María assumed the leadership of the alumbrado movement in Guadalajara after Isabel's arrest in 1524. María denounced herself to the Inquisition in 1525, in the wake of an edict of grace; she was arrested on charges of alumbradismo, Lutheranism, and Erasmianism in 1532. One of María's followers was Bernardino de Tovar. María was the cousin of Pedro Cazalla, who housed Francisca Hernández in Valladolid.

Cruz, Isabel de la. Franciscan tertiary, beata, and the first alumbrada to be arrested by the Inquisition in 1524. The record of her trial is not extant.

Flores, Bernardino. A parish priest in Pinto, Flores deposed against Vergara in 1530, to the effect that the latter criticized St. Augustine and disputed the accuracy of the Latin Vulgate Bible. Vergara recognized Flores in the publication of testimony, and responded fulsomely; that part of his defense confirms his status as a Renaissance humanist.

Fonseca, Alonso de. Archbishop of Toledo, 1524–34; died February 4 of the latter year. Attempted to intervene with the Toledo tribunal on Vergara's behalf, without success.

Gaspar Martínez, Diego. The despensero within the tribunal's prison, who distributed foodstuffs to the inmates. He discovered Tovar and Vergara's secret correspondence on April 11, 1533, and accordingly provoked the Inquisition's investigation into the secret correspondence and bribery that occurred both inside and outside the jail.

Gumiel, Cristobal de. Another of Vergara's clients and mediators, Gumiel, too, relayed secret letters to the imprisoned Tovar; he was duped into acting as a go-between through Vergara's false gift of an ecclesiastical prebend. His Inquisition testimony in December–January 1533–34 was highly damaging to Vergara's case.

Hermosilla, Bachiller. Notary for the Inquisition tribunal of Toledo, and an object of Vergara's bribery once Tovar was arrested. Vergara promised Hermosilla food and 15,000 maravedís a year in return for his assistance with Tovar's case. The notary consequently handed Vergara the names of the prosecution witnesses, spoke with him privately about Francisca Hernández's testimony, and—probably accidentally—let him know about the arrest order for Juan del Castillo.

Hernández, Francisca. A beata and alumbrada who, like María de Cazalla, did not follow any monastic rule. Hernández exercised her spiritual guidance in Salamanca and Valladolid, and among numerous Franciscans; Tovar was one of her early admirers. She was arrested by the Inquisition in 1529. The record of her trial is no longer extant.

Lucena, Gaspar de. Brother of fugitive Juan del Castillo, Lucena was arrested by the Inquisition on charges of abetting heretics. Where his brother was concerned, Lucena received and acted upon information from Vergara, including the news that a Latin arrest order for Castillo would be sent to Spanish officials in Paris.

Manrique, Alonso de. Archbishop of Seville and inquisitor general, Manrique was forced to leave the royal court in 1529 when he angered the queen. (He arranged a marriage that displeased her.) Manrique tried to intervene in Vergara's case, to the extent that he pressured the Toledo tribunal to speed up its prosecution. His efforts in that respect were not fruitful, but after Vergara was sentenced in December 1535, Manrique succeeded in having him transferred to the Toledo cathedral to serve the remainder of his penance.

Ortega, Juan de. The warden of the Inquisition's prison within the Toledo tribunal. His role in Tovar's and Vergara's subornation is indisputable. Ortega and his servant, Juan Sánchez, were suspended from their positions and investigated by the inquisitors after Tovar and Vergara's correspondence was unearthed.

Ortíz, Miguel. Part of Vergara's circle. Curate of the Church of San Pedro in Toledo, Ortíz was Tovar's friend, and reputed to be one of Francisca Hernández's followers. Ortíz studied Greek under Juan del Castillo. He also became one of Vergara's attorneys, and helped persuade the Toledo tribunal to diminish the penalty inflicted on Diego de Aguilar, Tovar's servant.

Ramírez, Marí. Servant of Francisca Hernández, and niece of Antonio de Medrano, one of Francisca's most ardent disciples. Marí was imprisoned in the same cell as her employer and mimicked her testimony.

Rodríguez, Hernán. Chaplain to both Vergara and the choir of the Toledo cathedral, and one of Vergara's most loyal clients. Rodríguez visited the Inquisition tribunal daily to check on Tovar's needs; he funneled Vergara's messages to Tovar, hidden in the foodstuffs he conveyed; and he passed bribes to the tribunal's warden and mozo del carcel. Rodríguez was arrested and penanced after his role in the subornation was discovered.

Sánchez, Juan. Otherwise known as the mozo del carcel, Sánchez was the warden's servant, and even more heavily involved than his master in the prison intrigues in Toledo. Sánchez and the warden were relieved of their responsibilities and subjected to interrogations in 1533, once the Toledo inquisitors realized the nature of Tovar and Vergara's correspondence, and Tovar's own machinations inside the prison.

Tovar, Bernardino. Older half brother of Juan de Vergara. Studied at the University of Salamanca; enthralled with beatas Francisca Hernández and María Cazalla. Arrested by the Inquisition in 1530 on charges of alumbradismo, through Francisca Hernández's testimony. Tovar's trial record has been lost.

Vaguer, Doctor. Another inquisitor attached to the Toledo tribunal. We know less about Vaguer than Yáñes.

Vergara, Juan de. Noted correspondent of Desiderius Erasmus, secretary to the archbishops of Toledo, Greek translator and theologian. One of the Spain's most famous intellectuals in the first half of the sixteenth century. Prosecuted and penanced by the Spanish Inquisition between 1533 and 1535.

Yáñes, Juan. Licenciate in canon law, and an inquisitor in the Toledo tribunal for twenty-five years.

Chapter Two

Erasmus and the New Testament

The Valladolid Conference of 1527

N o one would doubt Juan de Vergara's status as a Renaissance humanist and a Spanish Erasmian, yet his Inquisition trial reveals sides to him that such labels usually obscure. Vergara was trained as a theologian, but could identify himself as a lawyer; he saw himself as part of Spain's religious and cultural vanguard, but nevertheless moved in conventional and lofty circles all his life. The same sort of intellectual convolutions emerge from an even larger pool of evidence collected in 1527, in the northern Castilian city of Valladolid.

In the summer of that year, the Inquisition called some thirty-three of Iberia's most prominent theologians to Valladolid, and asked them to assess dubious, potentially heterodox excerpts from Erasmus's writings. The same clerics met and quarreled for more than two months, but never reached a collective decision on the problematic passages. In fact, they never even pondered all the material under review, for once plague struck the area in early August, Inquisitor General Manrique sent them home, and they never reconvened. Modern scholars have turned the 1527 Valladolid conference into a symbol whose meaning duplicates the scholarship on Vergara's prosecution: here, too, is a contest between the forces of reaction and progress, with predictable stances and participants; the meeting itself is supposed to signify only a momentary glitch in the swelling Erasmian revolution.[1] Yet the Valladolid deliberations are more important than the dominant historiography allows, for the Inquisition not only asked the theologians to debate orally, but to record their opinions as well. Most of the participants did as they were told, and wrote down their views on the excerpts from Erasmus's books; most of their reflections are extant. These surviving materials by Spain's clerical elite are priceless sources for questions about religious authority and the Spanish Renaissance.[2]

In 1527, the Valladolid delegates evinced the same elasticity as Vergara did seven years later: although not in any personal danger, they, too, oscillated between humanist and scholastic methods, and betrayed a potential gap between textual criticism and pious counsel. When they endorsed affective spirituality but dismissed the role of Greek in New Testament scholarship, their example warns us not to read devotion as interpretation; when they sanctioned Greek but valued Latin more, or defended Erasmus with dialectical reasoning, they enhance our understanding of Spanish humanism that much further. The Valladolid theologians adduced earlier and later sources, appealed to history as well as Church tradition, and advocated more or less hierarchy and tolerance in their relationships with each other and with the laity. They seldom adhered to a consistent position, and rarely accepted or rejected Erasmus's ideas in an absolute fashion. Their declarations confirm for Spain what we already know for Italy: Erasmus by way of his own writings, and Erasmus by way of his readers' responses, could amount to two very different phenomena.[3]

On April 24, 1527, Juan de Vergara explained the reasons for the conference to Erasmus himself. In a letter, Vergara relayed the tumult that had occurred once Erasmus's *Enchiridion militis christianis* had been translated into Spanish and published in Alcalá, sometime in 1524: "[The monks] began to shout continuously from the pulpits, the marketplaces, the shrines, the basilicas (for shouters of this sort are distributed everywhere), Erasmus is heretical, blasphemous, impious, sacrilegious. What more? More enemies to you suddenly arose from the vernacular translation of the book than from Cadmus's sowing of the teeth."[4] Vergara reported that in light of the calumny, Inquisitor General Manrique told the superiors of those monastic orders to stop their religious from attacking Erasmus openly, to abstain from future invective, and to leave the judgment of him to others. But Manrique also conceded that if the monks found anything wrong or dangerous in Erasmus's writings, which affected the public good alone, they ought to write it down, and it would be referred to the usual conference of theologians for evaluation. The inquisitor general's audience took him at his word: as Vergara recounted it, the monks stopped their sermonizing, immediately set off to find the errors in Erasmus's books, and became so involved in their task that they did not even have time to hear confessions during Holy Week.

Vergara went on to describe the ensuing events. On April 5, the religious orders presented their objections to the Suprema. In this second conclave, delegates from the Dominicans, Franciscans, Benedictines, and Trinitarians read their discoveries aloud, and repeated each other's findings to such an extent that Manrique finally ordered them to synthesize their objections. Vergara noted that Manrique wished to send the questionable passages to theologians at Alcalá and Salamanca, who in turn would assess the materials; ultimately, the inquisitor general imagined that the theologians would forward the most problematic sections to Erasmus or the pope or to both for clarification.

Vergara highlighted monastic intrigues as the impetus for the Valladolid conference, and other sources confirm the religious orders' enmity toward Erasmus in the mid-1520s. The head of the Dominicans, García Loaysa y Mendoza, spurned even the Latin edition of the *Enchiridion* because it deprecated purgatory and refused (famously) to equate monasticism with piety.[5] In 1526, Alonso Fernández de Madrid, the translator of the *Enchiridion* into Spanish, clashed with a Franciscan in Palencia when the latter affixed a list of Erasmus's errors to the pulpit; the same year, two more Franciscans circulated anti-Erasmian pamphlets in Salamanca.[6] Vergara was not incorrect to mention the antagonism between Erasmus and the friars. But viewing the conference against a backdrop of purely monastic enmity obscures its wider context, which was a speculative connection between Erasmus and Luther, and a simmering distrust of Erasmus that apparently extended to some part of the general public.

Scattered testimony shows that a theoretical link between Erasmus and Luther circulated in Spain much earlier and more consistently than historians have admitted. It was Diego López de Zuñiga, the polemicist commonly known as Stunica, who originally connected the two individuals in his first diatribe against Erasmus, published in 1520; he repeated the correlation in a letter to Vergara two years later.[7] In 1522, an imperial courtier told Erasmus that his letters had worked a miracle in Charles V's retinue, for now no one believed he was or ever had been a Lutheran: apparently someone *had* presumed Erasmus's sympathies for Luther at an earlier moment.[8] Finally, when the representatives of the religious orders were allowed to respond to Manrique in 1527, they blasted the Inquisition for ignoring the Lutheran danger that Erasmus embodied.[9] Stunica and his co-controversialist, Sancho Carranza de Miranda, were secular religious; Vergara, who had every reason to downplay antagonism to Erasmus in his letters, actually divulged widespread misgivings about him within the same epistles, and his comments were echoed by other witnesses.[10] It seems that the Valladolid conference of 1527 occurred in a climate of deeper, more widespread disapproval toward Erasmus than we often realize.

Because Charles V's troops began to sack Rome on May 6, 1527, the Valladolid assembly opened some weeks later than originally planned. On the afternoon of June 27, thirty-three theologians swore themselves to secrecy in front of the Suprema and two prosecutors for the Inquisition's Castilian and Aragonese secretariats. The deliberations began immediately afterward; the format and frequency of the sessions remained constant throughout six and a half weeks of meetings. The delegates met on Tuesdays, Thursdays, and Saturdays: with each new set of accusations, a single theologian would verbally expound the material under review, and deliver his own opinion on it. His verdict was followed by those of other attendees. We know, for instance, that on the first day of the meetings, the abbot and rector of the University of Alcalá, Pedro de Lerma, commented on the first set of passages, which pertained to the Trinity, and six of his peers succeeded him. In subsequent meetings the rest of the participants would speak until everyone had expressed his sentiments on the issue at hand; they then would take up the next topic, and start the process all over again. When Inquisitor General Manrique dismissed the group on August 13, it had progressed through four categories of a twenty-part repertory.[11]

Clearly the participants' opinions are unintelligible without understanding what they were reading, but the anthology of excerpts has a murky history, and it is impossible to determine its authors with certainty. Erasmus's most prominent Spanish adversaries, Stunica and Carranza, are unlikely suspects, because the one was in Rome by 1526, and the other attended the conference itself. Another of Erasmus's foes, Edward Lee, resided in Spain from 1525 to 1529 while conducting diplomatic missions for Henry VIII, and certainly could have contributed to the compilation; when the Valladolid repertory charged Erasmus with Arianism, a heresy from the fourth century, it conjured up Lee's earlier complaints.[12] Nevertheless, although many of the imputations in 1527 mimicked earlier controversies between Erasmus and his rivals, the Spaniards did not directly copy their grievances from previous invectives. The evidence suggests they were much more clever than that.

Whoever assembled the Valladolid propositions lifted many incriminating passages from Erasmus's apologiae against Lee and Stunica: they indicted his explanations of the alleged errors instead of his initial missteps, and thereby tapped a new source for their accusations. Their selection of excerpts from Erasmus's controversy with Stunica was especially deliberate, since the latter was a respected individual in Spain's academic circles, whose objections might have carried extra weight.[13] The Spanish repertory also reflected a meaningful shift within Erasmian controversies as a whole. The earliest polemicists had aimed their criticisms at Erasmus's 1519 revision of the Latin New Testament, as well as his annotations on it; and they had ordered their censures in biblical sequence. Under the major heading of "Matthew," for example, they would file everything wrong with Erasmus's comments verse by verse, so that their objections would follow the Bible's structure. The excerpts under scrutiny thus could cover a wide range of subjects, from the doctrine of the Trinity to specific renditions from Greek to Latin.

In contrast, the Spanish propositions looked like Stunica's second assault from 1522, in that they were arranged by theoretical topic instead of scriptural book, with anywhere from one to twenty objectionable passages or charges drawn from any number of works listed below the primary heading.[14] For example, a category entitled "Against the Eucharist" contained points drawn from Erasmus's prologue to his *Paraphrase* on Corinthians and his *Annotations* on Mark, among other publications. The Spanish architects also followed a European-wide pattern of moving from the exclusive indictment of Erasmus's biblical scholarship to accusations against all his writings on religion. Like their Parisian counterparts, who were acting simultaneously, the Spaniards, too, slammed the colloquy *Inquisitio de fide,* the edition of St. Hilary of Poitiers's opera (1523), and the *Paraphrases on Matthew* (1522): in the first two instances, they assailed distinct passages from their French peers; in the third they targeted the same selections but presented them with different wording.[15] The Spaniards also attacked Erasmus's *Modus orandi Deum,* whose first edition had only appeared in 1524, with a second in 1525. Their attention to Erasmus's later works, like their quotations from his apologiae, diminished the possibility that he had already exonerated himself in print. But if the Valladolid inventory consigned relatively more space to doctrinal and devotional issues, and absolutely none to specific problems of translation, it also included enough criticism of Erasmus's textual emendations to make clear the relationship between piety and philology. It would be misleading to characterize the Spanish repertory as "theological" over and against the more "grammatical" objections of its European counterparts, as if its protests had nothing to do with Erasmus's modifications of the New Testament's language.

Whoever they were, the creators of the Valladolid repertory were not straightforward as they culled material from Erasmus's works: they frequently isolated quotations, misidentified prose, and wielded paraphrases in an effort to make their suspect look as wicked as possible. They might label a passage as originating in Erasmus's *Annotations* when it really came from his 1521 apology against Stunica. Sometimes they refused to specify what, exactly, Erasmus had written, as when they noted that he "said many things in the *Colloquies*" against the veneration of saints, relics, and pilgrimages.[16] In one instance, they sliced a single paragraph into three different accusations, which they placed under three different topics: in the process they inverted the order in which the points had originally appeared.[17] Such maneuvers erased the quotations' surrounding language and obscured their meaning. One example of such obfuscation occurred with Erasmus's statement, "I do not see that what the Arians deny is able to be taught except by a ratiocination." Erasmus made that remark in his first response to Stunica, in the midst of an argument about ancient Arian heretics and 1 John 5:7; he proposed that the Arians' denial of the Trinity's unity of essence could not be overturned through that New Testament verse alone.[18] By the time Erasmus's comment appeared in the Valladolid anthology, it had lost its specific environment: "what" now implied that *everything* the Arians denied was undemonstrable by direct scriptural proofs. Whoever supervised the repertory wanted to obstruct the location and the circumstances of the excerpts; arranging questionable passages by topic instead of treatise made the context of the quotations that much more difficult to capture.

Finally, the collectors of the charges listed successive points as if they formed part of a common discourse, when they often had nothing to do with each other. Such an invention occurred in the first section of the inventory, which was devoted to offenses against the Trinity. Within that category, the first two passages came from Erasmus's 1521 apology against Stunica, and relayed his doubts over the canonicity of 1 John 5:7 and its effectiveness against Arianism. The third passage relayed the statement, "This is the moral foundation of the Christian religion, to revere everything among divine matters, but to sanction nothing except that which is clearly expressed in sacred letters"; this excerpt came from the *Modus orandi Deum,* and was originally part of a reflection on the differences between ancient and contemporary prayers.[19] In other words, the quotation from the *Modus orandi Deum* did not pertain to Arians, or to problems of speculative theology such as the Trinity's unity of essence. Nevertheless, the repertory's architects jammed all three quotations together, and then angled them to prove that Erasmus substantiated "the long-lasting and irrefragable heresy of the Arians."[20] By employing such techniques, the draftsmen of the charges were challenging the theologians to put the excerpts into their original milieus. But such strategies also implied an intellectual procedure called the mosaic method—a means of constructing a proof from pieces of discrete expositions. The mosaic method is fundamentally scholastic in its origins. It illustrates an approach in which an author's intention becomes less relevant than interpretative demands, and a work is as potentially malleable as its expositor's creativity. Flores's sermon on "Ite in castellum" exhibited similar intellectual parameters.

If issues of textual criticism inhered in the very fabrication of the repertory, they reverberated in the passages under review, which repeatedly raised problems of language, chronological distance, and practical as well as literary authority. The excerpts from Erasmus's writings addressed rhetorical style in the Bible and from there the attribution of its material, such as whether St. Paul composed the Book of Hebrews. The passages raised sanctity and scholasticism by commenting on the apostles' Greek and contemporary theological method. Notably, the material under review consistently invoked differences between the beliefs and customs of the early church and those of the contemporary one, whether in matters of confession, the papacy, or manuscript transmission. Entangled in the Valladolid propositions, then, were elements central to our most profound conception of Renaissance humanism. As the theologians responded to the first four categories of charges, they knew they were considering matters of the intellectual vanguard. Their reactions were remarkably intricate.

The Inquisition file that survives from Valladolid contains manuscript reflections from twenty-eight delegates. The Benedictine preacher named Alonso Ruiz de Virués, who later became entangled in Vergara's trial, also attended the Valladolid conference and responded to the passages under review, but his reaction now is missing from the AHN's file; nonetheless, in the first half of this century a scholar was able to transcribe it.[21] The greatest expanse of my sample, therefore, amounts to twenty-nine responses, with only one not in holograph. The authors of these documents were professors of theology, bishops and canons, imperial preachers and confessors, members of monastic orders and rectors of universities. Out of eight regular clerics, three were Dominican, three Franciscan, one a Benedictine, and the other an Augustinian; three participants were Portuguese, another had resided for at least five years in Bologna, and yet one more held a see in Albania.[22] Several delegates were also inquisitors, and at least ten had studied at Paris.

The Valladolid theologians were a diverse group, and they responded to the charges in markedly disparate ways: not only the length but the profundity of their responses varied wildly. The Portuguese Pedro Margallo, professor of moral philosophy at the College of St. Bartholomew in Salamanca, wrote six and a half folios; Diego de Astudillo, a member of the Dominican college of San Gregorio in Valladolid, composed two. Alonso de Córdoba, professor of nominalist theology at Salamanca, considered the charges at length and adduced references from Augustine, as befit a member of that religious order. Fernando Matatigui, professor of Scotist theology at Alcalá, framed his impressions in single-sentence reactions. Some participants responded to everything, others seem to have answered only part of the accusations, while still others left no reactions at all to some of the charges under consideration; as the conference progressed, the number of replies lessened in general, but I do not know whether that reflects a refusal to write on the later material or just a diminution in what has survived. Silence does appear significant when it occurs in the midst of an exposition, but how to interpret it is another matter, since participants could decline to record their opinions for very different reasons.[23] More important, the lacunae mean that the body of evidence constantly shifts, yet at no time do we possess single or even only several responses to the passages under review. As a result, we can draw conclusions from the replies.

The first accusation the theologians debated on June 27 was a familiar one: Erasmus's treatment of the verse called the *comma Johanneum,* 1 John 5:7, which read: "There are three who bear witness in heaven, Father, Son, and Holy Spirit, and these three are one." The comma was recognized as the major proof-text against the Arian heresy because it supported the Trinity's unity of essence. Erasmus had had the nerve to omit it from both the Greek and Latin texts of his first two editions of the New Testament, dated 1516 and 1519: he had used Greek as the archetype for the Latin, and he did not find the line in any of the Greek manuscripts he consulted.[24] Lee and Stunica rebuked him for the excision on the grounds that Lorenzo Valla had not contested the comma's authenticity.[25] Later, in his third apologia against Lee, Erasmus explained why he had omitted the verse, and noted that if any Greek manuscript had contained it, he would have included it. An Irish text quickly appeared with the comma added in the margin by a contemporary hand.[26] Erasmus restored the line in subsequent editions of the New Testament, but the Valladolid censors still wrote that he attacked the verse relentlessly, defended corrupt manuscripts, and thereby protected and even pleaded the Arian cause.[27]

All twenty-nine theologians responded to these allegations about 1 John 5:7, and twenty-three explicitly professed a belief in the comma's legitimacy, including Francisco de Castillo, a Salamancan Franciscan, who declared that

"First, I believe that testimony of blessed John, 'Tres sunt . . . ,' to be from the canon of sacred Scripture." Still, a few delegates questioned exactly how inviolable the verse really was, and participants disagreed as to whether the comma's sanctity was determined simply by papal and conciliar references to it. One contingent pointed out the papacy's failure to define an authentic scriptural text, and argued that delegates should not proclaim the comma's canonicity when the Church itself had not done so. Another group asserted that customary invocation of the verse was enough to prove its authenticity.[28] The conflict reveals that at least some participants would concede the lack of a conclusive version of the Latin Bible; their recognition of that fact matches Vergara's acknowledgment of the same point. But the majority did not entertain such explosive issues in their written responses; instead, they concentrated on the more obvious aspects of Erasmus's alleged errors.

Erasmus's treatment of the comma indicated that the Latin biblical text was amendable in light of the Greek, but most participants read the charge literally and refused to consider its ramifications. Eight delegates bluntly affirmed that Erasmus really could not find 1 John 5:7 in the Greek manuscripts he consulted, restored it when he did, and hence already had corrected his mistake. Lerma's reaction was typical: "That he says that that triplicity of heavenly testimony was not found by him in a Greek manuscript, he amply demonstrates; and seeing that he does not omit that verse in his translation, it may be passed over."[29] Another approach was to go outside the charge in search of exculpatory material. Royal preacher Gíl López de Bejar, professor Antonio de Alcaráz, and the rector of the Spanish college at Bologna, Miguel Gómez, maintained that Erasmus expounded the comma brilliantly in his *Paraphrase* of 1 John: logically, that exposition proved that he accepted the comma as part of the canon. Gómez and Jacobo Cabrero, the Albanian bishop, even defended the omission with one of Erasmus's own criteria for amending texts, for they pointed out that the comma was missing from the writings of the early church fathers, who surely would have used it in their polemics had it been available.[30]

But literality, extra evidence, and a lack of patristic testimony could not sway others who argued on the simple basis of Latin superiority, and contended that Erasmus should not have preferred Greek in the first place. Like Lee and Stunica before him, Juan de Quintana, who moved in imperial circles, stated that Erasmus's Greek manuscripts were fallacious. Diogo de Gouvea, head of the Portuguese college at the University of Paris, insisted that the comma had to be legitimate because of the authenticity of the whole epistle of John; Erasmus should have remained silent until the right manuscript came along, and anyone who doubted the verse's veracity was comparable to "a burned-up heretic."[31] In all, fifteen out of twenty-nine delegates saw only Erasmus's fault in expurgating the line, and refused to allow any circumstances to mitigate the omission.

His reason for restoring the comma in 1522 did not make them any happier. While numerous participants felt that Erasmus should be exonerated because he eventually returned 1 John 5:7 to the New Testament, for others the reinstatement just deepened suspicions about his orthodoxy. In the *Annotations* on his New Testament translations, Erasmus wrote that he finally included the comma to avoid slander: ten theologians thus decided that his decisions about the verse signified more than just a philological quandary. Córdoba summed up their position by noting that Erasmus "openly implies that he added that testimony because he finds it written, not because he thus believed it or felt it must be believed."[32] Francisco de Vitoria, the famous commentator on Aquinas and controversialist on native Americans, claimed that Erasmus's rationale left the reader doubtful, and therefore must be removed or revised. Even López de Bejar, who seemed to understand Erasmus's interest in Greek, wished he would bow to majority opinion and declare the comma's rightful inclusion in canonical Scripture.[33]

The Valladolid repertory also challenged Erasmus's outlook on Jesus' divinity, and cited in particular his remarks about Romans 9:5. Erasmus's complete commentary follows; the dates in brackets signify the editions of the *Annotations* in which his statements appeared.

Romans 9:5. "Who is God over all things." [1516–22: Unless this bit is added on, as we do come upon certain added-on bits.] [1516–27: Certainly in this passage Paul openly pronounced Christ as God. And in fact the Greek manuscripts that I have seen agree.][34]

When it appeared in the Spanish accusations, Erasmus's gloss took the following form:

On Romans 9, although the most obvious authority is that of the apostle speaking of Christ, "Who is God blessed forever," and this is the clear, frank, and obvious meaning; and also in which, as the same Erasmus testifies, all the manuscripts agree, he resorts to the most impudent evasion as he says, "unless this bit is added on, as we do come upon certain added-on bits," etc.[35]

According to the inventory, the annotation proved that Erasmus wavered over Jesus' part in the Godhead. The implication was that Erasmus backed Arianism, but the theologians responded to his textual criticism instead.

Only one of the sixteen delegates who replied, Miguel Gómez, was entirely comfortable with the idea that scriptural passages might have been appended. In contrast, Francisco de Vitoria thought Erasmus's annotation weakened the Bible's authority and scandalized the faith; Lerma found the gloss offensive and wanted it torn from the book; Antonio de Guevara, inquisitor and bishop, called the commentary completely heretical and scandalous. Others pondered Erasmus's language and wondered whether he really claimed that Romans 9:5 was tacked on: Bernardino Vázquez de Oropesa, a professor of theology at Salamanca, and Alonso de Córdoba thought he did not, although to their minds the ambiguity did little to lessen the insult. If inquisitorial secretary Luís Coronel spoke publicly what he wrote privately, he may have prompted his peers' uncertainty about Erasmus's meaning, for he proposed that the comment was innocuous if it were read scholastically; he also noticed that Erasmus had deleted the remark from the latest edition of his *Annotations.* But even Coronel could not evade completely the question of whether Erasmus's gloss diminished confidence in the New Testament's authenticity, although he tried to delay answering it: he stipulated that he would speak on the matter when he and his counterparts reached the category labeled "on the authority of sacred Scripture."[36] He declined to endorse or refute his peers' reproach.

Not all of Erasmus's editorial musings produced the same level of antagonism. The Valladolid propositions also included his annotation on Luke 1:35, in which he suggested that the angel's statement to Mary should read that the Christ "would be born" rather than "would be born of you"; here Erasmus had adduced Greek and Latin manuscripts, as well as the eleventh-century commentator Theophylactus, as the basis for his emendation. Significantly, out of the twelve theologians who reacted to Luke 1:35, only five rebuked Erasmus for his comments; several delegates said the omission of *ex te* (of you) was wrong, but offered no reason why, while Quintana alone referred to Erasmus's codices and insisted they were corrupt. Lerma, who objected strenuously to the proposal for Romans 9:5, dismissed the remark about Luke by declaring that Greek manuscripts did not contain the prepositional phrase, and noting that Lefevre d'Etaples had already removed it; he implied that Erasmus's alteration had a precedent, however recent. Even Córdoba, who found the annotation on Romans erroneous and heretical, thought the one on Luke was acceptable.

The reason for the delegates' different reactions probably lies in the circumspection of the one gloss and the ambiguity of the other. Erasmus's decision about Luke 1:35 was limited to that verse alone and explicitly depended on manuscripts: although the Valladolid proposition neglected his reasons for deleting the verse's prepositional phrase, the seven respondents who allowed his comment presumably knew the *Annotations* and were affected by his fulsome rationale therein. Furthermore, Erasmus had stipulated that "ex te" was missing in Latin as well as Greek manuscripts, and thereby supplied an extra measure of security from texts that most of the delegates regarded as preeminent. In contrast, Erasmus's reflections on Romans 9:5 suggested a hypothetical scenario—appendages to the Bible—which might occur in any part of Scripture, and the Spaniards found that equivocation dangerous. Quintana warned that if the genuineness of biblical passages were debated on impulse, "then nothing of authority shall remain in sacred Scripture, because I may say that any particular clause whatsoever is added on . . . and so the authority of sacred Scripture will perish."[37] His response recalls Flores's statement to the inquisitors three years later: both interpreted philological investigation as a threat to sacred writings.

Valladolid's charges rebuked Erasmus's alterations of the Bible's vocabulary as well as his remarks on its composition. One of his most famous modifications of its language occurred in the second edition of his New Testament in 1519, when he substituted "discourse" for "word," or *sermo* for *verbum,* in John 1:1.[38] Lee and Stunica had found the change rash, and had berated him for it; Erasmus had answered that rendering "word" as "discourse" or "communication" or "speech" or "voice" was hardly a criminal matter in a private book. The Spanish repertory quoted his response.[39] It also included two more offenses that centered on rhetoric: on Mark 6:3, Erasmus called Joseph "the stepfather of Christ"; on Romans 8:3, he remarked that "because Christ assumed the character of a criminal, he was a sort of hypocrite."[40]

Where these three charges were concerned, ten out of twenty-three respondents affirmed that Erasmus's language was wholly acceptable, while seven rejected it as fruitless, curious, and novel. Six others accepted one passage but spurned another: so Estevam de Almeida, a Portuguese delegate, condemned the use of "stepfather" but recognized that "hypocrite" could have a positive meaning, while Pedro de Vitoria argued the reverse. In general, fewer participants objected to the use of "sermo" because it occurred frequently in patristic writings and had authoritative precedents, although some elevated a competing strand of religious authority when they insisted that "sermo" violated the customary reading of the Church. A number rejected Erasmus's use of "stepfather" because that term had negative connotations in their own epoch: they thought it could denote a second husband, as well as the husband of a woman whose children were by another man; in their opinion, Erasmus had implied that Mary had either married twice or cuckolded Joseph. Others reacted to the term "hypocrite" as if its sense were permanent across the centuries and always evil.

A significant number of the respondents displayed some flexibility toward Erasmus's annotations and alterations of scriptural language, particularly when the changes could be discovered in recognized sources. But the assembly as a whole was less amenable to the straightforward remarks that Erasmus could make about saints, in particular about Jerome, the traditional translator of the Latin Vulgate. The Spaniards' charge had an elaborate history. In the first polemic that Stunica launched against Erasmus, he attacked his omission of the comma Johanneum, noted Jerome's inclusion of the verse in the Vulgate, and pronounced Erasmus's Greek manuscripts fallacious. In reply, Erasmus tried to turn evidence about Jerome against his adversary: he retorted that Jerome really doubted the authenticity of 1 John 5:7, actually trusted Greek manuscripts, and ultimately altered the common reading of the Church by allowing the comma to stand.[41] Both men tried to use Jerome's status for their own ends, but in the process Erasmus also observed that that church father was reckless, imprudent, and inconsistent. The Spanish architects of the repertory deliberately entwined his description into their complaint about the comma itself. I have italicized the relevant phrases:

Erasmus in the *Annotations* of 1 John 5 defends corrupt manuscripts, *rants and raves against the blessed Jerome,* pleads and even defends the Arian cause. And for instance that passage, "There are three who bear witness in heaven, the Father, Son, and Holy Spirit, and these three are one," he attacks with a relentless war, he spits out all judgments, he even piles up frivolous reasons to the contrary, *he attacks the divine Jerome with these words: "Although that man, namely Jerome, very often is impetuous, too little prudent, often changeable and seldom constant to himself."*[42]

When the theologians perused the charges, they simultaneously saw that Erasmus had emended Jerome's text and abused him personally.

The twenty-five respondents as a body censured Erasmus's affront to Jerome's dignity, although some also tried to exonerate him by interpreting the charge literally and refusing to consider its implications. Accordingly, a few wondered if his depiction of Jerome were true, although they went on to deplore it. Miguel Carrasco, theology professor at Alcalá and client of Juan de Vergara, left it to others to decide whether Erasmus's characterization of Jerome fit, but recognized that Erasmus himself had behaved in an uncivil, impudent, and brash fashion. Guevara could believe that Jerome was rather fickle, but asserted that Erasmus still spoke impertinently. López de Bejar daringly claimed that Erasmus's remark was apt even if its terms were inappropriate.[43] Seven others worried less about the justice of Erasmus's statements and concentrated instead on his insolence, which they found infuriating. The most vehement reaction came from Gouvea, who envisioned Erasmus as ruining the status of preachers and sermons through his comments on holy people and texts. He fumed, "What authority will preachers of the Word of God have in the pulpit, if they cite Jerome's testimony in sermons? What steadfastness in these things that Jerome translated, if the statements of his translation are produced against heretics?"[44] Even those who tried to excuse Erasmus's remarks on grounds of pertinence, accuracy, and context clearly regretted them: Coronel conceded that he personally never would have written such words about Jerome, for they plainly displayed irreverence.[45]

The Valladolid repertory suggested that Erasmus had weakened the New Testament's authority by altering and criticizing its text and its translator. It also charged that he denigrated the Bible and Catholic doctrine when he proposed that certain dogmas were deduced from Scripture rather than expressed in its narratives. In several publications Erasmus observed that "only the Father was called true God in the Gospel," and that remark provoked some of the hottest debate at the conference.[46] Much of the argument revolved around what Erasmus meant by the expression: the Spaniards tried to determine whether he was thinking of "true God" as the literal denomination *verus Deus,* or whether he wanted the clause to encompass deductions as well; they disagreed over whether Erasmus expected "Gospel" to include just the first four books of the New Testament, or all of it.

The way they read Erasmus's expression had a material effect on their rejoinders. Francisco de Vitoria, who expounded the proposition to the assembly, carried some participants with him when he objected that since "God" had to signify "true God," Jesus was labeled true God whenever he was called God; he solved the problem through Thomistic realism, and then asserted that Erasmus's notion of the "Gospel" was not confined to the first four books of the New Testament. Erasmus's intent mattered less than the fact that his statement was scandalous, dangerous, and worthy of expurgation. Nevertheless, Vitoria finally acknowledged that if Erasmus really meant "true God" as a literal utterance, and limited "Gospel" to just the first four accounts of the apostles, then his declaration could be tolerated. Most of his peers agreed with him, although they also found Erasmus's aim obscure.

Other suspicious passages also involved scriptural and patristic expressions or the lack thereof; the delegates had time to consider excerpts that concerned the process by which the Holy Spirit came to be called a member of the Trinity. Some of the charges emerged from Erasmus's edition of Hilary of Poitiers, the fourth-century Father: there Erasmus alleged that Hilary hesitated to name the Holy Spirit as God because his reverence for the Bible prevented him from uttering what it did not express.[47] This time there was no question of excusing the suspect by narrowing his terms: Castillo, Córdoba, Almeida, Juan de Arrieta, and, reluctantly, archdeacon Antonio Rodríguez de la Fuente summoned examples from the New Testament and the church fathers to disprove Erasmus's statement. Several delegates insisted that Hilary had pronounced the Holy Spirit as God in Book Two of his *De trinitate,* although Gómez, Alcaráz, and the canon Pedro de Ciria contended that they personally could not find the cognomen "God" openly bestowed on the Holy Spirit in Scripture, or in Hilary's writings either. Gómez then repeated his tactics toward the comma Johanneum, and asserted that the church fathers would have cited a biblical equation between the Holy Spirit and God if one had existed. Alcaráz resorted to the now familiar ploy of declaring that Erasmus's error was one matter, the divinity of the Holy Spirit another.[48] But out of the seventeen theologians who wrote on this proposition, only six allowed Erasmus's suggestion about the Holy Spirit and the New Testament, the Holy Spirit and Hilary, or both.

Erasmus did not consider scriptural and patristic style in order to chart the various combinations of words in sacred literature. Instead, his remarks highlighted the historical development of Christian theology and practice, stressed the differences between sixteenth-century Catholicism and ancient Christianity, and were supposed to engender the critical imitation of an era that he perceived as chronologically and spiritually closer to Jesus. Within the Valladolid repertory, Erasmus's historical sensitivity was plain in his comparison of the Greek and Latin New Testaments; it was equally clear in his juxtaposition of patristic dogma and practice against their sixteenth-century analogues. Moreover, as he tried to prove to Stunica that Jesus was openly called God a mere two or three times in the Bible, he portrayed the diffidence of the apostles as equivalent to the reluctance of the Fathers.[49] When the theologians began to debate the plausibility of historical difference between their Christianity and the primitive church's, some fused Erasmus's musings on the apostles with those he offered about individuals in the early church, such as Hilary.

Even though history and philology were utterly entangled in the charges, just six delegates reacted to the historical overtones of the hypothesis that Jesus was seldom called true God in the Gospel. The issue was whether Jesus' identification with the Godhead emerged only gradually in the apostolic epoch, and the six Spaniards who replied rejected Erasmus's idea out of hand.[50] Córdoba wrote that the statement should be damned. Pedro Ciruelo, a professor of Thomistic theology at the University of Alcalá, contended that since the entire New Testament witnessed Christ as God, some disciple must have said it out loud; besides, the apostles did not write down all the words they preached. Quintana tried to make the same point from the opposite tack: he, too, maintained that Christ's divinity was proclaimed throughout the New Testament, but stipulated that the evangelists preached what they transcribed. He found Erasmus's remarks insulting to men in such a state of perfection; he consistently stressed the divine qualities of early Christians over their human ones.[51] His attitude toward the apostles exhibits the same expansive sense of sanctity that he and his peers displayed toward St. Jerome. They responded in a similar way to the historical notion that St. Hilary vacillated over naming the Holy Spirit as God in the fourth century.

Seventeen participants—a much higher number—treated the historical question of exactly when the Holy Spirit was proclaimed as divine, and by whom. Several theologians viewed the Nicene Council in 325 C.E. as a pivotal moment in the development of holy nomenclature; if Erasmus meant his statement about the Holy Spirit to apply to figures who preceded or attended that council, he could be right, although books from the period should be perused for safety's sake. Alonso Enríquez, nephew of the admiral of Castile and the highest-ranking attendee, explained Erasmus's point in greater depth, and Lerma agreed with him: the church fathers recoiled from descriptions of the Holy Spirit because they recognized the limits of their own understanding; they hesitated to advance their own opinions lest they contradict sacred letters.[52]

Still, a clear majority at Valladolid objected to the notion that the Holy Spirit's divinity was only gradually recognized, whether that process of identification concerned only Hilary or all the members of the early church. Almeida thought such ancients as Erasmus described never existed, because the articles of the faith were in place in the fourth as well as the sixteenth century. As a bishop and a saint, Hilary would have been bound to endorse those articles; he must have confessed the Holy Spirit as God: "Blessed Hilary dared to proclaim the Holy Spirit God, since these words, 'The Holy Spirit is God,' is one of the articles of the faith which was proposed must be believed by the baptized. If therefore he was a bishop and a saint, how then did he not dare?"[53] A number of Almeida's companions agreed with him. Hilary, and early Christians in general, believed in the same doctrine of the Trinity as their early modern counterparts. They confessed that the Holy Spirit was God even if they failed to write it down.

In most of the excerpts presented at Valladolid, Erasmus's esteem for primitive Christianity was simply implied, although emulation of that age guided many of his devotional priorities and recommendations. But a line from the 1524 edition of the *Modus orandi Deum* made his preference overt: when he wrote, "Perhaps this is the moral foundation of the Christian religion, to revere everything among divine matters, but to sanction nothing except that which is clearly expressed in sacred letters," he seemed to endorse the principle of *sola scriptura*. The Spanish repertory framed this quotation as additional proof of Erasmus's love for Arians and rejection of the comma Johanneum.[54] But none of the Valladolid delegates turned the extract toward Arianism; instead, eight tied it to Luther.

At first, twenty-one out of twenty-eight respondents pronounced the sentence from the *Modus orandi Deum* heretical as quoted, although some softened their stance afterward. Extenuating evidence could lessen the statement's heterodox aura. As Carranza pointed out, Erasmus had modified the remark in the second edition of his *Modus orandi Deum* in 1525; he had intended the comment to refer to private individuals alone; he was only echoing the sentiments of previous doctors, such as the Pseudo-Dionysius. Additionally, Coronel and Enríquez raised Erasmus's other works as contrary evidence: in their opinion, he could not have meant the statement literally, because he himself employed other authorities than Scripture and frequently submitted himself to the Church, which obviously promoted practices that the Bible lacked.

Numerous respondents—sixteen out of twenty-eight—found these arguments persuasive to some degree, if only because they became confused over Erasmus's aim, like Quintana and Vázquez de Oropesa, or acquiesced despite their better judgment, like Francisco de Vitoria.[55] Four theologians contended that Erasmus was not mimicking Luther in the excerpt, because he had already relayed their differences in *De libero arbitrio*; four others recognized that Erasmus never meant to echo Luther, but wanted the passage in question censored in any case.[56] From a practical angle, the four participants who disputed a Lutheran connection but endorsed censorship can be classified with fourteen others who persistently contended that Erasmus's statement was heretical, because all eighteen finally advocated the same solution to the controversy. A majority of the theologians—sixteen—finally believed Erasmus never meant the line as his own, or could be persuaded into such an opinion. But twenty out of twenty-four also evinced great unease over the sentiment simply because it was in print.

Nevertheless, in certain instances the Valladolid participants seemed to side with Erasmus in his affection for the early church. One of the topics they debated was the proper role of argument and coercion within Christianity; they had to decide whether Erasmus disparaged past and present debates over orthodoxy, as well as contemporary labors to enforce it. In his first apologia against Stunica, Erasmus contended that perhaps the Arians and, by default, heretics in general, could be coaxed into orthodoxy more readily through devout endeavors instead of probing ones. He wrote: "Perhaps it would have been better to effect this—that we may be restored with God—by pious studies instead of fighting it out with curious ones, such as in what way the Son may differ from the Father, or the Holy Spirit from both."[57] In the *Paraphrase on Matthew,* he counseled that heretics probably should be reserved to God's judgment, and suggested that adolescents be subjected to a cate-chetical examination on the meaning of their baptismal vows. Finally, in the colloquy *Inquisitio de fide,* one of Erasmus's characters called excommunica-tion something that terrified only children, and went on to reserve the real power over the human soul to God.[58]

Most of the attendees agreed with Erasmus's statement that pious studies were better than inquisitive ones: nineteen out of the twenty-three respon-dents favored the former, with or without qualifications. They seem to have understood Erasmus's comparison in the same way, as a contrast between moral theology and a speculative, dialectical, and potentially contentious counterpart. Although some participants cautioned that Erasmus's critique of disputation should not apply to early efforts to define the faith—and others insisted that contemporary scholastic inquiry was spiritually beneficial, too—slightly more than half the respondents endorsed Erasmus's outlook without reservation. Carranza wrote that such doctrine would "teach our disposition and incite the will to the love and charity of God, turning us from curious studies and useless debates, which are so effective for a quarrel, and of too little use for the education of the understanding."[59] Virués concurred that love was better than contention, Carrasco repeated St. Paul's dictum that the end of the Law was charity, and Martín de Samunde rhapsodized that Eras-mus's notion was charming. Thus the bulk of the delegates accepted the value of pious study over controversy to some degree. They went on to reproach, at least quietly, an institution that was founded on the soundness of confronting heretics: the Spanish Inquisition.

Matthew 13:25–30 detailed Jesus' parable about servants who wished to gather the tares too soon and would consequently endanger the wheat grow-ing alongside. Erasmus identified the tares as pseudoapostles and heretics, and suggested in his *Paraphrase* that Jesus' instruction to tolerate the tares rather than rip them up indicated that Christians should endure religious offenders.[60] Out of the sixteen Spaniards who responded, twelve called Erasmus's idea Catholic, pious, and indicative of the Church's mercy toward the heterodox; even Guevara, an inquisitor, declared that Erasmus's commentary on the tares could be overlooked, although it certainly would make his job more difficult. But if a sizable proportion of the delegates agreed that heretics occasionally could be ignored, their endorsement of mercy went only so far.

In the prologue to the same *Paraphrase,* Erasmus considered ways to rejuvenate Catholicism, and pondered whether children should undergo an examination about the significance of their faith. He thought they could be asked if they considered their baptism valid; if they responded affirmatively, they could renew in public the promises made by their godparents, and the ensuing ceremony would have a stirring effect on the audience. Besides appearing to repeat a sacrament, though, Erasmus recognized one more obstacle to his plan: persons might choose to *reject* their baptism instead of endorsing it. He then noted that such a renunciation should be prevented if at all possible, although if it occurred, it might be better to leave the offenders alone until they came to their senses, and in the meantime only exclude them from the sacraments. The Valladolid repertory included his proposal for patience but, typically, omitted the surrounding material that would have put the quotation in context.[61]

Regardless, the Spaniards reacted to the milieu of the excerpt as well as its actual content, and their responses are illuminating. Six out of thirteen thought religious instruction for older children was a wise suggestion; Lerma and Ciria recognized that Erasmus had been referring to the rites of catechization and confirmation. Nonetheless, not a single theologian favored Erasmus's "second proposition," in which he advised only minimal interference with adolescents who spurned the faith. Even Gómez labeled such counsel "neither sound nor accepted," although up to this point he had acted as Erasmus's most eloquent defender. Matatigui found the hands-off approach erroneous, Alcaráz and Rodríguez de la Fuente thought it unpleasant, and Lerma believed it implausible: he doubted that any boy would resist the faith in church, in front of the entire town; and if he did, he should be dragged back to it by force, fear, whips, and even the threat of death. As Córdoba noted, "happy the compulsion that compels toward the good."[62]

The last proposition entertained by the Valladolid group also revolved around a form of constraint, this time from Rome. The passage in question came from the opening of the colloquy *Inquisitio de fide*: it accused Erasmus of doubting the efficacy of excommunication. Out of fifteen respondents, nine dismissed the charge either because of Erasmus's other works, such as *De libero arbitrio* (Gómez), or because Erasmus pretended to be a heretic in this particular dialogue (Almeida), or because he intended the piece as a joke (Rodríguez de la Fuente). But most also expressed a negative opinion of the *Colloquies* as a whole, and wanted them removed from the public arena, restricted to a learned audience, or corrected by their author; their Italian counterparts also found that work especially perilous.[63] It was Erasmus's tone that proved offensive: the Spaniards condemned the sarcasm, slander, and drollery in matters of ecclesiastical tradition and authority. The delegates favored pious studies, but disapproved of ones that employed parodies to advance their arguments.[64] Instead, they wanted writers to offer explicit statements of respect toward the ceremonies and authorities of the Church.

The Valladolid sources look like straightforward testimony, despite their kaleidoscopic content; but I expect my readers to doubt whether we can use them at all, given the environment in which they were composed. The theologians met at the request of the inquisitor general; they expounded their views in front of the Suprema, deposited their statements with inquisitorial notaries, and lodged, in certain instances, with Inquisition officials.[65] Furthermore, the repertory raised wrongs against the Inquisition as the fourth category out of twenty, immediately after transgressions against the Trinity, Jesus, and the Holy Spirit; and the arrangement of the list was not accidental: it appears as if its architects intended to inflame inquisitorial hostility and compound the sensitivity of the delegates' public discussions. Finally, evidence suggests that at least some of the theologians responded to the potentially charged atmosphere and framed their responses carefully, whether they endorsed, allowed, or repudiated the lines they were scrutinizing. Rodríguez de la Fuente signed Lerma's written replies on the first group of accusations, while Matatigui issued his opinions as single sentences.[66] Guevara prefaced nearly all his responses with a profession of belief in the particular doctrine under review, and in one instance even reiterated part of the Nicene Creed, although his orthodoxy was not ostensibly in question.[67] Almost all his peers acted similarly when it came to the comma Johanneum.

Yet to turn such signs into proof that the participants disguised their views will not do, for a variety of reasons. At the start of the conference, the delegates swore the usual oath that explicitly constrained them to secrecy, but their pledge had included an extra condition: that nothing they said in the course of their deliberations, even casually, could be used by anyone else to damage their reputations. This constraint presumably included the inquisitors in the audience.[68] The same vow obliged them to offer their opinions as dictated by God and their consciences. And from a pragmatic standpoint, we generally cannot measure participants' testimony from inside the assembly against anything they composed outside it, since most of them never wrote another line on Erasmus either before or after 1527. The few who expressed sentiments elsewhere usually maintained the same stances, with the exception of Carranza, who followed Stunica's negative lead in 1522, and then shifted to a more positive outlook five years later.[69] More to the point, several of the delegates—such as Gómez, Cabrero, and Enríquez—usually endorsed Erasmus fervently. If they could express their viewpoints with zeal, their counterparts presumably could have too.

As for the chance that the specter of Luther prompted the theologians to treat Erasmus more harshly than they would have done in other circumstances, again we lack a comparative framework, for Erasmus's works only circulated prominently in Spain after Luther's had entered Spanish territory as well. The perception of a Lutheran threat undoubtedly had some effect on the opinions, but the question is in which direction: although several participants alluded to the "dangerous epoch" in which they lived, or connected Erasmus to Luther through the principle of sola scriptura, or repeated the aphorism that Erasmus laid the egg that Luther hatched, two others revealed a fear of pushing Erasmus into Protestantism by criticizing him too harshly.[70] Accordingly, the European atmosphere of religious contention may have curtailed some delegates' censure of Erasmus instead of augmenting it. If the participants restricted their enthusiasm for Erasmus as a result of Martin Luther, then they finally did not think Erasmus's exoneration was worth the risk. Such hesitation in itself would be highly significant.

I would contend that the statements from Valladolid contain basically authentic reactions to problems of historical change, textual criticism, and hierarchy. What they raise repeatedly is religious authority, whether construed as citation or power, or imagined as amendable or static; what they impart reveals the impossibility of sequestering their authors into discrete factions of humanists and scholastics, or Erasmians and anti-Erasmians. Their discrimination over interpretative methods, devotional messages, and status upsets the usual scholarly frameworks. It also enhances our appreciation of how the clerical elite handled its sources and conceptualized the Church in polemical circumstances. The intellectual preferences of these theologians amplify our understanding of the Spanish Renaissance.

The delegates' reactions to Erasmus's hermeneutics were complex. Ten out of twenty-nine linked his omission of the comma Johanneum to its absence in Greek manuscripts, and hence seemed to recognize Greek sources as the proper originals for the Latin New Testament. Nevertheless, if those delegates accepted the comma's deletion on the basis of seven Greek codices, they also condoned its restoration on the strength of a single manuscript and expressed relief at its reinstatement. Only Gómez and Cabrero enunciated the reasons behind Erasmus's expurgation; Cabrero alone maintained that Erasmus would still be justified in removing the verse because the evidence for it rested on a unique source. Just two more repeated Erasmus's own comment that he had been acting as a translator, not a dogmatist, and had worked as the manuscripts dictated.[71] The delegates exhibited no greater willingness or ability to pursue the matter further.

What makes such reluctance even more telling is that at least eight of the theologians at Valladolid were thoroughly acquainted with Erasmus's writings and presumably understood the foundations of his editorial decisions. Cabrero stated repeatedly that he had read Erasmus's works, while Coronel had perused the latest edition of the *Annotations*. Virués, López de Bejar, Enríquez, and Gómez called attention to *De libero arbitrio,* and insisted that Erasmus was not a Lutheran; Lerma cited the content of the *Modus orandi Deum*'s second edition.

Such familiarity with Erasmus's opera allowed the delegates to point out, as they frequently did, that they were being asked to judge material taken out of context. But nearly all declined to express their agreement with Erasmus's methods in any but the most limited terms. No one proposed to weigh the relative merits of the sources involved. No one revealed any theoretical understanding of the relationship between Greek and Latin manuscripts of the New Testament, or suggested that the comma Johanneum only appeared either in the margins of Greek manuscripts, or in late redactions of the same. In fact, even Erasmus's reputed supporters finally preferred to maintain the Vulgate rather than modify it according to its original languages: their loyalties paralleled those of the New Testament editors on the Complutensian Polyglot Bible, who have been called "extremely conservative philologists."[72] When the Valladolid Erasmians had to choose, they finally sided with tradition over evaluation.

A similar balancing act between convention and criticism, with a comparable resolution, occurred when the theologians addressed Erasmus's remarks on Jerome. A sizable minority was willing to distinguish between the man and the saint, but no one cared for Erasmus's focus on the former or thought benefits ensued from it. In the end, they preferred to stress Jerome's holy rather than human character; they emphasized his ecclesiastical status as a venerable authority, instead of his historical one as a resident of the late Roman Empire. That perspective allowed them to finally overlook Erasmus's charge that Jerome had a "changeable" nature—and the ramifications of Jerome's versatility were potentially enormous, as Erasmus well knew.

In his biblical commentaries, Jerome relied upon different texts than the ones he supposedly translated; he questioned the authenticity of the comma Johanneum in one gloss, but included it in his alleged version of the New Testament. If early modern Europeans really considered such contradictions, they eventually might wonder whether their customary Latin Bible really came from Jerome in the first place; although Erasmus had asked the question numerous times, the point never was raised at Valladolid.[73] In a way, the delegates were determined to maintain a certain reputation for Jerome against the evidence, just as they affirmed the comma Johanneum on the basis of a single manuscript. Consciously or not, the participants were acting on St. Paul's insistence that the church should display an essential unity that discrete texts and incidents must not shake. But at Valladolid that tradition of homogeneity led the theologians to deprecate historical events. On the whole they found ecclesiastical tradition more important than textual inconsistencies.

The same propensity to ally the present and the past guided the delegates when they pondered the nomenclature of the Holy Spirit and Jesus. Seventeen participants imagined that church fathers might have hesitated to call the Spirit God before 325 C.E.; nonetheless, they wanted to check those Fathers' works to see if Erasmus were telling the truth, and they asserted that St. Hilary never believed anything contrary to Catholic doctrine. Not one alleged Erasmian confronted whether and when the apostles identified Jesus with God. And some delegates promoted continuity so fervidly that their ancestors became their twins, as when Almeida insisted that his articles of the faith were the same ones that guided the earliest Christians. Even the most astute respondents could argue on the basis of long-standing prestige. For example, Cabrero attested the accuracy of Erasmus's manuscripts because they resided in the papal library:

Erasmus does not defend corrupt manuscripts, but emends them, nor was he bound to consider as corrupt the Greek manuscripts that he possessed. . . . because those manuscripts were offered to him from various libraries of religious orders and from the pope's library, where it must not be presumed that corrupt manuscripts of the Gospels and apostolic letters are kept.[74]

Many of his peers wrote as if the Arian heresy continued to threaten Christianity; Córdoba and Francisco Vitoria identified patristic arguments with scholastic ones, as if Christian intellectuals had used the same methods for the same ends throughout time, and produced texts that looked alike.[75]

The same preference for continuity enabled the participants to allegorize their scriptural authorities and cite them in a mosaic fashion, by pulling distinct texts into a common discourse. There is a certain coincidence between their methods and the repertory's. For instance, Córdoba insisted that he could convince an Arian of the Trinity through the straightforward use of the Bible; he then turned to Song of Songs 8:8–9 and expounded it with traditional metaphorical abandon, to the point that a threefold Godhead was present in the Old Testament. Such Christian treatment of Jewish Scripture was standard, of course, and Erasmus himself condoned it. But Córdoba and Quintana also revealed a limited sensitivity to New Testament milieus when they identified "eternal life," "true God," and "Son" as terms for the same thing in 1 John 5:20; found the phrase "eternal life" in John 17:3; and consequently insisted that Jesus was openly called true God in the Gospel. For Córdoba and Quintana, both 1 John and the Gospel of John were composed by the same person: if the expression *vita aeterna* had a single, stable meaning in 1 John, identical significance could be extrapolated to the same phrase in the Gospel of John, although two separate books of the Bible were in play.[76] A similar technique allowed Castillo to demonstrate that early Christians confessed the Holy Spirit as God, although his proof-text, Romans 10:10, specifically concerned Jesus.[77] Thus some of the delegates betrayed the same interpretative propensities as the producers of the repertory itself.

Much of the theologians' stress on textual homogeneity came out of scholastic traditions of biblical exegesis. Scholastic conventions could also affect their discursive style, whether through résumés of authorities or the invocation of syllogisms. In one remarkable passage, Coronel wrote that if he spoke as a dialectician, he could prove that Erasmus himself believed that Paul had identified Jesus as God: "I may speak in the manner of the dialecticians, [Erasmus] argued conditionally, from a preceding assertion to a consequent one, namely, in this way: if this clause is not added on, certainly in this passage Paul pronounced Christ to be God. But this clause is not added on. Therefore in this place Paul, etc."[78] Like Vergara, Coronel too moved between types of discourse for the purpose of persuasion.

The scholastic element within the Valladolid testimony is predictable: dialectical reasoning was the usual way to substantiate intellectual premises in the sixteenth century, and the participants were, after all, theologians writing in Latin. They were accustomed to studying God through Aristotelian logic. The repertory played on the delegates' expertise when it advanced Erasmian quotations, such as "the Father is called the origin of Himself because He may be from none other." The terminology of statements like these was remarkably unclear from a theological perspective, and could have prompted the delegates to trumpet their superior credentials and better style. But unlike their polemical counterparts from other parts of Europe, the Spaniards only found that Erasmus's vocabulary was inappropriate, and usually concluded that his propositions could have positive meanings. Amazingly enough, no one at Valladolid connected Erasmus's more casual language to his competence as a theologian. Even Carranza, who had berated him in 1522 for his use of unconventional terms and lack of professional qualifications, simply wrote in 1527 that his propositions were true, although not uttered in the style of more recent theology.[79]

The delegates' breezy attitude did not arise from the stance that words were unimportant, for no one maintained that Erasmus's alterations of Scripture were trivial. And the relative dearth of professional jealousy makes Spanish testimony startlingly different from its counterpart in other countries, in which Erasmus's inferior level of theological training was a cliché.[80] If the Spanish participants expressed some sense of hierarchy when it came to religion—for a few alluded to the difference in status between clergy and laity—the vast majority still displayed, at least implicitly, a certain elasticity toward the characteristics and practitioners of religious discourse.

Suppleness also distinguishes the Spaniards' opinions from those expressed by better-known controversialists. If the theologians shared Lee's, Stunica's, and Latomus's misgivings about Greek, at least a third recognized that it played a role in the assessment of Scripture, and declined to condemn Erasmus simply for having employed it.[81] Like Frans Tittelmans, most feared that criticism would wreck the Vulgate's prestige and Jerome's status, but some also accepted emendations to the Bible, albeit on a limited basis.[82] A few could extrapolate saints from their hagiographies, even if they finally worked from those individuals' place in tradition instead of history. And no one called Erasmus an Arian, although nearly everyone retained Arianism as a heretical category.[83] The relative pliancy of the participants' reactions may be due to the fact that they were responding to a polemic instead of launching one of their own; it really is the accusations from Valladolid that should be compared to the contentions of other Europeans. Still, the Spanish testimony furnishes a broader sample of hermeneutical stances than what individual controversialists can provide: it confirms a generally conservative drift in the face of textual criticism and history, but also exposes a certain forbearance toward rank and language.

Such evidence demands a more subtle exposition from the historian instead of the rigid contrasts of the older scholarly grid. Like the Vergara trial six years later, the Valladolid assembly does not verify discrete classes of humanists and scholastics in early modern Spain, but something far more delicate. Erasmus's reputed disciples at the conference did not embrace his notions unequivocally. The six who reacted to his advice on rebellious adolescents—Lerma, Matatigui, Alcaráz, Gómez, Ciria, and Rodríguez de la Fuente—unanimously condemned it. Four of the five who wrote on excommunication regretted the content and tone of the *Colloquies*; Lerma wished to excise or correct Erasmus's writings almost as frequently as anyone else.[84] Recommendations to expurgate or emend Erasmus's texts raise serious questions about how Spanish Erasmians read the very tracts that supposedly guided them: when coupled with the fact that Spanish translators omitted the more controversial sentiments of the *Enchiridion* and the *Colloquies*, it becomes clear that even Erasmus's disciples could treat his works selectively.[85]

The same sort of discrimination was equally prevalent among the alleged antagonists, for even the most persistent critics occasionally relented. Guevara, who considered many of Erasmus's statements useless and most of them heretical, wrote that his comments about the Inquisition were legitimate. Córdoba persistently censured Erasmus's remarks irrespective of their context or purpose, but thought the satire on papal excommunication was "open to a wholesome understanding"; Arrieta found Erasmus's advice on religious education beneficial, and wished such instruction occurred all the time.[86] Nearly everyone backed Erasmus's elevation of pious studies, and seconded his recommendation to pursue heretics in a more restrained fashion. But they also dismissed his approval of a relative religious freedom in the *Paraphrase on Matthew*: their censure illustrates the risk of assuming that a certain slant on spirituality connotes a particular outlook on tolerance.

The writings from Valladolid, like the declarations of Juan de Vergara, demonstrate that Spanish ecclesiastics envisioned religious authority in eclectic ways. In a number of instances, the delegates stressed custom over criticism and continuity over history, but they overwhelmingly favored affective piety over disputation. Often they could bear Erasmus's neglect of traditional language and structure, but they would brandish dialectic to exonerate his annotations, urge the censorship of his works even as they defended them, and sanction his Greek sources because they resided with the pope. Their preferences reveal that humanism and scholasticism could be practiced to a relative degree, that religious messages did not always correspond to particular interpretative methods, and that Spanish Erasmians did not practice as coherent a humanism as we have been led to believe. Indeed, the delegates persistently exhibited their intellectual autonomy through the nuances of their opinions and their inconsistencies.

The Spaniards' writings also demonstrate the potential opacity of intellectual practice in the early modern period: in two instances, their statements may only appear to endorse the emulation of the early church. The majority agreed that devout studies were more important than inquisitive ones. But they could have come to that conclusion for a thoroughly traditional reason, since Erasmus literally described such disputative pursuits as "studia curiosa." With that phrase, he raised the concept of curiositas, which had a history of condemnation from the Apostle Paul to Jean Gerson, and which Vergara had applied against Francisca Hernández. Similar difficulties of interpretation attend the delegates' reaction to Erasmus's exegesis of the wheat and the tares, because Erasmus's remarks did not differ substantially from the *Glosa ordinaria*'s. In such instances, it is almost impossible to know what motivated the delegates' approval—critical imitation of the early church, or customary regard for long-standing authority. What is certain is that their opinions could rely upon resonant intellectual schemes, although we too often describe their reasoning in overly reduced terms.

Such intricacy was amply exhibited by one delegate at Valladolid, Pedro Ciruelo. Ciruelo taught Thomistic theology at the University of Alcalá, commented on Aristotle, and looks like a thorough scholastic according to his modern reputation.[87] His statements from the conference seem to support that portrait, for he ostensibly rejected every philological or historical turn. He maintained that the comma Johanneum was canonical and insisted that the apostles called Jesus the true God; he affirmed that all the Fathers proclaimed the Holy Spirit as God, too, and he rejected Erasmus's treatment of Romans 9:5.

Nevertheless, there is a peculiar element to Ciruelo's responses, for he endorsed Erasmus's statements as soon as he censured them: at the end of each of his replies, he wrote that nearly all of the proposals under scrutiny were true or acceptable, including potential revisions to the Bible.[88] His citations of Scripture also differed qualitatively from ones offered by individuals such as Quintana and Córdoba. For example, when Ciruelo tried to prove that the earliest Christians referred to Jesus as God, he summoned evidence that actually was relevant in context, such as Romans 1:8, "I always give thanks to my God for you, because your faith is spoken of in the whole world." What he noted afterward was positively stunning, for he wrote "and speaking of his own epoch in chapter 10, [Paul] cites that verse of Psalms 18, 'their sound went forth into all the earth.' "[89] In that small phrase—"speaking of his own epoch"—Ciruelo betrayed an awareness of the gap of time between Judaism and Christianity. He exhibited the same perception in work on the Old Testament, although he continued to honor Jerome and defer to the Vulgate, at least ostensibly. If the Valladolid testimony reveals numerous twists in the intellectual priorities of Spanish clerics, Ciruelo's scholarship allows us to track the same curves in even more difficult texts. His writings further elucidate the paradoxes captured in 1527.

Chapter Three

A Converso and the Old Testament

The Literal Sense of Scripture

P edro Ciruelo offers us an exceptionally labyrinthine perspective on religious authority because he was a *converso* who studied Hebrew, translated the Pentateuch, and practiced textual criticism, while simultaneously scattering compliments to Jerome and the Vulgate throughout his manuscript prefaces. He is a consummate example of an early modern intellectual pulled in two directions at once. His work illustrates how Renaissance humanism could lurk beneath the most conventional exterior.

Until the end of the fifteenth century, the Iberian Peninsula possessed the largest Jewish population in Western Europe. Many of Spain's Jews converted to Christianity, voluntarily or by force, after the pogroms of 1391; another wave of conversions followed the Jewish Expulsion Edict of 1492. The Spanish Inquisition was founded in 1478 specifically to weed out reputedly false, formerly Jewish converts to Catholicism, and that institution prosecuted basically no one else during the first four decades of its existence. It thus would be easy to infer that Spanish ecclesiastics with exegetical ambitions stayed away from the Old Testament and Hebrew. It also seems reasonable to conclude that Spanish clerics who were conversos—who either converted from Judaism themselves or descended from Jews—had particularly powerful motives to avoid critical approaches to the first half of the Christian Bible. Yet Ciruelo pursued the history and philology of the Old Testament, and the manuscripts that relay his goals are extant. He presents us with an enigmatic corrective to the usual portrait of Spain as a font of intolerance: he disguised his intellectual priorities, and consequently confirms his country's bigotry; he also applied humanist techniques in his translations, and thereby reveals the potential flexibility of Spanish intellectual culture. If the Valladolid conference demonstrates the degree to which Spanish ecclesiastics valued traditional authority, the subject of Ciruelo and the Old Testament may disclose something equally meaningful, but in the opposite direction: the possibility of creative action in a venture packed with custom, in an environment where we might least expect such innovation.

When it comes to sacred literature, Renaissance humanists purportedly learned ancient languages, compared biblical manuscripts, and challenged defective readings in an effort to heighten their understanding of the Bible, the New Testament in particular. They scolded translators and chastised scribes. They are supposed to have confronted the Bible with one set of exegetical priorities, while their medieval predecessors pursued another. Not surprisingly, modern medievalists often have responded to this picture by emphasizing the continuity of intellectual endeavors among the twelfth, thirteenth, and sixteenth centuries. They have pointed to Andrew of St. Victor (d. 1175), who learned Hebrew and wrote commentaries on the Old Testament. They have emphasized the commentaries of Nicholas de Lyra (1270-1340), whose biblical glosses openly relied upon the eleventh-century Jewish scholar known as Rashi.[1] They have noted that medieval intellectuals displayed curiosity about the customs, proper names, and plants detailed in Scripture. And they have reminded us that the recovery of Aristotle's logical works in the twelfth century, with their emphasis on cause and effect, promoted in turn a new awareness of authorship, and from there a deeper interest in the human writers of the Bible.

Thus at least a smattering of medieval individuals knew the original languages of Scripture, sought its history, and cared about its authors; they noticed infelicities in the various versions of the Bible, and advocated the correction of that text in accordance with its prototypes.[2] Furthermore, it looks as if intellectuals began to pay greater attention to the literal sense of the Bible, beginning in the twelfth century and culminating in the fourteenth. And since respected experts, such as Augustine and Aquinas, defined the literal sense as the grammatical and historical meaning, and then as the author's intention, modern scholars may see only minute differences between the philological, historical, and contextual principles followed by medieval scholars, and ones practiced by their Renaissance successors.

From my standpoint, historians of Christian hermeneutics are both right and wrong simultaneously. Precedents to Renaissance techniques existed in the High Middle Ages. Nicholas de Lyra understood Hebrew, and noticed discrepancies between the Vulgate and St. Jerome's *De quaestionibus hebraicis*; he also censured the extravagant allegorizing that Christians applied to the Old Testament.[3] Conversely, Renaissance thinkers could reject textual criticism and history when the biblical text was at stake: Leonardo Bruni personally spurned the investigation of Hebrew, as did Erasmus; Giannozzo Manetti studied that idiom, but also combined deliberately Ciceronian orations with citations from the Pentateuch.[4]

Yet despite their antecedents and their own inconsistencies, Renaissance humanists who regarded the Bible could diverge from earlier practice in pivotal ways. They could pull their observations from Hebrew and Aramaic sources, rather than Jerome's Latin commentaries on those materials. They could turn textual incongruities into questions about the authentic translator of the Vulgate, instead of simply blaming Jerome's erraticism on the incompetence of scribes.[5] In sum, between the twelfth and fourteenth centuries, the number of intellectuals who critiqued sacred literature was small and the extent of their appraisals limited, despite their attention to languages, authorship, and history. If we recognize that some medieval individuals esteemed the textual study of the Bible, we must also admit that a far more numerous bunch stepped over the rind of the words in order to reach the fruit within.[6]

As for attention to Scripture's literal meaning, medieval interpreters expanded and altered their definitions of the literal sense even as they maintained the expression *sensus literalis*: that phrase could imply much more than grammar, history, and context. By the fifteenth century the sensus literalis could be divided into two parts, and if one meaning encompassed the history the words expressed, the other embraced the things the words signified, and then the *properties* of the things. The literal sense could hinge upon the author's intention, and include a metaphor if the author had meant to utter one. Then again, the Bible's foremost author was God, and since God proposed everything, thanks to His all-knowingness, every scriptural interpretation could be categorized as a "literal" one, at least potentially.

Disturbed by protracted chains of meaning that had little direct connection to the text itself, and moved by Augustine's dictum that Christian dogma could only be proven through literal explanations of the Bible, Lyra even devised a twofold literal sense. He expounded certain Old Testament passages according to their significance within Jewish history, and then offered *another* literal meaning for the same verses when they were cited in the New Testament.[7] Scholars often have presumed that Lyra's twofold literal sense signaled his willingness to treat the Old Testament within a Jewish context. But Lyra's appreciation for Jewish history was far less potent than the Christian imperative he inherited to find Jesus in the first half of the Bible. The result was that he invariably laid literal interpretations with Christian conclusions on top of Jewish history, law, and prophecy. With Deuteronomy 18:15, for example—"The Lord your God will raise up to you a prophet of your nation and of your brethren like me, and you will hear him"—he initially connected Moses' quote to Joshua, then turned the same quotation toward Joshua's successors, and finally applied it to Jesus. He also stipulated that the Christological slant gave the verse its principal meaning in both the Old Testament and the New. Jesus "was the great prophet to whom the other prophet's prophecies were ordained."[8]

Lyra's hierarchy came from a Christian tradition that handled Scripture as the expression of a single mystery, the Incarnation of Jesus as the Son of God. That legacy told Christian exegetes to enforce harmony upon the books of the Bible, to prefer spiritual readings of Scripture to literal ones, and to embrace religious truths over historical circumstances. Reverence for Aristotle could further justify the filtering of the Old Testament through the New. When that philosopher treated causes and effects, he argued that the last in order of execution was the *first* in order of conception.[9] In Matthew 22:37–39, Jesus condensed Mosaic Law by instructing his followers to love God with their heart and soul, and to love their neighbors as themselves; in Romans 10:4, Paul declared that Jesus was the end of the Law. According to one of the foremost apostles, then, Jesus consummated the Law in both his person and his version of it; with Aristotle's help, Jesus' statement on the Law could preface Exodus's, because last and first things were inextricably linked. Christianity thus was the "end" of Judaism, and must have preceded it. Lyra was not the only intellectual to absorb such emphases. Given the irresistibly Christian environment in which they lived, it would be unreasonable to expect later individuals to have ignored such weighty and authoritative lessons either. Even Erasmus pursued the history of the Church in order to forget it, for his highest interest lay in higher truths.[10]

With such powerful customs behind the exegesis of the Bible, any investigation of it in the sixteenth century must respect continuity as well as change; in fact, it is risky to posit change at all, since the difference between a conventional and an unusual exposition of Scripture can hinge on extremely subtle uses of language and delicate shifts in emphasis. The literal interpretation of the Old Testament in early modern Spain is full of such cryptic readings, and these readings illustrate in turn the distance between ourselves and the individuals we are studying, for we often cannot immediately grasp what we are scrutinizing. The challenges of these exegetical sources parallel in some respects the obstacles posed by records of the Inquisition.

Yet the search for confrontations with the Old Testament is worth the effort, because the topic reveals aspects of religious authority and information on the Spanish Renaissance that few academics have tackled (although scholarly inattention is now changing to interest).[11] Problems of language and history inhere in the very relationship that Christianity posits between the Old and New Testaments, however much the sixteenth-century faithful were taught to take that connection for granted.[12] Depending upon the interpreter and critic, the first half of the Bible might recount events about Jews or presage ones about Christians. Latin versions of the Psalms could contradict each other, depending upon whether they had been translated from the Greek translation of the Hebrew or from the Hebrew itself; blame for textual variations could be placed on translators, scribes, or, by the late fifteenth century, printers.

Notably, work with the Old Testament also entailed a decision to consider the Jews according to atemporal or contextual standards. Christian interpreters might treat Judaism as if it should mirror an Old Testament prototype, and react to historical change in that religion as a betrayal of the biblical model. But Christian scholars also could imagine Judaism as existing across time, and that vantage point could provoke their consideration of the Targums, the Aramaic translations of the Old Testament that were produced once Jews no longer spoke Hebrew routinely.[13] To a certain extent, then, early modern Christians could read the Old Testament as Hebrew or Latin, Jewish or Christian, and historical or allegorical literature. Their choices illuminate the ways in which they envisioned their religious past as well as their scriptural text.

Nonetheless, their preferences can be hard to detect, especially when they mingled critical impulses with traditional emphases. For instance, Pedro Ciruelo seems out of place in this book, because his writings look like the products of an intellectual polymath who practiced a full-blown scholasticism. Born around 1470, Ciruelo was a self-proclaimed orphan who studied the trivium and quadrivium at the University of Salamanca and then pursued theology at Paris. By 1502, he was teaching at the College of St. Antonio de Portaceli, in the Castilian town of Sigüenza; eight years later, he accepted the chair of Thomistic theology at the recently founded and eventually renowned

University of Alcalá. Like Juan de Vergara, Ciruelo, too, found his benefice shifted from San Ildefonso to San Justo y Pastor in 1519; by 1533 he had assumed the first teaching position ever underwritten for the Cathedral of Segovia; in 1536, he took up an identical spot at Salamanca's cathedral, where he died after Vespers on November 5, 1548.[14]

Ciruelo remained in university and cathedral circles all his life, and his writings apparently belonged to the more conventional currents of the European intellectual experience. He synthesized familiar textbooks, such as John Holywood's *Sphaera* and Thomas Bradwardine's *Geometria speculativa*. He commented upon Aristotle's *Posterior Analytics*. He also composed vernacular religious treatises in thoroughly medieval genres, such as the confessors' manual. Whether writing in Latin or Spanish, Ciruelo framed a great deal of what he had to say in an overtly dialectical format: his earlier works in particular often read like sequences of contradictory statements that he sometimes bothered to reconcile, but just as frequently did not. He liked number symbolism, and peppered his treatises with three's and seven's.[15] In some publications he relished allegories, to the point that he slighted the compatibility that should have connected the spiritual meaning of the text to its actual words: he once wrote that Simon of Cyrene helped Jesus carry his cross to Calvary and shouldered a burden that was not his own; Simon's example "signified hypocritical penitents, who carry the cross of penance not to mortify the flesh and their sins, but in order to be praised by men and reputed as holy."[16]

Ciruelo also did not hesitate to cite his scriptural authorities mosaically, or as clusters of discrete phrases that came from different books of the Bible. Sometimes he presented patchworks of verses as if they were coherent scriptural passages. In a work on plague and its spiritual remedies, Ciruelo summoned the following reference to support his point that plague destroyed human networks: "The impious will cease from uproar and those exhausted in strength shall rest; quarrels and reproaches will cease; the world mourned and vanished, and the height of the people is weakened, and [the earth] is infected by her inhabitants."[17] The problem is that this quotation does not exist in the Bible, at least not as Ciruelo cited it: the first phrase came from Job 3:17, the second from Proverbs 22:10, the third and fourth from Isaiah 24:4–5.

Ciruelo's fondness for dialectic, allegory, and proof-texts made up of unrelated passages stamps him as a scholastic, for these propensities are traceable to the intellectual methods promoted by the universities of the Middle Ages. His employment of scholastic technique is unexceptional: he hardly could have been exempt from that training when all professional theologians were indebted to it. Yet one area of his work complicates the labeling of his writings as pure scholasticism, for he did more than abridge Bradwardine or comment on Aristotle. He also made explicitly literal—word-to-word (*de verbo ad verbum*)—translations of the Old Testament from Hebrew into Latin.

In 1526, Ciruelo and his longtime collaborator, Alfonso de Zamora, presented a literal, interlinear, Hebrew-to-Latin rendition of Genesis to Toledan Archbishop Alonso de Fonseca, the same archbishop who employed Vergara as a secretary. In 1533, Ciruelo furnished Segovia's cathedral chapter with a manuscript that contained four Latin versions of the Pentateuch in parallel columns, taken from the Hebrew, the Aramaic Targum of Onqelos, the Septuagint, and the Vulgate. The Pentateuch encompasses the first five books— Mosaic Law—of the Hebrew Bible.[18] The Targums were the Aramaic paraphrases of Hebrew Scripture: their best-known examples were the Targum of Onqelos on the Pentateuch and the Targum of Jonathan on the Prophets. Both were employed by the third century C.E. Finally, the Septuagint was the most famous Greek translation of the Hebrew Bible: according to legend, it was rendered by seventy-two translators for Ptolemy Philadelphus in the third century B.C.E.; according to critics, its Greek text differed in important ways from its Hebrew model.

Ciruelo's work with such texts did not stop in 1533. Three years later, he dedicated a literal, interlinear, Hebrew-to-Latin translation of the Pentateuch to the University of Salamanca, and presented a similar rendition of Job, Psalms, Proverbs, Esther, Ruth, Ecclesiastes, and the Song of Songs to the same university in 1537.[19] The question of these translations' contribution to Hebrew scholarship—the extent to which they diverge from one another, and again from works produced by Zamora alone—has not yet been answered fully, and will have to be settled by an expert in Hebrew, which I do not read.[20] Still, Ciruelo's Latin prefaces to his translations are relevant to this book: his forewords, along with his occasional annotation, raise provocative findings about Spanish ecclesiastics' definitions of religious authority and the degree to which they could practice humanism and scholasticism at the same time. Ciruelo's introductions demonstrate the unsatisfactory results of casting Spanish clerics in dichotomous terms.

Ciruelo always followed the same basic outline in his prologues. He began by praising the Bible for guiding men and women to life after death. At first God's Word belonged only to the Jews, for He was especially revered among them; but because He wished to save all peoples, He inspired human agents to convey His teaching from Hebrew to Greek to Latin. Among such servant-translators, Ciruelo isolated Jerome as the most skillful, for others had never turned to the Hebrew at all, or else had altered the words or mixed up their order. Ciruelo then reiterated Jerome's advice to employ Hebrew for difficult readings in the Old Testament and Greek for trying passages in the New. He remarked that Jerome paraphrased the Old Testament, while he himself transferred its language literally. He also observed that his own translation finally would verify the superiority of the Vulgate by demonstrating that Jerome's work did not differ from the Hebrew in any meaningful way. Finally, Ciruelo concluded that his efforts would erase textual errors and silence Jewish calumny. In the more specific prefaces to the reader, Ciruelo expressed fears about the clumsiness of his Latin translation, explained how he had avoided or alleviated the challenges of moving from one syntactically distinct idiom to another, and hoped that his work would be useful.

Numerous elements in these prefaces were absolutely traditional. There was nothing new in Ciruelo's recommendations on the Bible's original languages: Augustine had issued similar counsel in the fourth century, Hugh and Andrew of St. Victor had done so in the twelfth, and Aquinas had enshrined the same advice one hundred years later. Nicholas de Lyra knew Hebrew well in the fourteenth century; in 1311–12, the Council of Vienne under Pope Clement V asked for chairs in Hebrew, Aramaic, and Arabic at Paris, Salamanca, and Oxford, among other sites. There also was nothing innately unorthodox or even suspicious about translating the Pentateuch or using it in Christian exegesis. In Judeo-Christian thought, the first five books of the Bible relayed Mosaic Law: the crux of that Law was the Ten Commandments, which God had revealed as compensation for people's inability to distinguish between right and wrong. The Ten Commandments, also called the Decalogue, were divine as well as natural law, and eternally bound human beings; they were as relevant to Christians as to Jews. Jesus had proclaimed as much in Matthew 19:18–19.

Ciruelo's literal style of translation was not novel either. His desire to produce a word-for-word, *de verbo ad verbum* rendition of Hebrew seems very much opposed to Renaissance humanists' appreciation for Latin eloquence—a goal they defined and pursued according to Cicero. In classical antiquity, Cicero had described the best translations as ones that conveyed the sense of the text (*transferre ad sententiam*) instead of its exact words. By the late Roman Empire, Christian intellectuals like Jerome agreed with the advantages of the transferre ad sententiam technique, but excluded the Bible from that method because the sanctity of Scripture precluded any changes in its vocabulary or word order.

Eventually the principle of literality that governed renditions of the Bible seeped into all renditions of all texts, even ones from Republican Rome. The literal technique dominated translation practice for centuries until a combination of circumstances revived Cicero's transferre ad sententiam alternative. In the late fourteenth and early fifteenth centuries, Greek scholars fled to Italy as the Ottoman Empire expanded in a westerly direction. These individuals were still familiar with ancient teachings on style because the cultural baggage of the Roman Empire had survived in Constantinople: some of them, such as Manuel Chrysoloras, who arrived in Italy in 1396, taught Greek and functioned as a sort of living conduit for the transmission of classical rhetoric. The 1421 discovery of Cicero's complete works on oratory hastened a process that was already under way.[21]

The result was a figure such as Leonardo Bruni, who benefited from Chrysoloras's instruction and Cicero's example, and consequently berated medieval translators for their concentration on single words and direct correspondences between them, instead of on whole phrases and larger blocks of meaning. The humanists' general preoccupation with eloquence even led some, such as Valla and Erasmus, to notice the crudeness of the Vulgate's Latin and the primitiveness of the apostles' Greek.[22] Of course, Valla's wish to make the New Testament sound like a composition from the late Roman Republic reveals as clear an indifference to history as scholastic realism, in which individual words signified unchangeable, exclusive meanings. But as far as modern scholarship is concerned, the recovery of classical rhetoric remains one of the primary characteristics of Renaissance humanism, and it would be notably absent in literal translations.[23]

Thus Ciruelo's interest in Hebrew and de verbo ad verbum translations does not make him a humanist, at least not automatically. His most obvious motives for rendering the Pentateuch also had little to do with textual criticism, since they turned on the status of St. Jerome and the authority of the Vulgate. In the prologue to the 1526 manuscript, Ciruelo described Jerome as the "most skilled" (peritissimus) of all translators, because he used the best Hebrew manuscripts and tried most diligently to restore the whole Old Testament to Latin readers. In the 1536 preface, Ciruelo wrote that he wished to prove the "undiminished truth" of the Vulgate and he insisted that the Vulgate hardly differed from the Hebrew except in certain, tacitly unimportant, phrases. Finally, in both 1526 and 1536 he noted that his own work would correct the printers' errors that corrupted Jerome's edition.

To all appearances, Ciruelo simply translated the Old Testament to magnify the position of Jerome and the Vulgate; his language suggested a wish to elevate ecclesiastical tradition and its most cherished authorities. When he chastised the mistakes of printers, he merely extended the cliché that scribes routinely muddled the biblical text. When he commented on the relationship between the Old and New Testaments—as in the 1537 prologue, which prefaced a translation of the Psalter and the books of Solomon—he also could treat the first half of the Bible as a figure of the second. Despite the fact that *we* tend to read "literal" as grammatical or philological, Ciruelo's de verbo ad verbum translations ostensibly had little to do with critical perspectives on the transmission of sacred literature.

Tagging his work as a product of humanism seems even less likely once we realize that Ciruelo's translations look like slender imitations of the Complutensian Polyglot Bible. Historians used to trumpet the Complutensian project as a symbol of the Renaissance in Spain.[24] Archbishop Cisneros began to plan this multilingual edition of the Bible after 1510; he took as his model the Old Testament that Origen had created in the third century C.E., which consisted of as many as nine Greek versions of Scripture, arranged in parallel columns over and against the original Hebrew.[25] Wherever appropriate, the Complutensian Polyglot presented the biblical text in Hebrew, Aramaic, Greek, and Latin. Its Old Testament entailed sequential columns of the Greek Septuagint, the Latin Vulgate, Hebrew with vowel markings, Hebrew without vowel markings, the Aramaic paraphrase of the Hebrew, and the same Aramaic without vowel markings. Cisneros's team made interlineal, literal—de verbo ad verbum—Latin translations only from the Septuagint and the Aramaic texts.[26] They left the Hebrew alone.

We can guess that Ciruelo benefited from the Complutensian Polyglot because he implied it: in his 1533 and 1536 manuscripts, he acknowledged that his Latin translation of the Aramaic came from his teachers of Hebrew. He learned that language from the scholarly cluster that directed the Polyglot's presentation of the Old Testament, which consisted of first-generation conversos Pablo Coronel, Maestro Alfonso de Alcalá, and Alfonso de Zamora.[27] Evidence that Ciruelo actually worked on the Polyglot itself emerges if we superimpose the dates of the project on the chronology of his teaching career. The Greek and Latin New Testament of the Polyglot came off the presses between 1513 and 1514. Scholars finished working on the Old Testament in 1515, although it required more than twenty-four months to print. The scholarly part of the project thus began in approximately 1510, which is the more conservative estimate, and lasted until the spring of 1515.[28] The same five-year period coincides almost exactly with Ciruelo's absence from his chair: the University of Alcalá's records show that he left his teaching position on April 12, 1511, and was reelected to it on January 7, 1516.[29]

The fact that Ciruelo learned Hebrew from the Complutensian editors of the Old Testament, used their Latin translation of the Aramaic, and most likely collaborated with them on the same enterprise does not bode well for his status as a humanist. The Polyglot's New Testament editors frequently tailored the Bible's original languages to Jerome's Latin instead of the reverse. For instance, at 1 John 5:7, the comma Johanneum, they translated the verse from Latin into Greek; they explicitly quoted Aquinas to justify the comma's inclusion.[30]

The New Testament team acted similarly in the case of Matthew 6:13: because the Vulgate omitted a clause found in most Greek texts—"for thine is the kingdom, the power, and the glory forever"—they also removed it from the Greek.[31] When they ran into a passage in which the Greek and Latin disagreed, as at 1 Corinthians 15:51, they offered both versions instead of deciding between the two. And on at least eight other occasions they knew of Greek readings that contradicted the Vulgate, but they still presented passages that supported Jerome in both the Greek and the Latin.[32] Although we know less about the hermeneutic principles that moved the Complutensian editors of the Old Testament, there is little reason to think that they acted differently: they clearly altered the sequence of the books, changed their division, and omitted critical vowel markings and accents.[33] In sum, Cisneros wanted the Polyglot structured in parallel columns so that everyone would see how Jerome's Latin matched other biblical languages, and his editors made sure that he succeeded in his aim.[34]

Esteem for traditional authority was reflected in other aspects of the Complutensian venture as well. It reproduced Jerome's biblical prefaces. Its main prologue recounted that the Vulgate's Latin Old Testament was placed expressly between the Hebrew and Septuagint, as if between the Synagogue and the Eastern Church, or as if two thieves were placed around Jesus in the middle, who signified the Roman or Latin Church.[35] This structure deliberately called up Jesus' crucifixion, and again Roman Catholic stereotypes about its supposedly tireless enemies, Jews and the Greek Orthodox. The same preface raised discrepancies between Latin manuscripts, and blamed them on the ignorance and carelessness of scribes.[36] The Polyglot gleaned its axioms of biblical interpretation from Aquinas and Lyra, whom it plundered for definitions of the literal sense and the reproduction of mnemonic devices. And its explanation of the allegorical sense of Scripture was packed with Old Testament examples; its ostensible interest in that part of the Bible lay in making it an expansive and detailed design of subsequent Christianity.[37]

The Complutensian Polyglot looks like a return to ancient Christianity because it emulates Origen's *Hexapla* and apparently operates on philological principles, but its content nonetheless preserved intact the codicils of medieval exegesis. Ciruelo's translations seem to echo the Polyglot's parameters. Both employed original languages, but venerated Jerome; both wished to correct textual errors, but attributed textual mistakes to copyists; both relayed texts de verbo ad verbum, and expressed the conventional relationship between the Old and New Testaments. Ciruelo not only borrowed the Polyglot's Latin translation of Aramaic, but its translation technique, its veneration of Jerome, and even its narration; as we shall see, he pulled sentences from its preface directly into his prologues.

And yet the story of Ciruelo and his biblical translations cannot end here. He may have relied upon the Complutensian Polyglot, but he did not blindly reiterate that project's preferences and language. Just as the clerics at Valladolid voiced small and large objections to Erasmus's writings, so Ciruelo reacted actively rather than passively to his sources. The changes he made in his literary authorities were often subtle, but they place him in the Renaissance as well as the thirteenth and fourteenth centuries. His promotion of textual criticism and his historical gaze upset the easy categorization of his works, despite their obvious debt to medieval models.

Ciruelo's decision to translate literally was explicitly self-conscious; he translated that way out of choice, not necessity, and he understood the rhetorical niceties he was violating. In his 1526 manuscript, he warned readers that he had used words or expressions that would not please Donatus, the fourth-century instructor of Latin grammar whose textbook was a standard reference; in 1536, he added that he had fallen into "barbarisms and solecisms," the former being grammatical errors, the latter deviations from rules of syntax. Ciruelo encountered such difficulties because of the profound differences between the Hebrew and Latin languages. As he observed, Hebrew formed certain verbs out of nouns: an equivalent process in Latin would result in *sacerdotare* out of *sacerdos*, or "to perform as a priest" from the word "priest" itself; and *pugillare* from *pugillus*, "to box" from "boxer."[38]

The solecisms, meanwhile, arose from the distinct rules that governed each idiom: Hebrew and Latin are inflected languages, but the same words in each do not always require the same cases of nouns after them. For example, the Latin verb *servire* (to serve) routinely governs the dative, but its equivalent in Hebrew takes the accusative; Ciruelo accordingly followed the Hebrew and rendered the First Commandment as "non servies de*os* alien*os*," whereas correct Latin syntax would dictate "non servies de*is* alien*is*."[39] Such constructions would have struck educated Spaniards as clumsy and ignorant, as Ciruelo well knew, but he thought his goal worth any potential reproach:

If perhaps anyone pursuing a more delicate Latin elegance should see that our translation does not sufficiently measure up to Latin eloquence, he may consider that this was done for this reason, that the original Hebrew language should be displayed by us in its phrasing, and so should the grammatical properties of its single words; which anyone attending to them will be able to grasp easily from our interlinear Latin gloss.[40]

Thus a reader would stumble over "non servies deos alienos," realize that the Hebrew for "servire" required the accusative case, and come to employ the manuscript as a teaching tool. More important for our purposes, Ciruelo recognized the difference between classical Latin style and its opposite; he realized he abandoned Latin eloquence because of his fidelity to the Hebrew original, and then explained the motive behind the awkwardness to his readers. He evinced a critical underpinning to what might have been a technique taken up by rote. He revealed an analogous discrimination when he commented on problems in the Old Testament text.

Ciruelo described his work as enhancing Jerome's status, but he blamed translators as well as scribes for discrepancies between the Latin Bible and its original languages. He consequently went much further than his most obvious authorities. The Complutensian Polyglot and Nicholas de Lyra only confronted the safest and most anonymous target when they inculpated copyists, since those individuals were three or four or a hundred times removed from the genesis of Scripture, and merely reproduced what the Holy Spirit originally had transmitted to a human agent. In contrast, Ciruelo suggested problems with Jerome's own translation in his three prologues, although the extent and placement of his criticism differed in provocative ways.

In his earliest translation from 1526, Ciruelo camouflaged his objections to the Vulgate with polemics against the Jews and praise for Jerome, which was an intelligent strategy: he used clichés to hide his criticism even as he appraised one of the most powerful religious authorities in sixteenth-century Europe. At the very end of the 1526 prologue, he noted that he wanted his work to silence the infidel Jews: "And [this translation is] the means by which we can refute the infidel Jews, who slander our Jerome as a distorter of sacred Scripture. For he nevertheless holds [sacred Scripture] far differently, as will be obvious if anyone wishes to compare his interpretation with the books of the Jews."[41]

Hence Ciruelo berated the Jews for censuring Jerome, and then admitted that their rebuke was correct, since he granted differences between the Vulgate Old Testament and the Hebrew original. He finally observed that his work would "elevate the preeminence of Jerome's rendition, wherever anyone can find it." As he explained, "We said specifically wherever it may be found, because we are not entirely certain that we have the interpretation of St. Jerome in and throughout all the common books of our Vulgate Bible; on the contrary, in his book *De hebraicis quaestionibus* he himself reproaches certain passages of our literature, which the common edition emphatically stated in his epoch."[42]

Thus Ciruelo ultimately raised the radical notion that Jerome did not render the Bible ascribed to him. The fact that he could mention such discrepancies in Jerome's opera shows that the subject was not reserved to the highest circles of the intellectual elite; it also illustrates a willingness to measure Jerome as a human being. Lyra had noted the same divergence between the Vulgate and Jerome's *De hebraicis quaestionibus,* but turned it in a completely different direction: in the second prologue to his *Postilla,* he used variation between the Vulgate and the Hebrew to question whether theologians should continue to use Hebrew at all.

In 1526 Ciruelo covered his critique with nods to conventional religious authority, as he chastised Jews and venerated Jerome. He employed the same strategies more extensively in the 1536 prologue to the University of Salamanca. As he described how sacred Scripture moved from Hebrew to Greek to Latin, he noted that translators changed the biblical text through caprice, their intellectual powers, and their linguistic skill. Their often whimsical alterations explained why "difference and variety" so frequently occurred in Old Testament manuscripts.[43] Yet Jerome had recognized such flaws, turned to the Hebrew source, corrected his predecessors' mistakes, and ultimately produced a Bible that faithfully reflected its original languages. In sum, Jerome "brought out in Latin the literal meaning of the Hebrew Scripture, certainly with the errors of previous translators being rejected."

In 1536, Ciruelo looked as if he aimed his negative comments solely against Jerome's predecessors; later he called that saint divine and reiterated the fidelity of the Vulgate to the Hebrew.[44] As for his own project, he insisted that he did not intend to produce a new Bible for the Church. He maintained instead that his manuscript would be useful "for repairing the errors and defects of scribes or printers, which happen daily in sacred letters out of their carelessness or ignorance, or out of the untaught audacity of certain smatterers."[45] By the end, he contended that the Vulgate would outstrip all other biblical paraphrases once it was "restored and emended"; still, deviations from the Hebrew were "hardly or most rarely found in it."

Once again Ciruelo complimented the Vulgate to disguise his tacit critique of it. In 1536, he asserted that there were two styles of translation: one worked according to words (*de verbo*), the other according to larger meaning (*per sensum*), as Jerome himself agreed. Ciruelo then declared that a reiteration of meaning (*sensus*) should be called a paraphrase instead of a translation, and cautioned that such paraphrases "very often change the words into another sequence from that which was in the original, and indeed they add some things, and remove some things from it." Ciruelo concluded that Jerome's rendition of the Old Testament was a paraphrase. In practical terms, through this line of reasoning Ciruelo placed Jerome in the flawed company of other translators, because the whole bunch translated paraphrastically and thereby changed, deleted, and added material to the biblical text. True, the impact of their alterations could differ qualitatively—the saint's modifications being smart, the others' stupid—but they ended up with the same fundamental results, namely, variation between the Latin and the Hebrew Old Testaments.

Finally, in 1536 Ciruelo observed that Jerome's Vulgate had failed to convince the Jews, who believed that any paraphrastic rendition of the Old Testament was flawed. He called such reasoning on the Jews' part ridiculous. But then he observed that he had produced his translation "in that way that the Jews long for it, without the addition, subtraction, or permutation of words" ("eo modo quo eam Judei desiderant, sine additione, substractione, aut permutatione verborum"). Ciruelo thus moved from a stereotype about the Jews and the Vulgate, to another cliché about their bad judgment, to agreement with their opinion. He gave the Jews what they wanted even as he deprecated their desire. Immediately afterward he again linked his work to refuting the Jews and elevating the Vulgate: his translation would help theologians and other educated men to argue with Jews and prove Jerome's accuracy, because Jerome's work "truly disagrees in practically no place from the true meaning of the Jews' Hebrew Bible, except in some phraseology of words."[46]

Of course, if Jerome's Vulgate really were no different from the Hebrew, and if its divergent phrasing were moot, then there would have been no need for Ciruelo's translations in the first place. Indeed, the zigzag quality of Ciruelo's prose makes him appear at first a model of inconsistency. Jerome possessed divine talents, but Jerome paraphrased. Translators before Jerome erred, Jerome recognized their flaws, and then Jerome committed the same sort of mistakes. Jews rejected paraphrases of the Old Testament, Jewish misgivings were absurd, but Ciruelo himself rendered the Old Testament according to Jewish standards of translation. In his 1536 preface Ciruelo wove critiques and tributes together in a nearly scholastic manner: approbation and reproach followed each other in dialectical fashion.

Significantly, Ciruelo abandoned such maneuvers altogether in his 1533 prologue for Segovia's cathedral chapter: that manuscript contains no Hebrew, and I suspect its absence amplified Ciruelo's candidness. The Segovia manuscript comprises four Latin versions of the Pentateuch in parallel columns: a literal rendition of the Hebrew, a translation of the Aramaic Targum of Onqelos, a transliteration of the Greek Septuagint, and the common translation ascribed to St. Jerome. In its preface, Ciruelo allowed that the translation of the Targum was made by his teachers; although he did not say so explicitly, both it and the Latin rendition of the Septuagint undoubtedly originated as part of the Complutensian Polyglot some fifteen years before. Ciruelo claimed to have accomplished the first column by himself, which was the de verbo ad verbum rendition of the Pentateuch from Hebrew into Latin.[47]

The Segovia foreword contains more theology and history, and a blunter exposition of both, than the 1526 and 1533 prologues; Ciruelo's injection of more narrative in particular may be attributable to his position as *magister* of that city's cathedral chapter. He detailed the benefits of natural law, "which shows us the good deeds that we must do, or the evil ones we may avoid." He frankly explained that God first gave the Bible to the Jews because "God was known *only* in Judea" ("notus in Judea solum erat deus"); seven years before, he had just emphasized the Jews' relative familiarity with God: "God was worth *so much* in Judea" ("notus tantum in Judea [erat] deus"). Ciruelo also expanded his treatment of the way holy doctrine was disseminated, that is, "through [God's] servants [and] prophets, then through the apostles and his other disciples, who wrote the canonical books of the Holy Bible for us."[48] He relayed the means by which the Bible went from Hebrew to Greek to Latin, and spent much time on Origen's contribution to that process.

The more ample history that Ciruelo provided in 1533 was paralleled by a more explicit measurement of the Vulgate against other Latin translations. Following his authorities—the Complutensian Polyglot and the Hexapla— Ciruelo placed his Latin Pentateuchs in parallel columns: his own translation, the one from Aramaic, the one based on the Septuagint, and the Vulgate itself followed in sequence. Notably, he positioned the Vulgate fourth among the texts, never described its location with the Complutensian Polyglot's metaphors about Jesus' crucifixion, and declined to pronounce the Vulgate pre-eminent among the four. Instead, he insisted that only his own work was a true translation, called the other three paraphrases, and urged his audience to solve any contrarities by comparison.

In fact the other three columns are rather paraphrases than translations, for they express the meaning of the text in other words, along with the addition, removal, and alteration of certain words, and by disregarding Hebrew phrasing, as any careful reader will be able to observe from the comparison of columns, whence a clearer meaning of sacred Scripture also will appear in vague passages. For what one of the translators said obscurely, another made clear, and vice versa; and where two or three of them may converge, the matter is proven by the rest.[49]

Here Ciruelo stated boldly what he had qualified before. Paraphrases of Scripture expressed the meaning of the Bible in other language. Paraphrases disregarded Hebrew phrasing. His rendition would illuminate "very many flaws of scribes, and the frivolous comments of certain affected expositors, and finally the imperfect erudition of certain translators of languages."[50]

Hence in 1533 Jerome became part of a crowd, not someone with divine abilities. Ciruelo never instructed his readers to follow Jerome as the final authority, never connected his own translation to promoting the Vulgate, and never referred to Jewish slander as additional grounds for his work. Moreover, in the same 1533 preface Ciruelo noted Jerome's ignorance of the Aramaic Targums, and went on to treat that unfamiliarity as an implicit imperfection. The Jews held the Targums in high esteem. The Targums were faithful to the Hebrew original; they could help anyone who wished to turn the Hebrew Old Testament into Latin.

If we summarize Ciruelo's criticism in his prefaces, we end up with the following points. Jerome's Vulgate was very different from the Hebrew origi-nal, as the Jews themselves knew. The Vulgate contradicted Jerome's biblical commentaries, and thus it was possible that at least parts of the common Latin Bible were not penned by him; Jerome had not employed the Aramaic ver-sions of the Old Testament, which were a valuable resource. Copyists, ex-positors, and translators of the Bible erred through their lack of erudition, and added things out of their own design. Even Jerome's translation really was a paraphrase, and paraphrases by definition altered the source.

If we step back and look at the theoretical trajectory that connects these smaller points, we end up with textual criticism, for Ciruelo acknowledged incongruities between the Hebrew and the Latin Old Testaments, and wanted to bring the latter into line with the former. He assessed which materials were available to Jerome, and remarked on the contrast between those books and his own; he recognized discrepancies within Jerome's opera, and declined to explain them away. He admitted conflict as well as continuity in the creation and dissemination of Holy Scripture.

This portrait of Ciruelo as a textual critic is sharpened by the annotations he provided in his 1536 and 1537 translations for the University of Salamanca. In those Latin marginalia, which are often in holograph, Ciruelo frequently preferred Hebrew readings to Greek and Latin ones, and did so with adjectives such as "truer," "better," "more skillful," and "more correct"; he also pointed to changes in meaning when passages occurred in apostolic writings.[51] Nevertheless, in the same manuscripts he also relayed variant readings without siding with either rendition, adduced New Testament citations of particular verses, and occasionally focused on etymologies—as Nebrija, for one, had done before him. His annotations and his prefaces illustrate combinations of intellectual impulses that we have only begun to chart.

Given his modern reputation, though, what is most exceptional about Ciruelo's case is the fact that philology lurked beneath the plentiful stereotypes. I would also argue that Ciruelo could view Jerome through a historical lens, or else he would not have highlighted the variation between the holy texts that he and that Father employed. In fact, Ciruelo seems to have had a taste for historical contingency, or the view that events and even Scripture were caused and affected by human beings as well as God. He demonstrated his historical bent in autobiographical details, in descriptions of his translations' evolution, and in the changes he introduced into the historical accounts of others. In the 1536 preface, Ciruelo noted that he never could have made his translation so easily as at that particular moment in time. He went on to explain that Spain had possessed many Jewish academies, that God illuminated the Spanish Jews with His grace around 1500, and that some Jews, who were extremely learned in Hebrew, took up the Christian faith devoutly and sincerely. Ciruelo in turn "seized upon the opportunity of this age," and started to learn Hebrew at forty; after twenty years, with God's help, he could moderately understand the Hebrew Bible.[52]

Certainly this account of learning Hebrew contains divine intervention: it was God who had promised to reveal His secrets in the Book of Daniel, God who fulfilled His promise by enlightening the hearts of the Jews, and God who chose Spain as the site for such conversions. Furthermore, as Ciruelo (at an advanced age) carried out his first translation, it was God who sustained his strength and heightened his mental powers. But the description was also personal and hence historical; Ciruelo underscored his own actions as much as divine assistance. After all, *he* was the one who had seized a unique opportunity, guessed the need for a literal translation of the Pentateuch, and coped with an ecclesiastical sponsor, Archbishop Fonseca, who finally was "absolutely indifferent and unconscientious" about the project. Ciruelo's zeal helped him to persist despite his enemies. He was an actor who benefited from, suffered in, and generally manipulated circumstance.

Ciruelo could control historical narratives as well, notably when he borrowed prefatory material from the Complutensian Polyglot. In 1533, he lifted that source's account of the Bible's translations over time, but propelled the story to temporal and disjointed ends over eternal and homogeneous ones. The Polyglot's narrative began with Ptolemy Philadelphus, the king of Egypt who commissioned seventy-two Jews to translate their Law from Hebrew into Greek in the third century B.C.E. Those interpreters produced the Septuagint Bible, which the Polyglot cast as an imperfect translation, one that was both lavish and splintered; its failings purportedly came from its Jewish translators,

who—coming to the king, translating the Pentateuch and the Prophets— explained about worshiping a single god in front of the king, and how no creature was God. From that angle is how they answered the king wherever they translated about the Trinity: either they would skip over it in silence or translate it enigmatically, lest they seem to have taught that three gods should be worshiped. They acted similarly concerning the Incarnation of the Word. Whence the translation of the Seventy sometimes is superfluous . . . [and] fragmented.[53]

The Polyglot filtered the Septuagint Old Testament through Christianity, and seconded traditional precedents. It suggested that the Jewish translators knew about the Triune Christian God, understood Jesus as the incarnation of that God, and hid evidence on such matters from Ptolemy, lest they mislead him about monotheism. It depicted the Septuagint's creation according to the unifying tendencies of Christian hermeneutics.

The Polyglot's historical narrative betrayed other consolidating impulses as well. It calculated chronology according to Jesus, so that the Septuagint was produced "before the Incarnation of the Lord, in the year 341 [sic], in the time of Ptolemy Philadelphus, King of Egypt." It stipulated that Aquila made his translation "after the Lord's Incarnation and Passion, [in] 124 C.E." It also presented the history of biblical translation as a wave of one version after another:

Then, after the year 53 C.E., Theodotion made a translation under Commodus. Then, thirty years later, the translator Symmachus clarified [it] under Severus. Then, after eight years, a certain translation of the Jerusalemite was found, whose author is unknown, which is called the common translation or the fifth edition. Then after eighteen years, in the time of Alexander, Origen arrived; who, seeing these imperfect translations, began to correct the Septuagint translation through the aforesaid later translations. Or, according to some, he only corrected and prepared Theodotion's translation, namely, supplying what was fragmented and trimming what was extravagant.[54]

The Polyglot accentuated the sheer succession of renditions, as if translator after translator "arrived" and confronted the Old Testament in some inevitable sequence. The apex of that chain was St. Jerome, who "most recently arriving . . . first corrected the Septuagint in Latin, with asterisks and obelisks. Afterwards, however, he immediately translated the Old Testament from Hebrew into Latin without asterisks or obelisks. And now the whole Roman Church uses this translation everywhere, although not in all the books," such as Psalms.[55] The Polyglot ignored the fact that Jerome's asterisks and obelisks functioned as critical marks, to denote where alterations had occurred. Instead, the Complutensian preface was more concerned with biblical translations as a divinely directed series of texts, rather than as products of discrete historical epochs and distinct human agents.[56]

Ciruelo treated the same individuals in the same order as the Complutensian Polyglot; he, too, portrayed biblical translations as a process ordained by God. Nonetheless, he reworked parts of his model's material, and the changes he introduced promoted history and conflict over providence and consensus. For instance, he declined to describe the seventy translators of the Septuagint as if they were Christian prophets, that is, as if they knew in the third century B.C.E. about the arrival of Jesus hundreds of years later; he excluded the Polyglot's statement about the translators and the Trinity.

Ciruelo's omissions did not arise from limited space, for he added to the Polyglot's account. He noted that Theodotion's translation was commonly used during Origen's epoch. He contended that Jerome initially decided to amend the Septuagint alone, and turned to the Hebrew original when he observed certain flaws that could not be covered up. He also asserted that the Septuagint continued to be read in the Church Offices until Pope Damasus (d. 384) pronounced in favor of Jerome's version.[57]

Ciruelo bolstered the Polyglot's history in important ways. As he explained how the Old Testament went from Hebrew to Greek to Latin, he promoted the agency of the saints, allowed different translations to exist simultaneously, and even credited the predominance of the Vulgate to a papal decree. If we combine these elements with his critical stance toward

Jerome and the Vulgate, it seems clear that he favored the methods of Renaissance humanism, despite his scholastic pedigree. Yet there is one final point to be gleaned from his manuscript prefaces, one that leads directly to his own history, and from there to the way he employed clichés in his prefaces.

Clues to Ciruelo's past are embedded in the changes he made to the narrative of the Complutensian Polyglot, in his 1533 translation for the Segovia cathedral. The Polyglot gauged chronology by Jesus' Incarnation, and flooded its account with references to it; the Septuagint was created before that event, Aquila's translation afterward. Easy as it would have been for Ciruelo to have replicated the Polyglot's language, he declined to use the noun "Incarnation" at all. Instead, he wrote that the Septuagint was produced "three hundred years before the advent of Christ," and stated that Aquila translated the Old Testament "after the birth of our Lord Jesus Christ."

It is difficult to believe that Ciruelo's preference for *birth* over *Incarnation* was not meaningful, even if he continued to call Jesus the Christ or Messiah. (As a Christian and a theologian in the sixteenth century, it would have been unthinkable for him *not* to have referred to Jesus as Christ.) If we survey other, similarly minute alterations, the drift of his exposition becomes that much more intriguing. I have highlighted the relevant distinctions.[58]

EXAMPLE I.

The Polyglot:
"Aquila, a certain Jew converted to *the* faith, *but later lapsed into heresy,* the first translator, made another translation from Hebrew into Greek in the epoch of the Emperor Hadrian."

("Aquila quidam iudaeus ad fidem conversus, sed postea in heresim lapsus, primus interpres, fecit aliam translationem de hebraico in graecum tempore Adriani imperatoris.")

Ciruelo:
"Aquila, a certain Jew converted to *our* faith, made another translation of the Hebrew Bible also from the Greek, in the epoch of Hadrian, Emperor of the Romans."

("Aquila quidam Iudeus ad fidem nostram conversus: aliam fecit hebraicae Bibliae interpretationem etiam graeca, id est tempore Adriani Imperatoris Romanorum.")

EXAMPLE 2.

The Polyglot:

> "After the year 53 C.E., Theodotion made a translation under Commodus."

> ("Deinde post annos liii. Theodotion fecit translationem sub Commodo.")

Ciruelo:

> "Theodotion, *another Jew, afterward confessed the faith of Christ,* and he made a third translation of the Greek Bible under the Emperor Commodus."

> ("Theodotion alius iudeus, postquam fidem Christi professus est, tertiam et edidit Graecae Bibliae traductionem sub Commodo Imperatore.")

In the case of the Jewish convert Aquila, Ciruelo added the possessive pronoun "our" to the question of the Christian faith, and declined to reiterate the line about heresy. When it came to Theodotion, he supplied details about that individual's formerly Jewish status.

Such small but evocative changes reverberate with meaning in light of Ciruelo's personal history: although he described himself as an orphan, the Inquisition archives at Cuenca reveal that he had plenty of relatives, although not the sort he would have wished to publicize. The Spanish Inquisition condemned Ciruelo's paternal grandfather to death as a Judaizer, or a Christian who purportedly practiced Jewish rituals. It disqualified four of his first cousins from holding public and ecclesiastical offices because of their Jewish ancestry; in 1553, it prosecuted one of those cousins and a nephew for heretical blasphemy. The Inquisition's confrontations with Ciruelo's family may not have stopped there, since depositions indicate that an uncle and the paternal grandmother either confessed to Judaizing or were convicted of the same.[59]

It is most unlikely that Ciruelo remained unaware of his ancestors' interactions with the Inquisition. Literary sources suggest that he underwrote memorial Masses for his parents in Molina de Aragón, the pueblo where many of his relatives resided.[60] His cousins and nephews knew about *him,* for they listed him in the genealogies they had to furnish at their trials.

It is a common misconception that the papal and Spanish Inquisitions routinely prosecuted Jews. Christianity defined Jews as well as Muslims as infidels, or persons outside the faith altogether; theoretically and typically,

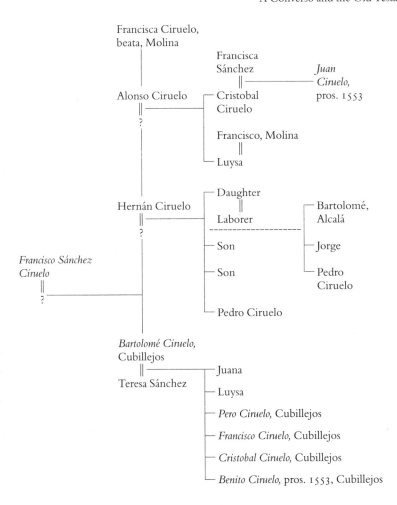

Note: Italicized names denote individuals disqualified from public office and / or prosecuted by the Inquisition tribunal at Cuenca, with dates of the prosecutions when available.

The first tier of children for Hernán Ciruelo is derived from Benito Ciruelo's testimony in 1553; the second tier comes from Cristobal Ciruelo's deposition in the same year.

Figure 3.1 Genealogy of Pedro Ciruelo's Family

inquisitors did not pursue infidels, because their job was to prosecute and thereby save heretics, and Muslims and Jews could not have fallen into heresy if they were not Christians originally. At the same time, though, definitions of Christian heresy included persons who followed both Christianity and the rituals and beliefs of another religion: thus Christians were liable to indictment if they observed Jewish or Muslim rites. In the case of the Spanish *moriscos* (converts from Islam), historians agree that that population only absorbed Christian dogma and ceremonies in a fragmentary way after being forced to convert in Castille in 1502. But the Inquisition's persecution of moriscos spiraled and ebbed in accordance with political and economic imperatives.[61]

The Inquisition's attention to Spain's conversos, though, was more persistent and intense. Thousands of Jews became Christians after 1391; they had been practicing Christianity for almost a century by the time the Spanish Inquisition was established. Hundreds if not thousands more converted in the wake of the 1492 expulsion of Spain's remaining Jews, and the speed with which they absorbed the tenets of their new religion is anyone's guess. The question is whether inquisitors really caught Judaizing conversos when they prosecuted the same between 1480 and 1520. The answer obviously hinges upon the individual case, but it also depends upon the semiotics of religious belief that we bring to the sources: we can read physical gestures and verbal statements as self-conscious signs of Judaism; we may ascribe the same gestures and statements to habit or whim. Our reactions to the evidence also turn on the way we imagine religious communities to endure.[62] Undoubtedly the Spanish Inquisition prosecuted Christians who deliberately followed Judaism. But it also arrested Christians who followed certain rituals out of custom and in relative ignorance of what those ceremonies signified.

Signs of Judaizing were codified quickly by the Inquisition and Spanish society, and so it is relatively easily to guess how Ciruelo's grandparents and uncle attracted the inquisitors' attention, although their particular trial records have been lost. They might have lit candles on Friday evenings, or rested on Saturdays, or blessed their children by placing their hands on their heads without making the sign of the cross.[63] They might have taken advantage of an edict of grace to confess that they declined to eat pork, and their confession would have resulted in penance; ten years later, they could have been indicted for something else, whereby their original confession would have compounded their second offense. They might have insulted their neighbors, who in turn retaliated by deposing before the Holy Office. They even could have been dead by the time the Cuenca tribunal was established in 1489, in which case its officials would have tried them posthumously: a guilty verdict would have entailed the exhumation and cremation of their bones.[64]

Dreadful as such persecution and punishment are to modern eyes, it is problematic to equate the inquisitors' attention to conversos with racial anti-

Semitism, because inquisitors focused on signs with religious import: bathing on Friday and resting on Saturday denoted respect for the Sabbath, while avoiding pork reflected adherence to Mosaic Law. The inquisitors were acting out of anti-Judaism. The genealogies the Inquisition required from converso prisoners and eventually *all* suspects owed as much to Christian clichés about heretics as to targeting Jewish bloodlines.[65]

Early modern Spain also could penalize the families of convicted heretics. Bartolomé Ciruelo's sons—Benito, Cristobal, Francisco, and Pero— were disqualified from holding offices that carried purity of blood statutes (*limpieza de sangre*): such measures eliminated candidates of Jewish ancestry. In 1553, Benito Ciruelo was prosecuted for heretical blasphemy when he allegedly said, "God has no power"; a nephew, Juan, was arrested the same year when he explained an Inquisition sentence as arising from greed.[66] Benito's and Juan's remarks prove nothing more than a certain hostility toward the Inquisition, while their indictments for "wicked statements" are absolutely typical of the epoch's arraignments.[67] But there also is no doubt that witnesses and prosecutors interpreted Jewish ancestry and inquisitorial conviction as both a sign and a magnification of religious liminality: a witness against Juan Ciruelo said the insult to the Inquisition rankled specifically because Juan was the great-grandson of Francisco Sánchez Ciruelo, the condemned.[68]

Pedro Ciruelo was already dead by 1553, so Benito's and Juan's arrests could have had no effect on him. The larger issue is whether earlier family history—grandparents condemned, an uncle who potentially confessed, and verifiable Jewish ancestry—affected his religious emphases, his methods, and even the subjects on which he worked. The problem is that any inevitable link between converso status and Old Testament translation destroys the scholarly agency of the individuals we are studying. Such a bond also fails to explain the endeavors of other conversos, such as Juan de Vergara, who had nothing to do with Hebrew. We know that Ciruelo did not always evince an affection for Hebrew, the Old Testament, or Jewish history in his moral theology: on one occasion, he composed a contemplative tract on the Passion of Christ. And thus neither a wider survey of known conversos nor a deeper perception of intellectual autonomy allows us to portray Ciruelo's ancestry as the *cause* of his translations. Moreover, his converso status did not predestine him to a life of personal discrimination and necessary subterfuge, because the application of limpieza de sangre statutes could be haphazard at best in early modern Spain. There is no reason to think that Ciruelo saw his career materially altered by such measures, any more than Juan de Vergara did.

At the same time, though, it is hard to see how Ciruelo's background did *not* condition his work to some degree, given his changes to the Polyglot's narrative and the emphases of some of his vernacular treatises: as we shall see, he made the Decalogue the centerpiece of works on penance and witchcraft. I have no proof that Ciruelo was a practicing Jew; I do not think that he was. Instead, I would contend that he occasionally effected a syncretism between Christian and Jewish teachings, and could even elevate the Hebrew text and Jewish history over the dictates of Christian hermeneutics. His scholarly and theological inclinations probably were intensified by his lineage, but they cannot have been governed by it. Consequently, I would argue only that Ciruelo's genealogy—or more specifically, his relatives' encounters with inquisitors—elucidates further his employment of his authorities. His past posed special risks beyond what most Hebraists routinely faced in the early modern period. All Christian scholars of Jewish sources could expect charges that they were "secret Jews, in league with Jews, [or] of Jewish origin" in the sixteenth century, but Ciruelo's family background and converso status heightened his predicament.[69] He solved the problem by echoing ageless platitudes to shield his own history.

If Catholic intellectuals customarily praised Jerome in the sixteenth century, so too did both Catholic and Protestant theologians vilify Jews. The defamation of Jews as obstinate, blind, hard-hearted enemies of Christ was habitual by the thirteenth century; three hundred years later, the Christian portrait of Jews could be even more vitriolic, for the latter often were depicted as the inversion of their theoretically virtuous Christian counterparts. Imagined as covetous, murderous, and above all deceptive—not least for speaking and writing in a language their contemporaries could not understand—the Jews watched their Sabbath be transformed into the witches' *sabbat*; their purported crimes included the blood libel, in which they performed a human sacrifice at Easter as a parody of Jesus' death and resurrection. There were no social, intellectual, or geographical limits to anti-Jewish calumny in early modern Europe. Erasmus routinely pitched anti-Jewish epithets at his Spanish controversialists; his insults had particularly deep meaning because he so obviously linked Spain with Jews, and again with conversos. Spanish conversos also could saturate their writings with anti-Jewish sentiments, particularly if those compositions had a polemical edge. The fifteenth-century archbishop of Burgos, Pablo de Santa María, berated Nicholas de Lyra's *Postilla moralis* for its reliance on Jewish exegetes, because everyone knew that Jews never told the truth about the Bible and could not be trusted; before his conversion in 1391, Santa María was Rabbi Solomon Halevi.

Christian Hebraists everywhere indulged in the same sort of stigmatization, which from a modern standpoint makes little sense: why should scholars of Hebrew insult the very people whose actions were not only described in their prized Old Testament, but whose closeness to God resulted in the Old Testament in the first place? The answer to the query is threefold. Early modern intellectuals prized quotation, and many of their literary authorities slandered Jews. Sixteenth-century scholars may well have believed the smears they inherited. Finally, writers could defame Jews as a distancing device, as a sign to their audience that they themselves were orthodox because they defined what was *not*. As I show in Chapter 6, Spanish writers on witchcraft could clarify Christian orthodoxy by describing its opposite, and the same dynamic occurred in translators' rationales: Nicholas de Lyra turned to Rashi as an authority, but warned his readers that Jews were deceitful; Giannozzo Manetti composed an anti-Jewish diatribe along with a translation of the Hebrew Psalter. Even Johannes Reuchlin chastised the Jews as enemies in his *De rudimentis hebraicis* (1506).[70]

Defamation of the Jews was a standard rhetorical device, especially for Hebrew scholars, and Ciruelo was no exception to this rule. Still, it is revealing to see where, exactly, Ciruelo employed anti-Jewish slander. Such calumny is missing entirely from the Segovia preface of 1533: there Ciruelo said nothing about Jewish implacability in the face of Christianity, nor raised the Jews' opinion that Jerome perverted Scripture. What Ciruelo did mention were the Aramaic Targums, which he commended as valuable and described as unavailable to Jerome. Yet as he applauded the Targums, Ciruelo simultaneously condemned the Talmud (the compilation of the rabbis' oral teachings) and subsequent rabbinical commentaries on those teachings, which were formed by the fifth century C.E. The Talmud had a particularly prominent place in anti-Jewish rhetoric, because it symbolized the extent to which the Jewish nation had moved away from Old Testament Judaism, or so twelfth- and thirteenth-century exegetes believed; in the opinion of numerous Christian scholars, the Jews' reliance on and reverence for their rabbinical traditions tainted their position as the People of the Book.[71] Judaism's alterations over time could conflict with Christian visions of that religion as a relic that eternally presaged Christianity.

Like any Christian intellectual, Ciruelo would have been familiar with the stereotypes about the Talmud, and he invoked two in his 1533 prologue: the Jews compiled the Talmud out of envy over Christianity's success; the Talmud twisted biblical passages into false meanings. Ciruelo interlaced these attacks with compliments to the Targums:

Yet . . . many greatly obscure passages . . . being discovered in their Hebrew Bible, the Jews brought forth an explanatory paraphrase for the education of ignorant Jews. Since Aramaic was not well known to Christians, that paraphrase was made in the Syrian language; we call the Aramaic edition the Targum. And because divine Jerome never wrote a word about that edition, [and made no] mention of it, truly it seems that the edition was brought forth after the time of the divine Jerome, that is, four hundred years after Christ. Also in that epoch, the Talmud of the Jews was composed in Antioch of Syria, out of envy of the Christian religion. And besides this Targum, the Jews have another, called the Jerusalemite Targum; they say the first of these Onqelos the Jew made, the second is called the Jonathan Targum by them, but this one is extremely rare among the Jews of our time, while the first in fact is sufficiently common. [The Onqelos Targum] is found in all their synagogues; this paraphrase is of great authority among all the learned men of the Jews, and is notably effective for confounding the Jews' brashness, insofar as they twist the Hebrew Bible to false meanings through Talmudic glosses. But the Aramaic edition construes the Holy Bible, for the most part, according to the true meaning, whereby learned men tried to secure this Latin translation from the Aramaic for me.[72]

By observing that the Targums were made in Aramaic because Christians did not know that language, Ciruelo insinuated the well-worn stereotype about Jewish secrecy; he voiced an analogous cliché when he connected the Talmud to Jewish jealousy. Yet he understood the historical context in which the Targums were created, knew that the Jews themselves held those texts in great esteem, and seemed to share their opinion, since he contended that the Aramaic edition was trustworthy.

As for the Talmud, it looks as if Ciruelo provided stereotypes about that source to distract his readers from his remarks on the Targums. He pointed up Jerome's ignorance of the latter, and subsequently noted that the Talmud of the Jews was composed in the same epoch "out of envy of Christianity." As soon as he contended that all learned Jews regarded the Targums with respect, he followed with the same Targums' utility for "confounding the Jews' brashness" with the Talmud; he finished with the Targums' fidelity to the "true meaning" of the Hebrew Old Testament. Ciruelo thus created an A-B-A structure of compliment, insult, and compliment: he was less vulnerable if he braided his accolades with censure. Ironically, although he seemed to loathe the Talmud in 1533, he would praise both it and the Targums over and against the Cabala in 1538.[73]

Ciruelo objected to Jews in more direct language in his other prefaces, although he placed his complaints in equally intriguing spots. In the general prologue from 1526, he contended that he could not have executed his translation more easily in another epoch, because of the number of converts who were so learned in Hebrew; he then remarked that he had no idea how these converts had gained such erudition, unless it was from working with the Jews themselves. He finally reminded his audience that no trust should be placed in the Jews whatsoever.[74] Such reasoning made his own translation worthless, since he had learned from first-generation converts, who formerly were Jews and who, according to his own slander of them, were deceptive. But I think Ciruelo worried less about intellectual backflips than about deflecting his audience from making a connection between Jewish teachers and his own education. The readers' preface reveals a similar trajectory: at the end of it, Ciruelo stated that he and Zamora had marked wherever the Jews and Jerome disagreed over the meanings of words, because they wished to refute the "obstinate insensibility" of the Jews.[75] They balanced a point against Jerome with one against unconverted Jews. In the 1526 manuscript, Ciruelo's anti-Jewish remarks were the last things readers encountered in both forewords. Their location meant that the two prologues always ended with an oblique reiteration of Ciruelo's orthodoxy.

Comments about Jews were even more straightforward in 1536, but so were the risks of Ciruelo's material. As soon as he mentioned that his translation would bolster the trustworthiness of the Vulgate—which implied that it was *not* reliable—he declared that his de verbo ad verbum technique would challenge the Jews' insolence. Immediately after noting the way the Jews greatly honored the Targums, he asserted that the Targums differed from the Hebrew truth in words and meaning—which was exactly the opposite of his point in 1533. In 1536, Ciruelo announced that his translation would help even the moderately learned dispute with infidel Jews, although by that year there ostensibly were no infidels of any sort left in Spain. He also claimed that the more important Jewish commentators—among them Rashi and Ibn Ezra, a celebrated exegete of the twelfth century—turned to the Vulgate for help with obscure passages. He finally alleged that when Jews taught the uncircumcised, they mixed lies with the truth.

In his Salamanca manuscript, Ciruelo again fixed his anti-Jewish comments according to the hazards he invoked. When he implied that his work would strengthen Jerome's, he followed with an observation about Jewish arrogance; when he referred to the Jews' own opinion of the Targums, he quickly dropped a comment that would belittle those Aramaic works as divine literature. Lastly, he adduced rabbis who had relied upon Jerome, noted that Jews treated Christians fraudulently, and thereby pursued two stratagems at once: to extol Jerome's knowledge over the rabbinical variety, and then to contrast, implicitly, his own converso teachers with unconverted Jews. The 1536 manuscript relays nearly all of Ciruelo's experience with Hebrew, from his education by conversos to his disappointment with Fonseca: his autobiographical reflections clearly evoked the first-generation converts who instructed him; they also might suggest, by extension, his converso grandparents who were burned as Judaizers. His story carried dangerous associations. Through anti-Jewish calumny, he deflected his own links to Jews and Judaizers, and reinforced his image as a faithful Christian.

Nonetheless, I would not wish to focus only on the functionalism of Ciruelo's anti-Jewish remarks: the result can narrow his writing to the point of one-dimensionality and make his attitudes more coherent than they really were. It certainly is possible that he distinguished between baptized and unconverted Jews, and disliked the latter. He could have viewed Jews as enemies of Christianity, but used their vilification to remove suspicion from his own endeavors. He also might have disparaged Jews because his models told him to do so, that is, because anti-Jewish remarks were expected in a prologue to such a translation. If Ciruelo slandered Jews out of scholarly and literary expectations, then the absence of anti-Jewish attacks in the Segovia manuscript, which featured Latin exclusively, might be important: although he disparaged the Talmud in the 1533 preface, he may have maligned Jews directly only when Hebrew was present. Yet no matter which prologue we review, Ciruelo seems to have expressed anti-Jewish sentiments whenever and wherever he praised Jewish sources (such as the Targums), Jewish opinion (such as esteem for the Targums), and Jewish priorities (such as de verbo ad verbum translations), as well as when he critiqued the Vulgate's Old Testament. Even if he scorned unconverted Jews, the evidence indicates that he shared their critical standards when it came to the Hebrew text of the Old Testament.

In the end, Ciruelo's translations reveal humanistic impulses in the midst of medieval authorities and techniques; he was a historical and philological critic who openly proclaimed the traditional authority of Jerome and the Vulgate. This polysemous impression of him is only intensified by a tract that he published in 1538, entitled "Ten Paradoxical Questions": the queries included such topics as the "rarification and condensation of bodies" and "the location of the earthly Paradise halted by God." The chapters evince increasingly abstract material as they progress; in every instance, Ciruelo presented their content dialectically. The ninth *quaestio* is the most relevant for matters of exegesis: it entails "a theological question on the various meanings of sacred Scripture."

Significantly, the title to the ninth inquiry was a ruse: despite Ciruelo's claim to assess the meanings of sacred Scripture, he only explored the literal one; and what he did with the sensus literalis was radical, for he addressed different meanings between the same passages in the Old and New Testaments. In the end, Ciruelo sanctioned the specific context of the biblical excerpt—its actual place in the text—as the crucial factor in its interpretation. By endorsing a Jewish environment for Old Testament verses, he recognized a potential disjunction between the Old Testament and the New. He was willing to tolerate and even welcome fissure between the two halves of the Bible on the grounds of historical context, although Christian tradition favored a consolidating hermeneutics.

Ciruelo packed his ninth question with earlier experts on the subject; he also wrote it according to dialectical structure, so that he first treated "things to be noted," then "conclusions," and eventually "doubts" that menaced the conclusions; the format duplicated Vergara's apologia. He invoked Gregory I's division of biblical interpretation into literal, allegorical, tropological, and anagogical modes of reading. He knew that the literal sense was the "basis and foundation" of biblical interpretation. He quoted Augustine's familiar statement that only the literal meaning of Scripture could effectively prove matters of the faith; he cited the same individual to verify that the literal sense pertained to what the author principally intended.[76] He confirmed that the sensus literalis was the grammatical, historical, and even metaphorical meaning of the words, so long as the author had intended an allegory. He repeated Aristotle to the effect that a multiplicity of literal meanings led to confusion and deceit, and followed Aquinas in asserting that God was the genesis of the Bible. He also lifted not only the title but the first paragraph of the ninth quaestio from Aquinas's Summa theologica, although he transposed the opening. He dropped the names of his authorities and copied their scriptural examples whenever possible.

But despite his adherence to custom, Ciruelo finally turned away from his sources' contentions. Despite the dialectical structure, he mentioned Aristotle exactly once in the ninth quaestio; Lyra, in contrast, filtered his biblical annotations through Aristotelian categories. Ciruelo collided with Lyra even further when he concentrated on possible literal meanings of a single excerpt. We may recall that Vergara cited Lyra as an irreproachable authority.

Ciruelo stipulated that the only biblical author who counted was the human one, rather than God. He also insisted that the literal meaning of a biblical passage came out of the author's intention: although God was the main author of the Bible, it was implausible that He should intend one thing primarily, since He intended everything at once. Moreover, if God intended everything at once, then all meanings of Scripture would be literal, although there could only be one literal sense, as all the authorities agreed. The larger issue was the identity between the Bible's human and divine architects; the difficulty was whether the human author and God had to have the same cardinal intention—something that celestial omniscience and omnipotence, not to mention Aristotle's notion of causation, seemed to demand.

Like Aquinas and Lyra, Ciruelo turned to the prophets to ascertain the matter: at the end of the Book of Daniel, for instance, the seer begged the Angel Gabriel to explain the wider meaning of his revelation, but the angel did not oblige; it looked as if the prophet could understand only a portion of what God wanted to forecast, although Aquinas was correct to think that prophets customarily understood things that were beyond the average person. Ciruelo concluded that synchronicity between God and a prophet might go only so far, and decided that the prophet could express "a literal meaning full of secret things"; God alone knew what those secret things were and what they presaged. But then Ciruelo pressed the cognitive break he had introduced: he noted that God bestowed spiritual meanings on Scripture, "whereby it very often follows in sacred Scripture that the meaning the prophet had was different from the one that God principally intended to signify through that writing."[77] His observation protected divine omniscience and Christian ends. But it also created a potential gap between what the human and divine authors of the Bible wanted to express.

The qualification that Ciruelo raised next was even more telling. If the literal meaning of Scripture were derived from what the human author principally intended to say, then what happened when the same passage appeared twice, once in the Old Testament and again in the New? The issue now was which human author controlled the literal sense, and Lyra had found the matter exceedingly clear: the two occurrences of the passage could have two simple, literal meanings. Thus Lyra understood 1 Paralipomenon 17:13 literally about Solomon—the verse read "I will be to him a father, and he will be to me a son"—and literally again about Jesus when the Apostle Paul called up the same verse in Hebrews 1:5. Because Paul intended that line as *proof* that Jesus was superior to the angels, and because things-to-be-proven only could stem from the literal meaning of scripture, Lyra believed the apostle's quotation of the verse must have a literal interpretation as well. But then he went on to elevate Paul's recitation of the verse because its counsel was more perfectly fulfilled. In Hebrews 1:5, Jesus was God's child by nature, whereas Solomon was just God's offspring through grace and adoption. Lyra's preference for a hierarchy determined by Jesus was not unusual; he always would raise the Christological meaning of a scriptural passage over its significance in Jewish history, despite his interest in the latter. The startling aspect here is the extent to which Ciruelo changed Lyra's predilections.

At first Ciruelo's exposition seemed no different from his predecessor's. He agreed that Paul's testimony in Hebrews 1:5 was literal because the apostle employed that verse as part of a larger interpretive point. And he, too, asserted that biblical passages had different literal meanings in the Old and the New Testaments:

"You shall not break from him," etc. . . . therefore in Exodus [12:46] those words in the literal sense were pronounced about the paschal lamb of the Jews, and in the Gospel of John [19:36], they were spoken about Christ, that is, certainly about the God of the Christians. And this second meaning in Exodus is not literal but allegorical—even if it is granted that Moses understood those words about Christ—because the sequence of the text openly produces a discourse about the paschal lamb.[78]

Until these lines, Ciruelo's exposition had been equivalent to Lyra's. But he declined to state that the Old Testament quotation in the Gospel was inherent in, presaged by, or simply better than its occurrence in the first half of the Bible. Ciruelo never suggested a fundamental identity between John and Exodus; on the contrary, he thought the two citations meant very different things where the literal sense was concerned. Even if Moses suspected he was talking about Jesus as he transmitted instructions about the paschal lamb, to read Christological import back into the Old Testament would make the lines in Exodus allegorical rather than literal.

Ciruelo never repeated Lyra's rationale that all prophets prophesied about the Messiah, that Moses was the greatest prophet of all, and that Moses thus anticipated Jesus; he did not exclusively turn the Old Testament's significance toward an invariably Christological object. Instead, he pinned the literal meaning of the Old Testament on that text's own succession of words: although Moses might have understood his remark in Exodus 12:46 about Jesus, the surrounding language "openly produces a discourse about the paschal lamb." Ciruelo's willingness to sever the two parts of the Bible is apparent even in his choice of vocabulary: in describing Christ as the "God of the Christians," and calling a Christological interpretation a "second meaning" for Exodus 12:46, he revealed his historical sensitivity.

Thus Ciruelo jolted Lyra's scenario in several ways. He allowed a split between the authorial intentions of the Old Testament and those of the New, and did not make one conform to the other, even when the passages in question came from prophetic figures. He stipulated that exegetes had to glean the sensus literalis from the language that surrounded the quotations in question. He flatly called Lyra a "daydreamer" (*alucinator*) because Lyra—despite his concern with Hebrew and Jewish history—would attribute allegories about Jesus to Jews in the historical books of the Old Testament, and then classify those metaphors as part of the sensus literalis. Ciruelo worried about the befuddlement of exegetical terms that could result from such free-floating explications. More important, he finally insisted that Old Testament writers be allowed to speak in a purely Jewish context, at least on occasion. His interpretative hierarchy initially raised the human author over God, but ultimately tied interpretation to the sequence of the text and the history it contained.

When it came to passages shared between both parts of the Bible, Ciruelo consequently narrowed the extent to which the reading of one could affect the meaning of the other. In the process, he expanded the number of literal senses beyond anything that Lyra ever imagined, and the more literal meanings he allowed, the closer he seemed to come to the position that language was referential, that is, that its meaning depended upon the circumstances in which it was uttered. It would be anachronistic to expect Ciruelo to have completely discarded scholastic realism, that is, the tenet that words expressed individual and unchanging realities: he spent twenty-odd years teaching Thomistic theology, and in the ninth question of the *Paradoxae quaestiones* he related the view that single words voiced single meanings. But when he observed that a scriptural verse could have not just two, but three or more literal meanings if it were invoked by different authors for different purposes, he shattered an interpretative method that Aquinas had practiced and that he himself presumably taught, called the *catena* (chain).

The catena worked through resonance, whereby one quote illuminated another, or a word expressed a quality that in turn could be linked to another phrase; at the Valladolid assembly, Alonso de Córdoba employed this technique to prove that *vita aeterna* had the same meaning in 1 John 5:20 as in John 17:3. Ciruelo preferred to emphasize instead the fact that the specific contexts, purposes, and hence meanings of literary authorities could differ, despite the identical vocabulary between them. As for multiplying the number of literal senses to more than two, Ciruelo demonstrated his case by citing the ways in which a single verse could appear in the Old and New Testaments, the sermons of a church father, and Church Offices on feast days, but serve varied purposes in each invocation. For example,

The same principle applies to that authority of Hosea 11, "I called my son out of Egypt," which is understood about the Jewish people, led out of Egyptian captivity. And it is cited in Matthew 2 about the child Jesus fleeing from Herod's persecution in Egypt. Third, it is read in the Gospel of the Mass of the Holy Innocents, and understood about the Gentile race, called by God to the Christian Faith and His Church out of Egypt, that is, out of the shadow of idolatrous infidelity.[79]

Ciruelo went on to list a whole page of sources that came from the Bible, but were employed in the missal for divergent ends; he understandably concentrated on passages from the New Testament rather than the Old, since there was no reason to make his argument more inflammatory than necessary. In any case, he had made his point: the presence of a single authority in both parts of the Bible did not automatically bestow the same meaning in each, because the significance of those lines hinged upon the purposes of their authors, and then upon their immediate literary context. A New Testament verse could not be pushed into its Old Testament source without changing into allegory, even if the Old Testament author intended it as such. And in the final analysis, the literal meaning of a scriptural verse hinged on the words that surrounded it.

Ciruelo never put the human authors of the Bible above God, but he certainly could augment their importance when it came to the literal meaning of the Bible. He also effected a new sort of balance between the Old and New Testaments, in which the former was not read as a mere shadow of the New, but was treated as a sovereign creation whose figures had their own immediate concerns, which could be distinct from the theology of an impending Christianity. Ciruelo's medieval predecessors also fixed on the importance of the literal, or grammatical and historical, meaning of the Old Testament; they, too, wanted to rid exegesis of extravagant allegories, to pursue original sources, and to amend errors in the biblical text. But they sought out the language and history of the Old Testament to clarify and secure the Christian signs that it contained; like Martin Luther, their interpretations of the Old Testament were governed by Christian authorities who told them to turn that work toward Christian truths.[80]

It is exactly this unifying impulse—to bind Jewish texts to Christian ends—which seems damped down or missing entirely in Ciruelo's ninth quaestio on the literal sense of Scripture. Despite the prominence of his references and the frequency with which he referred to them, he finally controverted his models for the sake of linguistic contingency and Jewish history, and his enthusiasm for such elements can help us understand why he translated the Pentateuch in a de verbo ad verbum manner. If the only way to arrive at the literal sense of Scripture was through the intention of the human author, and grasping that intention ultimately depended upon reading the text as it was written, instead of its later invocations, then word order and fidelity to the Hebrew became the key to the Old Testament's meaning.

Ciruelo's literal translations consequently had as much to do with context as tradition. His example allows us to glimpse innovative movement within a most conventional subject; apparently a converso theologian could critique the Old Testament without being indicted by the Inquisition, although readers surely recognized what Ciruelo was doing to his authorities. At the same time, though, his invocation of Augustine, Aquinas, and Lyra only proves once again the continuing force of precedent in the sixteenth century, for all that we denote it as the early modern epoch.

Chapter Four

The Construction
of the Shepherd

Certainly religious authority in early modern Spain affected more than Inquisition conclaves and biblical translations. Nearly all the individuals in this book were ordained to administer the sacraments; they consequently possessed a connection to the laity, even if they did not act on it. The issue, then, is how these ecclesiastics envisioned that relationship and construed their privileges within it. For most historians, the answer would be clear: the dynamic between the clerical and secular realms thrived on hierarchy and control, and priests as well as pastors simply turned their auctoritas toward the magnification of their own rank. Still, we have already seen the degree to which ecclesiastics can startle us with their combinations of intellectual emphases; the question is whether they may offer complementary shocks through their approaches to practical power.

Given their topics, the next three chapters could look like a tour of clerical hegemony, for they treat writings on ideal priests and bishops, guidance for the sacrament of penance, and exhortations against witchcraft. And yet the sources treated therein also reveal movement between the barriers we too frequently erect in Spanish history, whether those walls separate clergy from laity, humanism from scholasticism, or the distinct religious messages that humanists and scholastics allegedly offered. The texts in question encouraged inclusion and affection as well as rank and judgment. The authors provided their writings with references; their sources, and the way they read them, can reveal attitudes about the ancient church and degrees of historical sensitivity. The second half of this book diminishes even further our tendency to see early modern Spain as caught up in cycles of oppositional forces.

When it came to the application of practical ecclesiastical authority, the sacraments constituted the central arena for the interaction of priests and laity. Catholic theology presented baptism, confirmation, marriage, penance, the Eucharist, ordination, and extreme unction as so consequential because Jesus himself ordained them as the outward and visible signs of inward and spiritual grace. When the sacraments were administered to human beings, they conveyed that grace and thereby fostered human sanctification; their reception was crucial for everyone, including the clergy, but only priests could dispense the rites in question.

Such a system gave ecclesiastics great sway over the laity, at least theoretically, since the former managed rituals that the latter presumably wanted or were expected to desire; moreover, clerical supervision included demands about lay behavior that could be enforced by withholding the sacraments themselves. It thus is inviting to interpret the administration of the sacraments as an illustration of ecclesiastical dominion. For instance, imagining penance as an exercise in power is nearly a cliché of current scholarship. Laymen and women had to confess to a priest or friar before they could obtain the Eucharist; the inquiries launched and the answers expected can easily take on an intrusive and even coercive air to scholars at the end of the twentieth century.

Of course, ecclesiastical pressure depended upon some crucial conditions, such as whether priests were physically present to dispense the sacraments in the first place, or possessed enough education and integrity to execute them properly. The testimony for Catholic Europe suggests that neither prerequisite was assured for much of the sixteenth century. Juan de Vergara held at least eight benefices, one of which was a curacy at Torrelaguna; that particular position would have entailed the *cura animarum* (care of souls), which meant that Vergara himself should have been responsible for distributing the sacraments to at least a portion of Torrelaguna's laity. Needless to say, there is no evidence that Vergara ever took up residence in Torrelaguna: instead, he undoubtedly handed a replacement a share of the income that he received from that parish, and thereby provided his parishioners with a *mercenario* (priest-for-hire). By his own testimony, Vergara traveled constantly and frequently missed Divine Offices altogether; in the depositions against him, he taunted homilists who suggested that priests should preach to the congregations that supported them financially. He removed his brother from Francisca Hernández with two benefices. He bribed Cristobal de Gumiel with a false offer of another. Such details indicate that Vergara shared the usual outlook on Church offices in the first half of the sixteenth century, namely, that benefices were precious because of their income and privileges rather than their obligations and tasks. When Vergara shifted ecclesiastical posts among his family, or dangled the prospect of them before his contemporaries, he was merely enhancing his retinue's position through the intelligent deployment of his assets. His own qualifications, including a sense of vocation, were irrelevant to his accumulation and treatment of benefices, especially lesser ones; the same held true for Bernardino Flores, Antonio Medrano, and Guillaume de Croy, the latter the nineteen-year-old archbishop of Toledo.

Such practices and attitudes were not unique to Spain. Between 1492 and 1563, Italian cardinals persisted in pluralism, nonresidence, and nepotism, despite "a century of debate, tracts, memorials, and commissions" on ecclesiastical reform.[1] These princes of the Church could assemble vast ecclesiastical fortunes, while simultaneously evading obstacles to the acquisition of multiple benefices. It was forbidden to hold two or more benefices when the responsibilities of one involved the cura animarum, but papal dispensations could erase such incompatibilities. A cardinal also could resign an incompatible post to a specific individual, and because holders could name their successors, they usually put their relatives, most often their nephews, into the spots they relinquished. The result was the creation of ecclesiastical dynasties, since certain Church offices came to "belong" to particular families.[2] Meanwhile, a device called the *regressus* allowed prelates to take back the posts they resigned, should they lose their current holders. Cardinals even could benefit financially from the benefices they ceded, for pension schemes allowed them to distribute a percentage of their benefices' remuneration to themselves, their successors, or anyone else. Such strategies produced enormous wealth and influence. In 1556, for instance, Pope Paul IV ordered his cardinals to present lists of all the regressus they controlled: Alessandro Farnese, with the largest inventory, counted rights of reversion to posts involving ten cathedrals, twenty-six monasteries, three preceptories or teaching positions, and 133 lesser Church offices; he requested an extension in order to find the rest among his papers.[3]

Nonetheless, clear incentives to pluralism did not balance clerical incomes, even in the case of ecclesiastics lucky enough to secure multiple benefices. Monies were not fixed to clerical positions in any consistent way, even within the various tiers of cardinals, cathedral clergy, and parish priests. This diversity was compounded by the lack of financial requirements for ordination: men could become priests without adequate means for their support, since there was no inevitable relationship between taking orders and gaining an office. The mélange of clerical income was matched by a range of intellectual achievement, for seminaries customarily were absent and mandatory educational credentials nonexistent before 1563. All these conditions help to explain the actions and statements of someone like Cristobal de Gumiel, who became Vergara's go-between in hope of a benefice, clutched the false bequest of a benefice on his deathbed, and reported that he was no theologian and hence had no idea how Cajetan expounded Aquinas.[4] Gumiel was a desperately poor cleric: his indigence in turn enhanced his chance to be corrupted by a more powerful person, whether secular or ecclesiastic; his ideal payoff was a Church office and a consequently secured, minimum income. His belief that Vergara would deliver that post prompted him to disregard the Inquisition and his own safety. As for Vergara, his regard for his own finances and awareness of Gumiel's vulnerability meant that he had no scruples about feigning the gift, and knew his prey would snap at the lure. There is no reason to think that identical transactions and a similar lack of compunction were rare in any Catholic territory.

Even more significant conclusions, though, can be drawn from the examples of Vergara, Gumiel, and the Italian cardinals. Given their varying degrees of compensation, status, and education, as well as their general lack of vocation, it looks as if the Catholic clergy, as a self-identifying, professional class, simply did not exist for much of the early modern era.[5] Instead, Europe's Catholic priesthood was thoroughly heterogeneous and absolutely entrenched in secular affairs. The variation in its material resources, and its strategies for increasing those revenues, only heightened the chance that clergy and laity had more, not less, in common in the first half of the sixteenth century.[6]

We also know that ambiguities in the clerical estate—whether in terms of venality, poverty, or education—were addressed with newfound vehemence in the course of the epoch under review, as religious authors and authorities proposed an ecclesiastical order with a deeper appreciation of its responsibilities and a firmer awareness of its spiritual and practical position.[7] These individuals urged a different scenario from the status quo, one in which priests would reside in their benefices, preach to their congregations, and dispense the sacraments in a timely and thoughtful fashion. Italian examples of such reformers are particularly illustrious.[8] Gasparo Contarini (1483–1542), Venetian patrician, ambassador, and eventually a cardinal, advised residence and preaching upon the seventeen-year-old recipient of his treatise on episcopal obligation, *De officio episcopi* (1516). Gian Mateo Giberti (1495–1543), secretary to Pope Clement VII, envoy to Emperor Charles V, and absentee bishop of Verona, took advantage of the sack of Rome in 1527 to move to his diocese, whereupon he attempted to remake it in the image of St. Ambrose's fourth-century Milan.

Spain was not devoid of religious reformers either, and some of them appear in this chapter.[9] Canon lawyers such as Martín de Frías and Juan de Bautista published vernacular tracts on the visitation of dioceses and the instruction of priests, entitled *El tratado del modo y estilo que en la visitación ordinaria se a de tener* (1528) and *Doctrina de sacerdotes* (1535), respectively.[10] Juan Bernal Díaz de Luco (d. 1556), called Dr. Bernal by his colleagues, also possessed a canon law background but moved in court circles, eventually entering the Council of the Indies in 1531 and being ordained four years later. He accepted the bishopric of Calahorra in 1545, attended the Council of Trent until its second suspension in 1552, and managed in between to compose several significant works on the exemplary behavior of prelates and parish priests, including the *Instrucción de perlados* [sic] (Alcalá, 1530), the *Aviso de curas* (1539–51), and the *Carta desde Trento,* which was written in 1549 and published in 1553. As betrayed by their titles, in the *Instrucción de perlados* and *Aviso de curas,* Bernal offered straightforward guides to pastoral responsibilities. He wrote the *Carta desde Trento (Letter from Trent)* to the residents of his diocese of Calahorra and La Calzada, excusing his long absence and encouraging his flock to practice Christian virtues in the meantime.[11]

At the same time, the Dominican friar Domingo de Valtanás (1488-1565) enjoyed noble patrons, visited monasteries in southern Spain, and defended the Society of Jesus; he insisted that parish priests had a divine obligation to reside in their dioceses in the course of a polemic on "certain controversial moral issues" (1556).[12] His acquaintance and much more famous peer, Juan de Avila (ca. 1499–1569), skipped between the universities of Salamanca and Alcalá, contemplated a departure for the Indies, and became friends with the archbishops of both Seville and Granada. Maestro Avila founded colleges for the training of priests, promoted the Jesuits, and gained limitless fame as a homilist; between 1551 and 1565, he composed recommendations for the Council of Trent and the archbishopric of Toledo, as well as *pláticas* (discourses) on sacerdotal conduct.[13] Finally, Bartolomé de Carranza (1503–76)—the Dominican archbishop of Toledo, whose seventeen-year trial by the Inquisition was the most notorious of the century—attended the first and second convocations of the Council of Trent, and while there wrote one Latin work on the need for residence, the *Controversia de necessaria residentia personali episcoporum et aliorum inferiorum pastorum* (1547), and another on the ecclesiastical hierarchy and its responsibilities, the *Speculum pastorum. Hierarchia ecclesiastica in qua describuntur officia ministrorum Ecclesiae militantis* (1551–52).[14]

Like the alumbrados of the 1520s, or the delegates to Valladolid in 1527, clerics who wrote about pastoral obligations frequently knew each other and often had much in common.[15] Both Frías and Dr. Bernal acted as ecclesiastical judges for the bishop of Salamanca, and Bernal referred to Frías's guide to episcopal visitation in his own *Aviso de curas*. At times, Valtanás and Maestro Avila worked in the same geographical area, and like Dr. Bernal, they earnestly supported Ignatius of Loyola and his Society of Jesus.[16] Bernal and Carranza attended the Council of Trent's meetings in the 1540s and 1550s, and undoubtedly knew of Maestro Avila's *memorial* for the Spanish contingent there. Finally, three of the six—Juan de Avila, Valtanás, and Carranza—were indicted by the Inquisition, although their trials differed in both duration and the prosecution's motivation.

These individuals were active at approximately the same time, or between 1520 and 1570. They composed works that addressed the same subject: the proper conduct of parish priests and bishops toward both clergy and laity. They generally advanced the same points, from the desirability of clerical residence to the advancement of social harmony to restraint in financial expenditures. With the exception of Carranza, they deliberately wrote in the vernacular; they used identical vocabulary, from *reformación* to *ocio* to *disciplina,* or their Latin equivalents, and they cited the same authorities, from Chrysostom to Gregory the Great to John 21:15–17. There is no doubt that they conceived of themselves as attempting to reform their religious and even social environment, for their self-consciousness about their objectives was remarkably high. But given their explicit goals of amending the Church, the immediate issue is whether we want to label them as part of the Catholic or the Counter-Reformation.[17]

Until now historians have consistently linked Bernal, Carranza, Maestro Avila, and even Valtanás to the Catholic Reformation, a phrase that denotes an endemic movement for Catholicism's improvement, which began before Martin Luther's complaints, and allegedly favored an inclusive pastoral ethos over a combative one. Modern scholars have tied these Spaniards to the Christian humanism of Erasmus, as construed by Bataillon in *Érasme et l'Espagne*.[18] As these connections between the Catholic Reformation and Christian humanism have played out in the historical literature, they have reinforced the standard categories of the Bataillon argument, since scholars frequently oppose the Catholic Reformation to the *Counter*-Reformation— the latter term implies a reactionary phenomenon—and again to a regressive, proto-scholastic orthodoxy. The leading scholar on Carranza has remarked that the latter's Inquisition trial revealed a conflict between two types of Catholicism.[19] The same sort of divisiveness purportedly inhered in Vergara's Inquisition trial and the Valladolid conference.

Thus the paradigm of the Catholic and Counter-Reformation in Spain fundamentally parallels Bataillon's depiction of the Spanish sixteenth century: in both, a tolerant and progressive Catholicism is vanquished by a fanatical counterpart. This dynamic is not unique to Spanish historiography; the same pattern has commanded Italian scholarship as well for much of the modern era, and given the organizations and events of the sixteenth century, it is easy to see how it got there.

For example, the period between 1500 and 1600 can be construed as full of Catholic innovation as exhibited by the pious congregations created by the laity. In Cremona, the Barnabites began as an association of laymen that counseled men on marriage; in Milan, the Angels of St. Paul circulated freely during the day and practiced whatever charitable acts they chose, despite the fact that they were female. Like the Oratory of Divine Love, the Somaschi, and the School of the Most Holy Sacrament and Twelve Apostles, these groups relinquished the hallmarks of their older monastic counterparts, from chanting the Divine Office to wearing a particular habit. Instead, they left their constitutions vague and their initiative flexible, in order to attempt any charitable exercise that arose.[20]

Yet these decidedly inventive movements coexisted with religious classification and constraint. Paul III reestablished the Roman Inquisition in 1542; the Council of Trent provided Roman Catholicism with a clearly formulated soteriology between 1545 and 1563; Paul IV headed a papal regime from 1555 to 1559 that looks like the epitome of reaction. As a result, scholars have wrestled with ways to describe early modern Catholicism, because that religion encompassed such different-looking phenomena. For most academics, arranging Catholic history into an inimical relationship called "The Catholic and Counter-Reformations" has proven most compelling.[21]

And yet an ever larger contingent of Italian academics has stressed the continuities of the Catholic sixteenth century, and accented the movement of early modern clerics from the Catholic to the Counter-Reformation and back again. These scholars highlight collaboration between purportedly antithetical individuals, the exceptionalism of Paul IV's pontificate, and the ambiguity and failure that trailed the enforcement of orthodoxy, whether in terms of the Inquisition or the Index.[22] Other academics achieve the same outcome—the unification of Catholic history—by objecting to the very language in play: they find the label "Catholic Reformation" insufficient vis-à-vis the whole range of religious action in the sixteenth century, and argue that the phrase "Counter-Reformation" neglects the transitional and even modernizing tendencies of the Church after 1563.[23] The same inclusive impulses recently have appeared in Spanish history too, for we now have precedents for the Tridentine decrees in Castile, and the Catholic or Tridentine Reformation lasts between one half of the sixteenth century and the next.[24] But as subtle as such accounts of Spain can be, even they retain the notion of an intellectual and religious backlash as the sixteenth century progressed: they point to an increasingly rigid Catholicism that simultaneously took aim against the spiritual experimentation of earlier decades and Protestantism's refusal to disappear.[25]

This change in Spain's religious ethos allegedly was quickened by Philip II's promulgation of the Tridentine decrees in 1564. As Trent's *dicta* saturated the clerical hierarchy, the ecclesiastical elite began to perform its duties, however imperfectly, and to stress the distinctions between Catholicism and Protestantism: consequently, Spanish religious life became at once more centralized and more thoroughly spiritual.[26] Spaniards put their local confraternities under episcopal control and dedicated their shrines to more universal cults. They interiorized Catholic doctrine; they experienced and encouraged a heightened anxiety about their fate after death. By the end of the sixteenth century they were consumed with the afterlife and limiting their own and others' time in purgatory, for all that they imagined that afterlife in thoroughly material terms. Ultimately Spaniards poured their cash into testamentary bequests in ever-greater amounts—as the Church presumably wanted them to do—and affected the fate of their country. Their focus on purgatory meant that they committed assets to the dead instead of circulating them among the living.[27]

The authors under consideration here complement and emend this portrait, especially in the cases of Bernal, Carranza, and Maestro Avila. Their vocations and fortunes confirm that any division between a Catholic and a Counter-Reformation obscures more than it clarifies: it would be absurd to argue that these individuals belonged to one movement but not the other. The most prolific of them lived and wrote in the very decades, the 1540s to 1560s, which supposedly witnessed the triumph of a reactionary Catholicism within the rank and file of Spanish ecclesiastics. Like their Italian counterparts, Bernal, Carranza, Maestro Avila, and Valtanás attended, implemented, or echoed the deliberations at Trent. The fact that Bernal published a work in 1543 that Juan de Avila cited as much as twenty years later illustrates continuity rather than divergence between the pastoral priorities of one half of the century and the next. As for the Inquisition's attention to some of these religious reformers, not even Inquisition trials justify their depiction as the embattled advocates of a different sort of Christianity.

Maestro Avila was collared by inquisitors in the midst of the alumbrado crisis in the early 1530s, but was absolved of the charges; he went on to advise the archbishops who acted on the Tridentine decrees. Valtanás composed a vernacular work on Christian doctrine in 1555, and championed the Society of Jesus and episcopal residence in print in 1556, but only drew the inquisitors' notice in 1561. Finally, despite the hundreds upon hundreds of purportedly heretical statements presented against Carranza after his arrest in 1559, we know that political motives engendered that prosecution and directed its course. None of these prosecutions demonstrated that the Catholic hierarchy in Spain was rejecting one religious direction for another, and the defendants' deaths did not cancel their pastoral priorities: although their works ceased to be printed after the middle of the 1560s, their ambitions were preserved by individuals such as Martín Pérez de Ayala and Juan de Ribera.[28] Indeed, the only way to describe these clerics as somehow fundamentally, essentially subversive, is to ignore the decades in which they lived and the authorities with whom they collaborated. Their literary and professional careers were just as successful and complex as Juan de Vergara's. They should be viewed as part of the Catholic establishment.

Four of the ecclesiastics in this chapter worked in the middle of the sixteenth century; at least three also associated with and even embodied the highest ecclesiastical powers in the Peninsula. They lived and wrote at a time when a centralizing and spiritualizing impulse purportedly emerged from the Catholic elite. Yet these clerics offered different pastoral and devotional emphases in their written works, and their messages suggest that diversity was still possible in Spain between 1540 and 1570. Their divergence from one another also subverted their attempts to create a homogeneous clerical class, although they undoubtedly aspired to invest their peers with a sense of vocation and an awareness of their responsibilities. Finally, as they elevated the episcopate and the priesthood, they frequently posited the laity as collaborators in ecclesiastical power; and when they considered life in the world, they declined to disparage their contemporaries' physical and material well-being.[29] Their treatises even may prompt us to investigate further Spain's taste for the afterlife, since they neglected such accents altogether.

The references in these clerics' writings also complicate our tendency to infer humanist practice from the desire to amend Catholicism. Because the concept of Catholic Reform in Spain is so indebted to Bataillon, reformers in that country inevitably are interpreted as Erasmians; because the label "Erasmian" implies Renaissance humanism in the historiography, Catholic reformers in Spain also become Renaissance humanists. What makes such connections plausible is the general scholarly premise that the Catholic Reformation was ignited by a Renaissance humanism that turned on Christian sources.[30] Thus Contarini, Giberti, and their counterparts pursued the critical imitation of the ancients, but this time their models were the Latin Fathers of the Church. Furthermore, prototypes from the eastern half of the Roman Empire, such as John Chrysostom (ca. 347–407) and Basil (ca. 330–379), could be read in the original and in translation, since Greek had become available once more in the West. The Greek church fathers frequently were bishops in early Christianity, and their writings addressed the episcopal office and the duties of the clergy. Early modern clerics consequently could study the trials and triumphs of their ancient peers. The result, theoretically, was that ecclesiastics with reforming inclinations, such as Erasmus himself, recognized the distance between their Church and the primitive one, and tried to emulate the latter.

But again the Spaniards demonstrate the risks of reading at face value, for they referred to the twelfth-century Bernard of Clairvaux as frequently as the patristic Fathers in their writings, and turned to Cajetan to support their case for episcopal residence. They could quote the Bible mosaically; they could ignore change over time when they relied upon scriptural models. In some instances they explicitly rejected scholastic theology as irrelevant to their subject, and then employed its authorities and argumentative techniques anyway. But what is equally meaningful is that they also brandished apparently conservative methods in pursuit of drastic change.

From Martín de Frías's treatment of diocesan visitation, published in 1528, to Maestro Avila's treatise on the priesthood, written about 1563, the works entertained in this chapter were composed by men who currently or eventually were ordained, with a single exception.[31] As we shall see, the readership of these tracts is open to question, but their manifest goal was straightforward: their authors hoped to impress the full weight of the *cura animarum* upon ecclesiastics who should have practiced it. The Spaniards accordingly directed their works to archbishops, bishops, and parish priests, and handled the diocese and the parish as the center of religious life; they gave their writings such titles as *Doctrina de sacerdotes, Instrucción de perlados, Aviso de curas,* and *Tratado del sacerdocio.* Even Carranza's *Speculum pastorum,* which treated the ecclesiastical orders in nearly encyclopedic fashion, concentrated on prelates and priests. Such writings reinforce modern contentions that the secular clergy in the sixteenth century became a particularly attractive object of exhortation, even to monks.

In their writings, the Spaniards found it impossible to propose the correction of priests without also addressing their flaws. They thus described misconduct even as they urged better behavior. Their testimony confirms insights culled from Inquisition trials, curial records at Rome, and even synodal constitutions, insofar as they, too, reveal priests and bishops as thoroughly fixed in family circles and utterly susceptible to worldly attractions. At the same time, though, the immediate difficulty with using these texts for historical evidence lies in their literary and occasionally comprehensive character.

Tracts on priests often duplicated preceding ones, to the point that their descriptions should never be interpreted as eyewitness testimony to events, at least not without further evidence less prone to mimesis. For example, it is very clear that Bernal built his works from Frías's earlier treatment of visitation: he cited the latter as an authority, and magnified elements that Frías considered, such as the administration of the sacraments to the sick and the priest's explanation of baptism to midwives.[32] There is no way to conclude that Bernal physically observed situations in which these responsibilities went unfulfilled; it is impossible to claim that priests routinely failed to dispense the sacraments to ill people simply because he said so, when his remark was indebted, to a greater or lesser degree, to another literary source.

As for Frías's work, he seemed most interested in detailing every element that figured in a visitation, so as to render his text as complete as possible; but because he never furnished a hierarchy for the components he mentioned, we cannot deduce which ones he might have encountered in the visitations he physically carried out. Although it might look as if synodal constitutions—the recommendations endorsed by an episcopal council—ought to substantiate the Spaniards' literary testimony, such is not the case. Although directives of synods appear to divulge real misbehavior occurring at specific moments in time, they always, without exception, reiterate or modify preceding statutes.[33]

My caveats do not mean that we should discard treatises on priests and prelates as historical evidence, any more than the pitfalls in inquisitorial records oblige us to forego their details. Both kinds of sources preserve writers' attempts to persuade. Clerical authors always chose what to address and what to discard, even if they thought their duties entailed recording every particular that occurred to them; no matter how extensive their invocation of earlier authorities, they were engaged in an active process when they put their treatises together. If they repeated their predecessors, they apparently continued to find them dependable or apropos; if their works were reprinted, or carried in bookstores, or cited by others, their audience found the material relevant as well. Consequently, the descriptions that follow are not verbatim recordings of priests' and prelates' malfeasance, but rather can act as signs of the type of misconduct that a portion of Spanish ecclesiastics found particularly and consistently reprehensible across the sixteenth century.

According to Frías and Bautista, Bernal and Carranza, and Juan de Avila, parish priests in Spain sought cash and failed to perceive their obligations to parishioners and God. In sum, they lacked vocation, or as Maestro Avila put it, "if they enter into the Church, it's not because they choose to be low in the house of the Lord, but rich in the world; and if decent means of marrying offered itself to them, they would choose that."[34] The "riches" he mentioned were given greater specificity by Bernal, who decried bishops' seizure of Church funds and alienation of Church property; in his opinion, such prelates only viewed their offices as steps to greater worldly honors. Carranza seconded him, but with New Testament imagery: Jesus called those who anticipated, usurped, or ravaged the priestly office pillagers and thieves, as if they were hostile shepherds who wanted their own rewards instead of the health of their flock. And Frías complained of men who acquired Church offices through simony, administered the sacraments for pay, and abused their authority beyond what their synodal constitutions would allow.[35]

Patronage and poverty drove priests and explained their financial ambitions. In one treatise, Bernal pointed out the connection between Church property and loot for friends and family; in another, he noted that priests could be involved in vendettas that prevented them from leaving their homes at night to administer the sacraments, for fear their enemies would attack them.[36] (In such cases, he thought their superiors should force them to resign.) Maestro Avila tacitly acknowledged the pull of clientage when he stated that typical malefactors among the clergy were indigent and from villages: their "need for bodily food makes them haunt the divine mystery [of the Eucharist]," while the more limited milieus of their families gave them fewer means of advancement.[37] All the authors charged misbehaving clerics with ignorance, if only because of their lack of vocation; but Bernal went on to emphasize their obligation to improve themselves through reading, and spent little time sympathizing with the poverty that probably drove them into the priesthood in the first place. He suggested that clerics could better themselves if they would only make the effort; he accented their self-sufficiency in the emendation of their performance. His assumption of literacy and his belief in education were exhaustive.[38]

In contrast, when Maestro Avila attempted to explain stupid, aimless priests, he gave more weight to environmental causes. He recognized that such clerics were poor, that they lacked connections to potentially influential men, and that they were confounded in their attempts to provide for themselves. Their lack of vocation led to a situation in which they said the Divine Offices because their prebends obliged them to do so, while they were ignorant because they had no means of learning what they needed to know. Maestro Avila tied the ineptitude of confessors in particular to the lack of relevant lectures in Castilian universities: lessons on theology and canon law were not serviceable because confessors did not want to undertake such protracted studies—and could not have afforded them in any case.[39] But despite his appreciation for social, economic, and even educational contexts, Avila was not optimistic about the clergy's self-improvement. Instead, he favored group learning and discipline, whether for priests already in orders or future candidates; he thought the problem lay in the utter dearth of preparation for the clerical office. He wrote that priests had been raised since childhood "without obedience, without the cloister, without devotion and with ruinous companions, going day and night wherever they fancied, carrying along with them the inclinations they inherited from Adam, without having a brake, nor anyone to reprimand them."[40]

These Spanish clerics perceived the clergy as diverse, and were not happy about their conclusion: in 1547, Carranza characterized the estate to which he belonged as "tam promiscua turba sacerdotum" ("such a haphazard gang of priests").[41] The gang was chaotic because of its different levels of income and education. The gang's members were riotous because of their often pervasive ties to the secular community, whether through patronage or bribery or feuds, or even possessing a benefice in a person's hometown. Indeed, clerics might belong fundamentally to a neighborhood, as Bernal was well aware; such "local men" could run into significant difficulties when they dispensed the sacraments:

I fear that in locales where the priest is alone and a native of the place, or very well known in the village, certain women shall dare to conceal certain weaknesses of the flesh, seeing that the priests know the persons with whom they've sinned. The women worry that their partners will be discovered, even if they don't name them, because of some detail that they'll have to reveal, or because of some suspicion against them that already is in the village; especially if these women are kinswomen of the priest.[42]

Bernal's construction of this particular scenario may have had as much to do with his own illegitimacy as with anything he ever heard or saw. But evidence for clerics' entrenchment in their communities comes from other sources too: in the wake of the Tridentine decrees, Cuenca's priests conceded that they personally would not watch bullfights, but they could not imagine how they could refuse their houses to friends and family who wished to see the spectacle.[43]

Bernal and his peers presented solutions for such problems, and the heart of their remedies lay in the frank directive that holders of the cura animarum should reside in their benefices. The least rigorous opinion on the subject came from Frías, who noted that the bishop's visitor must ask about residence, reasonable reasons for neglecting residence, and the capabilities of the substitute in the priest's place.[44] His colleagues were much stricter, and they derived their mandate from a variety of considerations. As a body, they considered taking money from the parish and then refusing to serve it a great injustice, and they attempted to induce shame over the inequity. Carranza wrote

Tell me, ecclesiastical pastor, with what law do you demand a stipend? by reason of nourishment and necessity? You will answer, "by divine law, naturally." . . . Why, if I owe you the tithe in divine law, are you not required by the same law to serve the Tabernacle? . . . What iniquity is this, that you bind the community with religion on account of your salary, and you, if you please, are free from religion, if you don't want to act as a soldier [of Christ]?[45]

Valtanás expressed himself in equally severe terms, to the effect that the tithe exacted in Toledo was irrational, that the rent was snatched from the sweat of the poor and then spent elsewhere, and that tithes and rents were handed over in the first place to help priests nurture their flocks.[46]

Bernal, too, indicted clerics who accepted money from the laity, but acted as if they were exempt from residence. In his treatise on bishops, published in 1530, he entitled the seventh chapter "on the personal residence that they are obliged to carry out," and wrote that prelates must try to live in their dioceses above everything else.[47] He spent just as much space on the subject in the expanded version of the *Aviso de curas,* first printed in 1543: there he insisted that priests should occupy their prebends personally, and live as close to the church as possible, in order to administer the sacraments as often and as quickly as needed.

Meanwhile, Valtanás regarded residence as part of natural, divine, and human law, and thought it absolutely irremissible except for a very weighty reason; he went on to venture that absent priests lost merit even if they could justify their absence; he knew that residence could not be properly fulfilled by a third party.[48] Carranza was even more direct in the treatise he put together after Trent's acrimonious sessions on the matter, which occurred from 1546 to 1547. Residence in churches was an obligation of natural and divine law; it was a great responsibility, and ought to be pleasing and agreeable to everyone. Neither status nor tradition could excuse a cleric from this duty. Arguing on such grounds supported an abuse, not a custom.[49]

The Spaniards' outlook was grounded in and magnified by their claim that Jesus himself had commanded the personal residence of the clergy in John 21:15–17 and John 10:1–16. To produce residence from the first excerpt required some interpretative effort; its context was Jesus' third appearance to his disciples after his death and resurrection. In John 21:15–17, Jesus and Peter exchange the same dialogue three times: Jesus asks Peter if he loves him, Peter replies that Jesus knows that he does, and Jesus responds, "Pasce oves meas" ("Feed my sheep"). The fact that the order to feed the sheep was given by Jesus himself, and the recipient of the order was the foremost apostle and predecessor to the papacy, swelled the passage's significance. The verses were also rife with three's, symbol of the Trinity and the holiest of numbers in Christian hermeneutics.

The Spaniards accordingly interpreted the lines from John 21 in the most sweeping and serious way: the words "Feed my sheep" became divine law, because they were spoken three times by Jesus himself.[50] The statement was an absolute precept of the Lord; it was directed specifically to Peter, and hence became that apostle's personal responsibility. Yet the commission did not end there, for Peter's authority flowed to the papacy in turn, and again to all priests. What Jesus told Peter to do consequently filtered down clerical ranks and across centuries. The order to "feed my sheep" bound priests, bishops, archbishops, and popes to succor their parishioners.

Early modern clerics could find plainer instructions on residence in John 10:1–16, where Jesus described the ideal relationship between shepherd and sheep. In these lines, Jesus characterized himself as a good shepherd, remarked that he knew his sheep and they knew him, and said he would die for the flock. The authors we are studying were impressed with that sacrifice, and affected by the Latin verb *cognoscere,* which they properly translated as the Spanish *conocer*: both verbs entailed knowing a person instead of a fact, and suggested acts of observation and perception. To feed one's sheep, then, was a holy and direct assignment enjoined on every priest responsible for the care of souls; it involved spiritual and corporal food, just as the sacraments entailed material substances with spiritual import. The only way to "know" the sheep in the way Jesus envisioned was to live among the flock.

But for all the evocations of the New Testament, when it came to personal residence these clerics were forced to rely on other authorities too. Even if they had attempted a sola scriptura foundation for their counsel, Jesus' words to Peter, as well as his parable about good shepherds, required interpretation. The New Testament verses presented only implicit signs that residence was necessary, to wit, if a good shepherd dies for his sheep, then he must be physically present in order to do so. To complicate matters further, the Church Fathers neglected explicit treatments of episcopal residence because they presumed that bishops would live in their dioceses, as Carranza himself admitted.[51] The Spaniards assured their readers that "all the Fathers of the Church" interpreted the New Testament *toward* residence. But even one of their favorite patristic sources, John Chrysostom's *De sacerdocio,* failed to mention the topic.

Bernal and Carranza consequently turned to work by Cajetan, who died in 1534, to make their point: ironically, they employed the scholastic glosses of a famous contemporary to justify a return to the primitive church and a scriptural directive. Bernal grounded his arguments in Cajetan's commentary on Aquinas's *Summa theologica.* In the *Summa*'s II.II., quaestio 185, the fifth article asked "whether it was licit for a bishop to desert the flock committed to him because of some bodily persecution." Aquinas concluded that it was. Cajetan then extended Aquinas's article by exploring situations in which bishops could be absent, and ones in which they should not; in the process, he decried sophistic reasoning that claimed personal residence was fulfilled through a house in Rome, or the substitution of an expert stand-in. Bernal's presentation of Cajetan was legalistic in content, scholastic in structure, and only linked to Scripture through a single phrase from John 10—"a good shepherd lays down his life for his sheep"—which he did nothing to amplify.[52]

Carranza's use of Cajetan was more direct because he invoked the latter's commentary on John 21:15–17 instead of the gloss on Aquinas; still, he also cited the eleventh-century commentator Theophylactus and Aquinas's *Cathena aurea in quatuor Evangelia* in his argument. Given the difficulties and lacunae of the scriptural and patristic texts, Carranza and his peers obviously took advantage of any and every Christian source, including, on occasion, Erasmus, which promoted a divine sanction for episcopal residence.[53] Like some of their peers at Valladolid, they, too, used more recent writings as a guide to older ones. But in contrast to some of the theologians at Valladolid, they employed scholastic sources to correct rather than conserve the status quo.

Their expositions on residence duplicated the Spanish delegation's contentions at the Council of Trent. The coincidence is unremarkable, since Bernal and Carranza participated in the Council's sessions from 1545 to 1547, when episcopal residence prompted one of the most contentious debates and Bernal acted as one of its most persistent proponents.[54] The Spaniards wanted the Council to stipulate that the obligation to reside was grounded in divine law; they were convinced that without that criterion, any decree would lack requisite moral force.[55] Yet what struck them as a straightforward duty was actually a new rule that could affect every aspect of ecclesiastical life, for clerical residence threatened current conventions and power structures, including the boundaries of papal authority.

Residence made pluralism impossible. Without pluralism, ecclesiastics would see the diminution of their income, influence, and personal networks. Moreover, a requirement to reside struck directly at the prerogatives and even the purpose of the Roman Curia, whose officials routinely excused residence for others and never resided anywhere themselves: the Spanish argument turned what had passed for smart fiscal and familial policy into malfeasance.[56] A divine precept to reside also appeared to conflict with the pope's authority to grant exemptions from that obligation; for a portion of the Italian episcopate at Trent, Spanish claims looked like a plot to diminish papal power as well as their own, no matter how steadily the Spaniards upheld the papacy's right to dispense with the requirement. The Council's discussions of potential impediments to residence, and penalties for nonresidence, consequently assumed a singular importance.[57]

The Spaniards did not achieve the divine law clause when rulings on residence were approved at Trent in 1547 and in 1563; the Tridentine decrees insisted upon the obligation, but declined to specify where that duty originated. Nevertheless, Bernal and Carranza—who held the cura animarum as bishop and archbishop, respectively—took their own counsel seriously, since they resided in their sees years before Trent's directives were formally promulgated in Spain. In Bernal's case, he demonstrated remarkable coherence by arguing for residence in texts published over three decades, from 1530 until 1555; and by fulfilling his own counsel when he was not at Trent.[58] Yet what did these ecclesiastics want their counterparts to do, if they ever succeeded in forcing them into their parishes?

The Spaniards consistently promoted activity, for they all denounced lazy priests. An idle cleric was as bad as an absent one; there was nothing worse among Christians than an indolent pastor. Clearly Bernal and his peers expected priests to be busy, but when it came to specific tasks, their descriptions became remarkably variegated. Some stressed the clergy's role in Church rituals and sacraments. Frías asked whether clerics could read, sing the Divine Offices, fix movable feast days, and handle confessions; he suggested that a visitor ideally would watch each priest conduct a Mass.[59] Carranza, as befit a Dominican, mentioned Divine Offices too, while Maestro Avila emphasized the administration of the Eucharist and penance.

Interestingly enough, authors who underscored the priest's sacramental function also described clerics as enjoying a singular relationship with the divine, and again as intercessors for their parishes with God. Bautista noted that sacramental responsibilities placed ecclesiastics in a special position, for their work required them to possess a stable link with the Godhead.[60] Maestro Avila made the same point at greater length: the priest appeased the wrath of God toward the pueblo because the priest and God were friends (*amigos*); a priest's weapons were tears and prayer, with which he persuaded God to give up His anger. The cleric's arbitration was critical:

Although the pueblo with its wicked life may be so terrified that it neither has the courage to stand before His presence, nor dares to lift eyes to heaven, the Lord wishes that the priest will be such that with the cleanliness of his life, and friendly conversation and special familiarity that exist between him and God, he shall not be prostrate with terror like the pueblo; but instead may possess a holy courage to stand and come to the Lord, and beg Him, and importune Him, and bind Him, and conquer Him, so that, in place of the heavy whip of the just Judge, God may send the embraces of a loving Father.[61]

For Maestro Avila, the status of the clerical office derived precisely from its mediation with the divine, which was why he stressed the bridge of prayer. Although he also told curates to preach to the laity, help the poor, and visit the sick, he obviously envisioned their most important duty as the propitiation of God through prayer and sacramental sacrifice.

Other writers highlighted what we might call more social endeavors, because they reflected at greater length on more direct and numerous contact points between clergy and laity. Everyone cited the administration of the Eucharist as an important responsibility. But Valtanás underscored preaching as the centerpiece of a cleric's activities: a preacher himself, he had no doubt that a well-ordered and relevant sermon would affect the laity in positive ways.[62] Carranza wanted other good works as well as sermons, since "it is fitting that when the shepherd shall have sent out the sheep by means of preaching, he shall go before them by means of example."[63] He went on to note that when bishops visited the diocese, they should "preach, argue, admonish, confirm with holy oil, investigate in what way the sacraments may be administered. . . . Look into the customs of [their] subjects, repair churches, settle conflicts if such exist; and recognize and encourage good men."[64] Only from a personal visit could bishops attain the fulsome cognition that Jesus required of his Christian shepherds and set forth in John 10:3.

Meanwhile, Bernal's recommendations were as abundant as they were varied: in the case of both prelates and priests, he imagined them as continuously reading useful books, talking to learned, zealous, and virtuous people, and finally carrying what they had learned around the parish. Preaching was paramount for bishops, who should also provide decent homilists for smaller towns. Members of the episcopate ought to observe their surroundings and ascertain whether their synodal constitutions really matched their environment. Bishops were obliged to watch their judges and officials for bribery and corruption, to investigate the hospitals in their dioceses, and to ensure that their delegates conducted their visitations carefully.

Bernal only amplified the duties of parish priests. They had to wash their clothes and their bodies, and not start thinking that dirt and poverty signified the same thing, for only poverty was laudable.[65] They had to supervise the repair and cleaning of their churches, as well as any oratories in the area. They should avoid spending money on superfluous items. They must devote an enormous amount of time to the laity: the seventeenth chapter, "on instructing parishioners," is among the longest in the *Aviso de curas.*[66] Bernal advised curates to set up schools, with fixed hours, in which to teach children; he also wanted them to hand out educational goals as penance, such as learning whatever it was that the penitent in question did not know. He entreated priests to urge parents not to put their unmarried daughters in convents, at least not automatically. He told curates to know (*conocer*) their parishioners' ages, status, and means of support, so that they might better "counsel and support all of them, according to what each one should require."[67]

The guidance that Bernal, Carranza, and the rest offered was full of concern for the laity's physical well-being, albeit as construed by Catholic clerics. There should be nothing startling about the presence of material interests in these texts, since Jesus' directions to "Feed my sheep" carried such ramifications; Valtanás was acting on those implications when he remarked, "With their presence, bishops heal their subjects' illnesses of the soul, and remedy the necessities of their bodies." The proper function of a prelate was to tend his sheep with the pasture of doctrine and the fields of the necessities of life.[68]

Concern for the destitute was nearly omnipresent in these treatises, although individual authors might devote a relative amount of space to the problem of indigence and ways to remedy it. Just as near-contemporaries

Giovanni Botero and Pedro de Ribadeneyra construed their ideal princes as administrators, so Bernal drew the model priest as a sort of practical superintendent.[69] His ecclesiastics would try to prevent poverty before it occurred; they would survey the land and consult with others to determine what industry and craft, agriculture and labor would best suit the pueblo and enrich it. If a portion of the congregation became impoverished despite the best efforts, then priests should take up special collections from the parishioners, browbeat the rich, and even sell the church silver if the situation demanded it. Bernal bluntly wrote, "It is obvious that God would prefer a rational person to live, for whom He has done so much, rather than have people offer Him incense in silver vessels, or venerate the image of His cross in silver."[70]

As for more celestial concerns, such as purgatory, the saints, or testamentary bequests, the Spaniards expressed only a minimum interest in them, especially when compared to the amount of space they devoted to educating children, helping the poor, and administering the sacraments. Only Juan de Avila addressed the Virgin Mary as an intercessor for the pueblo; otherwise, references to the saints were entirely absent. Nearly all adduced the care of last wills and pious legacies as part of a priest's routine, but not one encouraged clerics to solicit that responsibility. Instead, these writings simply warned priests to carry out the Mass cycles committed to them in wills. The same concern was echoed in synodal constitutions and vernacular literature on death.[71]

Bernal was the most explicit as well as the most damning on the subject of unfulfilled bequests; since the amplified version of his *Aviso de curas* went through three editions between 1543 and 1551, his strictures deserve special consideration.[72] Just as the priest had an absolute responsibility to counsel the sick and the dying, so he must help the laity plan their testaments. In the arrangement of those wills, the dying should first consider settling their debts and only afterward entertain charitable gifts, especially ones for the poor of their own parishes. The dying should think about their servants, and whether the latter had suffered through their work.

Finally, Bernal noted that priests should not try to solicit numerous Masses from a dying person, as sometimes occurred; instead, it was critical to tell the laity the truth about how many Masses a priest could fulfill. Laymen and women were not obtuse; they knew when their *cura* accepted more Mass cycles than he could physically perform. The laity should never feel defrauded.[73] Bernal explicitly ranked testamentary Masses lower than works of mercy among the living, and explained:

If the Catholic Church, governed by the Holy Spirit, understood that the relief and satisfaction of the dead rested in a large number of Masses, more than in the works of mercy those dead carried out when they were alive, it would not so restrict the number of priests, since the Church does not wish someone to be ordained unless he has patrimony or a benefice.[74]

The Church placed relatively greater weight on charity performed in the here-and-now: if this hierarchy were not in play, then the ecclesiastical establishment would allow priests to earn their upkeep from Mass cycles for the dead. Bernal's own preference matched his description of the Church's: he wanted to shift the laity's and the clergy's attention away from memorial acts and toward benefits for the living. Given recent descriptions of the inflation that struck Spanish testamentary bequests in the latter half of the sixteenth century, his counsel was well placed and even prophetic. The average number of Masses requested in Madrid in the 1520s, in individual testaments, numbered ninety; that figure had climbed to 777 by the 1590s.[75]

Although scholars recently have argued that Spanish Catholics became obsessed with purgatory in the last half of the sixteenth and then the seventeenth centuries, we still know very little about the development of that propensity. It consequently is significant that vernacular treatises on clerics, which were composed and distributed either immediately before or during the period in question, could refuse to countenance that emphasis or else drastically limit it. The Spanish authors under review here addressed the clergy's duty to complete the Masses committed to them, but otherwise hardly developed the topic at all; the matter played a trivial part in their texts.

As for even larger arguments that early modern Catholicism began to highlight the individual over the community, and private sins over public ones, Frías, Carranza, and Bernal recognized the importance of social harmony and the role of the clergy in promoting it.[76] Frías adjured visitors to procure peace and concord in society by easing its members' angers and controversies; more abstractly, Carranza told his readers that a priest was nothing other than a minister of reconciliation, and cited 2 Corinthians 5:18 to prove it.[77] Bernal addressed the subject extensively: even before he was ordained or had received a bishopric, he sketched ideal clerics as if peacemaking were central to their job. In the *Instrucción de perlados* (1530), he told prelates to intervene personally in feuds and factions, because such conflicts engendered great harm to both bodies and souls. In the *Aviso de los curas* (1551), he devoted Chapter 19 to "how the priest has to work to put his parishioners in a state of charity and love with each other": there he adjured priests to detect enmities quickly, and to cure them with patience, mediators, and harsh penance, if necessary. Finally, in the letter he wrote to his subjects from Trent (1553), he begged them to refrain from suing and insulting their neighbors, "whose honor you are bound to protect and love as if it were your own."[78]

These texts reveal little evidence that their authors were attempting to heighten individual sins over communal offenses. On the contrary, the Spaniards sought to detach their readers, whether clerical or lay, from purely familial loyalties, and to direct their attention to wider matters of social stability; they accordingly spent much time confronting the enmities that could wreck their parishioners' emotional and physical well-being. Yet their apparent concern for their congregations may have entailed less than empathetic results, for a subtext to the Spaniards' treatises was the harassment of laymen and women into virtuous behavior.

With the exception of Bautista, the group could advise clerics to act aggressively in the face of lay recalcitrance. Sometimes the verbs they chose were illuminating: Frías described episcopal visitors as "rejoining, scolding, and supplicating" (*redarguendo, increpando, obsecrando*), and counseled that if the object of their correction would not accept it, then they had no choice but to go to the bishop himself for assistance.[79] Bernal's resolution that curas and prelates should "know" their congregations was capable of an insidious twist: in a likely extension of Frías, he wrote that priests who knew the lives of their parishioners subsequently could relay what needed punishment and emendation to the bishop.

Bernal then went into even more detail. He wanted clerics to pay special attention to strangers, because the latter sometimes lived with concubines whom they passed off as their wives; he thought priests should demand proof of the marriage. Once schools were set up, priests should tell parents to send their children to them, and if those admonitions did not work, they should turn to their superiors and especially "the authority of secular justice," which would compel the missing to attend. Bernal wished parishioners to seek out their priests on matters of unfamiliar or suspicious rituals, for the latter easily might involve superstition. He asked confessors to crack down on their penitents, because "gentleness" had relaxed "Christian discipline." And he proposed that overburdened priests schedule penance on a household basis, so that the laity would arrive for confession in some sort of order, and thereby eliminate crowds and carelessness.[80]

In the final analysis, Bernal's instructions were only more extensive than most of his peers'. Carranza used the same vocabulary when he contended that episcopal residence would restore Christian *disciplina,* and adduced St. Jerome to prove that discipline belonged to the priest; he explained that discipline connoted the seizure and restraint of those who neglected the salutary things of the law or committed an offense through malice.[81] It is true that Carranza and his cohort generally limited their recommendations on compulsion to the arena of public sin. They also presented clerics as potential objects of the same measures. But from a twentieth-century perspective it is too easy to read such counsel as coercion, to isolate discipline as the crux of their texts, and finally to interpret that discipline as the blunt exercise of practical power. Although historians insist that early modern "discipline" could be shared rather than imposed, and connote self-regulation as much as supervision by others, modern antipathy toward organized religion and secular bureaucracy makes such angles difficult to grasp, except as the inculcation of elite values.[82] When a status-laden group of clerics brandishes words like "observe" and "discipline" and "reprimand," the thrust of their terms seems very clear indeed.

But I would propose that reasons to refuse *disciplina* as control and compulsion, and again as the heart of these sources, lie in the very treatises under review. In fact, affection toward the laity permeates Spanish tracts on bishops and priests: if we really are pursuing alterity, then we have to consider that emotive element as seriously as any other, and not reduce it to the level of an insincere rhetorical ploy. These clerical writers did not veil their kindliness, but exhibited it through nouns such as *caritas* and *dilectio* in Latin, and *caridad* in Spanish. Their use of the words was always personal and often emotional; they expressed them about the very flock that ecclesiastics were supposed to supervise.

As Carranza explained it, a pastor's regard for his sheep was traceable to the interchange between Jesus and Peter in John 21:15–17, the same passage that proved Jesus had committed the flock to Peter, and then to Peter's successors. Carranza thought it highly significant that Jesus did not ask Peter about his wealth or the excellence of his family (*de generis nobilitate*), or even the knowledge that he ought to possess. Instead, something else was even more important, and hence Jesus interrogated Peter about love, the critical quality in a person who assumed the sustenance of Christians.[83] Moses demonstrated a similar feeling of love when he was examined about the pastoral duty in the presence of God. And Carranza contended repeatedly that the job of priests and prelates had nothing whatsoever to do with mastery.

See how I appeal to the emphasis of the words: Jesus does not say, "Act superior, wield power against my sheep," no matter how these words to that passage may be translated, but "feed my sheep." "Among you," he said, "it will not be thus, but whoever is the greater will be your minister" (Matt. 20:26). You will not therefore rule according to your will, but shall act like a pastor, not a lord.[84]

Carranza was consistent on this point: he relayed it in the *Controversia de necessaria residentia* as well as throughout the *Speculum pastorum*. Pastors should be modest and humble instead of proud. The cura animarum demanded ministry, not domination. Although a pastor was obliged to admonish the erring, he nonetheless should "endeavor much more to care for the subjects committed to him, than to correct [them]."[85]

Bernal's treatises frequently revealed limits to clerical superintendence as well: in the 1530 work on prelates, he wrote that bishops should seek to discover only what they could *licitly* know about their sheep. Equally telling evidence occurs in the materials that he composed after the first sessions at Trent were suspended in 1547. Stalled in that city because he and the rest of the Spanish delegation refused to proceed to Bologna with the other participants, Bernal penned a letter to his diocese in 1549, and simultaneously collected the lives of saints: in both compositions he expressed his attachment for his subjects and his dejection over his separation from them. As he closed the epistle, he wrote,

And because God is a faithful witness that today I desire nothing more than to find myself among you, in order to procure your salvation, I beg and charge you to make a special prayer to our Lord, begging Him to return me to your presence with His grace and favor that He knows I need, as a pastor of so many souls, and as inadequate as I am. Although it may seem as if I ask you for something that is to my benefit alone, spiritual goodness is so shared between the shepherd and his sheep that the prelate never receives some benefit from God in this case, that does not flow and communicate itself with his subjects.[86]

He portrayed himself as isolated from his flock and hence sorrowful.

Bernal and his peers saw no contradiction between discipline and love, so long as the former was employed for God and not for personal advantage. Rather, they seemed to view the one as a consequence of the other, at least ideally: as Carranza noted, "justice without mercy is not justice, but cruelty; while mercy without justice is not mercy, but silliness."[87] This ability to combine elements that strike us as distinct once again places us in an odd position. We can dismiss these clerics' invocation of love as a ruse, or react to their goal of eternal life as a disguise for particular interests inhering in the system. The problem is that such responses would replace the texts' open declarations with a past that reflects modern concerns. To complicate the situation even further, Bernal and his peers did address their personal profit as pastors, as we have just seen in the above quotation, but the way they conceived of that profit further challenges our expectations about them. In sum, they described themselves as working for their own salvation when they attended to the salvation of others. The connection between obligation and reward explains in turn how they could champion assertive measures when it came to the opposition or passivity of laymen and women.

As part of their efforts to construct more virtuous and competent shepherds, these clerics called upon divine judgment and personal responsibility. They wanted their audience to feel the weight of the cura animarum; they ended by transferring to the secular clergy the charge that basically had fallen upon friars since the thirteenth century, namely, custody for the souls of persons lower down the religious scale.[88] The ramifications of the arguments were very clear: priests and prelates were frankly advised that they would have to account for their parishioners' souls to God. And so the divine precept for residence came with a vivid announcement: if clerics practiced absenteeism and pluralism, or even simple indifference, the impact on their own afterlife would be catastrophic.

Valtanás, Bernal, Carranza, and Juan de Avila announced dire personal consequences for inept and absent shepherds. A pastor who did not tend his flock—by visiting, confirming, and nursing it—had much to fear after his own death.[89] The priest must render a report to God about the souls in his care, which would be nearly impossible to pull off unless he and the laity truly knew each other.[90] Anticipating that account should provoke a bishop into making visitations, unless he did not grasp the real possibility of his own eternal misery. Grasping the link between his own salvation and his parishioners' should quicken the priest's fulfillment of testamentary bequests, since "with what harm to both might a soul be lost out of the priest's own ignorance or negligence, or from not wanting to work; and how justly will that soul be howling constantly against the priest to God, if for one of these reasons it should be condemned."[91] Both Avila and Carranza bemoaned a situation in which priests and bishops had lost their fear of God's verdict upon them.[92]

Nearly all the Spaniards turned to the same scriptural text to document the clergy's accountability for souls in their care. Ezekiel 33:2–9 explained the watchman's duties to the people who chose him as a lookout. When that sentry saw the sword of God coming upon the land, he must sound the trumpet and alert the population; those who then failed to heed the trumpet died through their own fault. But if the watchman saw the sword approaching and neglected to alert the people, and the people subsequently perished, their blood was on his hands. Ezekiel 33:7–9 read:

So you, son of man, I have made a watchman for the house of Israel; whenever you hear a word from my mouth, you shall give them warning from me. If I say to the wicked, "O wicked man, you shall surely die," and you do not speak to warn the wicked man from his way, that wicked man shall die in his iniquity, but I will require his blood at your hand. But if you tell the wicked man, in order for him to be converted from his ways, and he is not converted from his ways, he will die in his iniquity, but you have delivered your soul.

Spanish clerics repeated this scriptural authority with its implications intact. With its assistance, Carranza proved that simple negligence made priests responsible for others' deaths, since "we kill as many as die daily from our silence."[93] Bernal spent entire chapters cautioning ordinands about the dangers their future office entailed.[94] And in a colorful metaphor, Frías wrote that mange could afflict sheep all the way to hell because of the shepherds' indifference; priests would keep their nails cleaner if they continually scraped the scabs from their flock, as Ezekiel commanded them to do.[95]

The clergy's salvation being bound up in the laity's reveals a rather different perspective on the potentially intrusive behavior of religious authorities. When Frías told episcopal visitors to scold parishioners, or Bernal wanted to harangue parents who refused to send their children to school, they were not just acting from the position that they knew what was best for the laity, although they undoubtedly thought that they did. Instead, they also were reacting to Ezekiel's admonitions about silence and responsibility, and were trying to safeguard their own resurrection by securing the same for their flock. Their awareness of their liability undoubtedly sharpened their insistence on preaching. They very often alluded to fear as they outlined their obligations; they consistently portrayed their duties as dreadful ones that should inspire nothing but awe in candidates for ordination. They cited the example of St. Chrysostom, who spent most of *De sacerdocio* describing his and St. Basil's panic over accepting the episcopacy. They noted that terror over God's judgment should promote self-knowledge, and from there awareness of one's aptitude and strength for clerical office. Notably, whenever they connected the laity and fear, they did so in terms of imitation: without exception, they imagined that secular women and men would worry about their own salvation if they witnessed their priests' anxiety over the same matter.[96] In this instance, priest and layperson were supposed to share the same disquiet over the same event.[97]

The notion of experiences and feelings imparted to both clerical and lay spheres immediately raises the problem of hierarchy. These authors decidedly wanted a professional clergy, that is, priests who conceived of themselves as special for deeper reasons than their income. But whether clerics-with-a-vocation should then insulate themselves from the laity, or focus on the distinctions between themselves and laypersons, were other matters, even in texts written by Spanish ecclesiastics in the middle of the sixteenth century. In reality, shepherds never could remove themselves entirely from interactions with their sheep, because they subsequently could not have done their jobs.[98] And because the Spaniards understood this truth about their office, most mapped out a sphere of appropriate collaboration between clergy and laity, while also trying to redress the undue susceptibility of priests to lay influence.

With the exception of Maestro Avila, who hardly mentioned laypersons in the works scrutinized here, these writers treated their flocks as allies. When Frías described the visitor's routine in a village, he envisioned asking the laity about the clergy's competence.[99] He also advised priests to inform midwives about baptism, to the extent that

in each place where the bishop or his visitor goes to visit, he must call all the midwives found in that place, and inform himself about each one, namely, whether they are accustomed to baptize infants being born, in the house and outside of danger, and how they must not do it. And when some danger exists or is presumed to exist, how they may baptize said infant, and on what part of the infant's body they cast the water. . . . And what words they say then, and if the formula is not well known to them, teach them, and so order it, under pain of excommunication, that each one of them shall learn the rite, or not practice midwifery. And he shall order the parish priest to teach them.[100]

In this instance Frías drew the ritual of baptism into the physical structure of churches and under the jurisdiction of priests, but he also deputized midwives to act in the clergy's place and handed them the sacramental formula. His restrictions on lay action accompanied the commissioning of it; he apparently thought that the priests' monopoly on the sacraments finally mattered less than the midwives' assistance. A decade later, Bernal would expand Frías's instructions and demand that *everyone* be taught how to baptize, "since the way things go, any of [the priest's] parishioners could find himself someday in a situation in which he would have to baptize some infant."[101]

Then there was the issue of lay initiative over and against the clerical variety. Bernal handled the matter practically rather than theoretically, through the description of concrete situations. For example, he explained that laymen and women often wished to create hermitages for their devotions: priests should investigate the structures of such buildings, because frequently they were not made well and fell down. If the construction materials were inferior, Bernal thought it wise to try and curb the laity's piety in this matter, even though stopping the project might depress the participants.[102]

As for the enormous crosses that parishioners tried to secure—which allowed them to outstrip other villages in processions—the priest first should try to convince them that the money could be better spent on books or chalices, assuming that the parish needed such items.[103] Only if such persuasion failed did Bernal advise the priest to turn to his bishop; immediately afterward, he railed against the spending habits of the clergy, who were just as liable to follow their impulses and buy themselves rich clothing when their churches lacked more important things.[104] He thus charged laypersons and priests with the same propensity to commit the same errors; if he stifled lay independence, he crushed its clerical analogue as well. He held both groups to a similar standard. Significantly, he did not rule out processions or crosses altogether, or label them as superstitious; instead, he presented the matter as a problem of relative worth.

Bernal adduced a further balance between the religious and secular spheres when he addressed clerical misdeeds, for he expressed his esteem for lay opinion both tacitly and candidly. When bishops attempted to reform the members of cathedral chapters, who always resisted their authority, they should preach against their belligerence from the pulpit; describing and indicting the flaws of those canons in public would spur recognition of their misdeeds in the wider population. Priests who went around with women, or pursued only the sins of the poor, soon would lose whatever sway they had.[105] If parishioners came to deprecate them, or spread rumors about them around the village, priests would forfeit whatever respect they enjoyed; if the clergy lost the laity's regard, its corresponding diminution in authority would harm laypersons as well. Laymen and women would not turn to such ecclesiastics for spiritual guidance. They would resist their priests' correction; they would hesitate over their administration of the sacraments, or not receive those sacraments in a suitable frame of mind. In sum, they would endanger their own salvation, and responsibility for their peril would fall on the priests in question.

It thus seems as if Bernal expected the secular realm to discipline the ecclesiastical one, as much as the other way around. He, and to a lesser extent his peers, divulged an acute awareness of and respect for the laity's capacity for anger; they also expressed faith in laymen and women's judgment. These small signs reveal parity as well as inequality in the relationship between the ecclesiastical and secular arenas. As Bernal put it, priests should not indulge in too much familiarity with their parishioners, for those friendships could compromise the sacrament of penance; on the other hand, it was just as bad for priests to separate themselves so thoroughly from the laity that they lived in great solitude and sadness, with no one to talk to.[106]

In the musings of these Spanish ecclesiastics, laymen and women hardly lacked influence: they could identify clerical wrongdoing, ruin an ecclesiastic's reputation, and provide priests with more or less camaraderie. Such reciprocity is demonstrated in other sources from the same epoch: municipal authorities demanded residence from their bishops, towns sued priests for their incompetence, and the laity occasionally took their complaints about sermons to the Inquisition.[107] If secular men and women refused to cooperate with the priest, they endangered his salvation as well as their own, and there is no reason to think that either the clerical or lay population was unaware of that hazard. In short, these authors worked toward the professionalization of the secular clergy, but in the process they did not separate the clergy absolutely from the lay universe: instead, they implied and invited the laity's assistance in carrying out what Christianity framed as a mutually beneficial endeavor.

The Spaniards could promote such collaboration because they envisioned their parishioners as rational. Indeed, the phrase "rational sheep" (*ovejas racionales*) occurs throughout most of the treatises under review, and the adjective was not accidental. The sheep's rationality dictated certain behavior for the shepherds. Because the sheep were reasonable, they must be persuaded instead of coerced; because some were wiser than others, their treatment must be individualized; because they were sensible, their approbation should be sought and their wrath feared, albeit not to the detriment of doctrine or morals. It was exactly that line between lay approbation and respect, and orthodox ritual and belief, that provoked some apprehension in these authors. When they worried about endorsing a hermitage, or purchasing a processional cross, or reproving penitents, they divulged that their authority could be challenged because of the secular community in which they lived.

Of course, all this counsel was moot unless someone were reading the texts in question. There is every indication that most of these authors tried to increase their audience by making their tracts emotionally moving. Four of the six practiced homiletic techniques in their prose, occasionally to the point of writing their treatises like sermons. They used the second-person voice and imperative verbs, relayed their own experiences, and inserted queries into their writing as if their public were going to read it aloud. Their literary efforts signaled a desire to widen their readership.

The evidence implies that several of these works circulated widely. Bautista's tract only went through one edition, but Bernal's expanded version of the *Aviso de curas* was printed in 1543, 1550, and 1551. Carranza's *Controversia de necessaria residentia,* published for the first time in Venice in 1547, appeared again in a collection of similar writings in 1562.[108] Finally, Juan de Avila's two *memoriales* for Trent, which were finally published in the twentieth century, were recopied in manuscript in their own epoch, and even translated into Portuguese.[109]

The explicit objects of these compositions almost always were ecclesiastics.[110] Maestro Avila composed his *Tratado de sacerdocio* as a guide for the clergy of Córdoba, on the occasion of a synod in 1563.[111] Frías envisioned his piece on visitation as similarly practical, for it would tell any bishop or episcopal visitor what to do and in what order. Bautista conceived of his *Doctrina de sacerdotes* as a companion piece to Archbishop and Inquisitor General Manrique's *Doctrina cristiana;* he composed it in Spanish to teach clerics less adept in letters. Bernal drafted his *Instrucción de perlados* in Spanish so that bishops could read it with less fatigue; he dedicated his first edition of the *Aviso de curas* to clerical friends, and in subsequent printings directed the same work to the parish priests of his diocese.

But although the Spaniards' works look as if they were read within ecclesiastical circles alone, some may have reached the laity as well. Two booksellers' inventories demonstrate that Frías's tract on visitation—collected in his *Tractatus perutilis,* also called the *Tractatus sacerdotalis*—and Bernal's *Aviso de curas* found a receptive following. In 1556, Juan de Junta's shop in Burgos possessed nine copies of Frías's work, and twenty-one of Bernal's; the same year, Juan de Ayala's bookstore in Toledo carried eighteen of Bernal's *Aviso de curas.*[112] These are substantial quantities for materials that were neither pamphlets nor broadsheets.[113] Furthermore, in 1556 Bernal's *Aviso* was priced at 51 maravedís in Burgos, and 34 in Toledo: a laborer's daily wage was 34 maravedís in 1551 in Cuenca, and if such compensation did not vary widely across Castile, then workers in Burgos and Toledo may have been able to purchase such treatises. Finally, historians have charted a literacy rate as high as 69 percent for Castilian men in the latter half of the sixteenth century; while the percentage of women who could read was much lower, there are signs that females acquired some learning through oral culture.[114] The lay population, as well as the clerical one, could read treatises on bishops and priests, both to themselves and to others.

It is at least credible that laymen and women could get hold of Bernal's *Aviso,* and decipher it when they did. Significantly, Bernal would not have excluded such individuals from his audience: although he frankly directed the last editions of the *Aviso* to the parish priests of his diocese, he also hoped it would benefit those wishing to be ordained, and "Christian readers" in general. Thus a text that argued for love, persuasion, and responsibility in religious authority—and recognized the laity's influence upon the same—was within reach of secular society. Bernal's enhanced version of the *Aviso* was printed three times between 1543 and 1551, and obviously sold well in bookstores; Spaniards found it relevant, whether they belonged to the religious or secular sphere. This evidence suggests in turn that the religious elite in Spain might successfully promote an inclusive enterprise based on mutual respect instead of a bellicose one aimed at clerical supremacy. The content and publishing history of Bernal's work imply an unexpected scenario: the *Aviso* deplored corrupt and oppressive priests, made that critique available to the lay sphere, and thereby provided the means for communities to criticize their ecclesiastics in turn. Catholicism was a hierarchical experience in the early modern period. But clerical testimony reveals that power existed on both ends of the scale, by design as well as inadvertently.

Given the pastoral messages of these texts, their authors could be classified as Erasmian, at least as historians usually construe that label. The Spaniards advised the imitation of Jesus, cited the Gospels and the Pauline Epistles, referred to the Greek Father Chrysostom, and focused on moral rather than speculative endeavors. Maestro Avila and Dr. Bernal described their objectives as irrelevant to scholasticism: they wrote that decent preachers needed a profound knowledge of Scripture, and reading Scripture connoted a different style, spirit, and skill from what occurred in scholastic theology.[115] They demonstrated as much self-consciousness about forsaking dialectic as Luís Coronel did about adopting it at Valladolid. At the same time, Bautista expressly based his *Doctrina de sacerdotes* on 1 Timothy 3, which outlined the qualities of the good bishop. Valtanás packed his work with biblical references; Carranza offered different versions of scriptural passages as they occurred in different languages. In this genre, at least, the Spaniards neglected the more combative elements of religious controversy: their writings on the episcopate and the clergy were remarkably free from comments about heretics, given the epoch in which they worked; their exemplary bishops and ecclesiastics had more in common with managers than martyrs. These texts thus reveal ample testimony about the Spanish Renaissance as it typically is described. But such a portrait would relay only a portion of the evidence.

If ancient sources appeared in the Spaniards' treatises, so did ones by medieval authors. These clerics cited Bernard of Clairvaux as frequently as Chrysostom; they may have referred to Gregory I's *Regulae pastoralis liber*, but Gregory was just as common an authority for the twelfth and thirteenth centuries as for the fifteenth and sixteenth: he was no more "reborn" in the Renaissance than Ovid or Aesop; his invocation cannot be read as reverence for the primitive church. Furthermore, when Juan de Avila composed his second memorial for the Council of Trent, and pondered the religious education of theologians, he noted:

> The theology that holy men write, which is solid—and in which the authors agree with one another—should be preferred to theology that does not meet these conditions. For this reason it seems that the theology of St. Thomas and St. Bonaventura is the most useful to be taught in the schools, although individually each student may read other good authors.[116]

In this instance Maestro Avila was not addressing biblical study or preaching, but a summary of knowledge about the Godhead. Given his topic, it was appropriate to turn to Aquinas and Bonaventura; he even was attempting a kind of symmetry, since those individuals were the consummate authorities of the Dominican and Franciscan orders. Yet when he created a list of religious references for a correspondent, he continued to demonstrate his acquaintance with medieval materials and to sanction, implicitly, scholastic conventions.

In a list of useful sources for the cura animarum, Maestro Avila enumerated the following materials in the following order as he treated particular topics. All the material below is his.

On the dignity of the ecclesiastical office:
St. John Chrysostom's *De sacerdotio*.
The tenth and eleventh chapters of St. Gregory's *De pastoralis*.
The examples used by St. Gregory Nazianzus in his *Apologia*.
St. Gregory of Nyssa's *Vita Moises* [sic], which contained appropriate examples. . . .

On the importance of the priestly office in the Old Testament, and the difference between that office then and now:
St. Ciprian's *De singularitate clericorum*.

Jean Gerson's forty-first sermon, in the second volume of his *Opera,*
f. 234. . . .

On the care of the priests' conversation, especially in the context of the Mass:
St. Bonaventura, *De praeparatione ad Missam.*
Jean Gerson, same as above, f. 231.
Dionysius the Carthusian, *De regimine et vita curam animarum habentium,*
arts. 13 & 14.
Ubertino [de Casale], *Arbor vitae crucifixae, in mysterio de Caena Domini.*

On the sacrifice of the Mass and the ensuing need to flee conversation with women:
Martín de Frías, *De arte et modo audiendi confessiones;* there he stuffs in, most
copiously, the testimonies of the holy Fathers.[117]

Maestro Avila did not hesitate to cite near-contemporaries as authorities, for
he not only mentioned Frías but Bernal in the same document. More important, he envisioned his references as offering discrete bits of information: his
list betrays no sensitivity to the literary context of the works in question or
awareness of the historical circumstances in which they were composed.

When it came to recommending the Fathers of the Church, Maestro Avila
promoted Chrysostom's entire tract, but also told his correspondent to read
certain chapters from Gregory's *Regulae pastoralis liber,* and to pursue specific
examples from Gregory of Nyssa and Gregory Nazianzus. He directed his
reader to precise folios in Gerson. He noted that Frías had stuffed citations of
patristic authors into *De arte et modi audiendi confessiones,* and apparently expected his audience to exploit Frías as an intermediary source instead of
turning to the originals. His repertory suggests a mosaic method of reading,
for he clearly was fond of *exempla,* which were the smaller anecdotes and
passages that preachers would cull from sanctioned sources in order to give
their own work extra prestige and persuasiveness.

The propensities that Maestro Avila divulged here occurred in his peers'
writings too. Bernal cited Isidore of Seville's etymologies as well as Chrysostom's fear of ordination. Carranza adduced Bernard of Clairvaux in the
midst of the church fathers—as if they were equivalent—and quoted him at
length.[118] Even when the Spaniards invoked patristic sources, they most frequently cited them as references, nothing more. For instance, they often
raised Chrysostom as a sacred authority, but rarely devoted any space to the
actual content of his *De sacerdotio,* and then merely restated it: the upshot was
that they relayed ancient materials as if they were self-evident proofs.[119] The

fact that they littered their reflections with patristic quotations meant little, because they never expounded them. Their readers would have found it difficult if not impossible to copy patristic examples from their treatises, despite the fact that imitation was enjoined on the audience.

When it came to emulating shepherds in the Old and New Testaments, here too the Spaniards evinced less contextual and historical sensitivity than their modern reputations would imply. Valtanás turned Moses into an absent bishop: he reported that as soon as Moses went to talk to God on Mount Sinai, the Israelites fell into all sorts of errors, although Moses obviously had the best excuse for nonresidence in the world. Frías treated Jesus' entrance into Jerusalem as the model for an episcopal visitor's arrival in a pueblo, despite the profound differences between one era and the next.

More examples lie in texts by Carranza. To promote kind rhetoric as part of the clergy's pedagogical mission, Carranza referred his audience to the spiritual verses Galatians 4:19, Ephesians 5:14, and finally Hebrews 12:12. The first citation reads "my dear children, with whom I am in labor again, until Christ is formed in you," and is part of a larger sentence; Carranza found its gentle quality in the phrase "dear children." His second excerpt stipulated, "Thus it says, 'Awake, sleeper, and arise from among the dead, and Christ will enlighten you.'" His third was the most applicable to his point, for it relayed the concomitant joy and grief that discipline might bring. Taken together, the references demonstrate that Carranza, too, could approach Scripture as a mass of independent lines; in this instance, he handled the New Testament like a jigsaw puzzle, although he also could demonstrate an awareness of context, as when he appealed "to the emphasis of the words" in John 21:15–17.[120]

Finally, in a move akin to Flores's interpretation of "Ite in castellum," or Valtanás's depiction of Moses as an ecclesiastic, Carranza summoned Numbers 11:11–14 and 11:17 to illustrate what happened to pastors who did not care for their flocks. Carranza informed his readers that Moses complained about his pastoral duties in those scriptural lines, and God consequently "diminished in Moses the spirit of the Lord." Yet Carranza twisted the passage in Numbers to his own interpretative ends. In fact, after Moses griped about his burden to God, the Lord told him to gather seventy elders of Israel and place them at the door of the tabernacle; the Lord then told Moses, "I will come down and speak with you, and I will take of your spirit, and will give it to them, that they may bear the burden of the people with you, and you may not be burdened alone."[121] Carranza presented Moses as losing the Spirit of God when he merely was sharing it; he depicted Moses as punished by the Lord when he was pitied by the same.

Thus this particular intellectual—and Carranza was an adept and esteemed theologian—could slight scriptural language and context in order to prove a point that rested on scriptural example. The analogue to Carranza's maneuver was citing Cajetan to bolster episcopal residence in John 21. And in the case of 1 Timothy 3—which explicitly detailed the qualities of a bishop, and might have constituted a particularly apt source for the Spaniards to employ— Bautista literally wielded its directives as criteria for the cura animarum in his *Doctrina de sacerdotes.* Unfortunately, he ignored historical change as he moved the biblical text into his own work: as a result, he entitled Chapter 5, "That a cleric has not been married more than one time," although the Third Lateran Council made the marriage of clerics unlawful and invalid in 1179. His contemporaries tended not to expound 1 Timothy 3 at all, which may betray their awareness that the Church had altered with the centuries.

Then there was Bernal, who presents us with an intricate combination of historical sensitivity and ahistorical concerns. In the *Aviso de curas,* he commented that if Aristotle had lived in the Christian epoch, that philosopher would have agreed that boy-priests must not associate with women. Here Bernal coupled an appreciation for Aristotle's historical epoch with a desire to employ him as a guide to Christian morality; he illustrates an almost constant conundrum within humanist practice, which was how to appreciate the historical distance of a source while continuing to invoke it for pedagogical purposes.[122] More striking still were Bernal's musings on holy bishops, whose lives he compiled while stranded at Trent between 1547 and 1551. He entitled his project the *Historiae sanctorum episcoporum, ex codicibus variis collectae et alphabetico ordine secundum eorum nomina digestae;* the very title of the manuscript raises the matter of criticism, with its description of "histories" that were "collected." The problem is whether Bernal assessed saints' lives as he gathered them, or merely listed them in a sort of annal.

The prologue to the *Historiae* reveals as many conflicts over history and tradition as Ciruelo's prefaces to his biblical manuscripts. Bernal carefully explained how he had taken up the work because of the leisure and consequent spiritual danger that surrounded him once the first Tridentine sessions were suspended in 1547. He then thought about the lives of his episcopal predecessors, who had acted with the greatest sanctity and highest diligence; he concluded that their example might spur him and his colleagues to imitate them.[123] He began to assemble accounts of these holy men, and as time went on friends and acquaintances sent him more materials; he finally decided to gather the narratives into a single volume, so that his contemporaries could find them more easily.[124] Bernal employed unfamiliar authors as well as definitive ones in his enterprise, and purely local texts scarcely read outside their dioceses. He knew that his reliance on obscure writers would irritate many of his readers, "who cannot bear anything to be read in history, which may not be signed and delivered by the testimony of some famous author."[125] But he declined to emend the potential errors of his sources, because he believed their illustrious cases might prove fruitful for others.

At first glance, it looks as if Bernal applied little or no discrimination toward his materials. Yet his awareness of what he was *not* doing was marked. He noted that he had taken on the job of collector instead of historian—"cum me hoc in opere non historiographi sed collectoris dumtaxat partes suscepisse meminissem"—and his explanation of his decision was akin to Ciruelo's rationale for translating de verbo ad verbum.[126] He clearly understood the pitfalls of refusing to rank literary authorities: if distinctions were *not* made, "then vain comments and ridiculous stories can be received as true histories, and bequeathed for Christian assemblies in churches," whereupon they ultimately would obscure Catholicism.[127] Nevertheless, Bernal contended that the urge to appraise had gone too far, and he described the appraisers themselves as if they were snobs who respected only the most celebrated authorities and spurned everyone else. His language presages the perspective of Michel de Montaigne, the famous French humanist, who belittled his contemporaries for reading famous names as signs of serious intellectual activity.

Significantly, Bernal's reasons for not winnowing his materials disclosed more historical imagination and critical acumen than the logic of his potential critics. He asserted that the most eminent Christian authors, such as Jerome, Eusebius, and the like, were fallible: esteemed as such men were, they could not have encountered or heard of every holy man, especially ones whose miracles and works were limited to certain dioceses.[128] Although virtuous individuals might be unknown to the masses, that was no reason to reject them as models or to disdain the sources that relayed their experiences. Because of the harshness of the times in which they lived, or the ignorance and barbarity of the peoples among whom they worked, there may not have been writers to memorialize their sanctity in fulsome narratives.[129] If their deeds were transcribed in fragments, that should not stop men from emulating them; obscure but holy Fathers should not be demeaned because they lacked an elegant history and the backing of an illustrious writer. Such neglect would amount to the greatest injustice.

Because Bernal's manuscript is exceedingly rare, I have been unable to observe his presentation of the actual histories. We know from the *Historiae's* title and prologue that he arranged his materials in alphabetical order; it seems unlikely that he provided much editorial comment to the narratives. Certainly the register of the *Historia's* contents—the *Catalogus sanctorum episcoporum,* which Bernal sponsored as a companion volume—betrays no substantial criticism. Instead, it describes Ambrose at greater length than Augustine, mentions discrepancies in feast days, and occasionally records Bernal's investigative anecdotes, such as the fact that he once celebrated Mass beneath the headless body of St. Athanasius, or heard that the remains of St. Blaise lacked an arm.[130]

Bernal presents us with numerous dilemmas, and most of them are similar to ones we have already encountered. He insinuated the fallibility of the saints when he noted their inability to acquire the lives of every holy man; like some of the delegates at Valladolid, as well as Juan de Vergara, he implied that sacred authorities were human as well as holy. He relied upon historical imagination to demonstrate why some bishops had gained only local fame. He understood that accounts of a life, even a saint's, had to be written down by people. But if he pressed the emulation of the ancients, he also based that imitation on breviaries. He never addressed the practical obstacles to copying a model from an earlier period in the Church, despite changes in ecclesiology, ritual, and doctrine; he declined to expound the sort of imitation that he wanted to take place.

Instead, when Bernal advised his readers to follow the archetype according to their own abilities, he was not acknowledging individual talents, but summoning a literary cliché. When he detailed the whereabouts of bishops' tombs and the condition of their remains, he revealed his implicit attachment to relics; by collecting the lives of 864 ecclesiastics, he demonstrated the persistence of the local in the wake of a council devoted to the church universal.[131] Like the ecclesiastics examined in earlier chapters, Dr. Bernal and his peers displayed some signs of Renaissance techniques, but exhibited scholastic ones as well. Their combination of purportedly incompatible methods did not stop them from promoting virtuous and loving shepherds. Their example undermines even further the notion that pastoral messages matched particular intellectual propensities in sixteenth-century Spain.

Chapter Five

The Formation
of the Flock

In the sixteenth century, clerical shepherds officially and frequently associated with their rational sheep during the sacrament of penance. The process of confession and absolution implied a hierarchical structure, since judgment and pardon were entangled in the exchange; moreover, this experience was supposed to occur yearly in a Catholic Christian's life, at least hypothetically.[1] It is no wonder, then, that modern scholars so often link penance to dominion, for its implications about ecclesiastical power are unmistakable. The preoccupation that medieval and early modern intellectuals evinced with the sacrament only compounds its importance to contemporary historians. Thomas of Chobham, subdeacon of Salisbury Cathedral, composed a guide to its proper dispensation by 1216; Jean Gerson wrote Latin and vernacular works on it in the early fifteenth century.[2] Erasmus mocked inept confessors in his *Colloquies,* and nascent Protestants railed against the way penance seemed to turn human salvation into a rote process of exchange.[3] Ecclesiastics repeatedly noticed penance from the thirteenth through the sixteenth centuries, whether as a developing sacrament, a means of consolation, or a symbol of confessional difference. It was a ritual of clear significance to the epochs in question.

Nevertheless, countless difficulties block our attempts to reconstruct penitential practice, for we cannot know exactly how confession was conducted, or what expiations were demanded, for the medieval or even the early modern period. Interchanges between priest and penitent were supposed to be secret, and hence transcriptions of them are absent; furthermore, confessors did not keep records of the penances they handed out to ordinary individuals.

Although Inquisition sources from Spain relate incidents of clerical solicitation—when confessors petitioned sexual favors from their female penitents—complete trials of such episodes are scarce, and the scenes they recount atypical.[4] As a result, academics who investigate penance tend to rely on literature about administering it, for tracts on the subject appeared consistently throughout the medieval and early modern eras.

We call such tracts confessors' manuals, and they immediately raise questions about religious authority because of their treatment in modern scholarship. Investigators habitually decipher confessors' manuals as tools of clerical supremacy in the early modern epoch, and imagine that penance's role in clerical hegemony became that much more important because of a change in the codification of sin. According to a highly prominent argument, confessors and preachers began to emphasize the Ten Commandments over the Seven Deadly Sins between 1400 and 1600, with marked effects on the psyches of individual laypersons and the position of individual priests.[5] This shifting paradigm of sin presumably infiltrated the confessors' manuals and affected penitents accordingly. Current interpretations of the manuals thus make them a fit object of inquiry for this book, because these sources allegedly speak to religious authority as citation as well as to religious authority as power: the Commandments, for instance, were literature as well as Mosaic Law, and hence were liable to different readings and interpretative methods, despite our tendency to envision them as a static and immutable source.

In fact, it is in connection with a purported alteration in the taxonomy of sin that the manuals have something to say about textual criticism. Were it not for the supposed rise of the Ten Commandments in this period, I do not think these sources would offer us much insight into the Renaissance, except perhaps in the sense of Renaissance humanism as humane-ness. In terms of modeling and historical distance, the manuals too often contain simple lists of questions that lack explicit sources or medieval precedents; most writers also kept their biblical references to a minimum. Still, the possibility that the Decalogue became the predominant way to classify sin between the fifteenth and seventeenth centuries raises the prospect of history and philology. Some citations of the Ten Commandments could be more faithful to the scriptural text than others, while violations adduced against the Decalogue could evince more or less sensitivity to change over time.

Many confessors' manuals were written in Spanish and published between 1492 and 1570. Like treatises on bishops and priests, they reveal the sorts of hierarchies that the clerical elite advanced and the intellectual foundations of its priorities. They confirm the importance of antecedents to early modern intellectuals, but also illustrate the emendation of models to more inclusive and ambiguous ends. The goals that clerical authors promoted in the vernacular manuals are especially meaningful for our depictions of the Spanish sixteenth century, because these writings undoubtedly touched a very large number of people.

Such tracts inevitably were composed by ecclesiastics, most of whom were regular clergy, and again primarily members of the Franciscan and Dominican orders: there was a long-standing connection between the mendicant orders and this particular sacrament, for all that Dr. Bernal and his peers urged bishops and parish priests to supervise it. Vernacular treatises on penance varied in length and depth, but concurred in both structure and content; they usually advanced according to the process of the sacrament itself. They typically began with opening exchanges between priest and penitent, proceeded to the recitation of the Lord's Prayer and the Ave Maria, and then considered the penitent's transgressions.

The manuals summarized evil and virtuous deeds according to a number of schemes, including the Seven Deadly Sins, the Decalogue, the fourteen acts of spiritual and corporal mercy, and the five senses. Authors always raised the difference between mortal and venial sins, for only the former carried the obligation of confession. They addressed the special cases that were reserved to the bishop for absolution; they treated the aggravating conditions that could shift a lesser sin into a more grievous one, such as fornication with a nun in a cemetery. They might finish with lists of misdeeds attributable to particular professions.

The confessors' manual was a genre that any literate cleric could attempt; we have examples penned by ecclesiastics who otherwise never appear in the historical record, as well as ones written by more prominent figures. An anonymous Hieronymite monk composed a manual called the *Arte para bien confesar* sometime after 1500, and then apparently died; a brother of the same religious order, who remained nameless as well, updated the text; and it went through numerous editions in the first half of the sixteenth century.[6] Hernando de Talavera, another member of the Hieronymite order and the first archbishop of Granada, wrote his *Breve forma de confesar* sometime after that city was taken from the last Islamic kingdom in Spain in 1492; his manual fits into his broader efforts with the newly converted.[7] In what would be one more entry in a long career, Pedro Ciruelo published the first edition of his *Arte de bien confesar* in 1514; Pedro Covarrubias, a well-connected Dominican, used much of Ciruelo's text for his own *Memorial de pecados* in 1515.[8] Domingo de Valtanás—who addressed episcopal residence, as we saw in the previous chapter—wrote a Latin manual on confession in 1526 and a vernacular one, the *Confessionario,* in 1555.[9] Finally, the Franciscan Juan de Dueñas published the *Remedio de pecadores* in Valladolid in 1545, and a Dominican named Juan de Pedraza had a *Summa de casos de conciencia* printed in Alcalá in 1568.

Because these clerics often proclaimed their own role in the penitential sacrament and referred to their personal experience in their tracts, their manuals can look like unparalleled sources of information on penitents, priests, and monks. Still, we should suspect the degree to which these sources reflected an external reality: like other materials in previous chapters, whatever referentiality the manuals possessed was mixed with literary imitation, and their mimesis of earlier sources could be revealed by their very titles. For instance, when Pedraza called his work a *Summa de casos de conciencia,* he was tying his publication to materials from the late twelfth and especially thirteenth centuries. That literary genealogy is critical to the assessment of the Spaniards' early modern texts, for medieval Latin models affected their conventions. Significantly enough, scholarly explications of those earlier prototypes have also shaped the interpretation of the later, vernacular part of the genre.

The forerunner to all confessors' manuals was the Latin tract called the *summa de casibus* or *summa confessorum,* Latin phrases that denote "a compendium of cases of conscience," or "a summary of confessors."[10] The summae de casibus appeared in European history as penance was codified and promoted as a sacrament. By the end of the twelfth century, penance had evolved into a chiefly private ritual between priests and penitents; this development occurred alongside a new prominence for transgressions of thought and an increasing emphasis on motive and contrition in the confession of sins. These trends in turn were only bolstered by the twelfth-century revival of Aristotle, because his logic elevated the relationship between causes and effects. The process behind the commission of sin consequently became that much more important in the sacramental rite. And this new stress on incentives and sorrow deepened confessors' responsibilities, for they now had to know the mental, emotional, and circumstantial landscape behind the transgressions that penitents recounted to them.[11]

The codification of penance was formally recognized by the Church when Pope Innocent III and the Fourth Lateran Council reacted to changes already underway and issued the canon *Omnis utriusque sexus* in 1215: henceforth, the sacrament became at least an annual obligation for all men and women who had reached the age of discretion, or six to seven years of age. The papal decree of 1215 presumably enlarged the potential number of penitents. The issue, though, was whether friars, monks, and secular clerics were ready to listen to the confessions that awaited them. The solution was the summae de casibus, which were written specifically to prepare confessors for their office: these texts were supposed to help priests and friars administer the sacrament of penance properly. Ecclesiastics such as Robert of Flamborough, Thomas of Chobham, and Raymund de Penyafort wrote their summae for the intellectual improvement of their peers, who in turn might carry out the cura animarum with a surer understanding of sacramental theory and a sharper awareness of sin.[12]

Historians agree that the first confessors' manuals were supposed to relieve a specific predicament within the Christian Church, but they dispute the impulses that prompted their composition: some scholars attribute the summae to canon law, others to moral theology.[13] The debate has not produced any firm results, because the summae usually blended the canonical and the pastoral so thoroughly that it is nearly impossible to distinguish them according to legal or moral propensities. Their multiple emphases make sense once we realize that they carried a twofold purpose: they taught clerical readers how to weigh the gravity of sins, and relayed Christian doctrine to them. In this respect they are comparable to vernacular treatises on the episcopate and the parish priest, since they, too, combined corrective angles with pedagogical ones. Nonetheless, modern students of the summae have found it difficult to account for the simultaneous presence of disciplina and dilectio in a single tract.[14] And so while everyone recognizes that confessors' manuals were fundamentally instructional, numerous investigators accentuate the insidious effects of the summae's pedagogy.

The most influential scholarship on the manuals highlights their judicial qualities and their exaltation of clerics as arbitrators: in this instance, historians persistently link auctoritas to augere, and treat religious authority as simply insatiable.[15] Purportedly, at least, the manuals and penance imposed ecclesiastical standards of morality on a secular population, and the attempt to "clericalize" lay society then provoked anxiety and guilt in the culture at large.[16] In this scheme, Church teachings on penance stressed self-examination and remorse, both of which helped to provoke an internal sense of transgression. But confessors also waffled over the definition of terms, such as contrition and attrition, which were critical to the penitential process; to make matters worse, scholastic culture depended upon the citation of authorities, but never agreed upon the best references to invoke, or stipulated that everyone's references should agree.

As a result, authors of summae could summon different authorities on the same topic, disagree with each other, and even hesitate to offer an opinion, although they still encouraged inquiry. And when confessors expressed that equivocality toward the sexual misdeeds of penitents, the results were particularly deleterious.[17] For example, a Dominican could interrogate married men and women about sexual positions and even the motives for sexual intercourse, and then offer only equivocal conclusions about the degree of sin the penitents had incurred. The sinners thus were commanded to examine their thoughts and actions, only to be told that what they confessed was a transgression of more or less gravity.[18] Modern scholars do not believe that this scenario encouraged peace of mind.

Accordingly, historians have contended that penance's combination of self-scrutiny, intrusiveness, and ambiguity heightened the instability of the moral universe and elevated the psychological distress of Europeans in general, all of which helped to secure acceptance of moral and social rules promulgated by the Church.[19] Certainly clerics were victims of the same anxiety; after all, priests had to comply with the same economies of sin and the same rites of confession, and they too must have suffered from equivocal answers. Nevertheless, the penitential system and the creation of a guilt culture finally worked to ecclesiastics' benefit, because clerics retained the formal power to absolve sins, for all that they confused people about moral missteps in the first place.[20] If demands for self-scrutiny induced shame and apprehension in everyone, whether ecclesiastical or lay, and the inculcation of guilt coaxed the entire population into acceptance of broader norms, confessors still remained at the top of the scale.[21] The Latin and vernacular manuals on penance supposedly played a critical role in these processes.

For the historians in question, this paradigm goes so far as to explain both the Protestant Reformation and the Catholic phenomenon called dechristianization. Thus Martin Luther rejected the Church because it was overly rigorous, Johannes Oecolampadius (1482–1531) knew what he was doing when he labeled confessors *psychotyranni*, and French Catholics in the eighteenth century turned away from a Christianity that trumpeted only fear and guilt.[22] Early modern Catholicism had only itself to blame for such developments: it promoted relentless inquiry and an impenetrable vocabulary in its sacramental theology, and reaped the consequences. Its increasingly harsh trajectory was simply reinforced when it deserted the Seven Deadly Sins—pride, avarice, luxury or lust, wrath, gluttony, envy, and sloth—for the Decalogue.[23] New stress on the Commandments replaced flexible misdeeds, subject to discrete interpretation, with specific laws found in Scripture. The change signaled a metamorphosis from a vaguely communal sense of sin to one that elevated offenses against God. Infractions that touched society, such as wrath and greed, were supplanted by faults that relied upon God as the arbiter, such as blasphemy. The Decalogue presaged a morality that turned on an internal sense of sin, while furthering a relationship to the divine that relied upon trepidation.[24]

The historians who created this scheme did not develop their arguments from Spanish evidence, or specifically direct their conclusions toward the Iberian Peninsula. Yet their arguments have achieved such authoritative status that they have infiltrated treatments of religion everywhere. Hence the Counter-Reformation in Catalonia revolutionized confession, and confessors' manuals in turn became critical elements for the dissemination and inculcation of a new, reformed morality; the manuals "devoted considerable space to sexual difficulties," including ones likely to affect the clergy.[25] Such literature helped project "hostility to sex . . . onto the faithful," and change the Catalan Church from a nonclerical, nonsacramental Catholicism—fixed in local communities and marked by agrarian rituals—into a religion defined by clerical privilege, the reception of the sacraments, and the performance of social obligations, albeit within the same small locales.[26]

When penance is the specific focus of inquiry, and not just part of a larger story about Spanish Catholicism, the effects of the historiography become even clearer. As the sixteenth century progressed, Spanish priests allegedly became even more vulnerable to the Church's increasingly rigid discourse on morality, for they were part of the system; as the Church's strictures became more severe, they suffered accordingly.[27] Yet priests enjoyed power despite their travails, because their role in penance made their relationship with the laity inherently unequal. For all their personal vulnerability in the wake of the Tridentine decrees, clerics were finally allowed and even encouraged to enforce their preeminence. Confessors derived their understanding of penance from literature, that is, the manuals, that evinced an authoritarian tone; they acted, essentially and consistently, like conservatives, who tried to inculcate, maintain, and extend the constituted authorities, whether religious or political.[28] These confessors pursued ever more detailed inquiries into their penitents' sexuality, leaving "many married persons with a pervasive sense of uneasiness and guilt about their sexual relations." The need to confess sins fully and "the incessant demand for slavish obedience to the confessor" effectively placed penitents under clerical thumbs.[29] Ultimately, the power dynamic within the sacrament was duplicated in the culture at large, and the best ecclesiastics were ones whose comportment would mark them as "morally distinct from and superior to secular society."

As Spanish clerics and their European counterparts distinguished their conduct and status from the laity, that process was furthered by the promulgation of the Ten Commandments over the Seven Deadly Sins as the measure of moral transgression.[30] Therefore, the most recent scholarship on Spain encourages us to see three large developments in the moral universe of the Catholic sixteenth century. Priests corrected their own behavior, bettered their understanding of doctrine, and consequently won greater respect and more acquiescence from the laity. The laity in turn cast their religious concerns inward and began to deprecate the material world, to think of themselves only as individuals before God, and to neglect their communal environment. Eventually, the Catholic population was divided into two separate and ever stricter camps of ecclesiastics and laypersons; that same population had absorbed lessons about difference, distance, and trepidation when it came to the Creator and even the priesthood.

Despite the frequent acknowledgment that priests were casualties of the same religious system, scholarship on penance and sin encourages us to read Catholic history as a competition between clerical and secular values in the early modern period. These arguments duplicate, in structure if not in content, other dichotomies in Spanish history for the same period. They reinforce the image of a Spain divided in two—whether those blocs consisted of Erasmians and scholastics, the laity and the clergy, or the material and spiritual worlds—and stratified vertically.

For all their popularity and eloquence, the usual contentions about early modern penance become remarkably tenuous in light of Church structures, ecclesiastical practice, and the confessors' manuals themselves, whether in Latin or the vernacular. Penance may have evolved into a chiefly private transaction by the early thirteenth century, and we might suppose that privacy was a prerequisite for the interrogation of penitents; nevertheless, the sacrament always entailed publicity, from the environment in which confessions occurred to the satisfaction imposed on the penitent.[31] Then again, it is difficult to imagine confessors' manuals as instruments of clerical control when clerical absenteeism made the very reception of penance doubtful for many Catholics, even into the sixteenth century. If penance had been dispensed regularly, most Catholics would have received it only once or several times a year, which looks like a rather slim foundation for ecclesiastical despotism.[32]

As for the summae de casibus, their most obvious features do relay an interest in motives, contrition, and an increasingly elaborate arrangement of misdeeds. Numerous medieval summae evinced interrogatory formats; by the middle of the thirteenth century, many writers also began to arrange their manuals alphabetically—which should have eased interrogations—and all of them spent a number of folios on sexual sins. In this last regard, the early fifteenth-century tract by Jean Gerson, entitled *De arte audiendi confessiones,* probably is the most notorious, for it spends a great deal of space explaining how to cajole adolescents into admissions of masturbation.

Yet the summae's devotion to motive, detail, and sexual misconduct did not translate wholly and inevitably into confessional practice. The summae cannot be read as recipes for the administration of penance because they were written as reference guides: their earliest incarnations often outlined the most difficult aspects of the sacrament, but over time they came to delineate every element of the rite. In 1225, Raymund of Penyafort, general of the Order of Preachers, angled his *Summa casuum* toward sins against God, transgressions against neighbors, and the description of irregularities in canon law; in 1518, Sylvester de Prierias propelled his readers from "absolution" to "abbesses" to "abrogation," and dedicated thirty-one folios to varieties of excommunication.[33] By the fourteenth century, the typical summa simply embodied the realm of potential situations a confessor might encounter. It amounted to an encyclopedia.

The Latin manuals also treated the confessors' discretion as a crucial part of the sacramental process. No confessor ever grilled a layperson or a cleric over all the sins that the summae offered for consideration, because he was supposed to target only the transgressions that were relevant to the penitents at hand. If treatises on priests and bishops candidly insisted that human beings should be treated as individuals, penitential tracts implied the same thing, since they presented different professions, ages, and circumstances as liable to particular misbehaviors. Furthermore, every author of a Latin confessors' manual, from Thomas of Chobham to Archbishop Antoninus of Florence, and Alain de Lille to Cajetan, warned their clerical audience about superfluous and inappropriate questions, and exhorted their readers to hesitant rather than meddlesome queries.[34] Such instructions weaken the connections that modern scholars routinely make between the manuals' content and the depth and range of real confessions.[35]

Manuals in Spanish, like ones in other European vernaculars, followed their Latin prototypes to a greater or lesser degree, and reveal the same corrections to the usual paradigm. Guides to penance in Spanish or French or

German were reference works as well, with censures against aggressive questioning; they were no more transcriptions of penitential practice than their Latin archetypes. At the same time, though, the Spanish texts also diverged from their Latin models in important ways, and those differences should further diminish our scholarly presumptions about this literary genre. One crucial distinction lay in the matter of audience. Historians always have rightly supposed that Latin summae were composed by clerics for their own peers. But they have erred in tying the vernacular sources to the same constituency alone. In fact, Spanish authors presented laymen and women as part of their readership too, either through direct statements or evocative rhetoric.

Sometimes the Spaniards openly included the laity in their audience, as when Ciruelo noted that "the present treatise . . . in our common language of Spain not only will be useful for confessors who have to examine the consciences of their penitents, but also for discerning laypersons, who with this discourse will be able to execute well the Apostle's counsel that says, 'Now a man shall inspect himself,' etc."[36] Valtanás proceeded with the same expectations, for he simultaneously issued directions for priests and penitents, and frankly remarked that the latter—who, after all, could be ecclesiastics as well as laypersons—should prepare for their recitation of sins with the help of a confessionario.[37] Covarrubias wrote his Memorial de peccados for his own use, "so that when [I] hear confession, I have it on hand"; then he adopted the first-person voice of the penitent in his exposition of the general confession, and the second-person one as he relayed the priest's potential responses. Even as late as 1567, the Archbishop of Valencia, Martín Pérez de Ayala, explicitly directed his confessors' manual to penitents as well as priests in his diocese.[38]

Finally, although the anonymous Hieronymite tried in 1507 to reserve parts of his manual to the clergy, by directing Latin marginalia to confessors alone, he undermined his own scheme by using Spanish in the main body of the text.[39] At times, he would imitate the confessor's voice: "You, sinner, where will you appear? Over there the just will hear the sweet voice of our Redeemer . . . but over there the wicked and the sinners will hear the sad and bitter voice that will condemn them to endless fire. . . . So look, look with great perseverance, and with all your powers, into your heart."[40] Elsewhere the Hieronymite relayed the sequence that penitents followed, which included an apology for being late, and assumed their persona, as when he wrote: "I express to God . . . my enormous fault, that I do not love God, nor have I served Him whole-heartedly, and with as much love and fervor as I ought."[41]

Although scholars have tried to divide vernacular manuals from Italy ac-

cording to a predominantly lay or clerical readership, that effort will not ac-
commodate the Spanish sources.[42] The Spaniards dropped Latin into their
treatises, including the form of absolution, but they also included sufficient
rhetorical clues and substance to reveal the laity as part of their audience.[43]
When we combine such subtle signs with explicit allusions to readership,
the Spaniards clearly presumed that the laity would read their works. Testimony from another type of source demonstrates that their beliefs were not
outlandish.

If works on the ideal priest appeared in Spanish bookstores, their quantity
was minuscule in comparison to the numbers of vernacular confessors' manuals that surfaced in the same venues. The manuals were routine items in the
devotional publishing boom that swept sixteenth-century Spain, and they
were offered at prices that should have enabled all but the destitute to get hold
of them. In 1556, Juan de Junta's shop in Burgos stocked three copies of
Archbishop Antoninus's *Defecerunt,* in Spanish translation; fifty-one copies of
a *Confessionario* by the fifteenth-century canonist Alonso de Madrigal; and
thirteen copies of Ciruelo's *Arte de bien confessar.* The *Defecerunt* was priced at
either 30 or 51 maravedís, Madrigal's work at 20 or 25, and Ciruelo's at 12 or
34; the higher prices reflected work that was bound.[44] Even more emphatic
findings emerge from the stock of Juan de Ayala's bookstore in Toledo,
which was inventoried in 1556 as well. In Ayala's emporium, a customer
could choose from 500 anonymous *Confisionarios breves,* 952 anonymous *Confisionarios,* 4 copies of the *Espejo de conciencia,* and 314 of Ciruelo's *Arte de bien
confesar;* although anonymous titles would have been eliminated by the 1559
Index, at least hypothetically, there were plenty of explicitly authored works
to take their place.[45] Prices in Toledo were similar to ones in Burgos, with
Ciruelo's manual selling at 10 maravedís for an unbound copy. That sum is
quite significant: laborers in Castile very easily could have purchased the *Arte
de bien confesar,* as well as other examples of the genre.

The quantity and prices of Spanish confessors' manuals reinforce what we
have gleaned from their content: this literature was geared to penitents as well
as confessors, and it could fall into anyone's hands. Such inclusivity signals a
critical difference between the Latin summae de casibus and their Spanish
counterparts, and even more distinctions occurred too, the most fundamental
of which was the Spaniards' recognition that they were poised between two
competitive objectives, comprehensiveness and utility. On the one hand, they
wanted their manuals to include what was imperative for the sacrament of
penance; on the other, they could not copy the exact content of the summae
without making their own materials extremely cumbersome, a predicament

they candidly admitted.[46] As they attempted to balance the encyclopedic with the essential, they selected what to treat and what to discard. It is difficult to claim a similar process of discrimination for the writers of the summae de casibus, who very often equated value with illustration—witness Prierias's thirty-one folios on excommunication—and who did not envision carrying their manuals in their pockets. These differences actually make the vernacular manuals better sources for investigating religious authority and a changing moral ethos, than penitential literature explicitly cast as exhaustive. The texts under review here necessarily involved authorial discretion, despite their clear imitation of Latin and even other Spanish models. Given their attempts to reach a lay as well as clerical audience, their authors deliberately circulated a particular morality to the widest possible readership.

The next question is what moral gauge Spanish clerics preferred to invoke. Notwithstanding scholarly arguments about a shifting moral calculus in this period, we find more evidence of syncretism than substitution when we evaluate the Spaniards' preferences for various arrangements of misdeeds. In the first half of the sixteenth century, Spanish manuals preserved both the Seven Deadly Sins and the Decalogue, and arranged them sequentially; the same is true for their Italian analogues. These authors routinely positioned the Ten Commandments before the Seven Sins, but very few expressed any difference in rank between the two economies; instead, they left the impression that they were equivalent in authority. They even might rate the Seven over the Ten by giving more space to transgressions against the former's code. For instance, Talavera labeled pride and spiritual sloth (*accidia*) as violations of the First Commandment, and thereby arranged his material as if the Decalogue governed the Seven Sins; nonetheless, when it came to the length of his expositions, he spent more time on pride and spiritual sloth than any other misdeeds under the Mosaic subheading. Italian manuals demonstrate the same propensity in even stronger ways, for their authors devoted many more folios to avarice than to any of the Commandments, although they ordinarily addressed the Ten before the Seven.[47]

Such structural clues are amplified by the Spaniards' overwhelming tendency to blend the substance of the two taxonomies, to the point that they force us to ask when the Decalogue really signified the Ten Commandments; this literature, too, illustrates the potential deceptiveness of sixteenth-century discourse, since it is all too easy to mistake headings for content.[48] Spanish authors might call up Exodus's formal admonitions, but more frequently than not they went on to inject the Seven Deadly Sins into them. Talavera's title highlighted the Ten Commandments as the axis of his manual, but he reproduced the sixth precept as "You shall not be luxurious" instead of "You shall not commit adultery." Covarrubias knew what the Sixth Commandment prohibited, but adduced love songs (*cantares de amores*), shaving, and lavish apparel as infractions against it; he followed that exposition with one against luxury, which contained queries about adultery, among other things.[49] The Hieronymite, too, connected the sixth precept to luxury.[50]

The tendency to fuse the wording of the two taxonomies was eased by relentless allegory: the Fourth Commandment, on honoring parents, frequently turned into a lecture on obedience to civil lords; the third precept, on observing the Jewish Sabbath, became an injunction to keep Church feast days. In these respects, the Spaniards were merely following their authorities, for earlier writers of manuals demonstrated the same tendencies, whether in Latin or the vernacular. Although historians contend that Gerson in particular accelerated the change from one moral system to another, his vernacular and Latin texts exemplify the tendency to syncretize the two economies: for example, he listed the Decalogue's precepts in the *ABC des simples gens* while surrounding them with septenary formulas, and routinely phrased the Sixth Commandment in terms of luxury.[51]

The larger point is that we cannot read the Decalogue as a symbol of moral change when these writers so often transformed it into the system they were purportedly discarding. As in Erasmus's use of curiositas, or the Complutensian Polyglot's critical apparatus, confessors' manuals may raise a sign we think we recognize, such as the Ten Commandments, but then fail to produce what we expect. For Spanish works on penance in this period, I have found historical and philological insight applied to the Decalogue in just one instance, namely, by Ciruelo, who knew the actual language of the precepts as a Hebrew scholar and reproduced them in his manual, albeit in Latin translation. He consistently exhibited closer and more historical readings of Exodus than his peers. He explicitly kept adultery as the center of the Sixth Commandment, for he wrote that that offense was more injurious to one's neighbor than all the rest, and hence had been forbidden explicitly.[52]

Ciruelo also treated the Commandments with some awareness of their purely Jewish context. His peers routinely included the offense of not tithing under the First Commandment, and Ciruelo did so as well, but he also inserted material on offerings and sacrifices, which he advised for an extraordinary reason:

God wants to be visited and recognized by His servants; and they should not appear before Him empty-handed, without bearing some part of the goods which God has given them for His service and the maintenance of His ministers; and in order to make a public declaration that they are God's vassals, and whatever goods they have, are from Him.[53]

Notwithstanding his acontextual use of "vassal," Ciruelo explained these sacrifices through their earliest Jewish history, as literal demonstrations of God's community; he infused the Jewish meaning of such offerings into a Christian exposition. He went on to render the Third Commandment as a directive to keep the Sabbath holy, and then tied the meaning of "Sabbath" to "rest."[54] Finally, and uniquely, he even reproduced the actual language of the First Commandment in Latin—"Non habebis deos alienos coram me" ("You shall not have other gods before Me")—and expressed the gist of it as the "loyalty or fidelity that man owes to God."[55] His elevation of the first precept also was palpable in terms of space: he spent twenty-two folios on that commandment alone, and covered the remaining nine in a mere twenty-seven.

Ciruelo's infusion of the Decalogue's language and historical setting into his treatise was singular among confessors' manuals in the first half of the sixteenth century. Its novelty did not hurt its circulation, for the *Arte de bien confesar* went through twenty-two editions between 1514 and 1560; its very popularity could support the idea of a shifting moral ethos, since Spaniards plainly found its more literal exposition of the Decalogue appealing. But Ciruelo's acumen with the Old Testament did not override his intellectual inheritance, and it is consequently untenable to posit his manual's success as proof of a new biblical foundation for Christian morality. Ciruelo preserved septenary formulas throughout his text, from seven principal interrogations on the Sixth Commandment to seven varieties of idolatry. He called adultery a type of luxury, fastened the Third Commandment to feast days as well as the Sabbath, and allegorized the language of the fourth and fifth precepts to include spiritual and temporal parents, and spiritual and emotional murder. He also transcribed the First Commandment as more than just "Non habebis deos alienos coram me." Notably, the way he and his colleagues rendered that mandate raises further obstacles to viewing the Decalogue as a sign of a particular codification of sin.

Without exception, Ciruelo's colleagues took their version of the First Commandment from Matthew 22:37–39. They supplied it as a variation of

You shall love the Lord your God with all your heart and all your soul and all your mind; this is the first and greatest commandment. And the second is similar to it, that you shall love your neighbor as yourself. On these two commandments depend all the law and the prophets.

163

instead of working with Exodus 20:2–6:

I am the Lord your God, who brought you out of the land of Egypt, out of the house of bondage. You will not have strange gods before me. You will not make a graven image for yourself, nor the likeness of any thing that is in heaven above, or in the earth beneath, nor of those things that are in the waters under the earth. You will not adore them, nor serve them; I am the Lord your God, mighty, jealous, visiting the iniquity of the fathers upon the children, until the third and fourth generation of them that hate me; and showing manifold mercy to these who love me, and keep my Commandments.

The Spaniards preferred Jesus and Matthew over Moses and Exodus. Their choice arose from the same interpretative conventions that led Christian intellectuals to direct the Old Testament to Christian ends.

The Spaniards would have found their choice justified by Aquinas and then by Aristotle. As we have seen in medieval and early modern exegesis, Aristotelian logic stipulated that the last in order of execution was the first in order of conception, and Aquinas worked that "Aristotelian metaphysic of final causality" into his theological system. For Aquinas and his Christian successors, Jesus' fulfillment of the Law came before the Law itself, in both chronology and importance. Accordingly, the Commandments became a subordinate, intermediate step between the Law's original conception and final execution. Aquinas explained that the two precepts of Matthew were the primary and general principles from which the ten of Exodus flowed as more specific precepts. The Decalogue was still obligatory, because God had proclaimed it; it was part of divine law. But its recapitulation in the New Testament took precedence over its expression in the Old.[56]

Between 1492 and 1568, every Spanish author of a vernacular confessors' manual used Jesus' summary of the Law in his transcription of the First Commandment. Even Ciruelo prefaced the phrase "you shall not have other gods before me" with "you shall love the Lord Your God with all your heart, etc."; he would preserve that reading in a witchcraft treatise explicitly centered on the Decalogue.[57] Covarrubias followed him and noted "the First Commandment has two parts: the first is 'adore your Lord God,' the second 'serve him alone.'" Their contemporaries, too, redacted the precept in terms of love. Talavera wrote, "the First Commandment, in short, is to adore only one God, to serve Him, honor Him, and love Him above all else."[58] Dueñas gave the first maxim in its New Testament version as well, while Pedraza remarked that "The Ten Commandments are summarized or contained in two, which are of natural law: You shall love God with your entire heart, and your neighbor as yourself. . . . From these the ten particular precepts follow, as conclusions from general principles."[59]

Pedraza's reliance on Aquinas was obvious, and Valtanás's rendition was no different: the Commandments were reduced to two general mandates—to love God above all else, and one's neighbors as oneself—that functioned as the proper objectives of all ten precepts.[60] Even by the 1550s and 1560s, when it looks as if Exodus were invoked more frequently for the First Commandment, the quotation was always accompanied by bits of Matthew 22, as if authors were balancing their authorities. Martín de Azpilcueta used the language of the Old Testament in his rendition of the Decalogue, but summarized the latter according to the "two [Commandments] that presuppose all the precepts of the Decalogue as first principles."[61] The same habit of listing Exodus's rendition first, and then inserting Matthew's, also occurred in Pérez de Ayala's *Breve compendio* (1567).[62]

Like other sources we have examined, the confessors' manuals involve problems of alterity: when it comes to the Decalogue, their authors employed terms that we can identify, but which can utterly mislead us; we expect Moses when we would do better to imagine Jesus. Moreover, when the Spaniards phrased the First Commandment as if it pertained to affection instead of judgment, their proclivity should threaten modern equations among the Decalogue, an Old Testament God, and a Christianity that was marked by anxiety.[63] These authors had a clear ability to meld what we customary sever.

Still, it seems fair to ask whether the purported effects of the Decalogue could have permeated confessors' manuals even if literal renditions of the Commandments were not there. Prevailing arguments about early modern morality teach us to expect emphases on the ethereal, the individual, and the hierarchical in texts on penance. But the Spanish religious elite did not advocate separating the soul from the body, the individual from the community, or the clergy from the laity in sources about confession or the episcopate. Western Christianity did not reject the body, despite its attention to managing it, and neither did its spokespersons: whether in the sixth or the sixteenth century, Catholicism was not a dualistic religion, split between the spirit and the flesh.[64] Even writers on confession could envision Christians as neighbors in a decidedly physical world; they portrayed penitents, whether clerical or lay, as intelligent collaborators in their own justification; they construed their readers as rational sheep. Instead of merely advocating a line of control that moved from the top down, these clerical authors opened up the relationship between priest and penitent to mutual correction. They promoted a muted religious authority through a medieval genre, in the same way that writers on the episcopate and the priesthood advanced change through scholastic reasoning.

The Spaniards' works make it impossible to dismiss the importance of the communal milieu and even the physical body to clerical authors, if only because they continued to employ the Seven Deadly Sins as a taxonomy. Pride, avarice, and envy connoted human relationships, for they depended upon evaluating one's position against others'. As Talavera remarked, pride appeared

when someone thinks, or gives to understand, that the good that he possesses comes from himself; or that if God gave it to him, it was on account of his merits; or when he deprecates other equals, or those greater than himself; and when he wishes to be reputed, held, or respected above all others, in anything that may be good or bad, spiritual or corporal.[65]

In the last line of the quotation, Talavera seemed to be reflecting distinct categories of the flesh and the spirit; still, the sin he expounded would surface most easily through speech and gestures. Pride's presence in the heart, attested by the verbs "thinks," "gives to understand," and "wishes," was discernible through observation, when sinners forced other people to recognize their excellence, or deprecated their equals or superiors. Even accidia, which was the last of the Seven Sins and signified spiritual sloth, could be expressed physically, since it prompted curiosity, talkativeness, and movement from place to place.[66]

There is nothing mysterious about linking the Seven Deadly Sins to the social environment, at least according to modern visions of their effects. What is arresting, though, is the degree to which these writers tied the Ten Commandments to material and neighborly surroundings as well. Some of those connections occurred because the Spaniards read the Decalogue as the Seven Sins. But the Spaniards also had a precedent for expressing social concerns through the Decalogue itself, for Isidore of Seville (ca. 560–630) had divided it into two parts, and had stipulated that the first three mandates entailed sins against God, the rest transgressions against people. Thus early modern writers could expound the Decalogue as if it pertained to wider human society, and not just the specific relationship between the human and the divine. The Commandments' very language could imply failings against the community, since the fifth precept against murder and the seventh against theft depended upon the injury of others.

But the Spaniards fastened other maxims to society as well. Covarrubias read the Eighth Commandment—against bearing false witness—in terms of judicial processes, which might cause feuds; Ciruelo isolated adultery as the gist of the sixth precept because it did the most damage to neighbors.[67] All noted the ruinous effects of scandal, which presupposed observation, gossip, and a larger context than just single individuals or specific households. They even prodded overtly internal precepts into social harm, as when Valtanás explained that the Ninth and Tenth Commandments prohibited the wish to murder, rob, and fornicate.[68] The Spanish manuals finally demonstrated the importance of the larger environment by accentuating the sins most likely to befall the practitioners of various occupations. However clichéd their ties between specific professions and certain misdeeds, their lists revealed the social contexts in which sins were likely to occur.[69]

I consequently would argue that these authors aimed at the same ends as writers on bishops and priests: they, too, wished to reinforce penitents' regard for the general good over concern for their families alone, to the point that Covarrubias grounded all his taxonomies of sin on the challenge of living well and peacefully within a community.[70] Still, the Spaniards' attention to the material world occurred alongside exhortations to self-criticism; those exhortations may lend credence to the modern notion that the manuals encouraged an interiorized religiosity and individual feelings of guilt. Every Spaniard began by asking penitents to prepare for the sacrament. These authors presumed that such groundwork in turn revolved around the contemplation of past behavior; they thought it crucial that penitents recall and regret their transgressions.

Accordingly, Ciruelo asked his readers if they had studied their consciences, reduced their sins to memory, and formed a resolution to correct their lives.[71] Pedraza wanted penitents to perceive their faults by examining their conduct through the Ten Commandments and the Seven Deadly Sins; he also thought they should brace themselves for confession by rehearsing their sins out loud and mustering both sorrow and regret over them. He stressed the emotional impact of what amounted to a spiritual exercise: "And it would be good if every time the penitent says 'I accuse myself, father, of such-and-such a sin,' he should have a special pain from it; because as the heart speaks with so many blows, it shall eventually bequeath a perfect pain for the penitent's past life in its entirety, which is the contrition that justifies the soul."[72] The confessor should help this process along through the use of shame or fear.

The Hieronymite's manual was unparalleled in recommending a replete self-criticism in emotional terms. It started with an admonition to "bring the penitent to compunction and contrition, and put fear and terror of Judgment Day into him," which was framed in the second-person voice.[73] The same monk told his readers to work themselves into a contrite state by considering how much they deserved to be damned; he instructed them to prepare for confession by trying to recall all their sins since the age of six. He enumerated sixteen adjectives that characterized a good confession, among them simple, humble, pure, faithful, frequent, clear, discrete, voluntary, and shameful; some of these conditions obviously entailed an internal sense of error. And the Hieronymite also repeated the eight "circumstances of sin" that should govern the penitent's narrative, or questions of who, what, where, for whom, how many times, why, in what manner, and when, all of which might deepen the sense of sin even further.[74]

Clearly a deliberate and comprehensive assessment of misbehavior, and a corresponding awareness of culpability, played a meaningful role in Spanish visions of ideal penitential practice. Not only was the confessor supposed to elicit a fulsome account of serious transgressions, but penitents should evaluate their sins beforehand and summon up appropriate feelings of guilt.[75] It was no accident that Ciruelo linked his manual's utility to the apostle's recommendation to "inspect oneself"; to an extent, that emphasis was predictable because contrition played such a prominent role in the theological discourse on this particular sacrament. And yet the secondary literature insists that the scrutiny and sorrow demanded by these treatises, as well as their Latin prototypes, amounted to a license for religious coercion and triggered the formation of a guilt culture. When most historians put the summae's demands for self-examination together with the same texts' persistent inquiries into sex—and only cryptic answers about sin—they find a dynamic that imparted more culpability than consolation.[76]

Scholars have singled out the summae de casibus's attention to sex to illustrate the imposition of monastic ideals and shame on the lay population. They point to the sheer extent of queries about masturbation and bestiality, incest and sodomy, wanton intercourse within marriage and fornication without. Latin authors assessed sexual positions according to their potential obstruction of procreation, and ended by labeling as sinful any posture except the missionary one. The summae decried oral and anal sex as sins against nature; they inveighed against intercourse during menstruation, pregnancy, and church feast days. Confessors as well as penitents could fall under the same proscriptions, with masturbation and homosexuality being particularly relevant to a monastic environment. But if clerics suffered even more from new codes of sexual behavior, or on occasion issued relatively "laxist" opinions about conjugal sexuality, on balance the Latin summae promoted a fundamentally pessimistic approach to sex, even in the case of married men and women.[77]

Given the Spanish manuals' emulation of their Latin predecessors, their authors could hardly omit the category of sexual misbehavior: in fact, all of them addressed that particular topic under either the Sixth Commandment or the third deadly sin of luxury. As with other matters of content and structure, though, the Spaniards did not literally replicate their models' discourse, and their discrimination with sex becomes particularly important in light of the prevailing scholarship. Remarkably, in nearly every instance the vernacular texts excluded elements of the most replete sexual interrogatories. They might address the same categories of sexual sin, but they almost always abbreviated their comments on the misdeeds in play; they issued positive statements about sex between married couples, and deleted the luxurious proclivities that supposedly tempted those pairs.

Covarrubias pursued a typical breakdown of carnal transgressions—fornication, adultery, rape of a virgin, deliberate birth control, sex in a sacred setting, sex with a menstruating or pregnant female, and lascivious intercourse with a wife, "as if she were a stranger"—but omitted any consideration of sexual positions.[78] Pedraza neglected to consider sodomy. Talavera rebuked sex on feast days, and with pregnant and menstruating women as well; he, too, adjured modesty in married sex, so that the couple would act like a husband and wife, instead of a pimp and his whore.[79] But Talavera also explained the rationale for marriage in terms of companionship as well as procreation, and ignored the topic of sexual positions. Ciruelo preserved the usual cases, or fornication, adultery, defilement of virgins, incest, sins against nature, and luxury within the matrimonial state. Yet in his exposition of such transgressions, he devoted a single line to bestiality, eliminated the consideration of sex during holy seasons, and erased the bans on oral and anal sex for married couples. He lessened the prohibition of masturbation between husbands and wives; he also neglected to treat sexual positions. He declared that intercourse between married couples could be as virtuous an act as any other, and asserted that sex between husbands and wives for pure pleasure was not sinful.[80]

So far as their content was concerned, none of the Spaniards' points about sex was original. Yet it is worth remembering that these authors engaged in a critical process when they produced their manuals. They chose what sexual items to include in the face of their Latin authorities; they decided how much space to devote to particular issues; the diminutions and omissions in their texts were not accidental. Furthermore, between 1500 and 1555 Ciruelo's *Arte de bien confesar* went through more editions than any other vernacular confessors' manual in Spain: given the degree to which it circulated, its emphases are especially important. In comparison to its Latin predecessors, it reduced the importance of sexual sin within the confession as a whole; it affirmed the worth of married sex, and then disseminated that message throughout Castile, to lay as well as ecclesiastical audiences, and penitents as well as confessors. Rather than inflicting clerical values upon secular men and women when it came to sex, Ciruelo mitigated those ideals in favor of working with lay realities, however much his recommendations depended upon Christian morality.

Ciruelo and his peers may have diminished the summae's sexual content out of fear they were teaching the laity what it did not already know; that concern was a commonplace in the literature as a whole. They followed another tradition when they explicitly prohibited unnecessary queries in their expositions of sexual sins. Yet I suspect their excisions meant even more than respect for married couples, concern for the sexually inexperienced, or adherence to typical counsel, for detailed interrogations about sex could work to the clergy's disadvantage.

The most provocative evidence of such a scenario comes from a Spanish translation of Antoninus's *Defecerunt,* which remarks that confessors should not ask minute questions about sex because "sometimes such things afterward are narrated in the plazas for ridicule and scandal at the priests' expense."[81] Apparently confessors as well as bishops and parish priests could fear the exasperation of the laity and their mockery: if they took the cura animarum seriously, then they had to esteem secular lives as well investigate them. The Spaniards' curtailment of sexual material reveals a certain deference toward moral sexual activity, however construed, as much as a reaction to purely practical considerations of space; after all, these authors could have chosen other areas to abbreviate. When they compressed the manuals' interrogations on sex, they were weakening the barrier between the clerical and lay spheres.

Given their perspective on married sex and sexual sin in general, it also seems meaningful that these ecclesiastics treated women as relatively equal to men; they indulged in fewer sexual stereotypes than we might have imagined. Ciruelo thought both men and women were liable to adultery and illegitimate children and could be equally responsible for abortions, either through potions or blows.[82] Valtanás disputed the notion that sex during menstruation was a mortal sin; he insisted that the absence of a bloodstain did not imply a lack of virginity, and overtly sympathized with a woman's tribulations in marriage.

> The harshest estate a person can take on is matrimony, especially for the woman, who from being free is captured and subjected to a thousand miseries and needs and dangers; and the greatest of all is that she has to live her entire life—eating and sleeping and conversing—in one house with one man. . . . And for this reason it is said that a woman is not herself who says yes to marriage.[83]

Lest we interpret his statements as a recommendation for the female religious life, Valtanás also rejected the forced entry of daughters into convents: "a man must not make a person a nun if such a vocation does not come very much from the heart, and the woman has thought about it for numerous days, and asked for it very many times."[84]

I would contend, then, that Spanish manuals belie the secondary literature, for they offer a more positive vision of laymen and women, and married sexual activity, than scholarly treatments of them have implied. Nevertheless, these tracts might have provoked psychic distress in one final regard: their sheer variety may have enhanced clerical power by confusing penitents over the gravity and even the definition of sins. Whereas in Chapter 4 literary heterogeneity undermined clerical attempts to consolidate authority, now the intellectual variety of the same clerics purportedly cemented religious control.

Spanish manuals disagreed among themselves, as even a casual inspection of them would show. Despite their similarities of form and content, they might contain more or less exposition, so that Ciruelo relayed the significance of the Decalogue in theoretical terms, while Talavera merely broke its precepts into specific queries. Valtanás, uniquely, advised penitents to repeat the confession by themselves fifteen times in fifteen days. Covarrubias devoted forty-four folios to questions on particular professions, and Pedraza detailed thirty-nine cases that fell under the seventh precept against theft. Dueñas began his treatise with a dialogue between personifications of "justice" and "confession." Pedraza shifted the First Commandment toward witchcraft, while Pérez de Ayala turned that precept against Protestants.[85] Whether the manuals' diversity stupefied their audience is impossible to say; that conclusion seems to reveal less about sixteenth-century readers, and more about modern reactions to the texts' alterity. Still, the sources' variety could affect ecclesiastics as well as laypersons, and in ways that might fluster as well as boost the confessor's authority.

Modern scholars have not sufficiently considered the possibility that vernacular manuals could amount to weapons for penitents against priests: from this angle, their very heterogeneity could work to the penitents' advantage. Given the prevalence, prices, and language of the manuals, it is plain that laywomen and men were reading them. If they had access to them, then there was nothing to prevent them from objecting that the manual *they* owned, or had borrowed, or had heard orally, had posed different queries, topics, and instructions for priests and penitents. In other words, the very contrasts of the vernacular texts raised the prospect of contesting confessors. And so the diversity of the manuals should have worried the clergy as much as the laity, because they had to confront penitents' informed expectations, which might well vary from their own.

We know that challenges to clerical authority could occur during penance: an Italian manual from 1510 warned its readers "not to argue with the confessor in the act of confession, the latter being as learned and intelligent as he should be."[86] If the Italian text cautioned against such altercations, they probably occurred, or at least the Italian author thought they were plausible. The same Italian source even preserved a space for disagreement by default, by opening the possibility of contention if the confessor were *not* "as learned and intelligent as he should be."

Other materials relay reproaches that actually took place, although for a much later period. In a pueblo of Tenerife in the eighteenth century, a Franciscan attempted to seduce a female penitent "by telling her that her husband was unfaithful, and that he alone would love her." His object promptly informed him that the Virgin was watching his every move, and that he was sitting in Jesus' place; he quickly desisted.[87] I would guess that such reprimands were far from rare in either Spain or Italy, given the entrenchment of priests in their local communities, the availability of confessors' manuals in the vernacular, and the evidence of such works' circulation. We already know that laypersons could make ecclesiastics' lives miserable, through ostracism or rumor or outright disrespect. But the Spanish manuals on confession provided even further means for lay power, not just by narrating the sacramental rite, but by listing the particular sins that could inhere in the ecclesiastical estate.

One of the most startling angles to the Spanish treatises is their exposition of clerical misbehavior, given that their authors expected the laity to read them. The sins of priests saturate the texts in question: no matter which manual we consider, it enumerated the moral errors of ecclesiastics. Talavera centered the evil of accidia on the chanting of the Divine Office; under the

First Commandment, he placed the flaw of singing counterpoint in a riotous manner, as well as pronouncing Mass more than once a day, except on the Nativity of Jesus, when a priest could celebrate the mysteries three times.

Talavera also detailed the shoddy conduct of ecclesiastics who only said Mass for money or while drunk. He stipulated that priests sinned who swore without great necessity, failed to pray before going to bed, and committed sacrilege during their dispensation of the sacraments:

Next, the priest sins who does not entirely protect the custom of the Church in all the things that pertain to this sacrament [of baptism], which would be lengthy to recount here; but he especially sins if, in the blessing of the font and the catechism, and the other acts that occur in the baptism, he jokes around, laughing and not paying attention; and if he pronounces the rite so fast that even he does not hear it or understand it, as many wicked clerics perform it in this epoch, on account of our sins.[88]

Talavera's points were unremarkable. Ciruelo cited the moral failings of ecclesiastics who set a bad example and thereby scandalized their subjects; he identified clerics with offenses against the Seventh Commandment, because they so often engaged in hidden theft. Covarrubias produced numerous sins under the Third Commandment that would have applied to ecclesiastics as well as laypersons, such as behaving badly *in* a church on a feast day, behaving badly *outside* a church on a feast day, and breaking fasts. He also included the query, "if you are a priest, and administered some sacrament while in mortal sin."[89]

Such castigation was reinforced by the constant stipulation that clerics would find the vernacular manuals useful; this dual audience of clergy and laity, which must have been perceptible to every reader, announced that confessors as well as penitents needed guidance. Moreover, a number of the sources offered positive portraits of confessors that might contradict their readers' personal experience, as when Valtanás instructed priests to listen to confessions with "good grace," and even "invite" disclosures. He went on to warn his clerical audience, and thus his lay one, that secrecy was an absolute prerequisite of the rite; he remarked that confessors should not inquire into details in order to gain some advantage over the penitent.[90] Dueñas entitled his seventeenth chapter "how much kindness and sanctity the confessor has to have in order to hear the faults and sins of the penitent"; in the nineteenth, he mentioned "how the confessor should be virtuous in life and conscience."[91] Even the Hieronymite spent the ninth chapter of his treatise on the desirable attributes of confessors, which readers, whether secular or ecclesiastical, might well use to measure their own. If treatises on priests and bishops openly prohibited clerical despotism, confessors' manuals offered the same warning implicitly.

These sources gave their readers a standard, however variegated, against which to gauge the conduct and intelligence of their religious authorities, and the assessment did not stop with confessors: when Covarrubias included queries about the sins of prelates, abbots, abbesses, nuns, archdeacons, archpriests, cathedral canons, and prebendaries, he was fostering the public assessment of those ecclesiastics as well. Remarkably, the Spanish materials explicitly asked their readers to discriminate among the clergy, because they charged them to avoid fools and seek out suitable confessors instead. Dueñas explained that duty to penitents over three full folios; he pictured the confessor as virtuous and knowledgeable, clear and discreet, with sufficient judgment to absolve the sinner and enough sense to distinguish between mortal and venial faults.[92] Ciruelo told his readers to seek a license from the bishop that would enable them to confess with other clerics, if their own happened to be an idiot [sic]. Even as late as 1567, or in the midst of what we commonly call the Counter-Reformation, Pérez de Ayala still set down five characteristics of a good confessor and adjured the laity to find one, although he also challenged exemptions from confession with approved priests in the diocese.[93] He seemed to be operating from the standpoint that any cleric with a license was qualified to administer penance after Spain's promulgation of the Tridentine decrees; but he also assumed that penitents could distinguish between better and worse confessors within that sanctioned group.

By and large, then, the authors of Spanish confessors' manuals envisioned their readers as rational sheep, and expected ecclesiastics to treat them as such. Sharing many of the same values as their counterparts in Chapter 4, they, too, promoted competence and obedience as if those qualities pertained to religious as well as secular circles. They listed clerical sins, and enjoined their readers to reject ecclesiastics who were incompetent or corrupt. They stressed activity—whether mental, physical, or emotional—in the process of salvation, and directed that counsel to laymen and women as well as clerics. Their manuals' net effect was to promote a religious authority in which each end of the spectrum exerted influence upon the other.

Undoubtedly some readers will object to my conclusions on the grounds that vernacular works on confession simply helped the laity subject itself to a clerical elite. In this scheme, when laymen and women were given the criteria to judge and repulse inept ecclesiastics, they assisted the professional formation of the clergy. By cooperating with the system and its established authorities, laypersons reinforced the line between the clerical and lay spheres; by demanding that ecclesiastics fulfill their obligations, they helped create a body that would wield jurisdiction and judgment at their own expense.

Although formally correct, this scenario strikes me as substantially crude, for it flattens the potential of the past in order to confirm contemporary expectations about bureaucracies. Such an approach plays with the notion of lay autonomy and power, but finally brings us back to the clergy's control of the masses. It encourages us to end up with a conspiratorial ecclesiastical sovereignty, and a lay population that apparently was too witless to grasp what it wanted or what it was doing. How much more complex and alien the Spanish sixteenth century would be if it contained instead penitents who corrected confessors, confessors who respected their penitents, and an intelligentsia that welcomed more ambiguous trajectories of authority in pursuit of a religiously orthodox end.

Chapter Six

The Bewitching
of the Sheep

In an exemplary parish, priests and lay-persons might act for each other's mutual benefit; certainly the vernacular literature on confession and the episcopate promoted a certain reciprocity between the ecclesiastical and secular spheres. Yet the clergy's pastoral responsibilities also included the discovery and eradication of heresy, and it is difficult to imagine how religious authorities in the early modern period could endorse anything but strict lines of control where apostates were concerned. In the case of the witch, historians have argued for generations that the definition and persecution of that particular heretic fundamentally enhanced ecclesiastical supremacy. Theological and judicial elites construed the witch by marrying high demonology to popular ideas about harmful magic; the same intellectual aristocracy then sold that always libidinous, overwhelmingly female servant of the Devil to the European masses via sermons, pamphlets, and public executions.[1] By the fifteenth century, the witch's portrait was drawn and her status set as an enemy of God and the Christian community. Her arrest was sanctioned by popes; her characteristics were disseminated through the most infamous of witchcraft treatises, the *Malleus maleficarum,* printed in 1486–87.

The persecution of witches was supposedly hastened by the sixteenth century's respect for the Bible, and more specifically the Old Testament: more indictments were another consequence of the Decalogue's newfound prominence. When European intellectuals plumbed the Old Testament, they discovered the Commandments' prohibition of idolatry and Exodus's stipulation that witches should not be allowed to live. Once "the obligation to worship God correctly was put at the summit of Christian ethics, and idolatry was made the prime offense, witchcraft became, at least for clerics, a far more serious matter than it had been when still subsumed under one or other of the deadly sins."[2] Notably, the rhetorical habits of the religious elite matched their recent scriptural preferences: because ecclesiastics were disposed to order things through binary opposition or inversion, they presented the Commandments and their transgressions as sets of antitheses. They couched the Decalogue according to an "idiom of contrariety," and then carried that language into distinctions between the witch and the baptized Christian, the sabbat and the Mass, and the demonic and Christian communities.[3]

Significantly, although Vergara never mentioned the Commandments in front of the Inquisition, his vituperation of Francisca Hernández revealed all the hallmarks of such dichotomizing discourse, and included potential connections to the diabolical. Other ecclesiastics, whether Catholic or Protestant, found a perfect fit between a biblical text to which they were newly attentive and their penchant for dialectical constructions. Scholars believe that the Decalogue reinforced the witch stereotype for the general public as well: the Commandments were specific and forceful, they were constantly reiterated, and their obligations must have been clear. The latest research stipulates that anyone who took the Bible seriously must have defined magic and witchcraft as violations of God's Law, whether they belonged to Catholic or Protestant congregations.[4]

Nevertheless, ultimate responsibility for the existence and prosecution of witches finally lay with the intellectuals who invented witchcraft as a heresy and promoted it as an indictable transgression: without the efforts of priests, pastors, and judges, the masses could not have tied white or black magicians to the Devil so easily. It was Europe's elite that first characterized love magicians as demonic agents; the same group provided a rationale that could link destitute and hostile widows to the Devil. The European clergy condemned magic that had nothing to do with worshiping Satan or demons, and the point of their efforts can be summed up in a single line: to protect themselves and their institutions from rivalry.[5] Thus, ecclesiastics in Italy and Scotland, France and Spain allegedly are interchangeable with each other in terms of their methods and their goals. They created witches and pursued them; they surveyed the Old Testament and filtered its descriptions of sin through binary modes of thinking; they outlined the orthodox by diagramming its opposite. Their actions and their writings eased the evolution of clerical hegemony.[6]

True, dialogue might have existed between higher and lower elements of society, and been concealed by the divisive rhetoric of the religious elite;

demands for the witch's prosecution also could come from lower levels of society.[7] But in this scheme, the more important point is that churchmen advanced a sort of cultural proscription, directed mainly against the population at large, when they railed against superstition and witchcraft. Their project "was nothing less than to alter the cultural habits of ordinary Europeans across a broad spectrum of their daily experiences."[8] And so efforts against witchcraft were part of the social control carried out by both the Catholic and the Protestant Reformations in the sixteenth and seventeenth centuries. The dominant scholarly paradigm argues that witch-hunting in early modern Europe was not a peripheral phenomenon, but played a central role in that era's religions, for it was the flip side of pastoral efforts treated elsewhere in this book.[9]

Still, we know that the shape, speed, and even objects of witchcraft prosecution differed across space and time. Arrests in Scotland assumed much larger proportions than ones in England, while indictments in Ireland were almost entirely wanting.[10] Witchcraft trials were more frequent and intense in the western and southwestern regions of the Holy Roman Empire, where autonomous domains were smaller; the empire's more centralized states either avoided witch-hunting altogether or stopped it quickly once it began, contrary to earlier assumptions about witch panics and state-building.[11] Witches in Venice searched for treasure and practiced love magic, ones in Lorraine primarily damaged crops, and local environments obviously contributed to visions of demonic practice: in 1609–10, Basque suspects said that child witches guarded herds of toads, a detail that reflected their predominantly pastoral economy.[12]

European witchcraft and its prosecution is so variegated in the early modern period that it can assume prismatic qualities, and Spanish testimony does nothing to contradict that impression.[13] Castile experienced almost no mass arrests of witches in the sixteenth and seventeenth centuries, but tended to prosecute single individuals, while secular courts and the common populace in Aragon pursued both particular malefactors and groups of the same.[14] The feats of Spanish witches could include everything from harming crops and murdering infants, to seeking buried treasure and charming prospective husbands.

Like their Italian counterparts, who might baptize playing cards for luck, Spanish suspects also inserted Christian symbols and events into their rites. They could reverse elements of the Mass, as when Basque malefactors consumed a black Eucharist and drank the Devil's urine out of a silver cup that looked like a chalice.[15] They might apply scriptural examples to contemporary emergencies: one parish priest tried to cure a sick child by having the youngster consume wine out of a cup with "Eli, Eli, lama sabacthani" written on the bottom of it; that phrase came from Matthew 27:46, and recorded Jesus' cry on the cross.[16] In 1524, Inés de Alonso invoked Jesus *and* the Devil to find her clients' missing spouses, with an incantation that copied the first lines of the *Pater Noster*.[17] And in the early seventeenth century, women in Madrid expected the saints to help the divinatory powers of beans. A spell from 1638 read:

> With Saint Peter and Saint Paul,
> and the Apostle St. James,
> and with the blessed St. Ciprian;
> throw the lots [beans] into the sea;
> dead you throw them,
> alive you remove them;
> so may you remove these lots alive and true for me:
> if so-and-so has to come,
> go into the road.[18]

A bean "went into the road" (*salga en camino*) if one landed apart from the others after being thrown; in that case, the person in question would arrive. The rite alluded to the miracles wrought by Jesus and his followers, turned now toward a more mundane purpose.

Testimony on early modern witches is so diverse that it nearly defies attempts to condense it. It also offers us a number of obstacles, which combine the difficulties of Inquisition trials with the impediments of pastoral treatises. When we can find accounts of witchcraft, they very often survive as part of a legal case, with all the problems of mediation intact. When judicial and religious authorities addressed witchcraft, they could invoke literary tropes and common fables as well as legal depositions, and all these elements might affect the final version of a verdict or a report to the Suprema. Learned treatises on witches demonstrate the same stumbling blocks, since their authors might pull descriptions from their experience or their references. Nevertheless, up to now most historians have approached Spanish witchcraft as a straightforward arrangement of oppositional groups: our propensity to sort the subject into blocks complements other taxonomies in Spanish history, from distinguishing Erasmians from scholastics, to detaching the individual from the community.

For example, scholars consistently sequester Basque witchcraft from the Castilian variety, and go on to identify the first as a Northern European stereotype, the second a Mediterranean one.[19] In this scheme, Basque suspects harmed crops, murdered infants, and poisoned their enemies in a rural milieu; they met in orgiastic sabbats, possessed toads as familiars, and made explicit pacts with the Devil, while their Castilian or Mediterranean peers allegedly tended toward love rituals, divination, and healing, and usually acted alone in an urban environment.

Academics have partitioned other aspects of Spanish witchcraft as well: they commonly insist that the Spanish Inquisition as a body was not interested in persecuting witches in the early modern period, then oppose inquisitors to Spanish judges and the masses, and finally contrast the Inquisition in Spain with other, less tolerant authorities in Western Europe.[20] In modern treatments of witchcraft the Spanish Inquisition turns into a benevolent force, and that benevolence in turn makes Spain a positive example vis-à-vis its European neighbors. The irony of this interpretative angle is profound. Unlike scholarly narratives about Erasmus and Spain, ones about witches turn Spanish exceptionalism into a positive attribute.

Reasons for Spanish leniency toward suspected witches may lie in the Inquisition's 1526 ban on confiscating their property: in the wake of that prohibition, inquisitors could have ignored the accused because prosecution would not result in any financial gain for the tribunals in question.[21] Nevertheless, the most frequent argument by far for Spanish magnanimity involves a rationalism that inquisitors alone purportedly absorbed and propagated. Thus, the Suprema usually viewed witchcraft with skepticism, and conveyed that attitude to its local tribunals, especially regarding flight to the sabbat, called transvection. The dissemination of such disbelief eventually affected provincial authorities: hence, inquisitors in Cuenca became increasingly incredulous about witchcraft and sorcery over the course of the sixteenth century, and consistently refused to read folk magic as diabolism.[22] In Aragon, where witchcraft belonged to secular as well as inquisitorial courts, inquisitors saved lives whenever they could seize control of witchcraft cases; even their colleagues in the Basque country reacted cautiously when faced with a witch's confession.[23] Most scholars accordingly transmit a story of rational and prudent inquisitors contesting gullible and ignorant judges and masses. The result is a narrative about early modern Spain that is nearly as suspenseful as Bataillon's.[24]

For all their drama, academic conclusions about Spanish witchcraft often exhibit as many pitfalls as typical presentations of the Spanish Renaissance. For example, the geographical distinction between Northern and Mediterranean witches does not fully relay the details of the cases, because we have found demon-worshiping suspects in Córdoba, Cuenca, and Toledo; unearthed female love magicians in the Pyrenees; and discovered demonic familiars among suspects in Andalucia.[25] Then again, insistence upon the Inquisition's skepticism and rationality neglects the intellectual and religious environments of the inquisitors themselves.

All too often scholars have treated transvection as if it were the decisive factor for categorizing their subjects: if an inquisitor doubted the actuality of a witch's flight, he was a rational man.[26] Yet early modern intellectuals possessed sources that said nightflight could occur through illusions as well as in reality, and in either case the Devil and his demons could be to blame; if an inquisitor attributed transvection to hallucinations, he might still preserve diabolical intervention in the scenario, because the Devil was the father of lies.[27] Spanish inquisitors took part in a literary and theological culture that did not distinguish between superstitious and diabolical rites. They recognized that witchcraft involved potential infidelity toward God, whether the rituals at hand concerned love magic or the actual invocation of demons.[28] When inquisitors declined to turn witches over to the secular arm, or to sentence them to perpetual imprisonment, their decisions should not connote modern sensibilities.[29]

If we approach Spanish witchcraft from the angle of pure power relationships, we may find classification equally difficult to achieve, for a rigid distinction between folk magic and orthodox Catholicism becomes as unreliable as a split between incredulous and gullible factions of the population. Clerics assumed the roles of cloud conjurers, rabies healers, and judges of locusts; Inquisition records relay how priests carried out the excommunication of aphids, complete with formal decrees.[30] Laymen and women invoked the Trinity in rituals, and peppered ceremonies with the figures, literary accounts, and number symbolism of Christianity. When the village of Usún experienced drought in the early sixteenth century, the residents, including the priests, carried a statue of St. Peter down to the local river and threatened to submerge it unless Peter himself interceded with rain. Three times the participants repeated the phrase, "Holy Peter, help us placed in this necessity, that you may obtain rain for us from God"; they finally warned the effigy of its imminent drenching if they did not receive rain within a certain period of time.[31] Menacing a statue, not to mention exiling an insect, may look like the purest sort of popular magic to us, but Christian texts and concepts were embedded in the very rites in question. Usún's populace apparently guessed that Peter would be particularly leery of water because he nearly had drowned, as documented in Matthew 14:30; a similar familiarity with Christianity was demonstrated by the same population's use of the number three in its invoca-tion.[32] As for the excommunication of locusts, villagers obviously understood the power of that rite in its ecclesiastical context. Spanish sources on witch-craft demonstrate repeatedly that lay religion could be learned and learned religion could be popular, and their testimony matches evidence from other parts of Western Europe.[33]

When Spanish clerics complained about sorcerers, they undoubtedly hoped to reserve Christian rituals to clerics acting inside churches; they wished to amend an environment in which laypersons and even priests turned Christian formulas and objects toward curative or prophetic ends. Yet any explanatory strategy that forces ecclesiastics into a homogeneous mass, and ignores their own motives for their actions, only reduces the culture it intends to illuminate.

I would argue instead that we cannot overlook clerical differences in the name of an overarching object, because details could affect agendas in signifi-cant ways. Spanish authors might construe their witches and their godly communities along more or less gendered lines, and with more or less em-phasis on ecclesiastical status and material happiness. Like their peers who wrote on penance or the episcopate or even Erasmus, they could also sum-mon distinct authorities for their arguments, or turn identical sources to various ends. Contrary, then, to presenting witchcraft texts as a uniform body of literature, I would prefer to highlight their diversity, and thereby encom-pass the nuances of at least a fraction of the evidence.

Two witchcraft treatises from Spain betray dissension as well as conso-nance on what might strike us as the most straightforward of topics: even on this subject, the Catholic elite of Europe's most thoroughly Catholic country revealed intellectual fluidity over concepts and counsel. Readers are already acquainted with one of the authors in question, Pedro Ciruelo; the other, Martín de Castañega, is not unknown to the historical record either. Cas-tañega was a Franciscan friar who spent most of his long life in Burgos and the Basque country. In 1516, Pope Leo X ordered him released from an Inquisi-tion prison, where he and a companion were held for publicly defending a monk already condemned by the Inquisition. By 1531, Castañega figured as the custodian of Santa María de Jesús in Navarrete; twenty-four years later, he was acting as the guardian for the monastery of Aránzazu in Guipúzcoa. Castañega's only surviving publication is the *Tratado de las supersticiones y hechicerías* (*Treatise of superstitions and sorceries*), which was printed once in Logroño, in 1529.[34] Ciruelo issued the *Reprobación de las supersticiones y hechi-*

cerías (*Reprobation of superstitions and sorceries*) in 1530. The Ciruelo piece went through eight more editions between 1538 and 1628.[35]

Scholars have reacted to Castañega's and Ciruelo's treatises with interest: they have edited them, translated them into English, and cited them in broader surveys.[36] Such regard seems appropriate. Castañega's *Tratado* does not appear in the bookstore inventories from Toledo and Burgos in the 1550s, but it was cited by at least two authors in the sixteenth century, one of whom used it for a treatise written in Nahuatl, the Aztec language.[37] Ciruelo's *Reprobación* was the most frequently reprinted vernacular work on witchcraft in early modern Spain: it overshadowed that field to an even greater extent than his *Arte de bien confesar* dominated the genre of the confessors' manual. The *Reprobación* gained attention from the episcopate, for Dr. Bernal recommended it in his *Aviso de curas* and kept it in his library. It also attracted the notice of Baroque encyclopedists, who invoked it on such matters as locust conjuring and exorcism.[38] Copies of the *Reprobación,* at 34 maravedís apiece, figured in the 1556 inventory of Juan de Junta's bookstore in Burgos; it was priced at the same level as bound copies of Ciruelo's *Arte de bien confesar.*[39] Given the language in which they were written, and the extant references to them in the contemporary literature, it seems likely that Castañega's and Ciruelo's witchcraft texts circulated after they were published.

Certainly their authors intended that they should. In his dedication to the bishop of Calahorra, Castañega wrote:

Therefore wanting to enlighten simple Christians with the small spark that Christ wished to grant to me, and to serve your illustrious Lordship in it, I arranged and composed this *Treatise of superstitions and sorceries* in the Castilian language, so that episcopal visitors and parish priests, and even all the clergy of your very reputable and great bishopric, might have it in their hands, on account of the material being scattered: it is not sufficiently synthesized, detailed, or expounded, nor applied to the cases that occur. Which treatise, in my opinion, not only will be useful for the simple folk—to separate them from their errors and diabolical delusions—but even is necessary to remove much ignorance from many who deny the types of superstitions and sorceries that are written down here, although they presume to be educated.[40]

It is difficult to tell from this passage alone whom Castañega envisioned as "simple Christians" and "simple folk"; he may have been referring to the lower echelons of the clergy. His bishop, Alonso de Castillo, had an ecclesiastical audience in mind when he ordered clerics in his diocese to acquire the *Tratado,* and announced that his episcopal visitors would verify ownership of the volume as they made their rounds.[41] Notwithstanding the bishop's directions, Castañega aimed practical suggestions at the laity in other parts of the treatise. Because he wrote the *Tratado* in Spanish, it easily could have escaped a purely ecclesiastical readership.

Ciruelo's comments about his constituency were at once more equivocal and more inclusive. At first, he seemed to aim the *Reprobación* at even higher elites than Castañega, since the opening paragraph stipulated that he wanted his treatise in the hands of prelates and ecclesiastical and secular judges, who all too often overlooked the punishment of superstition and sorcery.[42] By the end of his prologue, though, Ciruelo wished to awaken the shepherds of the flock of Jesus Christ, who presumably amounted to village priests and confessors; in the middle of the same preface, he connected the *Reprobación* to his confessors' manual, which he certainly wrote for the laity, and noted that he wanted to warn "all good Christians and fearful servants of God" about the risks of superstitious practices. As we shall see, the *Reprobación* was packed with counsel for ordinary men and women, as well as criticism of ecclesiastics. The evidence is considerable that it migrated throughout Spain and among various social and intellectual classes.

Nonetheless, scholarship on these texts has tended to focus less on their readership and more on elements that reflect the general historiography of Spanish witchcraft. Academics primarily have asked which author was more skeptical than the other: Castañega's editors find their subject incredulous because of his equivocation toward healers and neglect of the Devil's mark; his willingness to tie the witch's sensations to the imagination, and to attribute cures to natural causes, make him rational.[43] Other students have read Ciruelo's methodology as "more objective and modern" than his contemporaries', and have described him as imbued with a new scientific spirit in his drive to classify.[44] Then there is the matter of referentiality, or the degree to which the *Tratado* and the *Reprobación* transmit rituals that actually were carried out by men and women in sixteenth-century Spain. Scholars usually have presumed that the two Spaniards were relaying spells and ceremonies that their contemporaries practiced: as a result, these treatises allegedly can tell us what real life was like for the Spanish masses, and illuminate more obscure passages in sixteenth-century literature.[45]

In contrast, I would second more recent contentions and argue that such questions are not the right queries to put to these works.[46] Like every other text in this book, Castañega's and Ciruelo's treatises were part of a larger literary genre and indebted to multiple literary authorities. Their reliance on Augustine and Gerson, William of Auvergne and Aquinas, makes it difficult to verify connections between what they might have witnessed and what they wrote. Even if they alleged their own experience, their intellectual culture was so obliged to references that they could surround the potentially authentic with the literary. For example, Castañega stated that he had conversed with suspected witches, and had observed autos-da-fé in which witches were turned over to the secular arm: "Of these I knew and saw some burned and reconciled, in which one said the demon made him deny God and his faith, but that the demon never succeeded in making him deny Our Lady; and he was a little old man, and he was reconciled, and knew his sin."[47]

Here Castañega seemed to rely on a real incident, and made his witch male, but he most frequently targeted the female variety throughout his text. Elsewhere he reported that "experience" linked poor women and indigent clerics to the Devil, and showed that students embarked on necromancy "every day," but his comments were as platitudinous as suggestive of direct observation. Ciruelo, meanwhile, may have listened to confessions of superstitious activities, but there is no evidence he ever came close to a witchcraft trial, although his seventeenth-century glossator turned him into an inquisitor to boost the *Reprobación*'s prestige.[48] As a result, the *Tratado* and the *Reprobación* cannot be treated as verbatim descriptions of sorcery and witchcraft, given the degree to which their authors depended upon literary precedents, although awareness of the legal cases also should prevent us from treating these works as if they were simply the intellectual fantasies of the religious elite.[49]

Whatever their degree of imitation or reportage, their opinions do not make Castañega and Ciruelo skeptics. The two theologians may have adduced natural causes for mysterious events, but they believed in demonic forces, albeit ones that were subservient to God: such credence in turn means that we cannot portray them as quasi-modern. Furthermore, their understanding of the implicit demonic pact, and metaphorical connections between the Devil and lies, gave demonic implications to their references to hallucination and delusion. Like their inquisitorial counterparts, Ciruelo and Castañega never had any reason to distinguish theologically between superstition and heresy, or between folk magic and demonology, although they might well differentiate between the two in the penalties they recommended. They could indict malefactors more or less severely on a practical level, but in no way do their treatises evince incredulity in the face of the Devil and his demons.

The most recent assessment of the *Tratado* and the *Reprobación* treats the two works as equivalent, and from there as Spanish examples of clerical efforts at christianization and social control.[50] Castañega and Ciruelo could be treated as a unit; their treatises support the modern notion that "high" demonology really pertains to pastoral literature. The Spaniards consistently raised penance, holy water and crosses, the reception of the Eucharist, and the study of Scripture as they sketched orthodox behavior; their recommendations echoed ones found in confessors' manuals. They urged recourse to village priests; they addressed the parish more often than the monastery; they thought bishops should be concerned with witchcraft because they had to answer for the souls of their flocks. Like their peers who wrote about the episcopate, they, too, extended the responsibilities of the clergy. They stressed the same authorities and sacraments.

They also characterized the demonic in similar ways. Both overlooked distinctions between the Devil and demons, handled devils as enemies of God, and stipulated that traffic with such agents constituted treason against the Deity. Connections to the demonic violated a Christian's baptismal vows; traitorous behavior of this sort was worse than betraying a secular lord. As for motives, the Devil wished above all to be revered by God and God's creation, but God in turn would punish such misdirected worship most harshly.[51] Castañega and Ciruelo went on to address the Devil's human servants in comparable succession. They began with the learned invocation of demons, treated the Northern European stereotype of the witch as if it were a subtopic of necromancy, and finally addressed what we would call white magic.[52] They recognized that witches could be male as well as female. They described the explicit demonic pact, whereby "with clear and formal words, repudiating the faith, [witches] make a new profession to the demon in his presence, who appears to them in the form and shape that he wishes to take; the witches giving him their entire obedience and offering him their body and soul."[53] Their witches anointed themselves with certain ointments, pronounced particular words, and flew through the air at night to carry out maleficent acts.[54] And both Castañega and Ciruelo decided that such transvection could occur in the imagination as well: they thereby reconciled the *Canon episcopi,* the pseudo-patristic decretal, with biblical examples of angels and demons carrying people through the air.[55]

Castañega explained that nightflight was proven through scriptural cases and the witches' own confessions, although God had to allow such events to occur in the first place. He also admitted that

just as we read and find that the demon and any good or bad angel, through their efficacy and natural power, can carry any man who acquiesced in it through the air, waters, and seas—God permitting—so we read that the senses can be snatched away from oneself, which the doctors call ecstasy, and in that state people may have revelations of great secrets, and things that occur in remote places, and think they are or have been in those territories.[56]

Castañega went on to cite Augustine as proof that the Devil could "disturb the human senses, as in a very heavy and serious dream, in such a way that the demon may make it appear to the person that he is in that place that the demon represents to him."[57] He concluded that the Devil could have explicit pacts with two types of ministers: some really traveled to distant lands with the Devil's help; others were led into a delusional state through the Devil's influence, wherein they experienced diabolical revelations of faraway and hidden things.

Ciruelo presented the same arguments more concisely. Some witches really quit their houses when the Devil carried them through the air, and what they saw, did, and said in that state of consciousness really occurred. On other occasions the witches did not leave their residences, but the Devil deprived them of their senses and they fell to the ground as if they were dead, and the Devil showed them in their fantasies that they went to other houses and places. In the second instance, none of what the witches experienced was true: they merely thought the events in their dreams had transpired in fact.[58]

Castañega and Ciruelo shared a similar outlook on such malefactors: whether they really flew or just succumbed to demonic hallucinations, they had rejected their baptismal vows and should be punished as apostatical schismatics. Any kingdom that allowed such necromancy to exist—and witches were necromancers in substance—could expect to incur the wrath of God. The Christian community could not afford to ignore such creatures.

Ciruelo and Castañega also endorsed the notion of the tacit demonic pact, and urged religious and secular authorities to inquire into the Devil's less obvious associates. In the clerical culture of early modern Europe, and the Middle Ages as well, the plausibility of an implicit demonic alliance rested on stereotypes about the Devil himself. In 1 Peter 5:8, the Devil was a lion, "seeking whom he may devour": he and his coterie actively sought to corrupt human beings.[59] Thus demons could invent spells or invade existing ones in order to tempt the practitioner; they could interfere in human rituals without an invitation. Even if rituals seemed to work through natural or divine causes, the Devil could be involved: a sorcerer could burn incense and thereby invoke the Devil's aid as if by a prearranged sign, just as friends engaged in private gestures whose meaning only they could glean.

From this perspective—which stressed authoritative precedents, the limited presence of the miraculous in the world, and rigorous ties between causes and effects—sorcerers had to be signaling to some intelligence when they performed their ceremonies.[60] Moreover, the Gospel of John reported that the Devil was the father of lies, and a vain ritual was an untruth because it could not work through either natural or divine causes. Ciruelo voiced the following syllogism: "because vanities are lies, and lies please the Devil, it is clear that the man who performs vain works serves the Devil, and sins very seriously against his God."[61] The final result meant that the most innocuous-looking ceremonies were liable to demonic intrusion, whether those rites were carried out privately or publicly.

When Castañega and Ciruelo separated the natural and supernatural realms from the demonic one, they condemned what we think of as white magic; their arguments consequently match some scholarly theses.[62] Their notion of the implicit pact allowed them to deprecate rituals that had nothing to do with the Devil, at least superficially, and in the process they seemed to undercut their audience's material happiness. They cautioned their readers to avoid healing by the oral and written spells, called *ensalmos* and *nóminas,* which included unknown words or symbols. They highlighted the dangers posed by local shamans, whether the latter pursued correlations between knotted belts and broken limbs, changed old prayers into new ones, or asked their clients to imbibe cups of water in which they had written certain expressions.[63] These Spanish clerics prohibited the use of spells to remove the evils provoked by witchcraft, called *maleficia;* they attacked public exorcists and conjurers of storms.[64] They seemed to target the same culprits on identical grounds.

Sometimes Castañega went so far as to encourage his readers to endure their afflictions without complaint. As he deplored the excommunication of locusts—a rite intended to prevent famine—he explained why prayers sometimes went unanswered:

God may not hear us or answer our petition as quickly as we wish, in order to test and make known our virtue and patience, because if God permits evils to test and demonstrate the kindness and virtue of a virtuous person like Job, much more shall He deny us the material blessings that we ask of Him for the same reason; and so many times He does not consent to the material blessings that people ask of Him when they ask for them, so that they may establish themselves more firmly in humility, and their virtue and patience may appear more clearly.[65]

In Castañega's rendition, Job was a paragon of human suffering and Christian forbearance, and readers should emulate him. What could have made the emphasis even more forceful were Castañega's links between the Devil and the physical world: he wrote that Christians easily turned into the Devil's servants if they were brazenly attracted to temporal riches; he implied that the reverse of the satanic was a purely spiritual milieu. His audience might well have inferred that the best security against demons lay in the rejection of the material world.

Not surprisingly, Castañega and Ciruelo handed clerics the task of defining and restricting the diabolical. Priests had to supervise their congregations, and flocks in turn must bow to the direction of their shepherds. As Ciruelo attested,

For greater clarity and the better instruction of good Christians, I wish to place here certain rules about nóminas and ensalmos. And these rules will be so true and Catholic that no decently educated man will be able to deny them. Which is a reason for other simple men and women, without education, to not find fault with them; because in God's community the faith of the lesser and the lowly is to be ruled by that of the greater prelates and the educated.[66]

Bishops and judges should interrogate figures who claimed extraordinary powers of healing; they should distrust men who allayed storms; they must not tolerate obstacles to their own authority in their own dominions.[67] At the same time, both clergy and laity should turn to Church ceremonies and lesser religious officials to preclude the Devil's invasion. Castañega adjured his readers:

And in order to free themselves from the snares and deceits of the demon, with the help of God, they should try faithfully to hear devotedly the High Mass on all feast days; and every time they can, to hear the sermons with much attention; they should confess with good confessors, at the very least when the Church demands it . . . and they always should be obedient to the commandments of the Church, and fear falling into some sort of excommunication, and even more being in an excommunicated state for some period of time. They should never create frivolities or other things not taught in Church; they may not pray orations or say words that are not used in Church, even if they appear devout; and when they have some doubt, they immediately may ask their village priest or their confessor.[68]

Castañega told his audience to "live with misgiving and fear of going against the faith of the Holy Mother Church and her commandments"; he seemed to encourage the scrupulosity that writers on confession spurned.[69] He was not alone in his emphases. Ciruelo, too, highlighted the divine wrath that would plague the superstitious, and recommended the *Pater Noster,* as well as the sacrament of penance, as preventative measures against demonic influence.[70]

Castañega's and Ciruelo's sentiments seem to fit current contentions about the European clergy and its fight against witchcraft. Their treatises apparently tried to eradicate lay healing, and to substitute instead an ethos of silent affliction. Their tracts could elevate spiritual goodness over material happiness; they undeniably planted ecclesiastics as the proper arbiters of secular lives. But if certain passages in the *Tratado* and the *Reprobación* match the scholarship, conflicting testimony survives in these treatises as well, although they seem to offer firm messages about ecclesiastical privilege. Notably, Castañega and Ciruelo reveal that "thinking with demons" did not inevitably produce dualities between the physical and spiritual worlds, the clerical and lay estates, or men and women.[71]

Castañega may have recommended Job as an example to his readers, but he also proposed solutions to his audience's suffering; he recognized the importance of their bodily well-being. When it came to nóminas, which were spells or prayers written on slips of paper, he instructed his public on the construction of orthodox ones, which hardly signals a neglect of earthly concerns.[72] He went on to list objects that his audience could employ in its quest for remedies:

> It is not wicked to use the water from the washing of the chalice, or where certain relics have been washed, either to drink or to cast over certain sick flocks of animals. Because without any superstition whatsoever, on account of their devotion, men sometimes ask for the oil from the lamp that burns before the statue of some saint, or before the Eucharist; and for the water from the washing of the wounds [i.e., the stigmata] of the statue of St. Francis, not in order to use the substance wickedly, but to receive it and use it with much devotion, wishing to cure their passions and sicknesses, or those of their flocks.[73]

Castañega did not impose a division between more and less suitable objects in this passage, for he addressed the illnesses of sheep as well as the emotional maladies of people. He also did not treat the search for physical cures as somehow inappropriate for Christians. He recommended only articles found in churches, but nevertheless advocated the employment of real objects, attained through human means, to help disorders. He presented spiritual and corporeal measures as if they were interrelated within Catholicism.

His contemporary amplified the same message. Ciruelo provided an extraordinary number of practical recommendations in his witchcraft treatise, and his advice prominently featured physical objects and the material realm. He wrote that good Christians should seek all the cures that human knowledge had to offer, whether the problem were disease, or the loss of honor and household. The same Christians should then commend themselves and their families to God and His saints, and pray for celestial help in what neither natural power nor human knowledge could reach.[74] Immediately thereafter, Ciruelo stressed the extent to which human efforts should go: "a man must do what he can through his own knowledge, or take the advice of those who know more, either teachers, or friends, or the experienced elderly"; he was not suggesting that suffering Christians remain isolated from the concern and direction of their larger communities, nor was he picturing assistance in purely clerical terms.[75] He recommended similar measures against storms, wherein villagers must pursue cures with all their might, and might fire guns at the clouds to make them disperse.[76]

Even his spiritual counsel involved the body and the material realm. When thunderstorms approached, the clergy should enter the churches, followed by the leading men and women of each parish; once there, a rush of activity should ensue, as candles were lighted, the missal was placed on the altar and opened to the Gospel, and relics were lifted from their repositories and positioned around the Eucharist. Ecclesiastics then would kneel on the altar steps, laypersons would prostrate themselves on the ground, and everyone would beg God collectively to dissolve the wicked cloud through His infinite power: they would supplicate Him "to deliver that family and the lands of that place from the damage that storm will be able to produce."[77]

When Ciruelo and Castañega condemned material pleasures, they had in mind the reckless pursuit of riches; to convey their disapproval of extravagance, they used adjectives such as "disordered" (desordenada) and adverbs such as "licentiously" (desenfrenadamente). But an extravagant quest for wealth was one thing, and reasonable happiness in the world something else again. Neither Spaniard promoted quiet anguish. Both pondered therapies for the dire situations that were far too apt to strike their neighbors, not to mention themselves. Indeed, if the Tratado demonstrated at least some concern for people's well-being, the Reprobación extended that regard to remarkable lengths. Ciruelo worried about human illness and crop damage. He treated his readers as if they were sufficiently energetic and intelligent to find remedies themselves, or to discover experts who possessed solutions. He recorded whole pages of strategies for eliminating pests such as locusts, and summoned Job as an illustration of the Devil's torment, not as a model for imitation.[78]

On the subject of the community and physical well-being, Castañega and Ciruelo conform to their contemporaries in earlier chapters. Spaniards who wrote about the episcopate and penance, parish priests and witches, decried vicious action in the world, but never expected their readers to deny their earthly existence. Even diatribes against the demonic allowed the clergy and the laity to cherish their material lives, although every theologian in Spain recognized that the lack of money and goods enticed people toward the Devil in the first place. Given the variation in *clerical* incomes in the sixteenth century, and the very real prospect of ecclesiastical poverty, priests could gravitate toward sorcery too, and Ciruelo and Castañega realized as much. The two Spaniards chastised the clergy directly in their tracts, and damned rituals that ecclesiastics might routinely recommend. Their attempts to define and condemn liminal practitioners and ceremonies stretched to the priesthood as well, and in Ciruelo's case, he expressly included the laity in that critical exercise.

The exploits that Ciruelo denounced with the greatest fury were perpetrated almost exclusively by ecclesiastics. Bishops were so careless that they allowed cathedral canons to mark fortuitous or ill-omened days in the calendars of breviaries, psalters, and missals. "Greedy and moronic clerics or friars" devised the superstitious strategies behind the Masses of El Conde and St. Amador, and the thirty-day cycles called *treintenarios,* which attracted so much censure in the texts in Chapter 4.[79] Local priests excommunicated locusts: they judged the insects, found them guilty, and gave them a span of time in which to either leave the area or face expulsion from the village.[80] Ecclesiastics also conjured clouds: they tricked people into thinking that demons produced storms and hail, and then offered to send the troublesome tempest elsewhere.[81] Ciruelo implicated exorcists, who almost inevitably were clerics, with the same fervor. Anyone who publicly exorcised energumens (the technical name for the possessed) must be suspected of necromancy. Laypersons who did the same were even more questionable, of course, because they never had been invested with power over demons; but priests who behaved as if they had a special gift for exorcism were always highly dubious.[82]

Castañega, too, stamped ecclesiastics as potential miscreants in the excommunication of locusts; he labeled them conclusive ones in the eviction of clouds. But he failed to criticize them to the same extent as his colleague, and merely noted that priests who exiled pests "deserved to be very harshly punished by their bishops and prelates."[83] Even fraudulent exorcists escaped his direct censure: although he described tricksters who debated devils and put energumens into trances, he never pinpointed ecclesiastics as the most plausible agents of the farce, or singled them out for reproof.[84]

In contrast, Ciruelo supplied his audience with a relentless appraisal of clerical wickedness, and treated his readers like rational sheep. He presumed that ordinary men and women would act upon his practical instructions about illness, clouds, and locusts; he believed they could discriminate be-tween legitimate spiritual authority and its opposite. He even appealed di-rectly to his readers' perspicacity about relics.

This sixth rule about nóminas also pertains to the relics of the saints that some people carry about with them. It certainly would be a more devout and useful practice for them to put the relics in churches or pure places, and take up the devotion of praying every day some prayers to those male and female saints whose relics those objects are purported to be. I say this for three reasons. The first is because in this epoch now there is much doubt and little certainty about the relics of the saints, for many of them are not authentic; and sometimes what they say about the splinter or timber of the boat really occurs.[85]

However cryptic his last phrase seems to us, Ciruelo's contemporaries would have guessed immediately what he meant by it: wooden fragments that seemed to come from Jesus' cross could be forged.[86] In the same treatise, Ciruelo went so far as to claim that people who pined after relics were placing their hope in dead things. He believed in the saints; he did not dispute the existence and potentially miraculous effects of their possessions. But he still wished laypersons to follow his example and discriminate among the relics offered for their veneration. If ordinary men and women, as well as clerics, had taken his advice, they might well have conflicted with the higher eccle-siastics who were supposed to be guiding their spiritual lives and supervising their pastoral activities.

Ciruelo imagined his audience behaving in even more assertive ways when it came to the bewitchment of storms: he wanted his readers to baffle cloud conjurers by asking them questions, which he cheerfully supplied.[87] A pru-dent individual might examine spell-casters as to why, if they possessed the power to cast out tempests, they could not draw them in again during a drought. A person could ask spell-casters why they had no incantations against the floods that rushed through the earth and destroyed fruits, animals, and even human beings. Finally, readers could raise the topic of fires, and quiz the conjurer as to why he was unable to lift the flames off the ground and send them through the air.[88]

Ciruelo thought his queries were reasonable. These vain practitioners claimed that demons delivered bad clouds, but sacred histories also reported that demons could move fires and floods: if conjurers could control one, they should be able to manage the others. Once the objects of the interrogation failed to explain their limitations, their audience would see the superstitious and diabolical foundation of their spells. Once we realize that cloud conjurers very often were priests, Ciruelo's scenario becomes positively startling, for he encouraged laypersons and ecclesiastics to debate such individuals and demonstrate their ignorance, without imposing any limits on the disputations in question. If his readers could contest their priests' activities with clouds, locusts, and demoniacs—as well as relics—then communication as well as stratification was supposed to occur in Christian practice.

In Ciruelo's version of witchcraft and sorcery, ecclesiastics were as likely to fall for the Devil's charms, and then to bewitch others, as their lay brothers and sisters. He thus extended the scope of potential malefactors to include the very religious authorities he exalted; he asked his whole readership to discipline suspects, whether the latter belonged to the clergy or the laity. Although he sprinkled the *Reprobación* with remarks about the ignorance of the populace and its necessary submission to the ecclesiastical domain, he mitigated those comments with other details. The whole trajectory of his witchcraft text implied some degree of collaboration and correction between the secular and religious spheres; it preserved and even augmented the mutual correction we have seen in confessors' manuals and treatises on the episcopate.

Notably, Castañega did not offer such a comprehensive list of offenders, or include the laity in the chastisement of culprits; he and Ciruelo attributed diabolical acts to different perpetrators, and thereby sketched different religious hierarchies. One diminished the range of potential heretics, but inculpated women and Jews with such intensity that he made up in depth what he lost in scope. The other widened the net of potential guilt, but excused ignorance and ignored witchcraft's most stereotypical agents.

Castañega could tolerate healers of rabies; he attributed their beneficial powers to their saliva.

Many doubt the power and gift that healers have, and by experience demonstrate, against rabid dogs and their poison. On this subject, it should be noted that natural powers are so hidden from human understanding in the present life, that many times we see . . . marvelous works and do not know the reason behind them, except that such is the property of natural things, and that it is hidden from us.[89]

Since men as well as animals could have different natural gifts, it was just possible that particular individuals were fashioned to heal through their breath or their touch, although they certainly were few in number. Ciruelo believed instead that people who claimed such natural powers were nothing more than vicious drunks (*borrachones viciosos*), at least ordinarily; anyone who attributed such healing to God was equally questionable. Secular and religious authorities should drive rabies healers out of town, for they not only spread superstition, but tricked their clients as well: they "robbed the households of the masses and damned their souls."[90]

The same sort of expansive critique distinguished Ciruelo's opinions over and over again. He condemned more practices than Castañega, and reserved more measures more frequently to the Church and its ministers. The *Reprobación* was 147 folios in length, the *Tratado* fifty-five; the former addressed more than fifteen types of witchcraft, the latter just a handful. Ciruelo condemned divination through the *Clavicula Salomonis* and the *Arte notoria,* prediction by dreams, belief in lucky and unfortunate days, and forecasting by fire, water, and the human palm, all of which Castañega ignored.[91] He tacked on more reasons to explain why the Devil sought public exorcisms and large audiences. He also issued more exacting instructions on legitimate spiritual remedies. In a storm, priests should not leave the church to confront the bad clouds, much less drag relics after them; doctors and surgeons must pray and make the sign of the cross when they treated patients, and ask God for the grace that their medicines could not supply.[92]

Ciruelo's categories of the superstitious were more abundant than his counterpart's, his patience with liminal practitioners much less. He refused to admit that healers and love magicians might be assisted by God, because miracles routinely occurred only in early Christianity. He tended to restrict the miraculous to the historical past, and used events in the Old and New Testaments to gauge the verisimilitude of purported wonders in his own epoch. He positively denied the possibility that amazing cures came from some natural power, although he would also expand the effects of nature to curtail the sorcerer's authority. Storms owed their origins to natural causes, and would not respond to incantations. Demons seldom pushed clouds around, because if God allowed them to do so, they would attempt it all the time. Thus Ciruelo swelled the circle of likely culprits and amplified demonic explanations for their alleged abilities. Castañega's outlook seems far more benevolent, given his more explicit acknowledgment of natural healing and his more limited treatment of sorcery.

But these texts are even more intricate than my exposition allows. If Ciruelo extended the number of suspects, he also lessened their guilt when they were ignorant. In the midst of his section on oral and written charms, Ciruelo noted that while the Church tended to tolerate such spells, confessors should not. He then wrote:

And I nevertheless say that in the secret audience of confessors, a distinction must be made between those who have entered into the superstition of ensalmos and nóminas; because for persons without learning, ignorance excuses them, or lightens the sin. This is true before they have been advised and corrected by wise theologians and prelates; because if they still persist in wishing to use ensalmos and nóminas after being advised, ignorance shall not excuse them.[93]

Immediately afterward, he noted that his critique so far should apply only to persons who were *not* ignorant. For the nescient remainder, there either was no sin committed, or only a venial one, or if it was mortal, it was not very serious, at least so long as their obliviousness lasted. Many things were sins in greater persons that were excused in lesser ones, on account of age or sense or knowledge.

Paradoxically, Ciruelo's exposition could amount to a tool for laity and clergy, since it allowed penitents to plead ignorance on his authority; if accused of implicit pacts with the Devil through the use of ensalmos and nóminas, they easily could claim that they never had been informed about superstitious behavior and its potentially diabolical implications. Castañega furnished similar ammunition to the laity because he, too, indicted conjurer-priests and excused natural powers of healing; his public could have turned either point to its advantage. But if Castañega's readers happened to be women or Jews or conversos, they would find themselves tied to the Devil essentially, without any means of escape.

Castañega and Ciruelo differed profoundly over the sex of the probable witch. Ciruelo paired men with women through every type of sorcery, including the practices of the *bruja;* he positively declined to tie particular bewitchments to females; he wrote much of his treatise as if demonic pacts, both explicit and implicit, were concluded by men. But Castañega so decisively bound women to witches, and then to the Devil, that his remarks on clerical conjurers scarcely echoed in comparison. Although he admitted in spots that witches could be male, he devoted nearly half the *Tratado* to the Devil's female disciples.

Castañega presented his readers with a mirror image of the Catholic and diabolical churches, and scholars have long appreciated his taste for inverted images. According to the *Tratado,* there were two congregations in the world, the Christian and the demonic: the former had sacraments, the latter excrements; the first featured a unified congregation, the second a broken one.[94] Catholic rituals entailed clear words and plain substances that could be located easily. In contrast, "diabolical excrements are in things not found in human life and conversation, such as unguents and powders made from rare materials, from animals and birds that are found with great difficulty, and with unknown and rhythmic words."[95] The Devil devised his rites as mockeries of their Christian counterparts.

Females predominated in Castañega's unholy flock because he applied inversion to the sexual realm; in this respect, he fits the latest historical arguments absolutely. Christ prohibited women from administering the sacraments, and so Castañega thought it fitting that the Devil invested authority in women rather than men.[96] He followed this detail with multiple clichés about female propensities for the diabolical. Women were more easily tricked by demons, as Eve herself proved. Women were more curious to discover hidden things: their nature denied them knowledge, and because they were ignorant and contrary by nature, they wanted recognition for their intelligence. They were more talkative than men, could not keep secrets, and consequently could not help but instruct each other—a conclusion that explained why witches were found in groups.[97] Women were more prone to anger and rancor, and asked the Devil for vengeance because they lacked the means to retaliate against their enemies. Finally, Castañega noted that females turned to demons for sex, especially if they had been inclined to lust as adolescents; he commented that old women were more susceptible to the Devil's deceits because they thought he would remedy their indigence. He linked demons to the whole female life span, because women were vulnerable in both youth and senectitude.

Castañega admitted that there was no difference between male necromancers and female witches; through much of his exposition he also used the masculine plural noun for "witch"—*brujos*—that would have encompassed both women and men. All the same, when he addressed sacrifices at black Masses, he highlighted the role of midwives who killed children; when he raised the genealogy of witchery, he fixed on a pedigree that ran from grandmother to mother to daughter. He also pointed to women as the guilty parties in fraudulent demonic possessions. When demons seemed to control a person's body,

The first thing to do is to note and examine, with much care, which spirits are those by whom the person is tormented, because through experience it is seen that some persons, especially women, through their own malice, pretend they are taken over by spirits or demonically possessed, just as they sometimes fake being the victims of maleficia or sorcery. They do this because of some dissatisfaction they have with their lovers or husbands, or because of the great carnal passions they have with someone, or because of the terrible temptations of the flesh that the demon ignites in them.[98]

Castañega then relayed an anecdote about a fellow Franciscan who had cured a similarly afflicted woman with a "solemn discipline of whipping" (*una solemne disciplina de azotes*). He finally remarked that no one should be surprised at the astonishing physical antics of the female possessed, or interpret such signs as proof of an authentic possession, because "a woman who makes up her mind for it easily produces frightening gestures, and the more so if the demon helps her."[99]

Some scholars have contended that the notion of false possession fostered female religious expression, however obliquely: early modern clerics read the signs of possession and religious ecstasy as one and the same, but if possession were only feigned, then demonic interference in women's spirituality could disappear.[100] Yet this suggestion comes undone as soon as we recall the conceptual link between the Devil and lies: when a woman faked her subjugation to demons, she revealed her attachment to them through the deception itself. Castañega took that connection for granted when he described women as the most likely perpetrators of fraudulent possessions; when he asserted that women easily could simulate the physical signs of possession, he invoked lies and carnality, the hallmarks of the Devil, at the same time. Even his account of authentic possessions rebounded to female guilt: women were puny, with frail hearts and brains, furious passions, and oscillating tempers, and hence constituted "open doors" for demonic proprietorship. With such remarks, Castañega sealed the correlation between the diabolical and the female. Women evinced their ties to the Devil when they fell prey to genuine possession, because their weaker nature made them vulnerable; when they faked that condition they betrayed the same bonds, simply because they lied. In Castañega's *Tratado,* the prospect of women as legitimate mediators between the earthly and the divine was positively remote.[101]

In contrast, Ciruelo pinned the responsibility for a false possession on the exorcist, and never treated the energumen as culpable in any way, or even as typically female. He also declined to indict another of Castañega's objects, one that also possessed stereotypical ties to witchcraft: namely, Jews, and from there Hebrew. Castañega opposed the cohesive Christian community to disparate ones populated by various groups of infidels, but he saved his most devastating remarks for Jews. He rejected the notion that circumcision fulfilled the function of a sacrament, and equated it with diabolical excrements. He also maintained a solid connection between the Devil and Hebrew: when he characterized demonic rituals as brandishing "obscure words, ugly and rhythmic, which require concentration and study," he was thinking of that idiom; when he accused cloud-conjurers of talking in a "Babylonian confusion," and gave examples of their speech, he flaunted Hebrew words in front of his readers. He then turned Hebrew toward vanity and infidelity, two qualities packed with demonic allusions:

> It seems a vain thing, and even a lack of faith, and a matter of the Jewish quarter (*judería*) or superstition, to use ancient Hebrew names in Christian and Catholic prayers, as if the old names were worth more than the new. And such names are especially dangerous for the ignorant who know little, because those Hebrew and Greek names may serve as a cover, so that other unknown, diabolical names are spoken with them.[102]

After all, the apostles and disciples had performed miracles in Jesus' name alone. The translator of the New Testament wrote the name of Jesus more than five hundred times; even Paul, who was born a Jew, declined to use Hebrew words for God in his epistles. In Castañega's opinion, Hebrew words were left in the ground once Jesus rose from the dead.[103]

Ciruelo never employed the noun or adjective for Hebrew in the *Reprobación,* and never mentioned Jews in that tract either, although he littered his biblical prologues with anti-Jewish calumny. In the case of nóminas—in which language played a crucial role—Ciruelo merely told his audience to avoid unknown words in their writings, and specified nothing more; given his ancestry, his silence was not casual. His neglect of this particular subject becomes that much more resonant once we realize that he deliberately corrected Castañega's *Tratado* with his own *Reprobación,* which is the conclusion I reached after reading the two works repeatedly and side by side. We know that Castañega's treatise was printed in 1529, and our earliest extant edition of Ciruelo's tract is 1538: a gap of nine years certainly would have allowed Ciruelo to obtain his peer's text and rework it. Yet the two works may have appeared in even closer succession than those dates imply.

There is no questioning the 1529 date for the *Tratado;* indeed, that version is the only one we possess and the only edition attested in the secondary literature. But the prologue to Ciruelo's *Reprobación* of 1538 mentions a previous publication of the treatise, and some secondary sources report its earliest date as 1530.[104] If this scenario were true—and we have nothing to contradict it—then Ciruelo published a correction to Castañega within a year of the *Tratado's* appearance. We thus can imagine Ciruelo as moved by more or less urgency in his task; more important, the emendations to the *Tratado* are plausible because the *Reprobación* appeared afterward, whether we want to place its imprint in 1530 or 1538. In sum, Ciruelo deliberately altered the *Tratado* and consequently transmitted a different sort of witch. His version reached a much larger audience.

Ciruelo simultaneously followed and emended Castañega's structure; he supplemented his theory, clarified his illustrations, and erased his anti-female and anti-Jewish ingredients. Both clerics observed the same subjects and sequence to a notable degree: they moved from a broad theoretical statement, to necromancers and witches, to the white magic of healers and nóminas, and finally to the conjuring of clouds, locusts, and the demonically possessed. On the last topics, though, Ciruelo modified his peer's design by transposing the order of the chapters.[105]

Tratado	*Reprobación*
—on the excommunication of creatures that lack reason	—on the damned superstition of exorcists
—on the conjurers of clouds	—on the conjurers of clouds
—on the conjurers of demoniacs	—on the excommunication of the locust, the aphid, etc.

Ciruelo preserved Castañega's middle subject, but reversed the ones around it: the two lists form an "X" when compared to each other. I do not know what the emendation means, as its significance seems equivocal.

In terms of content, in some respects Ciruelo copied Castañega's exposition, for he, too, explained how the energumen could take on the countenance of the dead and relay the departed's concerns. Both authors adduced the demoniac's possible calumny of bystanders, and cited the Devil's love of spectators.[106] Moreover, when Castañega first addressed the identity of the Devil's servants, he initially raised male necromancers, and then presented his readers with female witches; Ciruelo duplicated that sequence, as well as the phrase "brujas o xorguinas." But while Castañega entitled his first chapter "how the demon always wants to be honored and adored as God," Ciruelo devoted his initial one to the First Commandment, and demonstrated that God wanted honor and adoration from men, which in turn sparked the Devil's envy.[107] He furnished the step that Castañega omitted.

Ciruelo did more with Castañega's text than simply replicate its structure and language, for he also remedied what he thought it jumbled. When these clerics addressed exorcism, they invoked Jesus' cures of demoniacs in the New Testament. Castañega cluttered his account with myriad dependent clauses:

And the Pharisees, blinded by envy, denied Jesus Christ the first sort [of exorcism], which is through the authority, efficacy, and power that he had, with which he expelled demons; and they accused him of the second sort [of exorcism], saying that the demons obeyed him as a magician and a necromancer, because of the familiarity he had with Beelzebuth [sic]; and so they said by the virtue or power of Beelzebuth, prince of the demons . . . Jesus throws out [sic] the lesser demons, or the demons of less power, and also these lesser demons themselves obey Jesus, because of the familiarity and pact that he has with them. The Pharisees wanted to say nothing more than this when they told Jesus, at other times, that he had a demon.[108]

The challenge posed by the Pharisees was whether Jesus exorcised through his own divine power, or through the friendship of Beelzebub.

When Ciruelo turned to the same question, he supplied his readers with more lucid language and a sharper narrative. He explained that there were two modes of exorcism, one that depended upon divine authority, and another that relied upon the Devil's intervention. Castañega had tried to sort exorcism into three categories, and ended by muddling them all.[109] In contrast, Ciruelo's varieties were detailed in the Gospel, the first

When our Lord Jesus Christ cured a mute demoniac, and by force, with his divine power, cast out the Devil, even though the Devil did not wish it, and it was against his will. And the malicious Pharisees said that Jesus did it in Belcebub [sic]: they wished to say that Jesus performed the exorcism as a necromancer, on account of the secret pact he had with Belzebub [sic], who is the Devil. And even though our Lord did not deny that there were some exorcists who used that wicked method, he still proved to them . . . that he did not expel demons through a pact of friendship with the Devil.[110]

Readers of the *Reprobación* would have ended up with a more intelligible explanation of Jesus' power over demoniacs.

Ciruelo repaired other aspects of the *Tratado* as well. Castañega omitted the theoretical foundations of the implicit demonic pact, despite his clear references to Gerson; all his witches practiced the same rites, irrespective of whether they explicitly swore allegiance to the Devil. As Castañega relayed it, the only difference between witches with tacit and open pacts was that culprits with implicit agreements had not renounced their faith out loud, at least not in their own opinion.[111] In light of his authorities, Castañega's version of the implicit pact was extremely odd: he never told his audience how conjurers could belong to the Devil even if they failed to invoke demons or fly through the air. In contrast, Ciruelo explained the implicit pact according to its usual theory, and provided an example that fit centuries of demonology:

If someone—in order to cure another from headache or fever—should tie a piece of white paper or linen to the patient's leg, without anything else; or measure a ribbon according to the palms of the hands, or pass the person through a burning vinebranch, clearly it would be frivolity and a vain thing; because neither the paper nor the linen, in and of itself, has the natural power to expel the wicked humor that causes that pain from the head or the body. . . . But because the Devil is a friend of those who perform vain works, it frequently happens that with that blank paper or linen the patient gets well, and the Devil does this through certain secret methods that he knows . . . And he does it to trick simple people.[112]

All the authoritative elements were in the *Reprobación's* account, from the bonds between vanity and the Devil and lies, to the notion of the Devil as a truculent and covert threat to unsuspecting people. Ciruelo rebuked Castañega more directly too: when it came to rabies healers, "some doctors and theologians of little learning" tried to defend such tricksters with the idea of endemic powers, but their reasoning would not survive scrutiny.[113] Castañega had argued that the same individuals acted on natural gifts.

Even smaller details drew Ciruelo's attention and revision. At first, his counsel on wicked clouds looks interchangeable with Castañega's: both recommended ringing bells, assembling in church, and displaying relics. The point of difference lay in whether the clergy should go out to defy the cloud. Castañega suggested that ecclesiastics take the cross, proceed to where the cloud was arming itself, and begin to sing and pray appropriate antiphons, the litany of the saints, and passages from the Gospels. Ciruelo may have decided that Castañega's exposition was faulty: he insisted that if demons only rarely delivered storms, there was no reason for the clergy to contest a natural phenomenon. In his opinion, ecclesiastics should not go outside to confront the tempest.[114]

In the wake of the *Tratado,* the material that Ciruelo neglected was just as important as what he expanded or altered. He would chastise the presence of unknown words in the laity's prayers or conjurers' spells, but he never raised the possibility that those incantations could involve Hebrew. He ignored the cliché of multiple diabolical congregations, and overlooked the inheritance of witchcraft from earlier generations; he disregarded the trope of a demonic church that mirrored the Christian one. Obviously such themes could reverberate for a Spanish converso, even one who called himself an orphan. In sum, when it came to Judaism, Ciruelo did not pursue inversion, in spite of that target's prominent role in Christians' binary formulas, and Ciruelo's own taste for dialectic. It seems most likely that this feature of the *Reprobación* had something to do with Ciruelo's religious status. From one angle, he literally bridged the dichotomy between Christian and Jew; he may not have seen the value of that duality or wished to insert it into this particular work. What he did with the Devil and sex, and the Devil and women, was equally notable. He left out every carnal detail that Castañega included, such as descriptions of *incubi* and *succubi*; he also erased any special link between demons and women. Throughout the *Reprobación,* witches were as likely to be male as female.

The differences between Ciruelo and Castañega become that much more meaningful in light of their sources and contemporary arguments about early modern witchcraft. The two Spaniards turned their religious authorities to unexpected ends, and their choices illustrate their intellectual independence in a provocative way. Both called upon the Bible and Augustine, and Aquinas and Gerson in the course of their works. The fact that they employed Augustine and Aquinas simultaneously, and accepted both real and hallucinatory aspects of witchcraft, allows their example to undermine a recent proposal in the academy, which says they should have relied on one authority or the other, and thereby interpreted the witch's activities as primarily authentic or delusional.[115] But Castañega and Ciruelo moved easily from patristic to medieval writers, and back again. They also pondered notions that had been addressed by a host of predecessors, such as the implicit pact and transvection; and when they declined to cite the genesis of their ideas, we cannot pinpoint their sources with certainty.[116] Still, their dependence upon the Bible, albeit on different sections, is very clear; and so is their mixture of scholastic and humanist methods and styles. Their treatises reinforce conclusions from other chapters: ecclesiastics in sixteenth-century Spain resist easy categorization because they demonstrate autonomy as authors and readers, even in an intellectual culture dedicated to quotation.

On one level Castañega seems to belong to the Renaissance, because his appreciation for rhetoric was strong. He employed the usual modesty tropes about his own abilities: he could do no more than employ bits of his predecessors' wisdom; he could summon nothing that had not been written before, and he remarked that even Erasmus was in the same position.[117] He then raised the prospect of "human art and industry," admitted the grotesque character of his topic, and stipulated that he would give his subject "the best possible luster, with persuasive and rhetorical colors," in order to convince readers of the unfathomable.[118] Castañega culled most of his authorities from the New Testament. He also seemed aware of ecclesiastical history, for he employed the phrase "the primitive church." These facets of the *Tratado,* especially the mention of Erasmus, have led Castañega's editors to call him a humanist, but closer scrutiny of his text prompts a rather different impression.

The *Tratado* betrays a taste for the most negative features of scholastic method, namely, ahistorical readings and reckless metaphors that positively contorted its literary authorities.

Castañega's rhetorical goals could prompt him to slight the wider context of scriptural verses and neglect the development of both Judaism and Christianity. He sought to demonize Jews. To achieve that object, he characterized Jewish sacrifice as involving the blood of children, and backed up his claim with Psalm 105:37–38, which described the sins of Israel during the Jews' exile in the wilderness; he ignored the fact that the verses relayed particular misdeeds at a discrete moment in time.[119] He also proposed meanings for New Testament events that had little to do with the passages in question. As Jesus was seized in the garden of Gethsemane, the Apostle Peter sliced off the right ear of a guard who was participating in Jesus' arrest. Castañega pushed this episode to the point of absurdity in his quest to tie it to excommunication. He treated the guard as the excommunicated, identified Peter's sword with the episcopate's, and noted that excision of the ear symbolized the "[notification] and [denunciation of] the spiritual death of one who is disobedient and rebellious toward the church and her prelates, to the ears of the excommunicated and to the other faithful."[120]

Even allowing for the hermeneutic chain behind the allegory—the two swords, the ear, and an audience—Castañega bastardized the scriptural incident. The guard was not rebelling against any church, and no criticism of him occurs in the biblical passage; on the contrary, Jesus rebuked Peter for his impulsive violence.[121] Castañega's willingness to overlook the language and environment of Scripture in the quest for a scriptural example marks him as a partisan of scholastic method. In this instance, at least, he made an antique text shore up meaning, instead of deriving messages from the text itself.

He also pulled one of his most important themes from a quintessential piece of scholastic writing: the *Malleus maleficarum,* by the German inquisitors Heinrich Krämer and Jacob Sprenger.[122] Castañega never cited the *Malleus;* it probably was too recent to serve as an explicit literary authority, especially in a work packed with New Testament references. But it seems clear that Castañega plundered the *Malleus* for his musings on women and witches, since he hit the same points in nearly the same order: he apparently attempted to reiterate the *Malleus*'s most obvious elements. In Part I, qu. 6, the *Malleus* addressed "why is it that women are chiefly addicted to evil superstition"; in his own Chapter 5, Castañega expounded "why more women than men are diabolical ministers." If we list the contents of these respective sections, we end up with the repertories of women's negative characteristics shown in

TABLE 6.1
Female Attributes Outlined by the Malleus maleficarum *and*
Castañega's Tratado

Malleus	Tratado
excessive in goodness or vice	inheritance from Eve
garrulous	more credulous and impressionable
wrathful	intellectually weak, and hence curious
avaricious	talkative, hence teaches others
either loves or hates	wrathful
carnal	vengeful
more credulous and impressionable	weak intellect
talkative, hence teaches others	carnal
intellectually weak	avaricious
emotionally vindictive	
inheritance from Eve	
feebler in mind and body	
carnal	
wrathful	
vengeful	

table 6.1. It looks as if Castañega borrowed and narrowed the qualities that his German peers enumerated, for he invoked identical traits, or credulity, loquaciousness, anger, avarice, and lust.[123] He lifted his witches' activities from his counterparts' treatise, such as copulation with the Devil, infanticide, and vampirism. He, too, stipulated that midwives were particularly liable to witchcraft, and recorded how demons could transform themselves into incubi and succubi.[124] Moreover, both the *Malleus* and the *Tratado* addressed the exorcism of demoniacs and irrational creatures, as well as the conjuring of storms.[125]

If Castañega followed the *Malleus maleficarum* as a religious authority, then his taste for inversion has a lineage, because the *Malleus* was shot through with oppositional constructions and concepts; both treatises advanced by juxtaposing dichotomous statements, which in itself was a sign of their authors' scholastic proclivities. At the same time, though, recent paradigms tell us to expect the Old Testament in early modern treatments of witchcraft, and Castañega's *Tratado* lacks exactly this element; in this respect he contradicts the practice of his German peers.[126]

The sixteenth century allegedly witnessed a new appreciation for Mosaic Law in the wake of the Renaissance's accomplishments with ancient languages, and the Protestant Reformation's principle of sola scriptura. Fresh interest in the biblical text produced greater attention to Exodus; Exodus 22:18 in turn purportedly read "you shall not allow a witch to live," while witchcraft also contravened the First Commandment, with its stipulations against idolatry.[127] Elites and masses from Scotland to Italy thus had even clearer mandates to discover the mostly female witch and punish her accordingly, once the Old Testament emerged as a fundamental religious authority. But Castañega's example demonstrates that early modern intellectuals did not have to depend upon Exodus 22:18 or even the Decalogue in order to describe the witch and urge her arraignment: in fact, given the degree of anti-Judaism in his text, Castañega demonstrated a certain coherence by refusing to glean any positive counsel from the first half of the Bible. He grounded his critique on New Testament materials; if his scriptural sources did not explicate the heresy he was chastising, that detail simply shows how clerics could turn their references toward unforeseen objects.

If focusing on Mosaic Law was supposed to have led early modern intellectuals to idolatry and the indictment of witchcraft, then Ciruelo illustrates that trajectory fulsomely. He labeled his first chapter a declaration "of the great excellence and dignity of the first of the Ten Commandments of God; to demonstrate how great are the sins of superstition that go against this commandment."[128] He described the Decalogue's reception by Israel, explained that code as the immutable law of nature, and designated it as eternally in force. He qualified the opening three commandments as superior to the other seven, and within those three, made the first one peerless. What he stressed above all were the virtues promoted and the vices outlawed by the sin of idolatry.

Of virtue it says, "you shall love your God with all your heart and all your soul, and you shall adore your God, and serve Him alone." Of vice it says: "You will not have other gods before Me; you will not adore or serve them or their statues or forms." Of punishment it says, "I am a God who is very jealous of My honor, and toward whoever harms Me in it, I will punish him and all his descendents, children and grandchildren, until the third and fourth generation." Of the reward of virtue, it says: "I am very merciful to those who love Me well and serve Me loyally, and I will perform many mercies for them and their descendents through more than a thousand generations."[129]

As in the case of his confessors' manual, Ciruelo again worked Jesus' rendition of the First Commandment into Exodus's phrasing. And despite its dialectical flavor, his deliberate amalgamation of positive and negative precepts would result in conclusions that expressed as much mercy as punishment.

Ciruelo's willingness to filter the Decalogue through Christian forgiveness, both conceptually and literally, produced a more temperate policy toward witches than we might have guessed. He ended up slighting the very objects—women, Jews, and Hebrew—that his peers so often associated with European witchcraft. Although Ciruelo had access to the *Malleus maleficarum* in the library at the University of Alcalá, he declined to insert the most notorious sort of witch into his treatise.[130] Although he enumerated a large number of potential idolaters in the *Reprobación,* he also excused the ignorant and fixed on those who should have known better, namely, the clergy. I would conjecture that Ciruelo most often portrayed the witch as a male sorcerer, instead of a vampiristic, vengeful woman, because he relied upon a wider array of Mosaic examples, and more readings from the Bible and other venerable sources. Clearly idolatry was the subject at hand, but the question is what form it could take for a Spanish ecclesiastic in the sixteenth century.

Significantly, Ciruelo's culprits tended to match Old Testament malefactors who predicted and revealed events, questioned the dead, and hindered misfortune; he called up such examples in Deuteronomy 18:10–11, Leviticus 20:27, and 1 Kings 28:7. He never cited Exodus 22:18 in the *Reprobación*: notably, that infamous verse featured a word for "witch"—*mekhashepha*—whose occurrence in the Old Testament was unique and whose meaning was exceptionally obscure.[131] Nicholas de Lyra had followed the Onqelos Targum when he translated mekhashepha into the Latin *sortilegam,* or a female soothsayer; Lyra also advanced the connection between women and the Devil by tying soothsaying to carnal acts. But another Aramaic Targum could urge a genderless reading of Exodus 22:18 because it included men as potential sortilegi as well, and we know from Ciruelo's biblical translations that he was familiar with it: the Jonathan Targum read "My people, children of Israel, you shall not let anyone who practices sorcery live."[132]

Ciruelo also would have been familiar with Rashi's directive that Scripture did not distinguish between male and female.[133] And traditional Christian authorities promoted the same inclusive angle. The Greek Septuagint handled Exodus 22:18 as affecting poisoners of either sex, while the Latin Vulgate rendered mekhashepha as *maleficos,* a plural Latin noun with a masculine ending.[134] Meanwhile, Augustine and Aquinas portrayed men as well as women as plausible disciples of the Devil, and Ciruelo invested the *Reprobación* with concepts from both those figures. If we survey his witchcraft treatise as a whole, it looks as if Ciruelo read the Decalogue through a larger context of holy sources, instead of isolating a single verse and ignoring prestigious alternatives to it. His reading of idolatry conformed to the oldest and most authoritative sources in the Christian tradition.

Thus, Ciruelo grounded his *Reprobación* on the precepts of Moses and categorized all witchcraft as sins of idolatry; even the Spanish verb *reprobar,* from which he derived his title, means a "condemnation from God's law." Yet the wider context of Scripture, the difficulty of its interpretation, and the availability and eminence of other readings, may have prompted Ciruelo to scrutinize other materials in a quest for the Decalogue's meaning. His search deeply affected his portrait of the witch. The irony of the *Reprobación* lies in the contrast between its apparent textual fundamentalism and its actual emphases. Ciruelo acknowledged the Commandments as his essential religious authority, but also relied on other sacred sources to clarify their parameters. The results are most unexpected, since he slighted the female witch, treated laypersons as collaborators, and neglected to draw a line between the material and spiritual realms. He turned an allegedly intractable text—Mosaic Law— toward ends that in some respects, at least, had more to do with concord than division.

The *Reprobación* offers us further incongruities in its combination of scholastic form and textual criticism. Like Castañega and nearly every other individual in this book, Ciruelo's debt to scholasticism was plain. In his witchcraft text he paired oppositional statements to arrive at the truth, although he simultaneously spurned dichotomies between Christians and Jews, men and women, and clerical and lay discipline. He did his best to order his material into coherent categories: he divided nóminas, for instance, into ones that featured good, true words, and others that displayed false, wicked phrases. He also reserved the *Reprobación's* final chapter for answering common objections, which amounted to handling scholastic *dubia*.

Nevertheless, Ciruelo broadcast his critical methods simultaneously. When he addressed the attribution of fortune or calamity to particular days, he remarked that some fools associated luck with the numbers of specific psalms, and then explained that the Latin and Hebrew versions of Psalms were tallied differently. He called the alleged formulas of Solomon fraudulent, despite their promises of instant knowledge: "there are various books about this art in various lands, and in various ways some do not agree with others; therefore Solomon couldn't have written them all."[135] Finally, Ciruelo filled the *Reprobación* with Jewish and Christian history: he described Israel's exile and the reception of the Decalogue; he explained the miracles in the early church as fostering the conversion of both Gentiles and Jews. His religious communities were not motionless, but resulted from the evolution of people over time.[136]

Ciruelo's tract on witchcraft proved much more popular in Spain than Castañega's, despite the latter's sensational details: the *Reprobación* even infiltrated the Basque country in 1561, when its counsel on demonic possession literally was copied into a manual on the cura animarum, written for the clergy of Pamplona.[137] Ciruelo's work may have been reprinted so often because of its author's relative eminence, but it also offered readers a more complex semiotics of the witch than the *Tratado,* because its portrait lacked women and Jews as obvious suspects. The fact that early modern Spaniards preferred Ciruelo's vision is just as important as recognizing that the Catholic elite could produce different witches from different sources, as if in competition with one another. The lesson here is that even texts that seem to promote the most rigid sort of religious authority can divulge the autonomy of ecclesiastical authors, and the independence of their clerical and lay readers, in sixteenth-century Spain.

Epilogue

Clerical authors in early modern Spain read their sources and composed their books in a personalized fashion: ironically, their combinations of texts, methods, and messages recall the Burckhardt thesis, which posed the Renaissance as the birth of the individual. The first half of the Spanish sixteenth century did not generate a series of protomodern persons, some of whom happened to be priests and monks. But it did tolerate an intellectual environment in which ecclesiastics could implant greater or lesser amounts of tradition, history, and criticism into their arguments. It also permitted an assortment of pastoral messages to circulate at the same time, even if those teachings rebuked confessors and featured clerics as likely sorcerers. Religious authority in early modern Spain was not construed or applied in a univocal manner. Questions about it reveal energy and ingenuity where we too frequently see stasis and routine. Ecclesiastics could call up, discard, and muster again certain techniques and emphases: they were not locked into particular propensities, although the historiography implies otherwise. Inquiries into the hierarchies they constructed, whether intellectual or practical, help to weaken the polarities we customarily apply to the evidence, for the evidence itself denies dichotomies.

Investigations into religious authority demonstrate that Spain had a Renaissance, and that clerics participated in that phenomenon. But Spanish ecclesiastics-cum-humanists, like European humanists in general, executed their critical and historical concerns within a scholastic heritage, which they could notice to a greater or lesser extent. Juan de Vergara came as close to calling himself a Renaissance humanist as any Spanish intellectual could, and then wrote a dialectical apologia on refusing to name his collaborators. Bartolomé

Carranza could emphasize a phrase in the Gospel of John, and then move seamlessly to one in Matthew, as if the two formed a single expression. Dr. Bernal made his colleagues pay attention to Jesus with the help of Cajetan. Pedro Ciruelo described the physical transmission of the biblical text, but hesitated to endorse Erasmus's comments on the development of Christianity. And Pedro de Lerma endorsed Erasmus's elimination of the comma Johanneum, but declined to explain the preeminence of Greek biblical manuscripts over Latin ones. Like their European peers, the Spaniards fluctuated between historical sensitivity and pedagogical instruction, between the Church as a historical institution and an eternal, immutable truth.

All the figures in this book betrayed their debt to Aristotle; all wielded at least the New Testament; all used personal experience to bolster their contentions. Most of the intellectuals studied here knew or could have known each other. The majority moved in relatively high ecclesiastical circles; we can describe them as forming a sort of intellectual community. Yet when we survey them as a whole, what stands out most is their inventiveness. They employed scholastic method and authorities in the pursuit of radical consequences, as Bernal did with episcopal residence. They cloaked their creativity in stock phrases, as Ciruelo did in his prologues to his translations. A few, such as Miguel Gómez at Valladolid, would defend Erasmus with Erasmus's own reasoning; an equally small number argued in consistently scholastic ways for thoroughly conservative ends. But on the whole these ecclesiastics snap our expectations of coherence about their priorities, given the auctoritates they summoned and the way they employed them. They did not always invoke Aquinas to preserve the status quo; they did not inevitably cite the New Testament in order to change its text. Their literary success depended upon literary quotation, but they could manipulate their sources in ways we have not sufficiently explored.

The evidence reveals persistent subtleties in the way Spanish clerics made and employed their hierarchies of religious authorities. It also betrays unexpected nuances to their promotion of religious privilege. We already knew that bishops, priests, and monks were thoroughly established in the secular world in practice; what we did not necessarily grasp was that ecclesiastical writers fixed their clerics in the world by design. The individuals treated here were not alienated from secular environments, nor did they urge that sort of estrangement in their works. They threatened their readers with divine wrath, and urged the same audience to self-examination; but they never detached ecclesiastics from the community, or expelled laymen and women from religion, either. They promoted instead a complementary enterprise of spiritual correction and advancement that occurred in the pueblo. Valtanás berated priests who took their congregations' monies and then refused to preach. Castañega only deprecated money when the quest for it assumed outrageous proportions. Bernal worried over angering parishioners, and Carranza drew his ideal bishops and priests as peacemakers. Their example should spur further investigation of several large theses in the academy.

The Spaniards wrote prescriptive tracts, not abstract ones: as pragmatic and successful men, and holders of ecclesiastical offices, they knew that neighborhoods and families could be harmed by clerics themselves. Accordingly, in nearly every instance they adduced ecclesiastical sins in the midst of their pious recommendations, and many of them went on to raise their readers as judges of clerical misbehavior even as they attempted to elevate the priestly estate. Frías could never have described episcopal visitors as "rejoining" had he not conceived of dialogue in the first place; Ciruelo included quizzes for priest-conjurers because he expected his audience to use them. The fact that Vergara could disparage the cura animarum while proclaiming himself an Erasmian only illustrates the range of clerical voices in early modern Spain. The fact that most of these ecclesiastics pictured the laity—and the clergy—as rational sheep simply demonstrates the potential alterity of earlier discourse: the expression strikes us as an oxymoron, but many sixteenth-century thinkers employed it in a very serious way.

Clerical writers in early modern Spain were active, not placid, intellects, and so were their readers: bookstore inventories and literacy rates, printing histories and literary effects imply that these authors faced a discerning audience and discriminated themselves. This sort of dynamism deserves particular emphasis in the Spanish case because of Spain's position in European historiography. Spain routinely is construed as the "other" when it comes to its Western counterparts. This "exceptionalism" is supposed to emanate from a religious mixture of Jews, Muslims, and Christians, and then from an extreme Catholicism, which dated from the Spanish Reconquest, evolved in Spain's battle against Protestants, and surfaced again in that country's rejection of republicanism in the twentieth century.[1] Throughout its history, Spain allegedly shut the door on the best European tendencies toward tolerance, and the early modern period looms large in that process. If some of the very agents of those reactionary tendencies—ecclesiastics in the sixteenth century—pursued more flexible methods and messages than we suspected, then we have taken another step toward deepening the usual portrait of this particular country. Of course, my findings generally extend only to 1570, and they can be twisted to very different ends from the ones I intend: scholars may use the first half of the sixteenth century, with its intellectual and religious fluidity, to dramatize the backlash that allegedly occurred in the second half of the same era. But I would point out that the subtleties described here rarely are confined to specific chronologies.[2] If these Spanish clerics were capable of equivocation and nuance, then their successors undoubtedly were too.

Notes

Abbreviations

ADC   Archivo Diocesano, Cuenca
AHN   Archivo Histórico Nacional, Madrid
BN   Biblioteca Nacional, Madrid
BH   *Bulletín hispanique*
CHE   *Cuadernos de la Historia de España*
CSIC Consejo Superior de Investigaciones Científicas
DHEE *Diccionario de la historia eclesiastica de España,* 4 vols.
Exp. Expediente
FUE   Fundación Universitaria Española
Inqu. Inquisición
Leg. Legajo
MRTS Medieval and Renaissance Texts and Studies
RABM *Revista de archivos, bibliotecas, y museos*
Sec. Sección

Introduction

1. Flores was a well-known agitator for the rebels' cause. See the specific references to him in what remains the best account of the insurrection, Joseph Pérez's *La révolution des "comunidades" de Castille (1520–21),* Bibliothèque de l'École des Hautes Études Hispaniques, no. 42 (Bourdeaux: Féret & Fils, 1970).

2. Flores interpreted Matthew 21:2 according to the tropological, or moral, mode of biblical exegesis, which was one of the four standard methods of exposition that Pope Gregory I (ca. 540–604) transmitted in the West. For the history of Western exegesis, see Henrí du Lubac, *Exégèse médiévale: Les quatre sens de l'écriture,* 4 vols. (Paris: Aubier, 1959–64).

3. A variation of the verse occurs in Luke 19:30 ("Ite in castellum quod contra

est" ["go into the village which is opposite"]) that makes Flores's interpretation even more far-fetched.

4. Extensive portions of Vergara's trial have been transcribed in John Longhurst, "Alumbrados, erasmistas y luteranos en el proceso de Juan de Vergara," *CHE* 27 (1957): 99–163; 28 (1958): 102–65; 29–30 (1959): 266–92; 31–32 (1960): 322–56; 35–36 (1962): 337–53; 37–38 (1963): 356–71. Flores's testimony is in 27 (1957): 153–55. The manuscript of Vergara's prosecution is preserved in the Archivo Histórico Nacional in Madrid, Sección de la Inquisición, Legajo 223, número 7, henceforth denoted as AHN, Sec. Inqu., Leg. 223, n. 7. See Chapter 1.

5. "Estando este testigo en esta villa de Madrid en la posada del señor arzobispo de Toledo, y en su presencia teniendo platica sobre estas trasslaciones [sic] que nuevamente se hazen del hebrayco y griego en latin de la sagrada escriptura, dixo este testigo que tenía por muy mejor y más cierto la que usa la sancta madre yglesia ahora que no qualquiera otra traslacion que de nuevo se saque; porque es abrir puerto, para que teniendose alguna cosa por no cierta de la traslacion que usamos, que cada uno que se le antoje que las cosas substanciales de la sagrada escriptura de que no están bien trassladas. . . . Y estando alli presente el doctor Vergara . . . dixo que sanct agustin [sic], por no saber griego, no supo lo que se dixo en la declaracion que hizo en los salmos de david, en el libro que se llama de las quinquajenas; y este testigo dixo que le parecía muy mal aquella palabra, y muy desacatada, por ser aquel un libro a quien toda la yglesia universal tiene en muy grand veneracion." Longhurst, "Alumbrados, erasmistas, y luteranos," 27 (1957): 154.

6. "Callasen"; ibid., 154–55.

7. Ibid., 28 (1958): 162–63; 31–32 (1960): 346–48.

8. "Pues de quien tan falsa e sacrilegamente usa de las palabras evangelicas para levantar una cibdad, bien se deve presumir que usara de las proprias para levantar un testimonio." Ibid., 31–32 (1960): 346.

9. Or so modern academics usually have interpreted Vergara's travails at the hands of his accusers. See Longhurst's introduction to his transcriptions, ibid., 27 (1957): 99, as well as Marcel Bataillon's account of the trial, *Érasme et l'Espagne: Nouvelle édition en trois volumes,* ed. Daniel Devoto and Chales Amiel, Travaux d'Humanisme et Renaissance, no. 250, 3 vols. (Geneva: Librairie Droz S.A., 1991), 1:473–509.

10. On humanist pedagogy's often incomplete effects on Italian primary and secondary schools, see Paul F. Gehl, *A Moral Art: Grammar, Society, and Culture in Trecento Florence* (Ithaca, N.Y.: Cornell University Press, 1993); and Paul F. Grendler, *Schooling in Renaissance Italy: Literacy and Learning, 1300–1600* (Baltimore: Johns Hopkins University Press, 1989).

11. Paul Oskar Kristeller is the single most influential proponent of this argument, which has the advantages of relying on fifteenth-century definitions of *umanista* and recognizing medieval antecedents to Renaissance humanism. Nevertheless, the difficulty with Kristeller's scheme is its fundamental distrust of rhetoric and its tendency to limit humanists to particular professions, narrowly drawn. See "Changing Views of

the Intellectual History of the Renaissance since Jacob Burckhardt," and "Humanist Learning in the Italian Renaissance," both in Kristeller, *Studies in Renaissance Thought and Letters,* 2 vols. (Rome: Edizioni di Storia e Letteratura, 1985), 2:3–25 and 2:93–110, respectively; and idem, *Renaissance Thought and Its Sources* (New York: Columbia University Press, 1979). For an application of Kristeller's concerns, see Jerrold E. Seigel, *Rhetoric and Philosophy in Renaissance Humanism* (Princeton, N.J.: Princeton University Press, 1968).

12. Especially as stated by Eugenio Garin in *L'umanesimo italiano,* 6th ed. (Bari: Laterza, 1975), who believed that the Renaissance sense of historical distance provoked the formulation of a truly human consciousness. On Renaissance historicism in general, see Roberto Weiss, *The Renaissance Discovery of Classical Antiquity* (Oxford: Oxford University Press, 1969); Donald R. Kelley, *Foundations of Modern Historical Scholarship: Language, Law, and History in the French Renaissance* (New York: Columbia University Press, 1970); and Charles G. Nauert Jr., *Humanism and the Culture of Renaissance Europe* (Cambridge: Cambridge University Press, 1995).

13. Petrarca wrote epistles to Cicero that grappled with the latter's political decisions. See his *Letters on Familiar Matters,* trans. Aldo S. Bernardo, 3 vols. (Baltimore: Johns Hopkins University Press, 1985), 3:317–21. For Leonardo Bruni's thoughts on the correct way to translate, see *The Humanism of Leonardo Bruni: Selected Texts,* trans. Gordon Griffiths, James Hankins, and David Thompson, MRTS, no. 46 (Binghamton, N.Y.: MRTS, 1987), 217–29.

14. A point made by the leading specialist on the Spanish Renaissance, Francisco Rico, as well as by Garin. See Rico's *El sueño del humanismo, de Petrarca a Erasmo* (Madrid: Alianza Universal, 1993), 42–43. In this scheme humanists discovered, or at least newly valued, a historical dimension for human existence, rather than a purely providential one. Their awareness of history led them to a sense of contingency or relativism, and then to the realization that humans could control or alter their circumstances. Renaissance humanists became aware that "the world could correct itself as one corrects a text or a style" ("que el mundo pudo corregirse como se corrige un texto o un estilo"). Ibid., 44.

15. The difficulty, of course, is that conclusions about Renaissance historicism, philology, and modernity are as potentially teleological as Burckhardt's. Scholars of the Renaissance very often describe their subjects in terms of "how close" they came to nineteenth- and twentieth-century textual criticism.

16. For similar issues with John Colet, see Eugene F. Rice Jr., "John Colet and the Annihilation of the Natural," *Harvard Theological Review* 45 (1952): 141–63.

17. On the history and procedures of the Spanish Inquisition, see Joaquín Pérez Villanueva and Bartolomé Escandell Bonet, *Historia de la Inquisición en España y América,* 2 vols. (Madrid: Biblioteca de Autores Españoles, 1984), and Henry Kamen, *The Spanish Inquisition: A Historical Revision* (New Haven, Conn.: Yale University Press, 1997), which amends his *Inquisition and Society in Spain in the Sixteenth and Seventeenth Centuries* (Bloomington: Indiana University Press, 1985). On the Toledo

tribunal in particular, Jean-Pierre Dedieu, *L'Administration de la Foi: L'Inquisition de Tolède XVI–XVIII siècle,* Bibliothèque de la Casa de Velázquez, vol. 7 (Madrid: Casa de Velázquez, 1989).

18. John S. Contreni, "Carolingian Biblical Studies," in *Carolingian Essays: Andrew W. Mellon Lectures in Early Christian Studies,* ed. Uta-Renate Blumenthal (Washington, D.C.: Catholic University of America Press, 1983), 71–98; G. R. Evans, *The Language and Logic of the Bible: The Earlier Middle Ages* (Cambridge: Cambridge University Press, 1984); Beryl Smalley, *The Study of the Bible in the Middle Ages* (Oxford: Basil Blackwell, 1952).

19. *Praise of Folly,* trans. Betty Radice, *Collected Works of Erasmus,* vol. 27: *Literary and Educational Writings* (Toronto: University of Toronto Press, 1986), 146, 150–53.

20. Jerry Bentley, *Humanists and Holy Writ* (Princeton, N.J.: Princeton University Press, 1983), 128. In preparing the 1516 New Testament, Erasmus possessed a single Greek manuscript of the Apocalypse, which lacked the final leaf. He lifted the last six verses from the Latin and translated them into Greek. He fixed the problem in his fourth edition of the New Testament in 1527.

21. On the humanists' shifts between history and allegory, and the assumption of imitation, Anthony Grafton, *Defenders of the Text* (Cambridge, Mass.: Harvard University Press, 1991), Chapter 1. For one literary scholar, "the mutual entailments of authenticity and estrangement generate the central problematic of Renaissance humanism": Debora Kuller Shuger, *The Renaissance Bible: Scholarship, Sacrifice, and Subjectivity* (Berkeley: University of California Press, 1994), 51–52. For continuities between medieval and Renaissance historicism, Janet Coleman, *Ancient and Medieval Memories: Studies in the Reconstruction of the Past* (Cambridge: Cambridge University Press, 1992), 558–67.

22. Mary Carruthers, *The Medieval Book of Memory* (Cambridge: Cambridge University Press, 1992), 11–13. Richard Southern made an analogous point in his introduction to the memorial volume for Beryl Smalley: *The Bible in the Medieval World,* ed. Katherine Walsh and Diane Wood (Oxford: Basil Blackwell, 1985). Intellectuals in the Renaissance could level similar charges: see Grafton, *Defenders of the Text,* Chapter 1.

23. For a forceful statement that humanism and scholasticism were fundamentally contradictory, see Charles G. Nauert Jr., "Humanism as Method: Roots of Conflict with the Scholastics," *Sixteenth Century Journal* 29, no. 2 (1998): 427–38.

24. On "mythologies of coherence" and other pitfalls in intellectual history, Quentin Skinner, "Meaning and Understanding in the History of Ideas," *History and Theory* 7 (1969): 3–53. Erika Rummel, *The Humanist-Scholastic Debate in the Renaissance and Reformation* (Cambridge, Mass.: Harvard University Press, 1995), 13, has contended that crossover attempts by scholastics and humanists were amateurish demonstrations, calculated to disarm their opponents; I see more value in such ambiguities. Petrarca noted in his introduction to his earliest collection of prose letters that his epistles "were so different that in rereading them I seemed to be in constant

contradiction," and that "to be contradictory was my only expedient"; *Letters on Familiar Matters*, 1:9.

25. Historians of the Spanish Renaissance can be divided into three general groups: those who locate it in the early fifteenth rather than sixteenth century, those who posit Antonio de Nebrija as its initiator, and those who tie it to Spanish Erasmianism. The arguments of the first and third groups display some grave disadvantages; the second position is most consonant with a definition of humanism as historical and textual criticism, but it, too, can turn to messages rather than methods of interpretation. For the first approach, see Ottavio di Castillo, *El humanismo castellano del siglo XV* (Valencia: Fernando Torres Editor, 1976), and idem, "Humanism in Spain," in *Renaissance Humanism: Foundations, Forms, and Legacy*, ed. Albert Rabil Jr., 3 vols. (Philadelphia: University of Pennsylvania Press, 1988), 2:39–104; for the second, see Jose López Rueda, *Los helenístas españoles del siglo XVI* (Madrid: Instituto Antonio de Nebrija, 1973); Francisco Rico, *Nebrija frente a los bárbaros* (Salamanca: Universidad de Salamanca, 1978). For a collection of pieces about biblical scholarship in the Spanish Renaissance, which recognizes Nebrija's contribution, see Natalio Fernández Marcos and Emilia Fernández Tejero, *Biblia y humanismo: Textos, talantes y controversias del siglo XVI español* (Madrid: FUE, 1997). On Erasmianism, see nn. 26, 27, 30, and 31 below.

26. Bataillon, *Érasme et l'Espagne*, was not the first to propose a connection between Erasmus and Spain. Marcelino Menéndez y Pelayo, *Historia de los heterodoxos españoles*, ed. Enrique Sánchez Reyes, 4 vols., 2nd ed. (Madrid: CSIC, 1963) 1:58, 3:9–16, originally had a negative opinion of Erasmus's impact, but reversed himself by the end of his life. Adolfo Bonilla y San Martín, "Erasmo y España (episódio de la historia del Renacimiento)," *Revue Hispanique* 17 (1907): 379–548, envisioned only a circumscribed relationship between Erasmus and the Iberian Peninsula.

27. Although in the 1520s Erasmus "sera devenu l'ame d'une révolution religieuse espagnole," by the next decade "Par la mort et par la captivité, les liens se rompent qui rattachaient l'élite espagnole à Érasme"; Bataillon, *Érasme et l'Espagne*, 1:172, 530. For the persecutions wrought by the Inquisition, and the spiritual crisis of the late 1550s that pitted Catholic Reform against Counter-Reform, see ibid., vol. 1, Chapters 9 and 13.

28. Silvana Seidel Menchi has posited that Erasmus performed a similarly osmotic function for Italy, although her evidence comes from different types of sources, her definitions owe less to essential proclivities, and her treatment of Erasmus and his audience is much more subtle. *Erasmo in Italia 1520–1580* (Torino: Bollati Boringhieri, 1987).

29. Bataillon described Erasmus's Christian humanism as akin to any other "mouvement intellectuel libérateur"; *Érasme et l'Espagne*, 1:80. He framed the relationship between Erasmus's supporters and detractors with military metaphors (1: 241–42). He finally compared Spain's sixteenth-century conflict over Erasmus to its twentieth-century civil war, which began the year he finished his *thèse* (1:848–49). In a 1976 article, he repeated the dichotomy between "el humanismo español y sus

adversarios tradicionalistas," and noted that the former was "inspirado en Erasmo de Rotterdam" (3:34). The scenario recalls a standard motif for treatments of Italian religious history in the sixteenth century, namely, the purported chasm between *spirituali* like Giovanni Morone and *intransigenti* such as Paul IV. See Chapter 4.

30. Even the most recent scholars of the Spanish Renaissance, who are far more likely to connect it to a revival of antiquity rather than a devotional style, fall into an analogous pattern of elevating spiritual counsel over modes of interpretation. Significantly, nearly all continue to frame the subject as a dialectic, and to divide early modern Spain into camps of progressive and regressive forces. See Juan F. Alcina and Francisco Rico, "Temas y problemas del renacimiento español," in *Siglos de oro: Renacimiento,* ed. Francisco López Estrada, *Historia y crítica de la literatura española,* ed. Francisco Rico, no. 2, vol. 1 (Barcelona: Editorial crítica, 1991), 11, 13. Also Eugenio Asensio, "Tendencias y momentos en el humanismo español," ibid., 28; Francisco Rico, *El sueño del humanismo,* 20–23, 107–18, 125, 145; Joseph Pérez, "Introducción," in *El siglo de fray Luis de León: Salamanca y el Renacimiento* (Salamanca: Universidad de Salamanca, 1991), 18–19. The same propensity to read Spanish humanism as Erasmianism, and Erasmianism as a devotional message, is routine among social and cultural historians of Spanish religion. For an example, see Carlos M. N. Eire, *From Madrid to Purgatory* (Cambridge: Cambridge University Press, 1995), 27, 226, 513.

31. J. H. Elliott, *Imperial Spain 1469–1716* (New York: New American Library, Meridian Books, 1977), 158–59, 211–21. John Lynch, *Spain under the Habsburgs,* 2 vols., 2nd ed. (Oxford: Basil Blackwell, 1981), 1:70–73. Positive evaluations of Erasmus and Ignatius include John C. Olin, "Erasmus and St. Ignatius Loyola," in *Six Essays on Erasmus* (New York: Fordham University Press, 1979), 75–92; idem, "The Jesuits, Humanism, and History," in *Erasmus, Utopia and the Jesuits* (New York: Fordham University Press, 1994); and Marc Rotsaert, "Les premieres contacts de saint Ignace avec l'érasmisme espagnol," *Revue d'histoire de la spiritualité* 49 (1973): 443–64. On Erasmus and Juan de Valdés, see John E. Longhurst, *Erasmus and the Spanish Inquisition, the Case of Juan de Valdés* (Albuquerque: University of New Mexico Press, 1950), and Massimo Firpo, *Tra alumbrados e "spirituali": Studi su Juan de Valdes e il valdesianesimo,* Studi e testi per la storia religiosa del Cinquecento, no. 3 (Florence: Leo S. Olschki, 1990), Chapter 1. On Teresa de Jesús, see Jodi Bilinkoff, *The Avila of St. Teresa* (Ithaca, N.Y.: Cornell University Press, 1989), 79–81.

32. Alcina and Rico, "Temas y problemas del renacimiento español," 5. Astute criticism of the Bataillon thesis lies in Eugenio Asensio, "El erasmismo y la corrientes espirituales afines," *Revista de la filología española* 36 (1952): 31–99.

33. Shuger, *The Renaissance Bible;* Bentley, *Humanists and Holy Writ;* Eugene F. Rice Jr., *St. Jerome in the Renaissance* (Baltimore: Johns Hopkins University Press, 1985); Charles Stinger, *Humanism and the Church Fathers: Ambrogio Traversari (1386–1439) and Christian Antiquity in the Italian Renaissance* (Albany: State University of New York, 1977); Salvatore I. Camporeale, *Lorenzo Valla: Umanesimo e teologia* (Firenze: Instituto Nazionale di Studi sul Rinascimento, 1972).

34. For a chronology of Erasmus's patristic scholarship, see Olin, "Erasmus and the Church Fathers," in *Six Essays,* 33–47, as well as L. D. Reynolds and N. G. Wilson, *Scribes and Scholars: A Guide to the Transmission of Greek and Latin Literature,* 2nd ed. (Oxford: Clarendon, 1974), 142–46, and Bentley, *Humanists and Holy Writ,* Chapters 4 and 5. The Greek New Testament of the Complutensian Polyglot Bible was printed by 1514, or two years before Erasmus's edition; but the sale of the former was delayed, so that Erasmus's work appeared first on the market.

35. Scholars of Erasmus's textual criticism can be divided into two groups: those who posit the gist of his hermeneutics as the predominantly allegorical interests of the *Enchiridion,* and those who see his priorities shifting to an increasing concern with the letter as the foundation for the spirit. I fall into the latter circle; for examples of its arguments, see J. B. Payne, "Toward the Hermeneutics of Erasmus," in *Scrinium erasmianum,* ed. J. Coppens, 2 vols. (Leiden: Brill, 1969) 2:13–49, especially pp. 42, 49; Jacques Chomarat, "Les *Annotationes* de Valla, celles d'Erasme et la grammaire," in *Histoire de l'exégèse au XVIe siècle,* ed. Olivier Fatio and Pierre Fraenkel (Geneva: Librairie Droz S.A., 1978), 202–28; Bentley, *Humanists and Holy Writ,* 116; and Manfred Hoffmann, *Rhetoric and Theology: The Hermeneutic of Erasmus* (Toronto: University of Toronto Press, 1994), with important cautions in J. B. Payne's review, *Renaissance Quarterly* 49 (1996): 903–4. For the opposite angle, James McConica, *Erasmus,* Past Masters (Oxford: Oxford University Press, 1991), and Olin, "Erasmus and Reform," in *Six Essays,* 1–16.

36. A distinction that becomes clear if we compare Erasmus's *Colloquies,* for instance, to the very popular fifteenth-century work by Thomas à Kempis, *Imitation of Christ.*

37. Alistair Fox has detected the same problem in expositions of the English Renaissance. "Facts and Fallacies: Interpreting English Humanism," in *Reassessing the Henrician Age: Humanism, Politics and Reform 1500–1550,* ed. Alistair Fox and John Guy (Oxford: Oxford University Press, 1986), 18–23, 27–31.

38. Vergara's and his peers' frequent and pithy use of the noun and adjective *idiota* provokes difficulties in translation: in the Middle Ages, the word connoted only a lack of Latin, but in sixteenth-century Spain, the employment of it also seems to carry overtones from the modern English cognate.

39. See Nauert, "Humanism as Method," 432–33; see Chapters 1–3 below for evidence of such intersections. I disagree with Rummel, who grants that humanists could pursue eclectic methods and styles in the early Renaissance, but contends that the humanist-scholastic rift was fundamental during the Reformation. Rummel, *The Humanist-Scholastic Debate,* Chapter 1.

Chapter One. The Trial of Juan de Vergara

1. In contrast, *colegios mayores* in Salamanca and Valladolid were only a small part of the university community, and their members generally were excluded from posi-

tions in university government. See Richard L. Kagan, *Students and Society in Early Modern Spain* (Baltimore: Johns Hopkins University Press, 1974), 66, 109–29, 144.

2. In 1311–12 the Council of Vienne had directed various European universities to provide chairs in Hebrew, Aramaic, and Arabic, but the measure never was fulfilled in any consistent way.

3. The Polyglot's New Testament was printed between 1513 and 1514, the Old Testament from 1515 to 1517. Juan de Vallejo, *Memorial de la vida de fray Francisco Jiménez de Cisneros,* ed. Antonio de la Torre y del Cerro (Madrid: Imprenta Baily-Balliere, 1913); Mariano Revilla Rico, *La Políglota de Alcalá* (Madrid: Imprenta helénica, 1917); Bataillon, *Érasme et l'Espagne,* 1:24–47; Bentley, *Humanists and Holy Writ,* 70–112.

4. Assuming, of course, that professors delivered lectures and the students attended classes, a problem uncovered in Alcalá as early as the 1520s. See Kagan, *Students and Society,* 170–71. As for San Ildefonso's intellectual priorities, the linguistic professorships frequently were vacant, the Complutensian Polyglot owed less to humanist method than we previously believed, and students' liking for the college's specialty—theology—was rather meager. For the second point, see Chapter 3.

5. This would be true for those men who not only acted as professors of theology, but also gained their salaries from prebends.

6. The *colegios* required entering members to be between twenty and twenty-four years old. Kagan, *Students and Society,* 124.

7. On the Complutensian Polyglot's Old Testament, Vergara's tasks would have included the collation of the Greek Septuagint against both the Hebrew original and the Latin Vulgate; for the New Testament, he would have helped collect and correct the Greek originals against the Latin Vulgate. His renditions of Aristotle exist in manuscript, in the archive of the Toledo Cathedral; they have never been studied in depth.

8. Miguel de la Pinta Llorente, O.S.A., *El erasmismo del Dr. Juan de Vergara y otras interpretaciones* (Madrid: Sánchez, 1945), 11.

9. There is an account of the formal investiture of the San Justo y Pastor prebends in the AHN, Sec. de Universidades, Leg. 10, n. 20. The change was phrased as a promotion and attributed to the generosity of Cardinal Cisneros's testament. For Cisneros's will, see BN, Sección de Raros, Manuscript #13020.

10. Fernando Martínez Gil, *La ciudad inquieta. Toledo comunera, 1520–1522* (Toledo: Diputación provincial de Toledo, 1993), 25. In 1569, the Toledo cathedral employed some six hundred persons, most of whom were clerics. For a rich assessment of Toledo's population, see Richard L. Kagan, "Contando vecinos: El censo toledano de 1569," *Studia Historica. Historia Moderna* 12 (1994): 115–35.

11. Jean Michel Lásperas, "La librería del doctor Juan de Vergara," *RABM* 79 (1976): 337–59.

12. Bataillon, *Érasme et l'Espagne,* 1:476–78, 493; Pinta Llorente, *El erasmismo del*

Dr. Juan de Vergara, 27; and Longhurst, "Alumbrados, erasmistas y luteranos," *CHE* 27 (1957): 112–16, 119–25, especially p. 121.

13. In terms of Vergara's contributions to the Complutensian Polyglot, we now realize that the editors on that project demonstrated less philological sophistication than once assumed. See Chapter 3 below.

14. For the difficulties in drawing historically reliable stories from legal sources, see Thomas Kuehn, "Reading Microhistory: The Example of Giovanni and Lusanna," *Journal of Modern History* 61 (1989): 512–34.

15. Francisco de Vergara's most famous work was a Greek grammar, printed first in Spain and then in Paris and Cologne: *De graeca lingua grammatica libri quinque* (Alcalá, 1537).

16. The Dominican tertiary María de Santo Domingo, who forecast Spanish military victories and suffered Jesus' wounds on the cross, enjoyed such support. Vicente Beltrán de Heredia, O.P., *Historia de la reforma de la Provincia de España (1450– 1550)* (Rome: ad S. Sabinae, 1939), 78–142, and a corrective in Bernardino Llorca, S.J., *La inquisición española y los alumbrados (1509–1667),* Bibliotheca Salmanticensis, no. 32 (Salamanca: Universidad pontificia, 1980); Jodi Bilinkoff, "A Spanish Prophetess and Her Patrons: The Case of María de Santo Domingo," *Sixteenth Century Journal* 23 (1992): 21–35. Also see Gillian T. W. Ahlgren, "Francisca de los Apostoles: A Visionary Voice for Reform in Sixteenth-Century Toledo," in *Women in the Inquisition,* ed. Mary E. Giles (Baltimore and London: Johns Hopkins University Press, 1998), 119– 33.

17. Pedro Ruiz de Alcaraz, one of the first alumbrados arrested, decried the Franciscans' tendency to demonstrate their spirituality through physicial signs, but some friars did in fact treat other alumbrados as spiritual mentors: Angela Selke, *El Santo Oficio de la Inquisición: Proceso de Fr. Francisco Ortiz (1529–1532)* (Madrid: Ediciones Guadarrama, 1968), 237.

18. The work of Melquiades Andres Martín has been critical in setting up our modern understanding of the alumbrados, although difficulties remain, such as the dynamic between practitioners of abandonment (*dejamiento*) and believers in recollection (*recogimiento*), and the question of the alumbrados' mysticism. Some alumbrados moved between dejamiento and recogimiento before their arrests and then spurned one or the other of them afterward, as would be the case with Francisca Hernández. Once in front of the Inquisition, they also could try to deflect the charges by attributing their ideas to such authoritative figures as the Pseudo-Dionysius; such occurred with Pedro Ruiz de Alcaraz. The fact that alumbrado doctrine only resides in Inquisition sources significantly compounds the difficulties of investigating it, because we possess no descriptions of alumbrado practice or belief that were not composed in a coercive setting. See Melquiades Andres Martín, *La teología española en el siglo XVI,* 2 vols. (Madrid: Editorial Catolica, 1976), 2:198–259; Llorca, *La inquisición y los alumbrados,* 65–85, and appendixes; Antonio Marquéz, *Los Alumbrados, Origenes y Filosofia*

1525–1559 (Madrid: Taurus, 1972); Milagros Ortega-Costa, *Proceso de la inquisición contra María de Cazalla* (Madrid: FUE, 1978), 5–9. In her study of one of Francisca Hernández's most constant followers, Angela Selke has rightly argued for fluidity in our conception and portrait of the alumbrados: *El Santo Oficio*, 234–35, 237, 240–41, 261.

19. Throughout this chapter, I mention characters in ways that will prove least confusing to readers. As a result, I frequently specify women by their first names and men by their last, because of the problem of duplication. No hierarchy is intended.

20. Two of Francisca's most zealous followers were Medrano and Fr. Francisco Ortíz; she cured the latter of the sin of masturbation. See Angela Selke, "El caso del Bachiller Antonio de Medrano, iluminado epicúreo del siglo xvi," *BH* 58 (1956): 393–420, and p. 405 for this quotation about Francisca and the Incarnation. Also see statements from Medrano's 1530–32 trial by the Toledo tribunal, parts of which are reprinted in Llorca, *La inquisición española y los alumbrados,* Appendix II. For Medrano's earlier encounter with the Inquisition, this time in front of the Logroño tribunal, see *Proceso inquisitorial contra el Bachiller Antonio de Medrano (Logroño 1526-Calahorra 1527),* ed. Javier Perez Escohotado (Logroño: Instituto de Estudios Riojanos, 1988). Francisco Ortíz was seized by the Inquisition after he preached against Francisca's indictment: during a sermon in Toledo, he chastised the inquisitor general for persecuting the bride of Christ, alias Francisca herself, and he predicted that Toledo would suffer three years of drought as punishment. Selke, *El Santo Oficio*, 31–36, 41–49, 55–61.

21. Tovar and the two others—Antonio de Medrano and Diego de Husillos—ignored the Inquisition's directive. Instead, they established themselves in a residence facing Pedro de Cazalla's house, where Francisca was living; they subsequently received daily blessings from her, "from window to window," and even entered Cazalla's place on a regular basis. Selke, "El caso del Bachiller Antonio de Medrano," 398.

22. Vergara recalled, "[Mendoza] asked [Tovar] if his lovemaking with Francisca was progressing well, although in more polite language" ("[Mendoza] le preguntó si le yba bien de amores con ella, aunque por otras palabras más del palacio"). AHN, Inqu., Leg. 223, n. 7, f. 258r. Vergara's recollections about Tovar, Francisca, and Mendoza occur at the beginning of his written defense, which he submitted to the inquisitors in March 1534. Given the aura of sexual misconduct that had surrounded Francisca and her male followers since at least 1519, Vergara may have intended his statements in 1534 to resurrect that negative image. Testimony about Francisca's sexual relationships is difficult to assess: all of it comes from Inquisition trials, and much of it is contradictory. Witnesses against the beata and her circle implied repeatedly that she had sexual intercourse with her adherents, but two of her disciples, Medrano and Ortíz, insisted upon her chastity: Selke, *El Santo Oficio,* 180–84, and 180, n. 6. Francisca herself testified that a number of disciples harbored "wicked designs" (*mala intención*) toward her and kissed her on occasion. She included Tovar in this group—sometimes he would shave his beard in order to kiss her—but not Ortíz. Llorca, *La inquisición española y los alumbrados,* 70, n. 17, and Appendix, 289–93. See

now Mary E. Giles, "Francisca Hernández and the Sexuality of Religious Dissent," in *Women in the Inquisition*, 75–97.

23. "Ningun contentamiento mostraron de mi negociacion: al fin sin curar de más complimentos, tuve forma con el dicho Tovar como se fuesse luego a Alcalá." AHN, Inqu., Leg. 223, n. 7, f. 258r, for all the points in this paragraph.

24. For local reasons behind Isabel's and Alcaraz's arrests, which are difficult to pin down, see Alastair Hamilton, *Heresy and Mysticism in Sixteenth-Century Spain: The Alumbrados* (Toronto: University of Toronto Press, 1992), 57–60.

25. Augustín Redondo, "Luther et l'Espagne de 1520–1536," *Mélanges de la Casa Velázquez* 1 (1965): 77–86, argues persuasively that Luther was more of a phantom threat than a real one at this point in Spanish history.

26. The theologians arrived at their verdict despite the fact that Isabel, at least, had been preaching the same counsel since about 1512, or years before Luther intruded on his contemporaries' consciousness. There is every indication that Isabel and Alcaraz developed their ideas out of a purely Spanish milieu; furthermore, they were imprisoned even before Erasmus's works plausibly could have reached them, at least in their vernacular versions, for Erasmus's *Enchiridion* was only translated into Spanish in 1524. Luther's opera had been under inquisitorial interdict since 1521.

27. The text of the 1525 edict is reprinted in Marquéz, *Los alumbrados*, Appendix.

28. Ortega-Costa, *Proceso de la inquisición contra María de Cazalla*, 99–101. María presented a written statement of her confession on March 2, 1525; although the six-day "period of grace" for confessions had expired, she received a penance anyway. In the course of her statement she never admitted being one of the alumbrados, but noted her counseling of Franciscan friars, her presumption, and her acquaintance with Isabel de la Cruz. Unfortunately for María, like all confessions made under edicts of the faith, hers was transcribed, preserved, and produced after her arrest in 1532.

29. The admiral of Castile, Fadrique Enríquez, was the brother-in-law of the marquess of Villena, the old protector of Alcaraz.

30. During his trial, Castillo acknowledged Tovar's mediation with Francisca: see testimony included in Ortega-Costa, *Proceso de la inquisición contra María de Cazalla*, 397–98, 431–33.

31. Her testimony was confirmed by Medrano, at least in terms of Francisca's coterie; see Llorca, *La inquisición española y los alumbrados*, Appendix II, 283.

32. Sara T. Nalle, *God in La Mancha* (Baltimore: Johns Hopkins University Press, 1992), Chapter 4; idem, "Literacy and Culture in Early Modern Castile," *Past and Present* 125 (1989): 65–96; Anastasio Rojo Vega, "Un sondeo acerca de la capacidad de lectura y escritura en Valladolid, 1550–1575," *Signo. Revista de historia de la cultura escrita* 3 (1996): 25–40; Keith Whinnom, "The Problem of the 'Best-Seller' in Spanish Golden-Age Literature," *Bulletin of Hispanic Studies* 57 (1980): 189–98. Also see Chapters 4–5 below.

33. Nonetheless, Inquisitor General Manrique disputed Francisca's spiritual gifts at least in part because she was not in holy orders: Selke, *El Santo Oficio*, 73, 128.

34. Hence the confession of a defendant was regarded as the "queen of proofs" (*regina probationum*) by both the papal and Spanish Inquisitions. Edward Peters, *Torture* (Philadelphia: University of Pennsylvania Press, 1987), Chapter 2.

35. Alonso de Mexia, an inquisitor from the Toledo tribunal who deposed against Vergara in November 1530, also was a canon of the Toledo cathedral and on at least one occasion was asked about Tovar's case by his fellow-prebends. Stephen Haliczer estimates that 55.7 percent of Valencia's inquisitors held canonries, the majority of them outside the city of Valencia itself. *Inquisition and Society in the Kingdom of Valencia, 1478–1834* (Berkeley: University of California Press, 1990), 118.

36. Her testimony in the Vergara proceso consistently fixes on her status as a spiritual advisor, a sage, and someone, in short, who was wiser than her male companions.

37. Francisca's indictment in 1529 was the third inquisitorial investigation she had faced, although the previous two involved only suspicions about lascivious acts between her and her followers. Selke, *El Santo Oficio,* believes that the Franciscan hierarchy was so disturbed over Francisca's influence on its friars that it collaborated with the Inquisition in her arrest (33–34, 62–68). Without more detailed evidence, I would hesitate to endorse that scenario.

38. It was most unusual for inquisitors to find a defendant innocent: in weak cases, tribunals could suspend the proceedings, which allowed fiscals to renew them at some later date. Inquisitors could impose penances in doubtful litigations—when the fiscal had not fully proven his claim—as well as in instances of proven culpability. Punishments could include enclosure in one's own house or a monastery, or flogging, which usually occurred in the streets where the guilty had practiced their errors. *Sanbenitos*— a bastardization of the Spanish *saco bendito* (blessed sack)—usually were hung in the culprits' parish churches once they were discarded. Almost no one experienced imprisonment or wearing the sanbenito for life. Relapsed heretics, though, were another matter: they were transferred to the civil authorities and executed. Kamen, *The Spanish Inquisition,* Chapter 9.

39. Bernard Vincent, "Un espacio de exclusión: La cárcel inquisitorial en el siglo XVI," in idem, *Minorías y marginados en la España del siglo XVI* (Granada: Diputación provincial de Granada, 1987), 162.

40. The most important studies, exclusive of conference proceedings, would include Nalle, *God in La Mancha;* Haliczer, *Inquisition and Society in the Kingdom of Valencia;* E. William Monter, *Frontiers of Heresy: The Spanish Inquisition from the Basque Lands to Sicily* (Cambridge: Cambridge University Press, 1990); Jaime Contreras, *El Santo Oficio de la Inquisición en Galicia, 1560–1700* (Madrid: Akal, 1982); Jaime Contreras and Gustav Henningsen, "Forty-Four Thousand Cases of the Spanish Inquisition (1540–1700): Analysis of a Historical Data Bank," in *The Inquisition in Early Modern Europe: Studies on Sources and Methods,* ed. Gustav Henningsen and John Tedeschi (DeKalb: Northern Illinois University Press, 1986), 100–129. The sophistication of these studies generally has not extended to work on the Inquisition and witchcraft; see Chapter 6 below.

41. Testifying in November 1530, Inquisitor Alonso de Mexia recounted how Vergara complained "of the enormous injury [*agravio*] that had been done in imprisoning his brother, Bernardino de Tovar, saying that it had been the most excessive thing done in this kingdom, and saying 'soon we shall see the things that go on in the Inquisition, and the injuries that are done, which are so notorious, and the frauds and injustices that occur' " ("[Vergara] quexándose de grande agravio que se avía hecho en prende a su hermano Bernardino de Tovar, diziendo que avía sido la más exorbitante cosa que se avía hecho en este reyno; y diziendo, a poco veremos las cosas que pasan en la Inquisicion, y los agravios tan notorios que se hazen, y las burlerías y injusticias que pasan "). AHN, Inqu., Leg. 223, n. 7, f. 200r. Vergara admitted under interrogation that he spoke to each inquisitor privately, "negotiating for Tovar" ("negociando por Tovar"), after Tovar's own arrest; ibid., f. 241v. Gaspar de Lucena—another prisoner, and brother of two other defendants, Juan del Castillo and Petronilla de Lucena—told the inquisitors that Vergara and Vaguer were enemies. Ibid., f. 127r.

42. For Vergara's actions against Ruiz, AHN, Inqu., Leg. 223, n. 7, ff. 147r–150v; for the particular anecdote about the inventory in Alcalá, see f. 149r. Ruiz recounted his suspicions in the course of his own prosecution: the investigators did not substantiate Vergara's efforts, but a marginal note in a contemporary hand adduced that there was a "strong suspicion" of Vergara's involvement in the slander. See f. 147r, upper right margin.

43. Ibid., ff. 40v–41r. The fact that Gutiérrez's interlocutor, Gerónimo Ruiz, had enjoined him to secrecy apparently was irrelevant.

44. For the depositions of Cristobal de Gumiel, who acted as the go-between for Vergara and Hermosilla, see ibid., ff. 235r–237v; for Vergara's statement that he spoke to Hermosilla several times, and simply commended Tovar's case to him, see f. 242r.

45. The noun *mozo* signifies a young man, not a child; the term designates a helper or servant.

46. The Granada tribunal was just as architecturally complex: it included apartments for the inquisitors' audiencias, halls for torture, repositories for bread, charcoal, and birds, and cells for the indicted. Vincent, *Minorías y marginados*, 163. Francisco Bethencourt includes a seventeenth-century plan of the Seville tribunal in his massive *La inquisición en la época moderna: España, Portugal, Italia, siglos XV–XIX* (Madrid: Akal, 1997), 87.

47. See Dedieu, *L'administration de la foi*, 159–68, on the recompensed officials of the Toledo tribunal.

48. During his own Inquisition trial, which was provoked by his assistance to the Vergara family, Rodríguez attested that "he came [to the tribunal] because he was so ordered by doctor Vergara, namely, that he should come every day to see if Tovar needed something" ("dixo que venía porque asi le era mandado por el dicho doctor Vergara, que viniese cada día a saber si avra menester algo el dicho Tovar"). AHN, Inqu. Leg. 80, n. 13, f. 1v.

49. For this sequence of events, see ibid., Leg. 223, n. 7, f. 97r–v.

50. "Salían en él letras de color leonado que se podían leer." Ibid., f. 97r.

51. Ibid., f. 102r–v.

52. Ibid., f. 118r–v.

53. Rodríguez testified to these details on May 4, 1533: ibid., f. 106r. Tovar confirmed the same scenario on July 7, 1533: ibid., ff. 110v, 112r–v. Tovar personally made a rough draft in ink before attempting to write with fruit juice, and destroyed it afterward. Miguel Ortíz, who was entwined in Vergara's circle, knew about the secret correspondence and how it was conducted: ibid., f. 306r–v.

54. Investigators can find these details in Rodríguez's trial as well as in Vergara's. For the former, see AHN, Inqu., Leg. 80, n. 13, with the particulars of the bribery on ff. 3r, 4r. For the same specifics in Vergara's proceso, see ibid., Leg. 223, n. 7, ff. 106v–107r (Rodríguez's testimony in the Vergara case), and f. 307v (testimony by Miguel Ortíz). Rodríguez was first interrogated by the Toledo inquisitors on May 4, 1533; by June 9, he was described as a prisoner, and he was penanced on December 13, 1533, with a fine of 150 gold ducats. Significantly, Rodríguez waived the presentation of defense witnesses, and his employer Vergara would do the same. For more details on Rodríguez's involvement in Tovar's case, see below.

55. During their interrogation of Hernán Rodríguez, the inquisitors consistently named the despensero, Gaspar Martínez, as one of the suspected employees, along with the alcaide and the mozo del carcel. AHN, Inqu., Leg. 80, n. 13, f. 2r–v.

56. Sharon Kettering, *Patrons, Brokers, and Clients in Seventeenth-Century France* (Oxford: Oxford University Press, 1986), Introduction and Chapter 1.

57. Anthony Molho, "Cosimo de'Medici: *Pater Patriae* or *Padrino?*" *Stanford Italian Review* 1 (1979): 5–33.

58. Evidence about Tovar beating Diego lies in the transcript of María de Cazalla's trial: Ortega-Costa, *Proceso de la inquisición contra María de Cazalla,* 479; the evidence came from Cazalla's servant. For Diego's loyalty to his employer, see his own Inquisition proceso: AHN, Inqu., Leg. 79, n. 1, f. 18r–v.

59. AHN, Inqu., Leg., 223, n. 7, f. 310r; in this instance, Miguel Ortíz acted as Gumiel's confessor. See n. 86 below.

60. Ibid., f. 40r–v.

61. For Lucena's testimony under torture in 1535, see ibid., ff. 351r, 352r–353r.

62. Fonseca signed Gumiel's receipt of the false benefice in Madrid: ibid., f. 310r, and see n. 86 below.

63. What we do not know is whether Hernán Rodríguez continued to carry messages to the tribunal after his interrogation on May 4, 1533; if he did not, the likely intermediary was Cristobal de Gumiel. Rodríguez was arrested by June 9; see n. 54 above.

64. For Medina's comments about Vergara and Valdés, see AHN, Inqu., Leg. 223, n. 7, f. 182r–v.

65. That is, Tovar, Francisca Hernández, Marí Ramírez, Francisco Ortiz, Diego Hernández, and Gaspar de Lucena. Diego Hernández was a follower of Francisca's,

whom historians have described as mentally deranged because he supplied a grandiose list of suspected Lutherans to the Inquisition. Lucena fell into the category of abetting heretics through his alleged assistance to his fugitive brother, Juan del Castillo.

66. By and large the Inquisition asked the first two sets of calificadores to appraise Vergara's statements that pertained to the alumbrados and Luther. The two groups met in Toledo on April 19, 1531, and in Valladolid on May 6, 1532. For their decisions, called *votos,* see AHN, Inqu., Leg. 223, n. 7, ff. 20r–22v, 29r–32r.

67. On May 17, prosecutor Ortíz Angulo noted that Vergara "a embiado abisos y cartas . . . de fuera de la carcel, y rescibidos de dentro del dicho Tovar su hermano por mano y medio de Fernando Rodríguez, su capellan, y Francisco, criado del dicho doctor, y por otras personas que él y ellos saben y del alcaide y mozo del carcel del sancto oficio . . . poniendo mal nombre a los ministros y oficiales . . . del sancto oficio." Ibid., f. 96r. For the indictment, see ibid., ff. 134r–137r. The editor of Cazalla's trial devotes some space to explaining the sequence and circumstances of the secret correspondence, but sides with the older historiography on Vergara's arrest. See Ortega-Costa, *Proceso de la inquisición contra María de Cazalla,* 521–23, nn. 7–21, especially n. 15.

68. Critical information about these schemes and setbacks lies in the trials of Diego de Aguilar, Tovar's servant, and María de Cazalla. For Diego's proceso—which features interrogations of the prison warden, Tovar, and Diego himself—AHN, Inqu., Leg. 79, n. 1, ff. 1r–2v, 4r, 6v, 7v, 12r–v, 14v, 16v–17r. For confirmation from Cazalla's trial, see Ortega-Costa, *Proceso de la inquisición contra María de Cazalla,* 479–96. Tovar secured his domestic's liberty from their cell, either by pleading Diego's purported heart condition or by offering Diego's help for such mundane matters as sweeping the stairs. The prisoner who promised silence in return for extra food from the warden was Diego Hernández.

69. Diego de Aguilar confirmed some meetings between various prisoners and Francisca: AHN, Inqu., Leg. 79, n. 1, ff. 16r, 22r–v. Testimony in María de Cazalla's transcript also suggests that such rendezvous with Francisca took place, and implies the affection of the alcaide and the mozo for that beata: Ortega-Costa, *Proceso de la inquisición contra María de Cazalla,* 543, 545, 550, 552.

70. Angela Selke, "Vida y muerte de Juan López de Celaín"; Vincent, *Minorías y marginados,* 164–65; Eugenio Asensio, "El Maestro Pedro de Orellana, minorita luterano: Versos y procesos," in *La Inquisición Española: Nueva visión, nuevos horizontes,* ed. Joaquin Pérez Villanueva (Madrid: Siglo Veintiuno Editores, 1978), 793–94; Richard L. Kagan, *Lucrecia's Dreams: Politics and Prophecy in Sixteenth-Century Spain* (Berkeley: University of California Press, 1990), 140–44.

71. I believe that the Toledo inquisitors were especially sensitive to Vergara's insults because of Francisco Ortíz's earlier, public diatribes against their office. See n. 20 above. The links between Ortíz's and Vergara's cases deserve further investigation.

72. The transcribed letters are in AHN, Inqu., Leg. 223, n. 7, ff. 97v–99v, 104v–

105r, 118r–120v. A radically abbreviated version of the Vergara-Tovar correspondence was copied into María de Cazalla's trial record as well. There the letters are so curtailed that they amount to snippets of the originals. Ortega-Costa, *Proceso de la inquisición contra María de Cazalla,* 515–18.

73. Maldonado was the bishop of Mondoñedo until 1532, when he was translated to the episcopate of Badajoz.

74. For these details, see AHN, Inqu., Leg. 223, n. 7, ff. 113r–117r, especially 115v–117r.

75. "They ordered that he should have this city as a prison, and not leave it without the permission and order of their lordships, under penalty of 500 gold ducats for the extraordinary expenses of the Holy Office" ["mandaron que tuviese esta ciudad por cárcel y della no saliese syn licencia y mandado de sus mercedes, sos pena de quinientos ducados de oro para los gastos extraordinarios del sancto oficio"]. Ibid., f. 117v.

76. Two days earlier, on June 21, the inquisitors had interviewed Diego de Aguilar, who confessed that Tovar had attempted to counsel Catalina de Figueroa about compurgatory witnesses: ibid., Leg. 79, n. 1, ff. 16v–17r. On June 23, the inquisitors obviously wished to discover what Vergara knew about this particular episode.

77. Whether members of Vergara's retinue truly did not know the content of the secret correspondence is unanswerable: certainly Hernán Rodríguez, and then Diego de Aguilar, professed their ignorance under interrogation. Ibid., Leg. 80, n. 13, f. 2v; Leg. 79, n. 1, f. 12v.

78. "No alcanza que aya hecho hierro ninguno en avisar y escrivir al dicho su hermano lo que le ha escrito, porque le tiene por buen cristiano . . . y este declarante es su hermano, y ha tenido justo dolor de su prision y trabajo. Y demás desto, es su abogado. . . ." Ibid., Leg. 223, n. 7, f. 123r.

79. "Luego el dicho doctor dixo que apelava y apeló de la injusta prision y pidió que le den lugar para que pueda nombrar un procurador para seguir la dicha apellacion ante los señores del consejo de la sancta inquisicion. Los dichos inquisidores dixeron que lo verán y se le dará la respuesta en su tiempo." Ibid., f. 123v.

80. Vergara had known about Flores's, Silva's, and Pedro Ortíz's depositions through Hermosilla's and Gumiel's mediation. Bataillon believed that such inside information put Vergara on his guard, but that conclusion seems implausible, given Vergara's continuing actions on Tovar's behalf.

81. AHN, Inqu., Leg. 223, n. 7, ff. 124r–125v.

82. Modern historians have persistently stipulated that Vergara's imprisonment exemplified a crackdown on Spanish Erasmianism. The best examples come from Bataillon, who recognized the role of the secret correspondence in Vergara's indictment, but also labeled the period 1530–33 a gradual "snowball" against Spanish Erasmians, and concluded that Vergara's trial "nous restitue l'histoire concrete d'un érasmiste aux prises avec l'Inquisition." *Érasme et l'Espagne,* 1:508. Part of the reason

for Bataillon's emphasis lies in the fact that he worked from the depositions to the indictment, a trajectory made clear in his exposition.

83. AHN, Inqu., Leg. 223, n. 7, f. 156r.

84. For the publication of testimony, ibid., ff. 194r–201r.

85. Ibid., ff. 128r, 129r.

86. Gumiel's comment on puntos occurs in ibid., f. 237. On the secret rendezvous, see ibid., f. 236r–v. According to Gumiel, Vergara showed Archbishop Fonseca "a paper written in orange juice, and the archbishop said to [Vergara], 'Watch what you're doing, trouble could ensue,' and [Vergara] shut up and he knew nothing more" ("un papel escripto con zumo de naranja, y quel dicho Arzobispo dixo al dicho doctor, 'mira lo que hazeys, que puede venir pena.' Y el dicho doctor calló y no supo más"); ibid., f. 237r. The subject of "supo" could be either Fonseca or Gumiel himself. Miguel Ortíz confirmed Fonseca's awareness of the scheme; ibid., f. 306v. In March 1534, Vergara admitted that he had pretended to hand over the income from a benefice to Gumiel in order for the latter to flaunt the gift to Hermosilla, who in turn would presumably continue to cooperate with Vergara et al. in the hope of greater financial gain. Vergara noted that the trick was unknown to Gumiel himself, who tried to protect the precious gift even on his deathbed. Ibid., ff. 252r, 254r–v.

87. Vergara insisted that he had "de procurar de saber todo lo que tocava a la causa de Tovar y ansi lo procuró, y que la forma como lo procurava que no ay para que declararla, pues la obra era la que convenía a la defensa del dicho su hermano"; ibid., f. 243r; also see ff. 240v, 242r–243r. Twice he refused to answer the question.

88. Vergara recounted that "el qual dicho licenciado Gumiel, hablando con este declarante sobre las cosas que preguntava al bachiller Hermosilla tocantes al negocio de Tovar, dixo a este declarante quel Hermosilla por entonces no tenía lugar de mirar aquello que se le preguntava, porque estava muy occupado en tornar de romance en latín una cierta informacion que se avía de enviar fuera del Reyno contra un maestro Castillo. Y que desta manera lo supo este declarante." Ibid., f. 315r–v.

89. Fonseca directed his letters to the Toledo inquisitors on June 26, November 23, and December 7, 1533, and to the Suprema on December 8, 1533. His epistles demanded appropriate treatment for Vergara, and recognized that the secretary was only arrested after Fonseca's own departure from Toledo in June 1533. Ibid., ff. 211r, 227r, 229r, and 230r. Fonseca may have sent more epistles before his death on February 4, 1534: four folios in the transcript, occurring between ff. 232–233, have been excised with a razor, and the first two evince traces of the episcopal seal. In August 1533, the Suprema warned the tribunal twice about delay and aggravation to Vergara: ff. 159r, 161r.

90. Vergara's indictment does not illustrate a policy enacted from the top down, if the tribunal's superiors, namely, the Suprema, could not force it to act. It seems to present us instead with a conflict between two clientage networks that operated and overlapped in Toledo, which were hooked in turn to the larger incarnations of the

Inquisition and the cathedral. Unfortunately, this suggestion is undemonstrable, because no one has conducted research on the Toledo inquisitors and their circles, as opposed to the Toledo tribunal as an institution, in the sixteenth century.

91. Miguel Ortíz's lengthy deposition occurs in AHN, Inqu., Leg. 223, n. 7, ff. 306r–310r, with Vergara's response on ff. 313r–315v; although Ortíz spent most of his interrogation attesting Vergara's sabotage, the fiscal lifted only statements about Vergara and Erasmus as additional testimony. For Alonso Ruiz de Virués's deposition and Vergara's response, see ibid., ff. 310r–312v, 319r–320r. Virués attested that he and Vergara had argued over whether a priest could celebrate Mass without first receiving the sacrament of penance, which also found its way into the charges. Virués did not ratify his testimony until January 12, 1535, when he himself was under arrest, in the monastery of San Benito in Valladolid; f. 344r.

92. The quote comes from Robert Grosseteste. Edward Peters, *Heresy and Authority in Medieval Europe* (Philadelphia: University of Pennsylvania Press, 1980), 4.

93. On July 12, 1533, the fiscal demanded that Vergara should be put in "some prisons of this Holy Office where no one can see him or communicate with him . . . which he now can do very easily, being in the room he presently occupies, on account of its windows looking out on the street. And he has those windows open, and he has spoken to people passing through the street, and those who go by have spoken to him, as is notorious to Your Lordship" ("en unas carceles desto santo oficio donde nadie le puede ver ni comunicar . . . agora puede hazer muy facilmente, estando en el aposento que al presente está, por salir a la calle publica las ventanas del aposento donde está, y las tiene abiertas y ha hablado a personas que pasan por la calle, y los que pasan le han hablado a él, como a vuestra merced es notorio"). AHN, Inqu., Leg. 223, n. 7, f. 133r.

94. For Rodríguez, see ibid., Leg. 80, n. 13, f. 4r; for Aguilar, see Leg. 79, n. 1, f. 32v.

95. On the meeting of the calificadores in 1534, see ibid., Leg. 223, n. 7, ff. 324r–332v: the theologians here were Juan de Medina, Juan Ruiz de Ubago, and Juan de Villareal. Twelve months later, Medina and Ubago would help determine Vergara's final sentence; see below. Two earlier conclaves of calificadores had occurred in Toledo on April 19, 1531, and again in Valladolid on May 6, 1532: ibid., ff. 20r–22v, 29r–33v.

96. Ibid., f. 374r.

97. It seems as if the tribunal implicitly recognized Vergara's status as a patron, given the harshness of his sentence as compared to the relative leniency of Hernán Rodríguez's. The latter verdict only exacted a payment of 150 gold ducats.

98. See AHN, Inqu., Leg. 223, n. 7, ff. 384r, 385r–v for Manrique's letters and the commutation order.

99. "A los locos y dementes que son en muchísimas ocasiones los que dicen las grandes verdades y las supremas razones." Quoted in Pinta Llorente, *El erasmismo del Dr. Vergara,* 15.

100. Bataillon recognized that Vergara was hardly a typical defendant or even

Erasmian, for that matter, but nonetheless concluded that his prosecution pitted the tradition of "L'Église pensante et étudiante" against "l'orthodoxie policiere et inculte dont les moines et le promoteur fiscal se font les champions." Vergara's pride was that of "l'homme d'étude formé au libre jugement"; when he condemned Bernardino Flores, "Il méprise le moine ignorant de toute la hauteur de sa culture d'humaniste." *Érasme et l'Espagne*, 1:508, 497, 498. The dichotomies are obvious. For Pinta Llorente, Vergara's "bronco temperamento, la comezón crítica, la áspera realidad, un soberbio talento y la ninguna apetencia de prebendas y sinecuras motivan en él la independencia intelectual para señalar errores y corruptelas, deshacer entuertos y lugares comunes." *El erasmismo del Dr. Juan de Vergara*, 27. Pinta Llorente's portrait of Vergara could not have been more misguided in several respects.

101. AHN, Inqu., Leg., 223, n. 7, f. 281v.

102. Ibid., f. 285r.

103. In my exposition of Vergara's defense, I have employed both his oral declarations of November 8, 1533 and his written statements of March 6, 1534. The expanse of the oral deposition runs from ibid., ff. 201r–204r. Vergara submitted a total of four written defense statements, the first encompassing ff. 257r–285r, the next three ff. 286r–292v. The last three statements were additions to the first one. All four were handed to the inquisitors on March 6, 1534.

104. Ibid., ff. 290v–291r.

105. Peters, *Torture*, 30–33, 43–47.

106. On the notion of Francisca and María as a sect, see AHN, Inqu., Leg. 223, n. 7, f. 287r; on their vulnerability as female witnesses, see ibid., ff. 266r, 267v, 289v and 290v. According to a 1523 inventory, the library at San Ildefonso in Alcalá possessed a copy of the *Malleus;* the same section of it would be used to fulsome effect in Martín de Castañega's treatise on witchcraft and sorcery, published in 1529. Nevertheless, Spanish clerics could spurn the *Malleus* as well as imitate it: see Chapter 6 below.

107. AHN, Inqu., Leg. 223, n. 7, f. 259v; Vergara reiterated his opposition to "conventiculos" on f. 262v.

108. Ibid., f. 262v.

109. On the concept of curiositas, see Chapter 2.

110. AHN, Inqu., Leg., 223, n. 7, f. 280r.

111. "Especialmente siendo tan ocupado como era." Ibid., f. 203r.

112. "Especialmente no siendo en publico ni ante vulgo, sino ante un Arzobispo de Toledo y otros dos caballeros, de los quales el uno era letrado y eclesiastico." Ibid., f. 273r.

113. Ibid., f. 203r. On Juan de Valdés, Vergara reported that "le avia reprehendido asperamente el meterse en materias que no avia estudiado," f. 204r.

114. "La porfia no era utrum confessio sit de jure divino, sino utre [sic] reperiatur per ecclesiam determinatum quod sit de jure divine, quae est quaedam quaestio facti." Ibid., f. 277r.

115. "No se pueda proceder contra nadie ante determinationem ecclesiae. Ni sé

yo, que aya en la inquisicion autoridad para determinar de nuevo tales propositiones autoritative, cum constet tales causas ad Petri sedem esse deferendas." Ibid., f. 277v. Here and elsewhere in his defense, Vergara wrote macaronically, mixing Spanish and Latin in the same sentences.

116. Ibid., f. 278v.

117. See ibid., ff. 12r–14r for Flores's original deposition, and ff. 196v–197r for its publication by the fiscal.

118. "Este testigo es persona infame y criminosa del crimen *laese maiestate*; . . . Incitó la gente a robos, muertos, incendios, sacrilegios, y otros generos de graves y enormes delictos, segun que en este reyno es público y notório y por tal lo allego." Ibid., 272r. Although Vergara used many of the same adjectives against Francisca Hernández—criminal, infamous, perjuring—he did not accuse Flores of deliberate deceit or conspiracy. It may be that those qualities simply were not relevant where Flores was concerned. But Vergara would also have recognized that charges of fraud and intrigue against women had particularly sharp reverberations.

119. When certain bulls of renunciation for the Pinto prebend were presented in favor of Flores, the late Cardinal Cisneros had ordered Vergara to hold up the transfer. The same cardinal also wrote a very harsh letter against the resignation and conferral, which Vergara himself penned or even composed; as a result "the ones who negotiated" for Flores concluded that the business was in Vergara's hands, and that the latter was impeding the process. Ibid., f. 272v.

120. Ibid., f. 272r–v.

121. Ibid., f. 273r.

122. "Sino que le parece a él [Flores], que en cantandose una cosa en la yglesia, hoc est intra parietes templi, luego la yglesia, hoc est congregatio fidelium seu concilium aut Papa, lo appru eva letra por letra como al mesmo Evangelio." Ibid., f. 274v.

123. "Mas las ynterpretaciones de las lenguas no suffren glossas, como otros dichos en quanto se pueda hazer; ni sabría yo glossar ni excusar a sant Isidro, quando dize que 'acolytus' graece quiere dezir 'ceroferarius' latine." Ibid., f. 274r. *Acolyte* comes from the Middle Greek adjective *akolouthos,* meaning "following."

124. "Entre los quales yo huelgo de entrar de buena voluntad." Ibid., 275v. On all these points, see ibid., f. 275r–v.

125. Ibid., f. 275v.: "harto necio sería a quien a todos los frayles generalmente toviesse por necios. Entre ellos ay necios . . . como entre clerigos; y ní el habito les viste de necedad tampoco como de sabiduría." Vergara's statement is a trope on Erasmus's famous declaration in the *Enchiridion* that monasticism did not necessarily connote piety.

126. "No avia ni podía aver en España noticia particular de las opiniones de Lutero, ni libro de sus errores; porque a la sazón comencava la secta en Alemania, y solamente en España se sonava una fama general de un herege quien en Alemania se levantava." Ibid., f. 259r. Vergara's remarks on Luther are consistent with his other

comments on the importance of formal definitions of heresy: if the pope did not offer such a classification, then the label was moot.

127. Ibid., f. 262v.

128. "Ni se deve tener por bueno hablar desacatadamente en disfavor de los sanctos y de sus libros, antes excusarlos y glossar sus dichos con reverencia." Ibid., f. 274r. On his own renditions from Greek into Latin, Vergara remarked, "Aunque más vezes hablando en tales materias fue lo poner exemplo en la physica y metaphysica de Aristoteles que assimismo trasladé." Ibid.

129. At one point, Vergara narrowed the meaning of "prophet" to "those who see," or *videntes;* ibid., f. 281r.

130. The apologia lies in ibid., ff. 244r–249r. In its introduction, Vergara noted, "La qual es la que aqui va scripta de mi mano, puesta a manera de question segun stilo de theologos," f. 244r.

131. "E por ventura, si el promisso fuera proprio mio, más que ajeno, me determinara más finalmente a obedecer; mas tocando principalmente a quien de mi palabra se dio, muy grand . . . baxeza cometería yo, si haziendo lo que no devo, le destruyesse. Y mal se devría fiar de mi otra cosa de más sustancia, si en ésta mostrasse infidelidad y flaqueza." Ibid., f. 244r.

132. "Porque yo con la autoridad de tales personas sanease mi conciencia y mi obligacion." Ibid., f. 244r–v.

133. "Queritur, utrum Joannes, qui tam persona quam secreta ipsa accepit sub sigillo confessionis, extra tum veram pactore confessionem, teneatur illa ad preceptum superioris manifestare." Ibid., f. 245r.

134. For an identical structure in an overtly scholastic but vernacular treatise, see Pedro Ciruelo's *Hexameron teologal sobre el regimento medicinal contra la pestilencia* (Alcalá, 1519).

135. The question of natural law in Spanish theology might be a provocative one, given the typical connections among that law, morality, and the Ten Commandments; and Spain's substantial converso population, to which both Vergara and Ciruelo belonged. Vergara's placement of the oath in the realm of natural law was duplicated by Tovar's servant in his own trial: AHN, Inqu., Leg. 79, n. 1, f. 15v.

136. "Qui in hominem materiis moralibus solet praeceteris celebrare." Ibid., Leg. 223, n. 7, f. 245r.

137. See Chapter 5 below.

138. Rummel, *The Humanist-Scholastic Debate,* Chapter 1.

139. Here Vergara was manipulating the traditional links between infidelity and heresy, fidelity and the First Commandment, and the Commandments as the written version of natural law.

140. AHN, Inqu., Leg., 223, n. 7, f. 246r.

141. Such obligatory and spontaneous disclosure could occur when a heretic was privately turning men from the faith, or a person planned to hand over a city to its

enemies: by referring to the betrayal of cities, Vergara again alluded to the comunero revolt of 1520; ibid. Notably, Tovar's servant repeated Vergara's reasoning about secrecy, natural law, and danger; one can only wonder if Vergara, Tovar, and their entourage planned a common legal scheme between 1533 and 1535. For Diego de Aguilar's statements, see ibid., Leg. 79, n. 1, f. 15v.

142. Ibid., Leg. 223, n. 7, f. 247r–v.

143. "Que se estudiase la question si era obligado o no para dar alguna color [sic] a lo que avía negado; . . . escrivanse los doctores que lo dezían, y que quando le llamasen, dixiese todo lo que pasava, y llevase escripto el fundamento que le movió para no decir luego la verdad." Ibid., f. 237v.

Chapter Two. Erasmus and the New Testament

1. Bataillon, *Érasme et l'Espagne*, 1:253–57, 263–65, 285, 295, 298–99. For explicit quotations of Bataillon's points, see Lu Ann Homza, "Erasmus as Hero, or Heretic? Spanish Humanism and the Valladolid Assembly of 1527," *Renaissance Quarterly* 50 (1997): 79, nn. 2–4. Also see Miguel Avilés, "Erasmo y los teólogos españoles," in *El erasmismo en España*, ed. Manuel Revuelta Sañudo and Ciriaco Morón Arroyo (Santander: Sociedad Menéndez Pelayo, 1986), 175–94; and idem, *Erasmo y la Inquisición (El libelo de Valladolid y la Apología de Erasmo contra los frailes españoles)* (Madrid: FUE, 1980). For Erasmus's reaction to the conference, see Erika Rummel, *Erasmus and His Catholic Critics*, 2 vols. (Nieuwkoop: De Graaf, 1989).

2. The repertory, chronology of meetings, participants' opinions, and other assorted documents are in AHN, Inqu., Leg. 4426. The entire repertory of charges is transcribed in Antonio Paz y Melia and Manuel Serrano y Sanz, "Actas originales de las congregaciones celebradas en 1527," *RABM* 6 (1902): 60–73; it also can be found in facsimile and in Spanish translation in Avilés, *Erasmo y la Inquisición*. The opinions of the delegates were transcribed by Vicente Beltrán de Heredia, *Cartulario de la universidad de Salamanca: La universidad en el siglo de oro* (Salamanca: Universidad de Salamanca, 1972), vol. 6. Beltrán had intended to publish these materials in 1937, but decided Bataillon had treated the conference sufficiently. I have used Beltrán's transcriptions for my quotations of the opinions because they are more readily available to scholars; they nevertheless contain multiple errors, and must be collated against the originals. I have not cited any material that differs from the manuscripts.

3. On the importance of viewing cultural transmission as a reciprocal transaction, in which the recipients consciously shaped the message or text as they received it, see Anthony Grafton and Ann Blair, eds., *The Transmission of Culture in Early Modern Europe* (Philadelphia: University of Pennsylvania Press, 1990), Introduction. For an example of such a process in action, and the potential distinction between *Erasmus ex Erasmo* and *Erasmus ex Erasmi lectore,* see Seidel Menchi, *Erasmo in Italia 1520–1580.*

4. "Continuo clamare coeperunt pulpita, fora, templa, basilicae (nam nusquam non acclamatores eiusmodi disponebantur), Erasmum hereticum, blasphemum, im-

pium, sacrilegum. Quid multa? Plures subito tibi ex vulgata libri interpretatione, quam ex dentium semente Cadmo, hostes coorti." P. S. Allen, H. M. Allen, and H. W. Garrod, eds., *Opus epistolarum Desiderii Erasmi Roterodami,* 12 vols. (Oxford: Oxford University Press, 1906–58), vol. 7, Letter 1814, ll. 123–27.

5. Erasmus repeated the incident in several letters; ibid., vol. 7, Letters 1902, 1903, 1909.

6. The Franciscan in Palencia came up with thirty suspicious excerpts from the *Enchiridion* and the *Paraclesis;* the latter was Erasmus's introduction to his edition of the New Testament. See Fernández to Luís Coronel, ibid., vol. 6, Appendix 18, Letter 3, ll. 19–35. For the problems in Salamanca, ibid., vol. 7, Letters 1903, l. 15, and 1909, ll. 35–37; one of those monks, Francisco de Castillo, became a delegate to the Valladolid assembly.

7. Bentley, *Humanists and Holy Writ,* 210–11. Stunica's initial attack remains unedited, although Erasmus's response to that first assault has been: *Apologia respondens ad ea quae Iacobus Lopis Stunica taxaverat in prima dumtaxat novi testamenti aeditione,* ed. H. J. de Jonge; *Opera omnia,* vol. 9, part 2 (Amsterdam-Oxford: North Holland, 1983). De Jonge's *Introduction* to the *Apologia* is the best overview of this complicated interchange: ibid., 3–49.

8. Bataillon, *Érasme et l'Espagne,* 1:150. The guardian of the Franciscan monastery in Alcalá also coupled Erasmus and Luther in his sermons; see the letter that Alonso Ruiz de Virués wrote to the same guardian in protest, in Adolfo Bonilla y San Martín, *Juan Luís Vives y la Filosofía del Renacimiento* (Madrid: Imprenta del asilo de huérfanos de sagrado corazón de Jesús, 1903), Appendix 1, 693–98.

9. Vergara to Erasmus, *Opus epistolarum,* vol. 7, Letter 1814, ll. 155–58.

10. Vergara's comments occur in ibid., ll. 23–24. For more evidence of popular hostility to Erasmus, see Alfonso de Valdés's letter in Fermín Caballero, *Alonso y Juan de Valdés, Conquenses ilustres,* vol. 4 (Madrid: Oficina tipográfica de hospicio, 1875) 4:335; and Gíl López de Bejar's opinions from Valladolid, in Beltrán de Heredía, *Cartulario,* 82. Further evidence of antagonism lies in Sancho Carranza de Miranda, *Opusculum in quasdam Erasmi Roterodami annotationes* (Rome, 1522), who inserted himself into the quarrel between Erasmus and Stunica by repeating three of his fellow Spaniard's complaints from 1520; for Erasmus's response, see *Apologia de tribus locis quos ut recte taxatos a Stunica defenderat Sanctius Caranza theologus,* ed. Jean LeClerc, *Opera omnia Desiderii Erasmi Roterodami,* 10 vols. (Leiden: P. Van der aa, 1703–6), 9:401–28.

11. AHN, Inqu., Leg. 4426, unfoliated manuscript, 3–8. Francisco de Vitoria expounded the second category of charges on July 9; Francisco de Castillo followed with the third and fourth sections on July 27.

12. Cecilia Asso, *La teologia e la grammatica: La controversia tra Erasmo ed Edward Lee* (Firenze: Olschki, 1993), 57–58. As in the case of other antagonists, Lee's attacks have not been critically edited, but Erasmus's to Lee have been: *Apologia qua respondet duabus invectivis Edwardi Lei* in *Erasmi opuscula: A Supplement to the Opera omnia,* ed. Wallace K. Ferguson (The Hague: Martinus Nijhoff, 1933), 225–303.

13. Stunica studied under the Portuguese Greek scholar Ayres Barbosa, collaborated on the Complutensian Polyglot Bible with Juan de Vergara, and published his first polemic against Erasmus at Alcalá. See de Jonge's introduction to Erasmus's *Apologia*, 13–34.

14. Nonetheless, Stunica's 1522 *Erasmi Roterodami blasphemiae et impietates* only appears to be arranged topically: in fact, its initial chapters confront Erasmus's treatment of Matthew, subsequent ones address Mark, and so forth, so that its sequence follows the text of the New Testament.

15. For the Sorbonne's complaints against Erasmus, see Charles Du Plessis d'Argentré, *Collectio judiciorum de novis erroribus qui ab initio duodecimi saeculi . . . usque ad annum 1735 in ecclesia proscripti sunt et notati . . .* , 3 vols. (Paris: A. Cailleau, 1725–36; reprinted Brussels: Culture et Civilisation, 1963), vol. 2, pt. 1:53–77. In his *Six Essays on Erasmus,* Olin noted the Sorbonne's censures of Erasmus's preface to the Hilary edition: Appendix, 93–121. Identical excerpts were indicted in the fourth category of the Valladolid repertory, "Against the holy inquisition of heretics," charges 1 and 2; and by the Sorbonne, *Collectio judiciorum,* vol. 2, pt. 1:54, 69.

16. "Multa dicit in colloquiis quae propter prolixitatem eorum praetermittimus." Avilés, *Erasmo y la Inquisición,* 49.

17. The example comes from the *Modus orandi Deum:* the monks extracted three statements from a single section and put them under accusatory categories on the Trinity, Christ, and the Holy Spirit. Compare Desiderius Erasmus, *Modus orandi Deum,* ed. J. N. Bakhuizen van den Brink, *Opera omnia,* vol. 5, part 1 (Amsterdam: North Holland, 1977), 144–46, with accusation 3 under "Against the sacrosanct Trinity"; accusation 1 under "Against the divinity of Christ"; and accusation 2 under "Against the divinity of the Holy Spirit," in Beltrán, *Cartulario,* 18, 21.

18. For the statement and its context, see the *Apologia*, ed. de Jonge, 258.

19. *Modus orandi Deum,* ed. Bakhuizen van den Brink, 146.

20. Beltrán de Heredia, *Cartulario,* 17–18.

21. All of the originals from Virués, and half of those for Pedro de Vitoria, now are missing from AHN, Inqu., Leg. 4426; we know they disappeared sometime after 1937, because Beltrán de Heredia transcribed them. We also know that approximately five more theologians attended the conference but either left no record of their views, or their statements have been lost.

22. On the Portuguese attendees, see Bataillon, *Les Portugais contre Érasme à l'Assemblée Théologique de Valladolid (1527),* Miscelânea de Estudos em honra de D. Carolina Michaëlis de Vasconcellos (Coimbra: Imprensa da Universidade, 1930).

23. For instance, a delegate might have passed over a charge because he found it unimportant, although he frequently wrote as much; or because he hesitated to reply to something he did not understand, or because his opinion would have been negative.

24. The verse occurs in almost all the Latin manuscripts of the period, but in only four Greek ones. Bentley, *Humanists and Holy Writ,* 44, and Erika Rummel, *Erasmus's*

Annotations on the New Testament: From Philologist to Theologian (Toronto: University of Toronto Press, 1986), 132–33.

25. Since Erasmus had published Valla's *Adnotationes* on the New Testament in 1505, his removal of the comma from his own work in 1516 and 1519 seemed to contravene one of his favorite authorities, for Valla himself had not performed the same excision; Bentley, *Humanists and Holy Writ*, 95. Lee and Stunica claimed that Erasmus's Greek manuscripts were corrupt, and from the standpoint of modern scholarship they were correct: Erasmus employed Greek manuscripts from the Byzantine Church, which embodied a separate, late, and inferior process of transmission. As a result, the Old Latin version that Stunica championed was more reliable than the Greek that Erasmus used as a model and translated in 1519, but since Stunica did not know that, he deserves no credit for it. See de Jonge's introduction to Erasmus's *Apologia* against Stunica, 19–20.

26. H. J. de Jonge, "Erasmus and the *comma Johanneum*," *Ephemerides theologicae Lovanienses* 56 (1980): 381–89.

27. "Erasmus in annotationibus primae Joannis 5 corruptos codices defensat, in beatum Hieronymum debacchatur, arrianorum causam agit atque tutatur. Nam et locum illum, *Tres sunt qui testimonium dant in caelo, Pater, Verbum et Spiritus Sanctus et hi tres unum sunt,* bello inexorabili impugnat, suffragia omnia respuit, rationes etiam frivolas undique in contrarium coacervat, divum Hieronymum his verbis impetit: Quamquam ille, scilicet Hieronymus, saepenumero violentus est, parum prudens, saepe varius parumque sibi constans." Beltrán de Heredia, *Cartulario,* 17–18. On Erasmus's treatment of heterodoxy in general and Arianism in particular, see James D. Tracy, "Erasmus and the Arians: Remarks on the *Consensus ecclesiae*," *Catholic Historical Review* 67 (1981): 1–10.

28. See Beltrán de Heredia, *Cartulario,* 36 and 114, 53 and 71, respectively, for the evidence cited in this paragraph.

29. "Quod dicit se in codice graeco non invenisse illam triplicitatem de testimonio caelesti, abunde probat; et quoniam in sua translatione illud non praetermittit, transeat." Ibid., 76.

30. Ibid., 37, 67.

31. "Est ut hereticus comburendus." Ibid., 72.

32. "Aperte insinuat quod illud apposuerit, non quia sic credidit aut credendum sentiat, sed quia scriptum reperit." Ibid., 54.

33. "He should be warned and begged so that, complying to the opinion of the majority, he may affirm that passage to be from the text" ("Monendus atque rogandus est ut, majorum sententiae acquiescens, locum illum affirmet esse de textu"). Ibid., 79.

34. "Romans 9:5. *Qui est super omnia Deus.* [1516–1522: Nisi haec particula adjecta est, sicuti quasdam adjectas offendimus.] [1516–1527: Hoc certe loco Paulus palam Christum pronunciavit deum. Et consentiunt, quae quidem viderim graecorum exemplaria.]" *Erasmus' Annotations on the New Testament: Acts, Romans, I and*

II Corinthians, ed. Anne Reeve and M. A. Screech, facsimile of the final Latin text with all earlier variants, Studies in the History of Christian Thought, no. 42 (Leiden: Brill, 1990).

35. "Ad Rom. 9, cum sit patentissima auctoritas Apostoli de Christo dicentis, *Qui est Deus benedictus in saecula,* et hic sit planus, simplex, manifestusque sensus, in quo etiam, ut idem Erasmus testatur, omnes codices consentiunt, ad impudentissimam tergiversationem confugit ut dicat: 'nisi haec particula adjecta est, sicuti quasdam adjectas offendimus,' etc." Beltrán de Heredia, *Cartulario,* 20.

36. "De hoc autem quod dicit Erasmus adjectas esse in sacro canone particulas, an videlicet invalidet sacrae scripturae auctoritatem, cum deveniemus ad articulum cuius titulus est, 'contra auctoritatem sacrae scripturae,' dicam quod sentio." Ibid., 62.

37. "Tunc nihil autoritatis maneret in sacra scriptura, quia quacumque particula signata dicam quod est adjecta . . . et sic peribit auctoritas sacrae scripturae." Ibid., 97.

38. On the theological rationale for the substitution, see C. A. L. Jarrot, "Erasmus's *In principium erat Sermo:* A Controversial Translation," *Studies in Philology* 61 (1964): 35–40, and Marjorie O'Rourke Boyle, *Erasmus on Language and Method in Theology* (Toronto: University of Toronto Press, 1977), Chapter 1.

39. "Item in annotationibus Joannis 1 apologetice se excusans quod transtulerit, *In principio erat Sermo,* etc., 'quid,' inquit, 'erat piaculum si in libro qui privatim legitur pro Verbo dicam Sermonem, aut eloquium, aut orationem, aut vocem, aut aliud quod idem polleat?' " Beltrán de Heredia, *Cartulario,* 21. Erasmus justified the switch in the 1522 version of the *Annotations.*

40. See the relevant verses in *Annotations on the New Testament: the Gospels,* ed. Anne Reeve, facsimile of the final Latin text with all earlier variants (London: Gerald Duckworth, 1986) 125; and *Annotations on the New Testament: Acts . . . ,* ed. Reeve and Screech, 382.

41. *Apologia,* ed. de Jonge, 254.

42. "Erasmus in annotationibus primae Joannis 5 corruptos codices defensat, in beatum Hieronymum debacchatur, arrianorum causam agit atque tutatur. Nam et locum illum, *Tres sunt qui testimonium dant in caelo, Pater, Verbum et Spiritus Sanctus et hi tres unum sunt,* bello inexorabili impugnat, suffragia omnia respuit, rationes etiam frivolas undique in contrarium coacervat, divum Hieronymum his verbis impetit: Quamquam ille, scilicet Hieronymus, saepenumero violentus est, parum prudens, saepe varius parumque sibi constans." Beltrán de Heredía, *Cartulario,* 17–18.

43. Ibid., 45, 74, 80.

44. "Quid auctoritatis in praedicationibus habebunt Dei verbi praedicatores in cathedra veritatis, si citent Hieronymi testimonium? Quid firmitatis in his quae transtulit, si dicta suae translationis contra haereticos afferentur?" Ibid., 72.

45. "Verba autem quae in Hieronymum scripsit, ipse non scripsissem; irreverentiam enim prae se ferunt." Ibid., 59.

46. Ibid., 18. The formulators of the Valladolid charges drew that quotation from the *Modus orandi Deum,* but it had counterparts in the first two editions of the

Annotations, as well as the *Apologia* to Stunica. See the *Annotations on the New Testament: The Gospels*, 221, and *Apologia*, ed. de Jonge, 124–30, in which Erasmus attempted to prove that the equation between Jesus and God was only implied in certain scriptural passages. In 1522, Carranza attacked the same annotation as well as Erasmus's attempt to justify it to Stunica: *Opusculum*, ff. 3v–14v.

47. For Valladolid's rendition of the quotation, see Beltrán de Heredia, *Cartulario*, 21.

48. Ibid., 70, 26.

49. He had written "Perhaps one could suppose that [denoting Jesus as God] was seldom done by the respectful apostles, lest the ordinary ears of certain persons of that age not endure the name of God to be assigned to man; and thus it happens that those persons sooner recoil from evangelical doctrine than begin to learn the mysteries of the Gospel. In these circumstances, Christ first ordered his disciples to preach repentance, and to be silent about Christ" ("Fortasse suspicari poterat aliquis hoc parcius fuisse factum ab apostolis verentibus, ne id temporis quorundam aures profanae non ferrent homini tribui Dei vocabulum, fieretque ut prius resilirent ab evangelica doctrina quam coepissent evangelii mysteria discere. Sic primum Christus suis mandavit, ut penitentiam praedicarent, de Christo tacerent"). *Apologia*, ed. de Jonge, 124.

50. In contrast, twenty of the Valladolid theologians debated the more formal aspect of the question, which was whether Jesus was actually labeled "true God" somewhere in the books of Matthew, Mark, Luke, or John.

51. Beltrán de Heredia, *Cartulario*, 55 (Córdoba), 51 (Ciruelo), and 96 (Quintana).

52. Ibid., 78, 66.

53. "Beatus Hilarius ausus est pronuntiare Spiritum Sanctum Deum, cum haec Spiritus Sanctus est Deus, sit unum ex articulis fidei quem baptizandis proponebatur credendus. Si ergo episcopus et sanctus fuit, quomodo igitur non ausus est?" Ibid., 29.

54. Ibid., 18.

55. For Vázquez's confusion over Erasmus's intentions, see ibid., 112.

56. The first group that denied Erasmus's mimicry of Luther included Gómez, Enríquez, Ciria, and Virués; the second, which wanted the material censored, consisted of Rodríguez de la Fuente, Lerma, Alcaráz, and López de Bejar.

57. "Fortasse praestiterat hoc piis studiis agere uti nos idem reddamur cum Deo, quam curiosis studiis decertare, quomodo differat a Patre Filius, aut ab utroque Spiritus Sanctus." Beltrán de Heredia, *Cartulario*, 18.

58. Ibid., 22–23.

59. "Cum erudiat affectum nostrum et incitet voluntatem ad amorem et caritatem Dei, avertens nos a curiosis studiis et inutilibus disceptationibus, qui tantum valent ad contentionem, et parum ad intellectus doctrinam." Ibid., 43.

60. The Valladolid excerpt read, "On the paraphrase of Matthew 13, servants who wish to gather the tares too soon are those who think that pseudoapostles and heretics should be driven from public with swords and deaths, when the head of the household does not wish them to be extinguished, but tolerated, in case they may

come to their senses and be turned from tares into wheat. Because if they do not come to their senses, they may be reserved for his judgment, to whom finally they will cause suffering.' [Erasmus] says these things there" ("In paraphrase Matthei 13: 'servi qui volunt ante tempus colligere zizania sunt qui pseudoapostolos et haeresiarchas gladiis ac mortibus aestimant e medio tollendos; cum paterfamilias nolit eos extingui, sed tolerari, si forte resipiscant et e zizaniis vertantur in triticum. Quod si non resipiscant, serventur suo judici; cui paenas dabunt aliquando. Haec ille"). Ibid., 22.

61. Ibid. The Sorbonne cited the passage in its entirety: Argentré, *Collectio judiciorum*, vol. 2, pt. 1:54.

62. "Et felix necessitas quae compellit ad bona." Beltrán de Heredia, *Cartulario*, 59.

63. Seidel Menchi, *Erasmo in Italia*, 141, determined that ecclesiastical and inquisitorial figures in Italy tried to censor the *Colloquies* before any of Erasmus's other writings.

64. Even the Spanish translator of the *Enchiridion* felt the same way: although he rejected any criticism of that particular text, he told Luís Coronel in 1526 that if anyone slandered the *Praise of Folly* or the *Colloquies*, they simply would have to endure it. See Alonso Fernández de Madrid to Coronel, in Erasmus, *Opus epistolarum*, vol. 6, Appendix 18, Letter 3, ll. 50–52.

65. AHN, Inqu., Leg., 4426, unfoliated manuscript page 14, comprises a partial list of attendees and their accommodations, and places certain theologians in inquisitors' residences.

66. Beltrán de Heredia, *Cartulario*, 77, 89–91.

67. Ibid., 74.

68. "Assi mesmo que jurán de tener secreto en lo que en esta catholica congregacion se hablara y platicara, en special que no dirán cosa alguna de que a alguno de los que son aquí congregados, e intervinieren en la dicha congregacion, se pueda seguir algun inconveniente y sinistra opinion." AHN, Inqu., Leg. 4426, unfoliated manuscript page 3. While a number of the attendees were either prosecuted or deposed by the Inquisition in later years, among them López de Bejar, Virués, Carrasco, and Lerma, none of them could have known in 1527 that they eventually would become targets of Inquisition officials. López de Bejar, Virués, and Carrasco were involved, in one form or another, in Juan de Vergara's trial.

69. Delegate Francisco del Castillo circulated anti-Erasmian pamphlets immediately before the Valladolid assembly was convened; see n. 6 above. After the conference, Enríquez wrote a defense of Erasmus that was prompted by the Sorbonne's condemnation; it recited dissimilarities between Erasmus and Luther, and was placed on the 1551 Index: *Eiusdem Defensionum pro Erasmo Roterodamo contra varias Theologorum Parisiensium annotationes liber unus. Ubi docetur Erasmi doctrinam cum Martini Lutheri haeresibus nihil commune habere* (Naples, 1532). Virués mentioned Erasmus in his seven *Collationes* (1526), now lost; a vernacular letter (1526) to the guardian of the Franciscan monastery at Alcalá, and the last of his *Philippicae disputationes XX adversus*

Lutherana dogmata per Philippum Melanchthonem defensa (Antwerp, 1541): in each, he emphasized Erasmus's merits but also recognized his faults. Bataillon, *Érasme et l'Espagne*, 1:236–40; and Bonilla y San Martín, *Juan Luís Vives y la filosofía del Renacimiento*, Appendix, 693–98.

70. Among others who mentioned the trials of their era, see Beltrán de Heredia, *Cartulario*, 51 (Ciruelo), 59 (Córdoba), and 72 (Gouvea); the last relayed the anecdote about the egg. The two participants who cited the risk in pressuring Erasmus were Cabrero and Ciria (ibid., 36, 48). Vergara told Erasmus that representatives of the monastic orders leveled the same charge of trepidation at Inquisitor Manrique; *Opus epistolarum*, vol. 7, Letter 1814, ll. 155–58.

71. Namely, López de Bejar and Virués: Beltrán de Heredia, *Cartulario*, 79, 114.

72. Bentley, *Humanists and Holy Writ*, 97. See ibid., 91–111, on the editorial principles of the Complutensian New Testament editors.

73. The same perception of Jerome's inconsistency could lead intellectuals to argue that Jerome must have commented on the Bible before translating it. See Rice, *Saint Jerome in the Renaissance*, Chapter 7, on the various approaches to Jerome in the early modern epoch.

74. "Erasmus non defensat corruptos codices, sed eos emendat, nec tenebatur reputare graecos codices quos habuit fuisse corruptos. . . . quia illi codices sibi fuerant oblati ex diversis religiosorum bibliothecis et ex bibliotheca summi pontificis, ubi corruptos codices evangeliorum et apostolicarum lectionum haberi non est praesumendum." Beltrán de Heredia, *Cartulario*, 36. Cabrero was attesting the venerability of monastic libraries as well as papal ones.

75. Only Lerma copied Erasmus's own comment that no heresy was more extinct than Arianism. Compare ibid., 77, to Erasmus's second *responsio* against Lee, *Opera omnia*, ed. J. LeClerc, 9:277. For Córdoba's and Vitoria's remarks, see Beltrán de Heredia, *Cartulario*, 54, 116.

76. Erasmus had told Stunica that he was not forced to apply 1 John 5:20 to Jesus; *Apologia*, ed. de Jonge, 128. But Quintana asserted, "that opinion of 1 John 5 is actually recounted about the gist of this authority [John 17:3], since it is his exposition, and the gospel and the letter were brought forth by the same apostle and evangelist" ("illa auctoritas primae Joannis 5 jam allegata est de corpore huius auctoritatis, cum sit eius expositio, et evangelium et epistola edita sunt ab eodem apostolo et evangelista"); Beltrán de Heredia, ibid., 96. For Córdoba's exegetical gymnastics, ibid., 56.

77. Ibid., 47.

78. "(Ut more dialecticorum loquar), argueret a conditionali, cum positione antecedentis ad positionem consequentis, hoc videlicet modo: si haec particula non est adjecta, certe hoc loco Paulus Christum pronuntiavit Deum. Sed haec particula non est adjecta. Igitur hoc loco Paulus etc." Ibid., 61.

79. Ibid., 44. For a description of Carranza's polemic, see Rummel, *Erasmus and His Catholic Critics*, 1:157ss.

80. Rummel, *Erasmus and His Catholic Critics,* 1:4–5. The stipulation of Erasmus as a grammarian or philologist, rather than as a theologian, was a standard charge in the controversial literature.

81. Rummel, *Erasmus and His Catholic Critics,* vol. 1, Chapters 4, 5, 7; Bentley, *Humanists and Holy Writ,* Chapters 4 and 5; and idem, "New Testament Scholarship at Louvain in the Early Sixteenth Century," *Studies in Medieval and Renaissance History,* n.s., 2 (1979): 51–79; Asso, *La teologia e la grammatica,* 59–98.

82. On Tittelmans, see Bentley, "New Testament Scholarship at Louvain," and idem, *Humanists and Holy Writ,* 199–211.

83. The Valladolid repertory's allusions to Arianism—and their European colleagues' mention of the same—reflected Pauline strictures to expect cycles of heresies as trials of the faithful. According to St. Paul, heresies would recur and tend to take the same form.

84. Lerma favored expurgation or emendation in four instances: Beltrán de Heredia, *Cartulario,* 77, 79.

85. For comments by Alonso Fernández de Madrid, the *Enchiridion's* Spanish translator, on his alterations to Erasmus's language, see *Erasmo: El enchiridion, o manual del Caballero Cristiano,* ed. Dámaso Alonso, *Anejos* of the *RFE,* no. 16 (Madrid: S. Augirre, 1932), 104–5.

86. Beltrán de Heredia, *Cartulario,* 76, 59, 33.

87. As the Valladolid assembly occurred, inquisitorial secretary Alfonso de Valdés wrote about Ciruelo to the imperial secretary of Latin letters, Maximilian Transylvanus: in the letter, Valdés reported that Ciruelo was the only delegate from Alcalá who did not take Erasmus's part, and characterized him as more of an astrologer than a theologian. See Fermín Caballero, *Alonso y Juan de Valdés,* 4:336. Bataillon picked up Valdés's description and amplified it, so that Ciruelo became "an intrepid defender of orthodoxy." The authority of Bataillon's book made the portrait definitive. See *Érasme et l'Espagne* 1:17, 260 n. 8.

88. Avilés also recognized the hidden moderation of Ciruelo's replies. "Erasmo y los teólogos españoles," 184.

89. "Et capite 10 de suo tempore loquens, citat illud Psalmi 18, 'In omnem terram exivit sonus eorum.'" Beltrán de Heredia, *Cartulario,* 51.

Chapter Three. A Converso and the Old Testament

1. Herman Hailperin, *Rashi and the Christian Scholars* (Pittsburgh: Pittsburgh University Press, 1963).

2. Smalley, *The Study of the Bible in the Middle Ages,* Chapter 4; Evans, *The Language and Logic of the Bible: The Earlier Middle Ages,* and idem, *The Language and Logic of the Bible: The Road to Reformation* (Cambridge: Cambridge University Press, 1985); R. E. Brown, *The "sensus plenior" of Sacred Scripture* (Baltimore: Johns Hopkins Press, 1955). For medieval exegesis in general, the fundamental works are Ceslas Spicq, *Esquisse*

d'une histoire de l'exégèse latine du moyen âge (Paris: J. Vrin, 1944); and Lubac, *Exégèse médiévale.*

3. Christians' propensity to react to the Old Testament as if it prefigured the New came from their expansion of a Pauline verse. In 1 Corinthians 10, Paul wrote: "Haec omnia in figura contingebant illis," or "all these things happened to those persons"— the Jews in the Old Testament—"as a figure," that is, a metaphor. Although Paul was speaking of certain episodes in the Old Testament, his successors applied his sentiment in an unlimited way, so that "haec omnia" became any and all events under the Old Law. Lubac, *Exégèse médiévale,* 2:60–84.

4. On Bruni and Manetti, see Christoph Dröge, "Quia morem Hieronymi in transferendo cognovi . . . Les débuts de études hébraiques chez les humanistes italiens," in *L'Hebreu au temps de la Renaissance,* ed. Ilana Zinguer (Leiden: Brill, 1992), 69, 74–79; on Erasmus, see G. Lloyd Jones, *The Discovery of Hebrew in Tudor England: A Third Language* (Manchester: Manchester University Press, 1983), 31–32.

5. Jerome Friedman, *The Most Ancient Testimony: Sixteenth-Century Christian-Hebraica in the Age of Renaissance Nostalgia* (Athens: Ohio University Press, 1983), 13–15; R. Gerald Hobbs, "Hebraica veritas and traditio apostolica: St. Paul and the Interpretation of the Psalms in the Sixteenth Century," in *The Bible in the Sixteenth Century,* ed. David C. Steinmetz (Durham, N.C.: Duke University Press, 1990), 83–99; Shuger, *The Renaissance Bible;* Marjorie Reeves, "The Bible and Literary Authorship in the Middle Ages," in *Reading the Text: Biblical Criticism and Literary Theory,* ed. Stephen Prickett (Oxford: Basil Blackwell, 1991), 12–63.

6. For this ubiquitous metaphor, see Beryl Smalley, *The Gospels in the Schools, 1100–1280* (London: Hambledon, 1985), 37.

7. Lyra could attest the literalness of these Old Testament quotes in the apostles' discourse because the apostles deliberately invoked them; their literality in turn meant that they had probative value for Christian theology.

8. "Fuit propheta magnus ad quem prophetiae aliorum prophetarum fuerunt ordinatae." See Lyra's gloss, *Biblia Latina cum glossa ordinaria,* intr. Karlfried Forehlich and Margaret T. Gibson, facsimile reprint of the *editio princeps Adolf Rusch of Strassburg* (1480–81), 4 vols. (Turnhout: Brepols, 1992), vol. 1, Deut. 18:15.

9. Lyra actually cited this axiom—called the Aristotelian metaphysic of final causality—on Exodus 12 and the Passover, to the effect that Moses' sacrifice of the lamb had Christological meaning because "est tamen primus in intentione sicut finis respectu eorum quae sunt ad finem ordinata." Ibid., 1:64r, on Exodus 12. In the same passage Lyra referred to Paul's admonition in 1 Corinthians 10, "haec omnia in figura contingebant illis." See n. 3 above.

10. Shuger, *The Renaissance Bible,* 21.

11. See the work of Fernández Marcos and Fernández Tejero, *Biblia y humanismo.* Two fertile areas of investigation involve Luis de León and Cipriano de la Huerga, although investigators often possess a less than satisfactory understanding of either medieval exegesis or Renaissance humanism. Colin Thompson, *The Strife of Tongues:*

Fray Luis de León and the Golden Age of Spain (Cambridge: Cambridge University Press, 1988); Hipolito Navarro Rodríguez, "Una obra inédita de Fray Luis de León: *Expositio in Genesim* (Codex 83, biblioteca de la Catedral de Pamplona)," *Scripta theologica* 16 (1984): 573–78; Eugenio Asensio, "Cipriano de la Huerga, maestro de Fray Luis de León," in *Homenaje a Pedro Sainz Rodriguez*, vol. 3: *Estudios historicos* (Madrid: FUE, 1986), 57–72; and Gaspar Morocho Gayo, "Humanismo y filología poligráfica en Cipriano de la Huerga. Su encuentro con fray Luis de León," *Ciudad de Dios* 204 (1991): 863–914.

12. Prickett, *Reading the Text*, 1–12.

13. Hobbs, "Hebraica veritas"; Friedman, *The Most Ancient Testimony*, 39–47, 172; James H. Overfield, *Humanism and Scholasticism in Late Medieval Germany* (Princeton, N.J.: Princeton University Press, 1984), Chapter 7. The same issues were present in the late twelfth and especially the thirteenth centuries: Jeremy Cohen, *The Friars and the Jews: The Evolution of Medieval Anti-Judaism* (Ithaca, N.Y.: Cornell University Press, 1982).

14. "Ciruelo post vesperas naturae concessit." Salamanca, Archivo de la Catedral, Archivo Capitular, *Calendario*, entry for November 5, 1548.

15. Numbers were omnipresent in medieval biblical exegesis. Lubac, *Exégèse médiévale*, 2:25–32.

16. "Y este significó a los penitentes hypocritas, que llevan la cruz de la penitencia no por mortificar la carne y sus pecados, sino por ser loados de los hombres y ser tenidos por santos." *Contemplaces sobre la passion del nuestro señor Jesu Christo*, bound with Ciruelo's *Libro de la teología mística* (Alcalá, 1547), f. 25v. St. Augustine risked a similar malapropism when he identified Lazarus so strongly with a sinner: Smalley, *The Gospels in the Schools 1100–1280*, viii.

17. Ciruelo's rendition of the Latin reads, "Impii cessabunt a tumultu et requiescent fessi robore; cessabunt causae et contumeliae; luxit et defluxit terra, et infirmata est altitudo populi, et iterfecta est ab habitatoribus suis." *Hexameron teologal*, f. A7r.

18. In this book, Mosaic always refers to actions and precepts of Moses, mosaic to a scholastic technique for producing arguments out of discrete quotations.

19. Ciruelo's biblical translations include the *Interpretatio latina sacrae scripturae Veteris Testamenti ad verbum*, 1526, Manuscript G-1-4, Library of the Monastery of El Escorial. (A copy of this work also resides in the Archivo Histórico Universitario, Madrid, dated 1527.) Also see Ciruelo's *Versiones tres Penthateuci*, 1533, Manuscript Ref. B-411, Inventory 123, Cathedral Archive, Segovia; *Penthateuci Mosayci veridicam interpretationem ad verbum*, 1536; and *Libri septem, Job, Psalter, Proverbs, Ecclesiastes, Cantica salomenis, Esther, et Ruth*, 1537, Manuscripts 589 and 590, respectively, Biblioteca Universitaria, Salamanca.

20. Several of Zamora's manuscript editions of the Targums were edited and published between 1982 and 1987. For a succinct synopsis of his career and modern bibliography on him, see Carlos del Valle, "Notas sobre Alfonso de Zamora," *Sefarad* 47 (1987): 173–79. We possess no comparative work on Hebrew scholarship in Spain

and Germany; historians often trumpet the superiority of German Hebraists without noticing the concurrent achievements of Spaniards. Ciruelo's and Zamora's work, for instance, occurred after Reuchlin's *De rudimentis hebraicis* in 1506, simultaneously with Sebastian Münster's 1527 Aramaic grammar, and before the latter's literal Latin translation of the Hebrew Bible in 1535.

21. Stinger, *Humanism and the Church Fathers,* 58, 100–101. For a different view of Chrysoloras's contribution, see Seigel, *Rhetoric and Philosophy in Renaissance Humanism,* 120–21.

22. On Valla, see Bentley, *Humanists and Holy Writ,* 51–52. Erasmus made critical remarks to the same effect in several of his annotations on the Pauline epistles, which were included in the charges levied against him at Valladolid in 1527; see their facsimile reproduction in Avilés, *Erasmo y la Inquisición,* 40. Other polemicists later used history itself against this sort of criticism, and argued that the New Testament's Greek was appropriate to its age. Rice, *St. Jerome in the Renaissance,* 180.

23. Kristeller, *Renaissance Thought,* 101–4; Seigel, *Rhetoric and Philosophy,* viii.

24. *Biblia complutense,* 6 vols. (Alcalá, 1514–17). Treatment of the Complutensian Polyglot as a monument to the Spanish Renaissance was routine until the work of Jerry H. Bentley. See Elliot, *Imperial Spain 1469–1716,* 118; Lynch, *Spain under the Hapsburgs,* 1:60; Antonio Domínguez Ortíz, *The Golden Age of Spain 1516–1659,* trans. James Casey (New York: Basic Books, 1971), 223; Bentley, "New Light on the Editing of the Complutensian New Testament," *Bibliothèque d'Humanisme et Renaissance* 42 (1980): 145–56, and idem, *Humanists and Holy Writ.* Ironically, although many historians have relied upon Bataillon for their characterizations of the Polyglot, he doubted whether that project really evinced the philological desiderata of Renaissance humanism: *Érasme et l'Espagne,* 1:40–41.

25. Origen's *Hexapla,* so-called because of its usually six-column structure, was so enormous that it probably was not copied in its entirety, but its text of the Septuagint was widely reproduced and disseminated on its own. Jerome's remark that he had seen the complete *Hexapla* in Origen's own library only heightened its reputation.

26. When it came to their translation of the Aramaic, the Complutensian team specifically rendered the Onqelos Targum into Latin; it was deposited in the library of the College of San Ildefonso. Marcos and Tejero, *Biblia y humanismo,* 20.

27. Zamora seems to have been Ciruelo's constant collaborator as well as instructor: he copied the Hebrew for Ciruelo's 1526, 1536, and 1537 translations, and attested his friendship with Ciruelo in Hebrew colophons. Together they revised the Hebrew grammar that Zamora originally produced for the Polyglot. Zamora held the chair of Hebrew intermittently at the University of Alcalá between 1512 and 1544. For Zamora's colophons, see the one translated by José Llamas, "Documental inédito de exegesis rabinica," *Sefarad* 6 (1946): 305; for a description of Zamora and Ciruelo's 1526 grammar, idem, "Los manuscritos hebreos de El Escorial," *Sefarad* 1 (1941): 12–13. Llamas contended that Zamora was the actual translator for the Ciruelo manu-

scripts, and argued that Ciruelo's name served as a kind of window dressing: given Ciruelo's converso ancestry, as well as the autobiographical content of the 1536 manuscript, such assertions seem most unlikely.

28. The Complutensian Polyglot Bible was completely printed by 1517, but did not receive the papal license for distribution until March 22, 1520, and was not in circulation until 1521 or 1522. Marcos and Tejero, *Biblia y humanismo,* 210.

29. On Ciruelo's tenure, see AHN, Sec. de Universidades, Libro 716, ff. 25r and 71r.

30. Bentley, *Humanists and Holy Writ,* 44–45, 153, offers the same caveat about Lorenzo Valla's biblical scholarship. The Greek Codex Montfortianus, which contained 1 John 5:7–8, was forged by Erasmus's enemies after the Complutensian Greek editors finished their work; eventually four Greek manuscripts would contain the comma Johanneum.

31. Ibid., 96. As it turned out, their decision to erase the line was correct, because it had been added to the scriptural text from the Greek liturgy, but their decision nevertheless reveals more devotion to Jerome than to criticism.

32. Ibid., 98–103.

33. See Marcos and Tejero, *Biblia y humanismo,* 210–12, who confirm that we cannot identify with precision the Hebrew manuscripts employed by the Complutensian editors.

34. "The Pentateuch has three languages, namely, Hebrew, Aramaic, and Greek, which we view printed with the other three corresponding Latin translations in close proximity, so that in this way the Latin translation of blessed Jerome replies to the Hebrew truth" ("Pentateuchus quidem triplicem linguam habet, Hebraicam videlicet Chaldaicam et Graecam, quas imprimendas vissimus cum aliis tribus latinis interpretationibus juxta correspondentibus, ita ut Hebraicae veritati respondeat latina beati Hieronymi translatio"). Complutensian Polyglot Bible, volume 1, f. 2r. The "three Latin translations" to which the prologue refers include the one by Jerome. Nebrija declined to work on the Polyglot because Cisneros would not allow him to amend the Vulgate: "Epistola del Maestro de Nebrija al Cardenal," trans. Roque Chabás, *RABM* 8 (1903):493–96. Felipe Fernández-Armesto also recognized the divergence between Nebrija's and Cisneros's approaches through his analysis of the latter's preface to the Polyglot: "Cardinal Cisneros as a Patron of Printing," in *God and Man in Medieval Spain: Essays in Honour of J. R. L. Highfield,* ed. Derek W. Lomax and David MacKenzie (Warminster: Aris & Phillips, 1989), 157–58. For Nebrija as textual critic, see Bentley, *Humanists and Holy Writ,* 80–91.

35. "Velut inter Synagogam et Orientalem Ecclesiam posuimus, tanquam duos . . . latrones medium autem Iesum, hoc est Romanam sive latinam Ecclesiam." Complutensian Polyglot, vol. 1, f. 6r.

36. "It happens that wherever there is a difference of Latin manuscripts, or the suspicion of a corrupted reading (a thing which we see happen most frequently from the ignorance and also the carelessness of scribes), one must have recourse to the first

source of Scripture, just as blessed Jerome and Augustine and other Church exegetes suggest" ("Accedit quod ubicumque latinorum codicum varietas est, aut depravatae lectionis suspitio [id quod librariorum imperitia simul et negligentia frequentissime accidere videmus], ad primam scripturae originem recurrendum est, sicut beatus Hieronymus et Augustinus ac caeteri ecclesiastici tractores admonent"). Ibid., f. 1r.

37. Ibid., f. 6r.

38. In 1536, Ciruelo wrote: "necessario incidemus in vitia Barbarismi et Solecismi, nam ad ea nos coget huius operis ratio [et] verbi causa. Ad Barbarismum pertinent pleraque vocabula peregrina, necdum satis latinitate Donatis; format nam sermo hebreus quaedam verba a nominibus, quae nec apud Grecos, neque apud Latinos usquam audita sunt, ut a sacerdote sacerdotare [sic], pro eo quod est fungi sacerdotio . . . [et] a pugillo pugillare, id est, pugillum implere." *Penthateuci Mosayci veridicam interpretationem ad verbum* (Salamanca, 1536), f. 2v. In his last example, he used a late Latin form of the noun "boxer" (*pugillum*) instead of the classical *pugil*.

39. "Ad Solecismum vero cogent nos diversa verborum regimina apud nos et apud hebreos, quia non semper eosdem casus nominum exigunt post se eadem verba utrobisque. Nam 'servio' apud hebreos iungitur accusativo, ut in primo decalogi precepto dicitur hebraice, 'non servies deos alienos.'" Ibid.

40. "Si quis forte delicatior et latinam concinnitatem [sic] affectans viderit hanc nostram interpretationem non satis respondere latino eloquio, is expendat hoc ea ratione factum esse, quatenus illa originalis lingua hebrea nobis representaretur in sua phrasi, et quantum ad proprietates gramaticas singulorum vocabulorum eius: quas ex nostra interlineari glossa latina facile cognoscere poterit quicumque advertens ad eas." Ibid., f. 3r.

41. "Et modus quo possimus confutare infideles hebreos, qui nostrum Hieronimum calumniantur uti sacre scripture depravatorem. Quod tamen longe secus habet, ut videre licebit si quis interpretationem eius cum hebreorum voluminibus conferre voluerit." *Interpretatio latina sacrae scripturae Veteris Testamenti ad verbum* (Escorial, 1526), f. 4r.

42. "Diximus notanter sicubi reperiatur, quia non sumus omnino certi quod in omnibus nostrae communis et per vulgatae bibliae libris habeamus sancti hieronimi interpretationem; immo in libro suo, de hebraicis questionibus, taxat ipse quosdam locos litterae nostrae, quae suo tempore dictitabatur vulgata editio." Ibid., f. 4v.

43. "And in fact these men brought forth Latin translations for us out of Greek and Aramaic editions, not out of the Hebrew source itself. In which translations, besides the varieties, much less errors, of their manuscripts, they likewise imparted their own individual dissonances, namely, each according to the capacity of his intellect, and according to the degree of his erudition in languages. For this reason, then, difference, and even variety, happens so frequently among us in the sacred Scriptures of the Old Testament" ("Et hi quidem ex grecanis atque caldaicis editionibus, non ex ipso fonte hebraico, latinas nobis ediderunt translationes. In quibus ipsi praeter suorum prototiporum varietates, ne dicam errores, proprias etiam addiderunt dissonantias, scilicet

unusquisque pro captu intellectus sui, atque pro modulo suae eruditionis inperitia linguarum. Hinc igitur accidit apud nos tam frequens in sacris scripturis veteris testamenti differentia, atque varietas"). *Penthateuci Mosayci veridicam interpretationem ad verbum* (Salamanca, 1536), f. 1r.

44. Jerome "scripturae hebraicae literalem sensum latino sermone depromeret, reiectis scilicet erroribus priorum interpretum." Ibid. Obviously Ciruelo was capable of invoking different meanings for the sensus literalis; see below.

45. "Ad emendandos errores et vitia scriptorum, seu impresorium, qui quotidie accidunt in sacris literis ex eorum incuria, vel ignorantia, aut ex quorundam sciolorum audatia indocta." Ibid. Significantly, Ciruelo borrowed the term *sciolist* from Jerome.

46. "Adeo qui in nullo fere loco discrepet a vero sensu hebraice Bibliae Judeorum, quamvis in alia phrasi verborum." Ibid., f. 1r.

47. "And so through the grace of God, translating the sacred Hebrew Bible word by word, I produced a Latin one" ("Et quia per gratia dei, Sacra Biblia hebraica verbum verbo reddens, Latinam effeci"). Prologue, *Versiones tres Pentateuci* (Segovia, 1533).

48. "Hoc egit deus noster misericordiae pater clementissimus, loquens ad nos inprimis per servos suos (et) prophetas, deinde per apostolos et alios discipulos suos, qui canonicos libros sacrae bibliae nobis scripsserunt." Ibid.

49. "Aliae vero tres columnae potius sunt paraphrases quam interpretationes, nam aliis verbis sententiam litterae declarant, etiam additione, remotione, et permutatione verborum quorumdam, et neglecta phrasi hebraica; ut ex collatione columnarum quilibet diligens Lector advertere poterit, unde etiam clarior apparebit sensus sacrae scripturae in locis oscuris. Nam quod unus interpretum obscure dixit, alius declaravit, et vice versa; et ubi duo aut tres eorum conveniant, reliquiis arguetur." Ibid.

50. "Scriptorum vitia plurima, et sciolorum quorumdam expositorum commenta frivola, ac demum quorumdam interpretum eruditio linguarum imperfecta." Ibid.

51. In a random sampling, I found Ciruelo's critical remarks in *Penthateuci Mosayci veridicam interpretationem ad verbum* (Salamanca, 1536), ff. 9r (Gen. 4), 74r–v (Exod. 2), 87v (Exod. 12), 97v (Exod. 18), 125r (Lev. 4), and 222r (Num. 32); and in *Libri septem, Job, Psalter, Proverbs, et al.* (Salamanca, 1537), ff. 21v (Job 37), and 25v (Ps. 2). Although Ciruelo explicitly sanctioned traditional Christian exegesis in the prologue to his 1537 manuscript, in his marginalia he declined to draw the significance of the Song of Songs to Christian ends.

52. "Quare prope annos christiane salutis mille et quinientos hanc promissionem implere volens noster Deus, precipue in hac nostra Hispania (in qua erant multae Judeorum achademiae), illuminavit sua gratia plurimis eorum. Abstulitque velamen caecitatis a cordibus suis, quibus nonulli viri plane doctissimi in sacra Biblia hebraica baptismum, et fidem Christi devote susceperunt, effectique iam Christiani sincere, veraciter, et sine fictione ulla nos docuerunt veteris testamenti secreta literalia. Ego

igitur hanc temporis opportunitatem nactus, cepi iam quadragenarius litteras hebraicas ab eis discere." *Penthateuci Mosayci veridicam interpretationem ad verbum* (Salamanca, 1536), f. 2v. The phrase "ulla fictione" refers to the standard cliché about Jewish deception where Christians and the Hebrew Bible were concerned.

53. "Qui-venientes ad regem, Pentateuchum et prophetas transferentes-coram rege disputaverunt de uno deo colendo, et quomodo nulla creatura esset deus. Inde est quomodo ubicumque occurrebant ei in transferendo de trinitate, vel sub silentio praeteribant, vel aenigmatice transtulerunt, ne tres deos colendos tradidisse viderentur. Similiter de incarnatione verbi facientes. Unde translatio septuagintaduum quandoque est superflua . . . [et] diminuta." *Biblia complutense,* vol. 1, f. 5v.

54. "Deinde post annos liii. Theodotion fecit translationem sub Commodo. Deinde post annos triginta Symmachus interpres claruit sub Severo. Deinde post annos octo inventa est quaedam translatio hierosolymis, cuius autor ignoratur, quae dicta est vulgata translatio vel quinta editio. Deinde post annos xviii. tempore Alexandri supervenit Origenes, qui videns istas translationes imperfectas, coepit corrigere translationem lxxii interpretum per posteriores iam dictas translationes. Vel secundum aliquos solum translationem Theodotionis correxit et miscuit, scilicet supplens diminuta et resecans superflua." Ibid., f. 6r.

55. "Novissime superveniens . . . primo correxit translationem lxxii interpretum in latino cum astericis et obelis; postea vero transtulit immediate bibliam de hebraeo in latinum sine astericis et obelis. Et hac translatione nunc ubique utitur tota Romana ecclesia, licet non in omnibus libris." Ibid.

56. When the Complutensian Polyglot noted that Origen used asterisks and obelisks, and Jerome did not, that difference was nothing more than an antiquarian detail instead of a point about history.

57. On Damasus, Ciruelo wrote, "Quamvis ergo ante divum Hieronimum editio septuaginta interpretum in ecclesiasticis officiis legeretur . . . tamen post Theodosium Imperatore Christianissimum ex decreto Damasi papae editio Latina Sancti Hieronimi recepta est in lectione ecclesiastica." Prologue, *Versiones tres Penthateuci* (Segovia, 1533).

58. The following quotations from the Complutensian Polyglot occur in vol. 1, f. 5v; Ciruelo's two quotations come from the Prologue to the *Versiones tres Penthateuci* (Segovia, 1533).

59. I am most indebted to Professor Sara T. Nalle for finding and partially transcribing the 1553 Inquisition trial records of Juan and Benito Ciruelo in July 1990. The two trials contain all the genealogical material on the Ciruelo family; they are located in the ADC, Inqu., Leg. 193, Exp. 2175 and 2181. I have relied on Nalle's transcriptions for my discussion of these cases. Juan's and Benito's trials contain evidence of their ancestry because inquisitors quickly came to believe that heresy ran in families: over time, persons suspected of Jewish ancestry would be asked about the heretical backgrounds of their relatives, which in turn became part of the legal record.

60. The possibility that Ciruelo provided memorial Masses for his parents is noted

in Nicolas Antonio, *Bibliotheca hispana nova*, 2 vols. (Madrid: J. de Ibarra, 1788), 2:184–85, who culled it from Diego Sánchez Portocarrero, *Historia y antigüedad del muy noble y leal señorio de Molina*, Part 2, BN, manuscript, n.d. Part 1 of Portocarrero's work was published in Madrid in 1641.

61. Antonio Domínguez Ortiz and Bernard Vincent, *Historia de los moriscos*, 3rd ed. (Madrid: Alianza Editorial, S.A., 1997), and Henry Kamen, *Philip of Spain* (New Haven, Conn.: Yale University Press, 1997), 128–32.

62. For the belief that Spanish conversos remained Jewish, see Haim Beinart's introduction to his *Records of the Trials of the Spanish Inquisition in Ciudad Real*, 4 vols. (Jerusalem: Israel Academy of Sciences and Humanities, 1974–85) 1:xiii; idem, *Conversos on Trial: The Inquisition in Ciudad Real*, Hispania Judaica, vol. 3 (Jerusalem: Magnes, Hebrew University, 1981), 286–99; Yosef Kaplan, ed., *Jews and Conversos: Studies in Society and the Inquisition* (Jerusalem: World Union of Jewish Studies, Magnes, 1985); Angela S. Selke, *The Conversos of Majorca: Life and Death in a Crypto-Jewish Community in XVII Century Spain*, Hispania Judaica, vol. 5 (Jerusalem: Magnes, Hebrew University, 1986).

63. See the trials transcribed by Beinart, *Records of the Trials of the Spanish Inquisition*.

64. Such posthumous punishments occurred in the case of Juan Luís Vives's mother: Miguel de la Pinta Llorente, O.S.A., and Jose Maria de Palacio y de Palacio, eds., *Procesos inquisitoriales contra la familia judía de Juan Luís Vives*, vol. 1: *Proceso contra Blanquina March, madre del humanista* (Madrid: Instituto Arias Montano, 1964); Kamen, *The Spanish Inquisition*, Chapter 9.

65. Medieval intellectuals, too, invoked arguments about lineage when it came to heretics, but I doubt that anyone would contend that the Cathari or the Waldensians were perceived as "races" in the twelfth and thirteenth centuries. For an example of the racial argument about Spanish conversos, see Benzion Netanyahu, *The Origins of the Inquisition in Fifteenth-Century Spain* (New York: Random House, 1995).

66. On *limpieza de sangre* statutes, see Albert A. Sicroff, *Les controverses des statuts de "pureté de sang" en Espagne du XV au XVII siècle* (Paris: Didier, 1960). Benito's offense was transcribed as "dios no tiene poder," Juan's as "el dicho Ciruelo dixo, diciéndolo por los de este santo oficio, 'de algun cabo han de sacar su salario.'" Quotations are from Nalle's transcriptions, ADC, Inqu., Leg. 193, Exp. 2181 (for Benito) and Exp. 2175 (for Juan).

67. Beginning around 1540 and accelerating after 1572, local inquisitorial tribunals were ordered to send summaries of their cases, called *relaciones de causas*, to the Suprema. Current scholarship on the relaciones for Castile and Aragon reveals that blasphemy was one of the crimes most frequently prosecuted. Contreras and Henningsen, "Forty-Four Thousand Cases of the Spanish Inquisition (1540–1700)," 100–129. Contreras and Henningsen indicate that blasphemy, which the Inquisition denoted as *proposiciones*, constituted 22.5 percent of 25,890 trials for the Secretariat of

Aragon between 1540 and 1700, and 33.2 percent of 18,784 cases for the Secretariat of Castile during the same period. Also see Dedieu, *L'Administration de la Foi*, 280.

68. "Y aun le paresció mal porque ser como el dicho Ciruelo es bisnyeto de Francisco Sánchez Ciruelo condenado." Deposition by Pedro Hernández de la Parra, September 15, 1553, against Juan Ciruelo: ADC, Inqu., Leg. 193, Exp. 2175.

69. Friedman, *The Most Ancient Testimony*, 6.

70. On Manetti, see Dröge, "Quia morem Hieronymi," 76–79, and Gianfranco Fioravanti, "L'apologetica anti-giudaica di Giannozzo Manetti," *Rinascimento* 23 (1983): 3–32. On Reuchlin, see Overfield, *Humanism and Scholasticism in Late Medieval Germany,* Chapter 7; and John Edwards, *The Jews in Christian Europe 1400–1700, Christianity and Society in the Modern World* (London: Routledge, 1988), 52–54.

71. Cohen, *The Friars and the Jews*, Chapter 3.

72. "Verum . . . biblia Hebraica plurima loca valde obscura . . . reperientes, paraphrasim declarativam ediderunt ad informatione imperitorum judeorum. Quae ut christianis non pateret Caldeo, Siroque [sic] sermone facta est, quam ipsi Targum nos Caldaica editionem vocitamus. Et quia divus Hieronimus de illa nunquam fecit verbum, nullamque mentionem, verisimile apparet eam post tempora divi Hieronimi editam fuisse, hoc est, post annos Christi domini quadringentos. Quo etiam tempore Thalmuth iudeorum, ex invidia christianae religionis, in Antiochia Syriae conditum est. Et praeter hoc Targum, judei aliud habent, dictum Targum Hierosolimitanum; primum horum dicunt fecisse Onqelos Iudeum, secundum dicitur ab eis Targum Ionathe, sed hoc rarissimum est apud iudeos nostrae tempestatis, primum vero satis vulgatum est. Et in omnibus eorum sinagogis invenitur; est que magnae auctoritatis ista paraphrasis apud omnes doctores judeorum, valetque notabiliter confundendam Judeorum protervitatem, qua per glossas Thalmidicas Biblia[m] hebraica[m] ad falsos detorquent sensus. At Caldaica editio, per maiori parte, sacram Bibliam ad verum sensum interpretatur, quare mei doctores procuraverunt hanc translationem Caldaica habere Latinam." Prologue, *Versiones tres Penthateuci* (Segovia, 1533).

73. Ciruelo's work on the Cabala occurs as the tenth question to his *Paradoxae quaestiones numero decem* (Salamanca, 1538). Ciruelo's condemnation of the Cabala places him in the category of philological versus mystical Hebraists, a distinction often adduced by modern scholars.

74. "Hoc nam opus alio tempore commodius fieri non potuit, cum sint hodie apud nos multi fideles lingua hebrea peritissimi, qui sua eruditione singulari tanto operi sufficiant. Nam his deficientibus vix nobis esset unde ista peteremus, nisi ab ipsis professione hebreis; quibus certe fides a nobis habenda non est, cum sciamus apud eos prohibitum esse sub censuris gravissimis ne dogmata sua nos sincere doceant: nec ulla misteria nobis revelent." *Interpretatio latina sacrae scripturae Veteris Testamenti ad verbum* (Escorial, 1526), ff. 4v–5r.

75. Ibid., f. 5v.

76. "Item ut Augustinus dicit in epistola contra Vintium Donatistam, a solo sensu

literali potest accipi efficax argumentum ex sacra scriptura ad probanda ea que fidei sunt; non autem ex aliis sensibus, nisi forte apud fideles qui illos sensus spirituales recipiunt." *Paradoxae quaestiones,* ff. G5v–G6r. On authorial intention, "Secunda vero pars etiam ex dictis est manifesta, quia non omnis sensus autoris predicti, sed solus illum quem ipse principaliter intendit, est dicendus sensus literalis sacrae scripturae; ut docuit Augustinus in duodecimo libro suarum confessionum." Ibid., f. G6r.

77. "Quare sequitur sepius in sacra scriptura alius erat sensus quem habebat propheta ab eo quem deus principaliter intendebat significare per illam scripturam." Ibid., f. G6r.

78. " 'Os non cominuetis ex eo,' etc. . . . ergo in exodo illa verba in sensu literali fuerunt dicta de agno paschali Judeorum, et in evangelio Joannis loquuntur de Christo, vero deo Christianorum. Et hic secundus sensus in exodo non est literalis sed allegoricus, etiam si concedatur quod Moyses intelligebat illa verba de Christo, quia series textus manifeste facit sermonam de agno paschali." Ibid., f. G7r. Notably, Ciruelo took the verse itself from John instead of Exodus.

79. "Eadem ratio est de illa autoritate Oseae 11, 'ex Egypto vocavi filium meum,' quae intelligitur de populo Hebreorum educto a captivitate Egyptiaca; et citatur Matthei 2 de Jesu puero fugiente in Egyptum a persecutione Herodis. Tertio, legitur in evangelio missae sanctorum innocentum, et intelligitur de populo gentilium vocato a deo ad fidem et ecclesiam suam ex Egypto, id est, tenebra infidelitatis idolatriae." Ibid.

80. Friedman, *The Most Ancient Testimony,* 128–30.

Chapter Four. The Construction of the Shepherd

1. Barbara McClung Hallman, *Italian Cardinals, Reform, and the Church as Property* (Berkeley: University of California Press, 1985), 32.

2. Ibid., 111–17; on the same issues in France, Joseph Bergin, *The Making of the French Episcopate, 1589–1661* (New Haven, Conn.: Yale University Press, 1996), Chapters 4, 8. For similar points as they affected the Council of Trent's debates on episcopal residence, see Giuseppe Alberigo, *I vescovi italiani al Concilio di Trento* (Florence: G. C. Sansoni, 1959), 396–401, 422.

3. Hallman, *Italian Cardinals,* 36.

4. Obviously Gumiel could have professed ignorance to help his own Inquisition case. We will never know whether he truly was unacquainted with Cajetan, although the fact that he suggested that source to Vergara implies a certain familiarity with it.

5. Joseph Bergin, "Between Estate and Profession: The Catholic Parish Clergy of Early Modern Western Europe," in *Social Orders and Social Classes in Europe since 1500: Studies in Social Stratification,* ed. M. L. Bush (London: Longman, 1992), 66–85. Nalle also emphasizes such ecclesiastical variety in the diocese of Cuenca: *God in La Mancha,* Chapter 3.

6. Philip T. Hoffman noted the same for Lyon's rural clergy in particular; *Church*

and Community in the Diocese of Lyon, 1500–1789 (New Haven, Conn.: Yale University Press, 1984), 50–52, 65–69.

7. For the model cleric of the Tridentine Reformation, see Hubert Jedin and Giuseppe Alberigo, *Il tipo ideale di vescovo secondo la riforma cattolica* (Brescia: Editrice Morcelliana, 1985), as well as José Ignacio Tellechea Idígoras, *El obispo ideal en el siglo de la Reforma* (Rome: Publicaciones del Instituto Español de Historia Eclesiastica, 1963). One historian has recently dismissed exemplary works on the clergy as static and abstracted from reality: Bergin, *The Making of the French Episcopate*, 209. As we shall see, Spanish versions of such texts, particularly Bernal's, counter that evaluation.

8. For the individuals who follow, see Elisabeth Gleason, *Gasparo Contarini: Venice, Rome, and Reform* (Berkeley: University of California, 1993); Gigliola Fragnito, "Cultura umanistica e riforma religiosa: Il 'De officio boni viri ac probi episcopi' di Gasparo Contarini," *Studi veneziani* 11 (1969): 75–189; Adriano Prosperi, *Tra evangelismo e controriforma: Gian Matteo Giberti (1495–1543)* (Rome: Edizioni di Storia e Letteratura, 1969). Like Giberti, Jacopo Sadoleto (1477–1547) also used the sack of Rome to go to his see of Carpentras and battle the privileges of papal officials and cathedral canons: Richard M. Douglas, *Jacopo Sadoleto, 1477–1547: Humanist and Reformer* (Cambridge, Mass.: Harvard University Press, 1959).

9. Of the individuals described below, Bernal's and Carranza's thoughts on the episcopate have been relayed by Tellechea Idígoras in *El obispo ideal,* although Tellechea Idígoras puts very different questions to the material than my own, and highlights description over analysis.

10. Frías, *El tratado del modo y estilo que en la visitacion ordinaria se a de tener,* which is the last text in his *Tractatus perutilis* (Burgos, 1528); Juan de Bautista, *Doctrina de sacerdotes* (Seville, 1535).

11. Bernal's *Instrucción de perlados* [sic] (Alcalá, 1530) is the only extant edition of this work, and lacks the last five chapters. Dr. Bernal first published the *Aviso de curas* in a version of nine chapters in 1539, then disseminated a radically expanded rendition of the same work in 1543, which went through two more printings in 1550 and 1551. Significantly, the *Aviso*'s first nine chapters, which remained constant throughout all the editions, were almost entirely devoted to highly allegorical considerations of the priest's qualities: Bernal made the parish priest into a military commander, a navigator of ships, and a guide on the road. In the second prologue to the augmented version of the *Aviso* (1543, 1550, 1551), Bernal explained that his expanded treatise would address the priests' specific responsibilities. In this chapter I have employed the 1551 Alcalá edition of the *Aviso,* which lacks folios 3–10; the content of those missing folios is described in the introduction to Tomás Marín Martínez's edition of Bernal's *Soliloquio y Carta desde Trento* (Barcelona: Juan Flors, 1962). I have used Marín Martínez's edition of Bernal's *Carta desde Trento* in this chapter; in the introduction to that volume, Marín lists Bernal's complete opera.

12. Valtanás composed Latin and Spanish confessors' manuals in 1526 and 1555, respectively, as well as a *Doctrina cristiana* in 1555. The work under review here is the

tenth chapter of the *Apologia y declaracion sobre ciertas materias morales en que hay opinion* (Seville, 1556), entitled "De la residencia de los obispos."

13. I have specifically used Avila's *Tratado del sacerdocio, Pláticas sacerdotales*, and the *Primer* and *Segundo memoriales* for the Council of Trent, *Advertencias para el Concilio de Toledo (1565),* and various letters, all in his *Escritos sacerdotales,* ed. Juan Esquerda Bifet (Madrid: Biblioteca de autores cristianos, 1969). For Avila's opera, see *Obras completas del santo maestro Juan de Avila,* ed. Luís Sala Balust and Francisco Martín Hernández, 6 vols. (Madrid: Editorial católica, 1970–71).

14. *Controversia de necessaria residentia personali episcoporum et aliorum inferiorum pastorum* (Venice, 1547), trans. and ed. José Ignacio Tellechea Idígoras, facsimile edition with Spanish translation (Madrid: FUE & Universidad Pontificia de Salamanca, 1993); and *Speculum pastorum. Hierarchia ecclesiastica in qua describuntur officia ministrorum Ecclesiae militantis* (1551–52), ed. Tellechea Idígoras (Salamanca: Estudio teológico de San Ildefonso, Universidad Pontificia de Salamanca, 1992). Although the first redaction of the *Speculum pastorum* is dated between 1551 and 1552, the editor reports that the manuscript contains numerous additions that Carranza made while he was imprisoned by the Inquisition between 1559 and 1576.

15. The quantity and quality of the secondary material on the six individuals treated here vary widely. Frías and Bautista are disregarded in the historical literature. For Valtanás, see Alvaro Huerga's and Pedro Saínz Rodríguez's edition of the *Apología sobre ciertas materias morales y Apología de la comunión frecuente* (Barcelona: Juan Flors, 1963), as well as Bataillon, *Érasme et l'Espagne,* 1:583–84, 613. On Dr. Bernal, Maestro Avila, and Carranza, consult the bibliographies in the *DHEE.* Secondary work on Carranza is considerable, the bulk of it written by Tellechea Idígoras.

16. Bernal exchanged numerous letters with Ignatius of Loyola between 1543 and 1556, preserved in Ignatius Loyola, *Epistolae et instructiones, Monumenta historica Societatis Iesu,* 12 vols. with various numeration (Rome: Monumenta Historica S.I., 1964–68), vols. 26 and 28.

17. The classic exposition of Catholicism in this period, which presumes continuity rather than bifurcation across the sixteenth century, is Henry Outram Evenett's *The Spirit of the Counter-Reformation,* ed. John Bossy (Cambridge: Cambridge University Press, 1968).

18. See Marín Martínez's introduction to Bernal's *Soliloquio y Carta desde Trento,* 10. In Tellechea's entry for Carranza in the *DHEE,* the imagery of Bataillon, as well as allusions to the Italian *spirituali* and *intransigenti,* is palpable: see n. 19 below. Bataillon neglected to treat Maestro Avila in the 1937 edition of *Érasme et l'Espagne,* but included him in the 1950 Spanish translation of the same: *Erasmo y España,* trans. Antonio Alatorre (Mexico City: Fondo de Cultura Económica, 1950), xv–xvi, 479–80, 533–34, 752–53. Also see Bilinkoff's *The Avila of Saint Teresa,* 79–84. Valtanás, too, was labeled an Erasmian by his editors, Huerga and Saínz Rodríguez, and by Bataillon himself.

19. Tellechea Idígoras has described Carranza as "a spiritual man, of deep Pauline

inspiration and a marked Christocentrism," and concluded that "in reality, in Carranza's case, orthodoxy and heterodoxy did not clash, but rather two distinct ways of understanding Catholicism with two different languages" ("un espiritual, de profunda inspiración paulina y de un marcado cristocentrismo. . . . En la causa de Carranza no se enfrentan, en realidad, la ortodoxia y la heterodoxia, sino dos modos distintos de entender el catolicismo con dos lenguajes diversos"). *DHEE*, 1:360, col. 2.

20. For these examples and numerous others, see Eric Cochrane, *Italy 1530–1630*, ed. Julius Kirshner, Longman History of Italy (London: Longman, 1988), Chapter 7.

21. The impetus to divide Catholicism in two in the sixteenth century owes much to Catholic history in the twentieth. Modern scholars who knew Italy and Spain under fascism have their reasons for focusing on elements of early modern Catholicism that seemed to forecast Rome's cooperation with Mussolini and Franco. Genocides and world wars only heightened historians' appreciation of religious tolerance and nonconformity, while the explicit ecumenicism of Vatican II prompted some scholars to look for earlier signs of openness to religious difference. For a succinct review of the Italian historiography on the matter, with ample references, see William V. Hudon, "Religion and Society in Early Modern Italy: Old Questions, New Insights," *American Historical Review* 101 (1996): 783–804.

22. Eric Cochrane, "Counter Reformation or Tridentine Reformation? Italy in the Age of Carlo Borromeo," in *San Carlo Borromeo: Catholic Reform and Ecclesiastical Politics in the Second Half of the Sixteenth Century,* ed. John M. Headley and John B. Tomaro (Washington, D.C.: Catholic University of America Press, 1988), 31–46; William V. Hudon, *Marcello Cervini and Ecclesiastical Government in Tridentine Italy* (DeKalb: Northern Illinois University Press, 1992), and the bibliography cited in Hudon, "Religion and Society in Early Modern Italy," 794, n. 28.

23. John W. O'Malley, "Was Ignatius Loyola a Church Reformer? How to Look at Early Modern Catholicism," *Catholic Historical Review* 77 (1991): 177–93; Wolfgang Reinhard, "Reformation, Counter-Reformation, and the Early Modern State: A Reassessment," *Catholic Historical Review* 75 (1989): 383–404.

24. Bilinkoff, *The Avila of Saint Teresa;* Nalle, *God in La Mancha;* Eire, *From Madrid to Purgatory,* Book 1. Hudon, "Religion and Society in Early Modern Italy," has proposed the phrase "Tridentine Reformation" as a substitute for the old nomenclature.

25. Both Nalle and Eire draw a Catholic Reformation that lasted throughout the sixteenth century, but that nevertheless became obdurate over time. For example, Nalle, *God in La Mancha,* 32–37; Eire, *From Madrid to Purgatory,* 193, 195–96, 200, 203–4, on the "obsessive" outlook on death that Spanish Catholics found increasingly attractive; 119, 170–72 on the Tridentine decrees' encouragement of that obsession; 426 on the "necessity of mimetic behavior" that Trent advocated. Eire concludes that "spontaneous behavior was antithetical to the spirit of Tridentine and Baroque Catholicism: this was an age that sought to rigidly conform all gestures to established norms, especially in piety," ibid., 426. For the "grain of truth" that lies in

the term *Counter*-Reformation, see Eire, ibid., 507; on the silencing of opposition, ibid., 512. I would not deny the polemical angle of many clerical writers in the later sixteenth century. But I would propose that our stress on sectarian conflict has eclipsed other evidence of a different nature, whether for the first or second half of the period in question.

26. Older accounts are more likely to describe this process as the simple implementation of orthodoxy and rejection of experiment: see Elliott, *Imperial Spain 1494–1716,* 221–28. More complex evaluations of the phenomenon lie in Nalle, *God in La Mancha,* Chapters 2 and 6; and Eire, *From Madrid to Purgatory,* Book 1. For comparative purposes, Adriano Prosperi's *Tribunali della coscienza: Inquisitori, confessori, missionari* (Torino: Giulio Einaudi, 1996), would have been useful, but I obtained it too late to incorporate its findings.

27. Both Nalle and Eire describe this epoch as a "golden age" of purgatory: *God in La Mancha,* 191; *From Madrid to Purgatory,* 172. On religious centralization and spiritual interiority, see Nalle, ibid., 156–65, 174–79; Kamen, *The Phoenix and the Flame,* Chapters 3 and 4. On Spaniards' propensity to read the hereafter in terms of the here and now, see Eire, ibid., 193–94, 207, 248–49. Both Nalle and Eire appreciate the fact that Catholic clerics shared the same concerns and practices as their lay contemporaries, including anxiety over purgatory and bequests for memorial Masses. Still, for the clergy as the beneficiary of such emphases, see Nalle, ibid., 202–4; and Eire, ibid., 229, n. 128.

28. Both Ayala and Ribera were archbishops of Valencia, who acted on a similar balance between inclusion and stratification in their diocese. See Ayala's *Breve compendio para bien examinar la consciencia en el juyzio de la confession sacramental* (Valencia, 1567); and Benjamin Ehlers, "Christians and Muslims in Valencia: The Archbishop Juan de Ribera (1532–1611) and the Formation of a *Communitas Christiana*" (Ph.D. diss., Johns Hopkins, 1999), Chapter 2.

29. My texts confirm evidence supplied by Nalle and Eire from other sources, insofar as the Spaniards' pastoral theology demolishes the notion that the clerics tried to exercise their authority over a quiescent and even bullied laity. Nalle, *God in La Mancha,* 132–33, as well as the examples cited on pp. 49 and 109; Eire, *From Madrid to Purgatory,* 4–5, 192–93, 230–31; Kamen, *The Phoenix and the Flame,* 158–59.

30. Jedin and Alberigo, *Il tipo ideale di vescovo secondo la riforma cattolica;* Fragnito, "Cultura umanistica e riforma religiosa"; Olin, *Six Essays on Erasmus;* Cochrane, *Italy 1530–1630,* Chapter 7; William V. Hudon, ed., *Theatine Spirituality: Selected Writings,* Classics of Western Spirituality (New York: Paulist, 1996), Introduction.

31. Juan de Bautista was a canon lawyer only, but his case should not be construed as overly unusual: so was Bernal when he published the *Instrucción de perlados* in 1530. For the mixture of canon law and moral theology that could ensue in pastoral treatises, see Chapter 5 on the confessors' manual.

32. For Bernal's explicit reference to Frías, see the *Instrucción de perlados,* f. 13v; for

Bernal's development of Frías's details, see the *Aviso de curas* (1551), ff. 47v (administering to the sick) and 61v (baptism).

33. Bernal, *Instrucción de perlados,* f. 16v, told his readers—ostensibly members of the episcopate—to survey the "synodal constitutions of the entire kingdom, in order to take from all of them what was relevant for their bishopric" ("constituciones synodales de todo el reyno para de todas tomar lo que para su obispado conviene"). Any survey of synods from particular dioceses reveals that Bernal's recommendation was standard procedure.

34. "Estos, si entran en la iglesia, no es porque elíjan ser bajos en la casa del Señor, mas que ricos en el mundo; y, si se les ofreciera buen aparejo para casarse, aquello eligieran." Juan de Avila, *Tratado del sacerdocio, Escritos sacerdotales,* ed. Esquerda Bifet, 173.

35. "Alius vendit, alius rapit, alius praesumit sacerdotia divina; alius usurpat. Omnes isti vocantur a domino fures et latrones, sicut alieni pastores, quia non quaerunt ovium salutem sed propria tantum commoda." Carranza, *Speculum pastorum,* 51. For Frías, *Del modo y estilo,* f. A7r.

36. See *Instrucción de perlados,* f. 10v, where Bernal addressed the usurpation of Church property, and contended that it usually occurred in order to reward (*gratificar*) certain relatives or friends. On the dire effects of feuds, see his *Aviso de curas,* f. 49r.

37. After an exposition of bad clerical behavior, Maestro Avila wrote "La gente que esto hace es, ordinariamente, sacerdotes pobres y de gente de pueblo, cuyo necesidad del comer corporal [sic] les hace frecuentar aqueste divino misterio." *Tratado del sacerdocio, Escritos sacerdotales,* ed. Esquerda Bifet, 173.

38. *Aviso de curas,* ff. 35r–37r.

39. "Pues oir casos de conciencia, y de conciencia moral, donde? Que en siete o más universidades que en estos reinos de Castilla hay, en ninguna de ellas se leen; y poco aprovecha para este intento que se lea en ellas teología y derecho canónico, pues los que administran estos oficios no se quieren poner a estudios tan largos, y a muchos falta la posibilidad para mantenerse en las dichas universidades." *Tratado del sacerdocio, Escritos sacerdotales,* ed. Esquerda Bifet, 179.

40. "Sin obediencia, sin clausura, sin devoción y con ruines compañías, yendo de día y de noche a donde se les antojaba, llevándolos sus inclinaciones que de Adan [sic] heredaron, sin tener freno ni quien les vaya a la mano." Ibid., 172.

41. Carranza, *Controversia de necessaria residencia,* 295.

42. "Yo temo que en los lugares donde el cura es solo y es natural, o muy conocido en el pueblo, algunas mugeres se atreven a callar algunas flaquezas de la carne, viendo que los curas conocen a las personas con quien han pecado. Y temiendo que han de caer luego en quien son, aunque no les digan los nombres, por alguna circumstancia que les avrán de dezir, o por alguna sospecha que ya ay en el pueblo contra ellas; mayormente si son parientas ellas del cura." *Aviso de curas,* f. 86r.

43. Nalle, *God in La Mancha,* 49.

44. "E si los tales beneficiados residan y los sirvan por si, tuviendo justa causa de no resodir [sic], si tienen en su lugar puestos sus tenientes y vicarios abiles y sufficientes: y con licencia del perlado conforme al capitulo *relatum cum aliis, de clericis non residentibus.*" *Del modo y estilo,* f. A15v.

45. "Dic mihi, o pastor ecclesiastice, quo jure petis stipendium? qua ratione victum et necessaria? Nimirum respondebis iure divino. . . . cur si in jure divino tibi decimas debeo, non tu eodem jure tenebris in servire tabernaculo? . . . que iniquitas est, ut populum religione alliges ob tuum stipendium, et tu religione sis solutus, si nolis militare?" *Controversia de necessaria residentia,* 290–91. Obviously Carranza was capable of invoking the Church Militant.

46. *Apologia y declaracion,* f. 17r.

47. *Instrucción de perlados,* f. 12v.

48. *Apologia y declaracion,* f. 16r.

49. *Controversia de necessaria residentia,* 183, 299.

50. Or as Carranza put it: "et vere locus hic est, meo quidem judicio efficacissimus, qua verba illa tertio repetita, 'Pasce oves meas,' sunt verum et absolutum Domini preceptum." *Controversia de necessaria residentia,* 205.

51. Ibid., 282–83.

52. *Instrucción de perlados,* ff. 11v–12v.

53. After citing Bernard of Clairvaux and Alcuin on the fulsome responsibilities of bishops, Carranza summoned Erasmus's annotations on John 21 as additional ammunition: "It will not be irrelevant among the testimony of so many ancient Fathers to introduce the words of Erasmus, which seem to be especially apropos, even if the authority of this man may not be evidence for us" ("Non ab re erit inter tot antiquorum patrum testimonia etiam Erasmi verba afferre, quae maxime conferre videntur, etiam si eius viri auctoritas non sit nobis argumentum"). *Controversia de necessaria residentia,* 207, and for Erasmus's specific annotation, 208.

54. See Bernal's memoranda on impediments to residence, presented to the delegates in June 1546: *Concilium Tridentinum: Diariorum, actorum, epistolarum, tractatuum nova collectio,* 13 vols. in 7 (Freiburg: Herder, 1964), 5:590–94.

55. As Carranza noted in his *Controversia de necessaria residentia,* 47; also see Alberigo, *I vescovi italiani,* 421–22.

56. Alberigo, *I vescovi italiani,* 409, 413.

57. On the 1546–47 debates over residence, see ibid., Chapter 11; and Hubert Jedin, *A History of the Council of Trent,* 2 vols. (St. Louis: Herder, 1961), vol. 2, Chapter 9.

58. Besides their presence in the *Instrucción de perlados* (1530), injunctions to residence occur in the last three editions of the *Aviso de curas* (1543, 1550, 1551), in the *Carta desde Trento* (1553), printed with the *Soliloquio,* and in the synodal constitutions that Bernal promulgated for Calahorra in 1555.

59. *Del modo y estilo,* f. A21r.

60. *Doctrina de sacerdotes,* f. 29v.

61. "Quiere el Señor que, aunque el pueblo con su mala vida este tan atemorizado, ni tenga osadía para estar en pie delante de su acatamiento, ni ose alzar los ojos al cielo; que el sacerdote sea tal que, con la limpieza de la vida y amigable trato y particular familiaridad que hay entre Dios y él, no sea derribado con temor, como está el pueblo, mas tenga una santa osadía para estar en pie y llegar al Señor, y suplicarle, e importunarle, y atarle, y vencerle, para que, en lugar de azote pesado de justo Juez, envie abrazos de Padre amoroso." *Tratado del sacerdocio, Escritos sacerdotales*, ed. Esquerda Bifet, 148.

62. *Apologia y declaracion*, f. 16r.

63. "Oportet enim ut bonus pastor, cum emisserit oves per verbum praedicationis, vadat ante illas per exemplum." *Speculum pastorum*, 54. Significantly, Carranza's language implicitly ties speech acts (*verbum praedicationis*) to physical actions in the community.

64. "Praedicant, arguunt, admonent, sacro chrismate confirmant, explorant quomodo sacramenta administrentur. . . . Mores subditorum exquirunt, templa reparantur, dissidia, si quae sunt, componuntur; boni viri et agnoscuntur et foventur." Ibid., 102.

65. *Aviso de curas*, f. 46r.

66. Ibid., ff. 73r–77v.

67. "Para mejor aconsejar y socorrer a todos, conforme a lo que cada uno oviere menester." Ibid., f. 67r; on marriage and convents, f. 128r. Bernal's advice on convents echoes the counsel that Valtanás provided in his confessors' manual; see Chapter 5.

68. Valtanás noted, "Los prelados, con su presencia, sanan las enfermedades del alma de los subditos, y remedian las necessidades de sus cuerpos"; he continued: "A donde claramente se pone el officio proprio del prelado, ser apancentar [sic] los subditos con pasto de docrina, y pasto de mantenimientos." *Apologia y declaracion*, ff. 15r–v, 17r. In the latter quote, he was making a pun on *apacentar*, which means to tend a flock, and *pasto*, or pasture.

69. Botero (1544–1617) published *Della ragion di stato* in 1589; Ribadeneyra's (1526–1611) *Tratado de la religion y virtudes que debe tener el príncipe cristiano para gobernar y conservar sus estados* was printed in 1595. Botero's work in particular went through numerous editions and was translated into various vernaculars. See Federico Chabod, *Giovanni Botero* (Rome: Anonima Romana Editorial, 1934); Robert Bireley, S.J., *The Counter-Reformation Prince: Anti-Machiavellianism or Catholic Statecraft in Early Modern Europe* (Chapel Hill: University of North Carolina Press, 1990); and most recently, A. Enzo Baldini, ed., *Botero e la "Ragion di Stato:" Atti del convegno in memoria di Luigi Firpo*, Fondazione Luigi Firpo, Centro di Studi sul Pensiero Politico, Studi e Testi (Florence: Olschki, 1992).

70. "Porque notoria cosa es, que quiere más Dios que viva una criatura racional, por quien él tanto a hecho, que no que le offrezcan incenso en vasos de plata, o reverencien la figura de su cruz en materia de plata." *Aviso de curas*, f. 149r.

71. For an outline of the various Masses requested in testamentary bequests, see

Eire, *From Madrid to Purgatory,* 196–97; on problems completing such commissions, ibid., 215–21. Most of the Spanish authors treated in my work focused on difficulties with the trental or *treintenario,* a Mass cycle for the dead pronounced over a thirty-day period.

72. On the editions of the *Aviso,* see n. 11 above.

73. *Aviso de curas,* ff. 108r–110r, 114r, 125r–v.

74. "Si la iglesia catholica, regida por el espiritu sancto, entendiera que en el mucho número de missas estava el alivio y satisfaccion de los defunctos, más que en las obras de misericordia que quando vivos hizieron, no estrechara tanto el número de los sacerdotes, pues no quiere que se ordene sino quien tenga patrimonio o beneficio." Ibid., f. 110v.

75. Eire, *From Madrid to Purgatory,* 177.

76. For such contentions, see John Bossy, "Moral Arithmetic: Seven Sins into Ten Commandments," in *Conscience and Casuistry in Early Modern Europe,* ed. Edmund Leites (Cambridge: Cambridge University Press, 1988), 214–31; idem, *Christianity in the West, 1400–1700* (Oxford: Clarendon, 1985); idem, "The Counter-Reformation and the People of Catholic Europe," *Past and Present* 47 (1970): 51–70; and Jean Delumeau, *Sin and Fear: The Emergence of a Western Guilt Culture, 13th–18th Centuries* (New York: St. Martin's, 1990).

77. Frías, *Del modo y estilo,* f. A7r; Carranza, *Speculum pastorum,* 116.

78. *Instrucción de perlados,* f. 14r–v; *Aviso de curas,* ff. 81r–83r, but note that this chapter is misfoliated; *Soliloquio y Carta desde Trento,* 194–96.

79. *Del modo y estilo,* f. A6r.

80. *Aviso de curas,* ff. 26r, 73v, 84r.

81. "Ut qui, spretis salutaribus legis, aut torpentes neglegentia aut malitia incitati delinquerint, a vitiis suis ecclesiasticae censurae severitate, si opus est, coerceantur et publice corripiantur." *Speculum pastorum,* 46, 64–65. Also see the *Controversia de necessaria residentia,* 184, where Carranza mentions "ancient and true Christian discipline."

82. On the modern tendency to read discipline as coercion, see Hudon, "Religion and Society in Early Modern Italy," 793, 797–804.

83. "John 21:15–16, Petrus, interrogat eum Christus, non de divitiis aut de generis nobilitate, nec interrogat de scientia, quae in pastore est quidem summe necessaria, verum non sola; tantum hic interrogat de dilectione, haec enim est maxime necessaria super caetera omnia ei qui pascendas rationales oves suscipit." *Speculum pastorum,* 37.

84. "Vide obsecro emphasim verborum: non dicit, 'age superiorem, exerce potestatem in oves meas,' quamvis et haec illi tradantur, sed 'pasce oves meas.' 'Inter vos,' inquit, 'non erit sic, sed qui maior est, vestrum sit minister vester' (Math. 20:26). Non igitur pro arbitrio tuo imperabis, sed pastorem ages, non dominum." Ibid., 65.

85. "Pastoris enim est obedientes pascere et inobedientes corrigere, sed multo plus curabit pastor pascere subditos sibi commissos quam corrigere." Ibid., 66. Here Carranza is citing the sixth chapter of Gregory the Great's *Regulae pastoralis liber;* also see *Speculum pastorum,* 40, 56–57. Moreover, in the *Controversia de necessaria residentia,*

Carranza wrote "Secundo, episcopus et quivis alius ecclesiasticus pastor ex iure divino debet esse non dominus gregis sibi commissi, sed verus pastor, ergo eodem iure tenetur agere pastorem," 287.

86. "Y porque Dios es buen testigo que ninguna cosa deseo hoy más que hallarme entre vosotros para solicitar vuestra salvación, os ruego y encargo mucho que hagais oración particular a nuestro Señor, suplicándole que me vuelve a vuestra presencia con aquella gracia y favor suyo que él sabe que un pastor de tantas ánimas y tan insuficiente como yo ha menester; que aunque parezca que os demando cosa de mi provecho particular, es tan común el bien espiritual entre el pastor y sus ovejas, que nunca el prelado recibe beneficio alguno de Dios en este caso, que no descienda y se communique a sus subditos." *Soliloquio y Carta desde Trento,* 200, which Bernal printed in 1553, after his return to his diocese. For similar sentiments, see the prologues to Bernal's *Historiae sanctorum episcoporum* and *Catalogus sanctorum episcoporum,* both transcribed in "*El Catalogus sanctorum episcoporum del Obispo Bernal Díaz de Luco,*" ed. Tomás Marín Martínez, *Miscelánea conmemorativa del Concilio de Trento (1563–1963): Estudios y documentos* (Madrid-Barcelona: Instituto Enrique Flórez, CSIC, 1963), 373–459.

87. "Iustitia sine misericordia non est justitia, sed crudelitas; misericordia vero sine iustitia non est misericordia, sed fatuitas." *Speculum pastorum,* 97. Carranza attributed his quotation to Chrysostom.

88. Nalle points to similarly expanded responsibilities for Cuenca's secular clergy: *God in La Mancha,* 96.

89. Valtanás, *Apologia y declaracion,* f. 16v.

90. Bernal, *Instrucción a perlados,* f. 7r.

91. "Y con quanto daño de ambos se perdera aquella anima por su ignorancia o negligencia, o por no querer trabajar; y quan justamente estará perpetuamente clamando a Dios contra él, si por alguna de estas causas se condemnare." Idem, *Aviso de curas,* f. 107v.

92. Avila, *Tratado del sacerdocio, Escritos sacerdotales,* ed. Esquerda Bifet, 169–70; Carranza, *Controversia de necessaria residencia,* 261.

93. Carranza, *Controversia de necessaria residencia,* 261. Valtanás, too, cited Ezekiel, and summarized the prophet as saying, "If your subject should be lost because of your neglect, an account of his sin will be demanded from you"; *Apologia y declaracion,* f. 16v.

94. Chapter 9, ff. 29r–36v, of Bernal's *Aviso de curas* is packed with warnings about priests' duties and divine judgment.

95. "La qual lepra y sarna affaz de vezes se queda de por curar hasta el fuego infernal por el descuydo y negligencia de los pastores. . . . A causa de lo qual traen mucho más limpias las uñas que si continuamente anduviessen descarmeñando estas y otras tales sarnas y roñas de sus ovejas; como son obligados segun paresce por el propheta Ezechiel en diversos capitulos." *Del modo y estilo,* f. A2or.

96. Bernal, *Instrucción de perlados,* ff. 19v–2or, and idem, *Aviso de curas,* ff. 32v–36v; Juan de Avila, *Tratado del sacerdocio, Escritos sacerdotales,* ed. Esquerda Bifet, 169–70.

97. A point confirmed by Eire, *From Madrid to Purgatory,* 4, 230–31. The individuals I studied betrayed the same conviction as Nalle's and Eire's, namely, that divine judgment would occur immediately after their death: Nalle, *God in La Mancha,* 194, and Eire, ibid., 172.

98. Here I disagree with Nalle, who asserts that clerics in Cuenca were pressured to remove themselves from the secular world after the promulgation of the Tridentine decrees. Our evidence comes from different decades, but I doubt that Conquense religious were promoting and obeying a dualistic imperative even in the 1580s. *God in La Mancha,* 49, 90.

99. *Del modo y estilo,* f. 22r.

100. "En cada lugar donde el diocesano o su visitador fuere a visitar, deve de hazer llamar todas las parteras que oviere en el tal lugar, e informarse de cada una, si fuera de peligro acostumbran baptizar luego en casa las criaturas en nasciendo, y como no lo devan hazer. E quando ay o se presume aver el tal peligro, como baptizen la tal criatura; y en que parte le echan el agua. . . . E que palabras son las que entonces dize; y si no las supiere bien, enseñeselas y mandele sos cierta pena de excomunion que cada qual dellas las aprendan, o no usen del tal officio. E al cura que se las enseñe." Ibid., f. 32r.

101. "Pues segun las cosas suelen acaecer, a qualquiera de sus parrochianos se le puede algun día ofrecer caso en que aya de baptizar alguna criatura." *Aviso de curas,* f. 70r.

102. Ibid., ff. 55v–56r.

103. Bernal's reference to processions, crosses, and village competitions parallels anthropological findings from other sixteenth-century sources. See William A. Christian Jr., *Local Religion in Sixteenth-Century Spain* (Princeton, N.J.: Princeton University Press, 1981), 105–23.

104. *Aviso de curas,* f. 61v.

105. Ibid., f. 82v.

106. Ibid., f. 44r–v.

107. Nalle, *God in La Mancha,* 37, 109.

108. Jedin and Alberigo, *Il tipo ideale di vescovo,* 43, n. 32.

109. Rafael Arce, *San Juan de Avila y la Reforma de la Iglesia en España* (Madrid: Ediciones Rialp, 1970), 86, n. 3.

110. The exception may have been Valtanás, who placed his piece on residence in a collection of other tracts on multiple subjects.

111. See Esquerda Bifet's introduction to Avila's *Tratado de sacerdocio, Escritos sacerdotales,* 120.

112. William Pettas, *A Sixteenth-Century Spanish Bookstore: The Inventory of Juan de Junta* (Philadelphia: American Philosophical Society, 1995); Antonio Blanco Sánchez, "Inventario de Juan de Ayala, gran impresor toledano (1556)," *Boletín de la Real Academia Española* 67 (1987): 207–50.

113. Pamphlets and broadsheets could number in the thousands in such shops: Nalle, *God in La Mancha,* 114–18.

114. Nalle, "Literacy and Culture in Early Modern Castile," and idem, *God in La Mancha*, 126–27. For the most recent studies on literacy in early modern Spain, see the collection of articles in *Bulletin hispanique* 99, no. 1 (1997).

115. Juan de Avila, *Memorial segundo al Concilio de Trento, Escritos sacerdotales*, ed. Esquerda Bifet, 78–79; Bernal, *Aviso de curas*, f. 33v.

116. "La teología que escriben santos y que es sólida, y en la que concuerdan unos con otros, se debe preferir a la que estas condiciones no tiene, y por esto parece que la teología de Santo Tomás y de San Buenaventura es la más conveniente para ser enseñada en las escuelas, aunque en particular pueda cada uno leer otros buenos autores que hay." Juan de Avila, *Memorial segundo al Concilio de Trento, Escritos sacerdotales*, ed. Esquerda Bifet, 78.

117. Idem, *Epistolario sacerdotal*, ibid., 394–95.

118. Bernal, *Aviso de curas*, f. 33v; Carranza, *Controversia de necessaria residentia*, 269–74, and idem, *Speculum pastorum*, 34.

119. Bernal, *Instrucción de perlados*, f. 6r, features a long quotation of Chrysostom, but no exposition of that material. The same technique permeates the ninth chapter of Carranza's *Controversia de necessaria residentia*.

120. See n. 84 above, in which Carranza wrote "Vide obsecro emphasim verborum."

121. Carranza, *Controversia de necessaria residentia*, 289.

122. "Si aquel philosopho fuera de nuestra edad christiana, tuviera por necessaria gobernación que los sacerdotes mozos no trataran tan familiar [sic] y secretamente con las mugeres." *Aviso de curas*, f. 43r. On this sort of paradox, see Shuger, *The Renaissance Bible*, 51–52, and Grafton, *Defenders of the Text*, Chapter 1.

123. "Non enim exiguum illum fructum duxi, quem me ex hoc labore percepturum confidebam, ut eam inculpatam tot illustrium antecessorum meorum vitam, et res quamplurimas maxima sanctitate et summa diligentia ab eis gestas legerem." Prologue, *Historiae sanctorum episcoporum*, "*El Catalogus sanctorum episcoporum del Obispo Bernal Díaz de Luco,*" ed. Marín Martínez, 379.

124. "Quas ego historias cum nuper apud me esse animadverterem, facturum me cum christianis omnibus tum praesertim mei ordinis viris rem utilem et gratam existimavi, si eas omnes uno libro alligarem, et ipsorum in illis quaerendis molestiam hoc meo labore levarem." Ibid.

125. "Ut in historia nihil legere sustineant, quod testimonio celebris alicuius scriptoris testatum et obsignatum non extet." Ibid.

126. Ibid.

127. Ibid., 380.

128. "Quorum nomina et historiae eisdem regionibus inclusae diu fuerunt quibus dioeceses ipsae circumscriptae et terminatae sunt, ubi miraculis illi et rerum gestarum sanctitate floruerunt." Ibid.

129. "Verum constat viros multos sanctissimos olim extitisse, excellenti illos quidem pietate et religione insignes, nec non plurimis ac maximis miraculis illustres,

qui tamen (vel propter injuriam temporum, vel ob inscitiam et barbariem earum regionum in quibus versati fuerunt) scriptores haud sunt nacti per quos res ab eis gestae celebrarentur, et elegantis historiae monumentis comprehensae ad posteritatis memoriam servarentur." Ibid.

130. Bernal's catalogue is transcribed by Marín Martínez in ibid., 406–58. For these anecdotal details, see ibid., 411, 413. Bernal frequently cited one location for a bishop's remains, then noted that another source placed the body elsewhere. He also was quick to raise his personal experience.

131. Bernal attested his fondness for relics and his veneration for medieval figures of the Church in the case of Bonaventura, "whose body rests in Lyons, in the monastery of St. Francis. . . . where I saw his head and held his hands as I proceeded to the Council of Trent" ("cuius corpus quiescit Lugduni in monasterio Sancti Francisci . . . ubi ego vidi caput eius et manibus tenui dum ad Concilium Tridentinum proficiscer"). Ibid., 413.

Chapter Five. The Formation of the Flock

1. Problems with clerical residence could disrupt the sacraments in general, and it is not certain that penance was dispensed and received habitually even in the early sixteenth century. Lawrence G. Duggan, "Fear and Confession on the Eve of the Reformation," *Archiv für Reformationsgeschichte* 75 (1984): 153–75. Nevertheless, the explosion in printed, vernacular treatises on confession would seem to argue for the sacrament's important place in Europeans' consciousness.

2. Thomas of Chobham, *Summa confessorum,* ed. F. Broomfield, Analecta mediaevalia Namurcensia, no. 25 (Louvain: Éditions Nauwelaerts, 1960). Jean Gerson, *L'A.B.C. des simples gens, De arte audiendi confessiones, Examen de conscience selon les péchés capitaux, Le miroir de l'âme,* and *Modus brevis confitendi,* ed. Msgr. Pierre Glorieux, *Opera omnia,* 10 vols. (Paris: Desclée, 1960) 7:408–9, 8:10–17, 7:393–400, 7:193–206, and 9:84–86, respectively.

3. Erasmus, *The Shipwreck,* in *Ten Colloquies,* ed. Craig Thompson (New York: Liberal Arts Press, 1957); for Protestant complaints, see the descriptions in Steven Ozment, *The Reformation in the Cities* (New Haven, Conn.: Yale University Press, 1975), 22–32, 47–56. Ozment treated Reformation polemics as descriptions of practice, and concluded that the sacrament of penance was enormously burdensome for laymen and women.

4. Stephen Haliczer, *Sexuality in the Confessional: A Sacrament Profaned,* Studies in the History of Sexuality (Oxford: Oxford University Press, 1996).

5. Scholars express different chronologies for this development. Bossy, "Moral Arithmetic," 214–31, posits a slower rate of change that began in the fifteenth century and only crested after 1600; Haliczer, *Sexuality in the Confessional,* finds the metamorphosis "already quite marked" by that later date.

6. I have used the Toledo 1524 edition of the Hieronymite's *Arte para bien confesar.*

7. Hernando de Talavera, *Breve forma de confesar* (Granada, post-1492), ed. Miguel Mir, Nueva Biblioteca de Autores Españoles, vol. 1 (Madrid: Casa Editorial Bailly, 1911).

8. I have used later editions of Ciruelo's *Arte de bien confesar* (Valladolid, 1534), and Covarrubias's *Memorial de pecados* (Seville, 1521). Bibliographers and scholars consistently confuse Ciruelo's *Arte de bien confesar* with the Hieronymite's *Arte para bien confesar* because of their similar titles. The Hieronymite's manual fell under the prohibitions of the 1559 Index of Prohibited Books because of its anonymity.

9. Domingo de Valtanás, *Confessionario* (Burgos, 1555).

10. The formal title of *summa confessorum* did not appear in the literature until after 1280; for problems of anachronistic usage, see Leonard E. Boyle, "Robert Grosseteste and Pastoral Care," and "The *Summa confessorum* of John of Freiburg," in *Pastoral Care, Clerical Education and Canon Law, 1200–1400* (London: Variorum Reprints, 1981), I:9 and III:248, n. 18, respectively.

11. These developments occurred in a nonsynchronous way; for summaries of them, see Bernhard Poschmann, *Penance and the Anointing of the Sick*, trans. F. Courtney, The Herder History of Dogma (London: Herder and Herder, 1968); Cyrille Vogel, *Le pécheur et la pénitence dans l'eglise ancienne* (Paris: Les éditions du Cerf, 1966); Amédée Teetaert, O.Cap., "La 'Summa de poenitentia' de Saint Raymond de Penyafort," *Ephemerides theologicae lovanienses* 5 (1928): 54; Pierre Michaud-Quantin, "A propos des premières *Summae confessorum*," *Recherches de theologia ancienne et moderne* 26 (1959): 265–69; idem, *Sommes de casuistique et manuels de confession au moyen âge (xii–xvi siècles)*, Analecta Mediaevalia Namurcensis, no. 13 (Louvain: Éditions Nauwelaerts, 1962), 109–11; John Bossy, "The Social History of Confession in the Age of the Reformation," *Trans. Royal Historical Society*, 5th ser., 25 (1975): 21–38.

12. A pastoral angle strongly argued by Boyle against Thomas Tentler; see Boyle's "The Summa for Confessors as a Genre, and Its Religious Intent," in *The Pursuit of Holiness in Late Medieval and Renaissance Religion*, ed. Charles Trinkaus with Heiko Oberman (Leiden: Brill, 1974), 126–30. For Tentler's work, see n. 14.

13. For canon law as the dominant influence, Boyle, "The *Summa confessorum* of John of Freiburg"; for an opposing view in favor of pastoral theology, see Broomfield's introduction to his edition of Thomas of Chobham, *Thomae de Chobham summa confessorum*. The original title of Chobham's work was *Summa Cum miserationes domini*, derived from a psalm *incipit*.

14. Despite Thomas Tentler's avowals that "discipline and consolation can be complementary," his analysis ultimately depicts such elements as competitive where the summae are concerned: *Sin and Confession on the Eve of the Reformation* (Princeton, N.J.: Princeton University Press, 1977), 349. Also see Delumeau, *Sin and Fear*, 200: "The handbooks [summae] thus progressively drain off considerations of pastorship. They were less and less practical guides for the use of confessors and their congregations, and more and more autonomous works detailing a hard discipline: that of the 'cases,' itself tightly attached to canon law." Delumeau's appraisal of the summae's

development in the thirteenth century is the opposite of Boyle's; see "The *Summa confessorum* of John of Freiburg."

15. Tentler, *Sin and Confession,* passim; Delumeau, *Sin and Fear,* Part 2, Chapters 6–10. Adriano Prosperi's arguments in *Tribunali della coscienza: Inquisitori, confessori, missionari* (Torino: Giulio Einaudi, 1996) are undoubtedly relevant here as well, but I obtained that work too late to employ them.

16. Tentler, *Sin and Confession,* Preface, 52–53, 161–68, 231–32, and Conclusion; Delumeau, *Sin and Fear,* 197–200, 203–4, and 209, where the Church's efforts at christianization entailed "the mass diffusion of a rule of life conceived by ascetics"; also see Delumeau, ibid., 302, for the remark that the "guilt-instilling discourse of the church" was "elaborated by and for monks but aimed more and more toward laypeople, with a constant stress on sin." One of the chief avenues for that discourse was the sacrament of penance and the summae.

17. Tentler, *Sin and Confession,* 250–63; he concludes that "the theory of attrition and contrition might have supplied confessors with practical distinctions, based on the psychological motives of fear and love, to explain what kind of sorrow a penitent had to have. It did not. . . . Confessors were stuck with theological abstractions for their pastoral instruction." On the chaos purportedly induced by fuzzy definitions of sin, see ibid., 162–232, on the sexual transgressions of married couples.

18. Ibid., 162–63, 175–76, 207–8. For similar findings about clerics, confession, and sexual sins—and agreement that the combination elevated ecclesiastical power over the laity—see Delumeau, *Sin and Fear,* 214–20.

19. "The element of psychological guilt as a central sanction is vitally important. For while it is true that the encounter with the priest entails submission and shame, the heart of the system is reliance on internal feelings of guilt." Tentler, *Sin and Confession,* 347. Bossy, "The Social History of Confession," would agree with Tentler and Delumeau on the interiorization of penance as that sacrament evolved over time. But Bossy disputes the notion that individual sexuality became the focus of sin in medieval and early modern Europe, and he tends to weigh the pedagogical and pastoral aspects of confession more heavily than his peers.

20. Tentler, *Sin and Confession,* xix–xx; Delumeau, *Sin and Fear,* 197–98.

21. Tentler seems to reject the notion that the penitential system achieved clerical tyranny, because "[p]riests did not author a conspiracy; they participated in a system." Still, if "priests certainly participated in and were subject to this system . . . these male celibates also dominated it, while hierarchical and scholarly authorities articulated the rules that guaranteed that dominance." *Sin and Confession,* 364.

22. Ozment, *The Reformation in the Cities,* 22–32, 47–56; Tentler, *Sin and Confession,* 52–53, 349–62; Robert Bireley, S.J., "Two Works by Jean Delumeau," *Catholic Historical Review* 77 (1991): 78–88.

23. Bossy, "Moral Arithmetic." On the first of these taxonomies, the standard work remains Morton W. Bloomfield, *The Seven Deadly Sins* (East Lansing: Michigan State University Press, 1967). In Spain, the most commmon version of the seven sins

was signaled by the mnemonic device *saligia,* whose letters denoted *superbia, avaricia, luxuria, ira, gula, invidia,* and *accidia;* this formula was a relatively late one, popularized in Europe in the thirteenth century.

24. Bossy, "Moral Arithmetic," 216–17. Bossy asserts that the new prominence of the Decalogue elevated the sin of idolatry as well, and consequently facilitated the prosecution of witchcraft: ibid., 229. On potential connections among the Decalogue, idolatry, and witchcraft, see Chapter 6 below.

25. Henry Kamen, *The Phoenix and the Flame: Catalonia and the Counter-Reformation* (New Haven, Conn.: Yale University Press, 1993), 123–26, 323–24.

26. For the quotation, ibid., 327; see as well 131–39, 157–58, and 205. Kamen insists, often simultaneously, that the Tridentine decrees in Spain did and did not work. Thus the Counter-Reformation was "a true historical event within the consciousness of Spaniards and of Catalans" (430); but Trent "always had been a myth, an ideal to which the Church aspired but to which the Catholic people paid little more than lip-service" (ibid.). He surely is right to suggest that local communities remained the centers of everyday religion, for all that they absorbed the reforms offered by a more centralized Catholicism.

27. Haliczer, *Sexuality in the Confessional,* 103.

28. Ibid., 8–9, 205. Similar arguments play a powerful role in historians' assessments of early modern witchcraft. See Chapter 6.

29. Ibid., 114, 151.

30. Ibid., 9, 16, 21–22, 154. Haliczer owes his arguments to Bossy and Delumeau.

31. For descriptions of public penance, see Mary C. Mansfield, *The Humiliation of Sinners: Public Penance in Thirteenth-Century France* (Ithaca, N.Y.: Cornell University Press, 1995).

32. Duggan objected to Tentler's arguments on the grounds of clerical absenteeism and the infrequent reception of penance; see the former's "Fear and Confession on the Eve of the Reformation."

33. Raymund of Penyafort, *Summa textu sacrorum canorum* (Paris, 1720). Silvestro Mazzolini da Prierio, *Summa summarum quae Sylvestrina dicitur* (Strasburg, 1518), ff. 163v–194v. On Prierio, see Michael M. Tavuzzi, *Prierias: The Life and Works of Silvestro Mazzolini da Prierio, 1456–1527,* Duke Monographs in Medieval and Renaissance Studies, no. 16 (Durham, N.C.: Duke University Press, 1997).

34. See, for instance, Tommaso de Vio, *Summula Caietani* (Lyon, 1581), 66; Ciruelo, *Arte de bien confesar,* ff. 40v, 49r.

35. Although Tentler recognized that authors of summae expressed caveats about immaterial queries, he nevertheless thought such warnings could not outweigh the sources' "overwhelming detail." He tied their protracted enumeration of sins to their ultimate goal of discipline and control. *Sin and Confession,* 135–44.

36. "El presente tratado . . . en nuestra común lengua de España provechará no solamente para los confesores que han de examinar las conciencias de sus penitentes, mas también para los discretos seglares, [quien] con esta doctrina podrán bien cumplir

el consejo del apostol, que dize, 'Probet autem seipsum homo,' etc." *Arte de bien confesar,* f. 2r.

37. Valtanás, *Confessionario,* ff. 18v–19r, 42r.

38. Pérez de Ayala, *Breve compendio para bien examinar la conciencia en el juyzio de la confession sacramental* (Valencia, 1567), f. A3r.

39. He explained his reasoning as "así que los confesores se podrían aprovechar desto tratado de la dentro y fuera; los penitentes de solo lo que se dize y traía dentro de los capitulos." *Arte para bien confesar,* f. A2v.

40. "Tu, peccador, donde pareccrás? Alli oyrán los justos la dulce voz de nuestro redemptor . . . mas los malos y peccadores alli oyrán la triste y amarga voz que los condemnará al fuego sin fin. . . . Mira, mira pues con muy gran diligencia, y con todas tus fuerzas, pon [sic] tu corazon." Ibid., f. A4r.

41. "Digo a dios . . . mi grandíssima culpa, que no ame a dios ni le serví de todo corazon, y con tanto amor y tanto hervor como yo devía." Ibid., f. C1r.

42. Roberto Rusconi, "Manuali Milanesi di confessione editi tra il 1474 ed il 1523," *Archivum Franciscanum Historicum* 65 (1972): 107–56.

43. Ciruelo's *Arte de bien confesar* contains the Latin form of absolution, f. 61r–v, and so does Covarrubias's *Memorial de pecados,* ff. M3r–M7r.

44. Pettas, *A Sixteenth-Century Spanish Bookstore,* 7–8, 10, 13–14.

45. Blanco Sánchez, "Inventario de Juan de Ayala," 216, 218, 220–21, 225, 231, 233, 235, 237. By the 1550s, Ciruelo's *Arte de bien confesar* was simply denoted as the *Confessionario.*

46. I am not suggesting that vernacular writers never engaged in lengthy lists: Covarrubias spent forty-four folios on specific queries for various professions.

47. See the tables of content at the end of Rusconi, "Manuali milanese di confessione." Tentler admitted that a similar asymmetry existed in Italian manuals when it came to queries about avarice and sex, but he focused nonetheless on the sexual interrogations as particularly serious; for his rationale, see *Sin and Confession,* 223–26.

48. Bossy recognized that his historical subjects might relay more or less complete renditions of the Commandments; he also granted that the last seven Commandments were framed routinely as offenses against neighbors; "Moral Arithmetic," 215–16. Still, he cast the First Commandment as "fundamental to the entire system" (216), and stressed differences instead of similarities between the Decalogue and the Seven Sins.

49. Covarrubias, *Memorial de peccados,* ff. D4r, D6r.

50. *Arte para bien confessar,* f. C4v.

51. Bossy conceded that Gerson never deprecated the Seven Sins and continued to preach on them. But he also maintained that Gerson "treated the commandments as the rock of Christian ethics" and "held onto the scriptural text as far as possible"; "Moral Arithmetic," 222 and ibid., n. 14; also see 223. I would agree that Gerson produced "something coherent, persuasive, and reasonably memorable" in his Latin

and French works on penance, but not because he adhered to the Decalogue and ensured that it governed his writings. The contents of his works belie Bossy's assertions. Katherine J. Lualdi has examined confessors' manuals from France, and has found the same blend of Seven Sins and Ten Commandments as in the Spanish evidence. "Self and Society: Sacramental Confession and Parish Worship in Late Medieval and Reformation France" (Ph.D. diss., University of Pennsylvania, 1996).

52. *Arte de bien confesar,* f. 33v. Covarrubias would borrow Ciruelo's language for his own remarks on the Decalogue, idolatry, the implicit demonic pact, and the Sixth Commandment.

53. "Quiere Dios ser visitado y reconocido de sus siervos; y que no parezcan delante del vacios, sin llevar alguna parte de los bienes que Dios les a dado, que sea [sic] para servicio de Dios y mantenimiento de sus ministros; y para protestar que son vassallos de Dios y quantos bienes ellos tienen son del." *Arte de bien confesar,* ff. 12v–13r.

54. In his *Explanatio Symboli Apostolorum,* Erasmus would provide his readers with an analogous explanation: "But 'Sabbath' for the Jews means 'rest' " ("Sabbatum autem Hebraeis sonat requiem"). *Explanatio Symboli Apostolorum,* ed. J. N. Bakhuizen van den Brink, *Opera omnia,* vol. 5, Part 1 (Amsterdam: North Holland, 1977), 309.

55. *Arte de bien confesar,* f. 4v.

56. Aquinas, *Summa theologica,* Ia–IIae, qu. 100, art. 8.

57. See Chapter 6 below.

58. "El primero mandamiento, en suma, es adorar a un solo Diós, servirle, honrarle, y amarle sobre toda cosa." *Breve forma de confesar,* 4.

59. "Estos diez mandamientos se suman o encierran en dos, que son de ley natural: Amarás a Dios con todo corazon, y al proximo como a tí mismo. . . . De los quales se siguen los diez particulares, como conclusiones de principios generales." Juan de Pedraza, O.P., *Summa de casos de conciencia* (Alcalá, 1568), f. 107r. For Dueñas, *Remedio de pecadores* (Valladolid, 1545), ff. 67r–68v.

60. "Asi los de la primera tabla, como los de la segunda tabla, se reduzen a dos preceptos generales, que son fines de todos los preceptos, que son: Amar a dios sobre todas las cosas . . . y el proximo como asi mesmo." Valtanás, *Confessionario,* f. 46r.

61. *Manual de confessores* (Medina del Campo, 1555), 59.

62. Pérez de Ayala, *Breve compendio,* f. 45v.

63. I refer again to Bossy's assertion that the "strategy" behind the Decalogue was fear of God, although he knows his subjects "smuggled" the evangelical commandments into Exodus itself. See "Moral Arithmetic," 216, 221.

64. Caroline Walker Bynum, *Holy Feast and Holy Fast: The Religious Significance of Food to Medieval Women* (Berkeley: University of California Press, 1987), and *The Resurrection of the Body in Western Christianity, 200–1330,* Lectures on the History of Religion, no. 15 (New York: Columbia University Press, 1995), Introduction. Given many of the soteriological emphases in the first half of the sixteenth century, and Trent's decrees on justification in the second, Bynum's point about medieval Chris-

tianity should be extended to early modern Catholicism as well. For arguments about material happiness, witchcraft, and clerical attitudes toward both, see Chapter 6.

65. "Cuando alguno piensa, o da a entender, que el bien que tiene, que lo tiene de sí mismo; o que si Dios se lo dió, que fue por sus merescimientos; o cuando menosprecia los otros iguales o mayores que él, y cuando quiere sobre todos ser reputado, tenido o acatado, en cualquier cosa que sea buena o mala, espiritual o corporal." *Breve forma de confesar,* 7.

66. Ibid.

67. Covarrubias, *Memorial de pecados,* f. C6r–v; Ciruelo, *Arte de bien confesar,* f. 33v.

68. *Confessionario,* f. 72r.

69. An insight advanced by Lualdi, "Self and Society," Chapter 2.

70. *Memorial de pecados,* f. A6v.

71. *Arte de bien confesar,* ff. 2v–3r.

72. "Y por tanto sería bien que cada vez que dize 'acuso me, padre, de tal culpa,' tuviesse un dolor particular della; porque hablando el corazon con tantos golpes, viniesse a dar un dolor perfecto de toda la vida pasada, que es la contricion que justifica el alma." *Summa de casos,* f. 4r.

73. *Arte para bien confesar,* f. A3r. Dueñas couched his advice in similar language: "The first thing to think about is the great danger [the penitent] is in before the confession. Second, the very terrifying, austere, and no less terrible judgment of God our Lord. Third, His very excessive, generous, and immense mercy" ("La primera es el gran peligro en que está ante de la confession. La segunda es el muy espantoso, estrecho, y no menos terrible juyzio de dios nuestro señor. La tercera es su muy excessiva, larga, y immensa misericordia"). *Remedio de pecadores,* f. 26r.

74. *Arte para bien confessar,* f. B3r–v. The Hieronymite and his Latin predecessors attributed the eight-item list to Cicero; it gained much authority from its inclusion in Penyafort, *Summa textu sacrorum canorum,* 431–32.

75. Too much guilt, on the other hand, was just as reprehensible as a lack of it: numerous Spaniards expounded the sin of scrupulosity, which involved an obsessive fixation on personal failings.

76. Scholars may point out that sexual queries did not dominate the summae, and that confessors probably limited their interrogations on sexual topics. Still, "a celibate male clergy exercised control over a married laity through sacramental confession. One might justifiably invoke here the language of class conflict." Tentler, *Sin and Confession,* xix.

77. Ibid., 223–32, subtitled "The Negative Balance."

78. *Memorial de pecados,* f. D6r–v.

79. "Item, pecan si no guarda en habla y en obra la honestad [sic] que a tal acto pertenesce, la diferencia ha de haver del ayuntamiento de marido y mujer al del rufian y de su manceba." *Breve forma de confesar,* 18.

80. *Arte de bien confesar,* ff. 34r–40r.

81. "Y algunas vezes las tales cosas despues se relatar en las plazas por escarnio y

por escandalo de los sacerdotes." *Summa de confession llamada Defecerunt de Fray Antonino, Arzobispo de Florencia* (Toledo, 1524), ff. 24v–25r.

82. For abortion, see *Arte de bien confesar*, f. 31r, under the Fifth Commandment prohibiting murder.

83. "El estado mas áspero que uno puede tomar es el matrimonio, mayormente para la muger, que de libre se captiva y subjeta a mill miserías y necessidades y peligros; y el mayor de todos, que ha de bivir toda la vida-comer y dormir y conversar-en una casa con un hombre. . . . Y por esto dixo el otro: que no está en si la muger que dize sí para casarse." *Confessionario*, f. 35v. As in his treatment of episcopal residence, Valtanás puns here as well, this time on the play between "si" as oneself, and "sí" as "yes." For his comments on virginity, see ibid., f. 69r–v; he intended "to disillusion men, so that they may not think their wives have been unchaste with other men, on account of not seeing a trace of blood in the matrimonial act" ("por desengañar a los hombres, que no piensen que por no aver visto rastro de sangre en el acto matrimonial, por esso creen que sus mugeres han sido deshonestas con otro hombres").

84. "No deve hombre meter a monja a persona si no le sale muy de corazón, y sobre avelo pensado muchos días y pedido muy muchas vezes." Ibid., f. 55v.

85. Pedraza, *Summa de casos de conciencia*, ff. 11r–20v; Pérez de Ayala, *Breve compendio*, ff. 45r–46v. On connections between the Decalogue and the prosecution of witchcraft, see Chapter 6.

86. "E fuge come dal vento di contendere ne disputare cum il confessore in lo acto de la confessione siando luy docto y intelligente como debbe essere." Francesco da Mozzanica, *Breve introductione* (Milan, 1510), f. 2v., cited in Rusconi, "Manuali milanesi di confessione," 120, n. 2. Significantly, Rusconi characterizes Mozzanica's treatise as aimed at women (ibid., 144). Caveats about arguing with confessors were absent in the Latin summae de casibus.

87. Haliczer relays this incident in *Sexuality in the Confessional*, 115; he also notes that among the intended victims of clerical solicitation, the "largest single group" rejected their confessors' overtures (114). As Haliczer intimates, such rejection could involve the chastisement of a confessor.

88. "Item, peca el sacerdote que no guarda enteramente la costumbre de la iglesia en todas las cosas que a este sacramento pertenescen, que serían aqui luengas [sic] de contar; pero en especial peca si la bendicion de la pila y catecismo y otros actos que en el baptismo concurren, hace burlando, riendo e sín atencion, e si lo dice así apriesa que aun él mesmo no se oye ni se entiende, como por nuestros pecados muchos malos clerigos lo hacen en este tiempo." *Breve forma de confessar*, 10.

89. Ciruelo, *Arte de bien confesar*, ff. 33r, 40r–v; Covarrubias, *Memorial de pecados*, f. B8r.

90. *Confessionario*, ff. 17v–19r.

91. *Remedio de pecadores*, ff. 34r, 37r.

92. Ibid., ff. 30r–33r.

93. Ciruelo, *Arte de bien confesar*, f. 62r; Pérez de Ayala, *Breve compendio*, ff. 39r–41r.

Chapter Six. The Bewitching of the Sheep

1. For the classic statement of this paradigm, see Norman Cohn, *Europe's Inner Demons* (New York: Basic Books, 1975). A much more subtle exploration of the witch stereotype and its development lies in Edward Peters, *The Magician, the Witch, and the Law* (Philadelphia: University of Pennsylvania Press, 1978); a general rendition for a wide audience is contained in Brian Levack, *The Witch-Hunt in Early Modern Europe,* 2nd ed. (New York: Longman, 1995).

2. Stuart Clark, *Thinking with Demons: The Idea of Witchcraft in Early Modern Europe* (Oxford: Oxford University Press, 1997), 503–5.

3. Ibid., 35, 61, 64–65. Clark believes that religious polemics between Catholics and Protestants only heightened their propensity to divide and contrast; in his view, Christians in the sixteenth century became "addicted to something akin to Christian manichaeism." Although Clark recognizes scholasticism's potential impact on the witch's sexual identity, he does not connect scholastic method, with its dependence upon oppositional constructions, to the allegedly binary thinking of his subjects. Ibid., 64, 122, and see below.

4. Ibid., 490–91, 497, 502–8. Clark explicitly follows Bossy's argument on the renewed importance of the Decalogue, with all the psychological ramifications intact; he makes the same argument for the Commandments and witchcraft literature that Bossy and Delumeau promote for the Decalogue and confessors' manuals.

5. "Above all, pastors made up for any caution regarding malevolent witchcraft by their sustained and bitter attacks on its benevolent equivalent—popular magic." Clark, *Thinking with Demons,* 522. On witchcraft as a "counter-institution competitor" for Christian allegiance, a challenge to universal domination, and a rival of the official priesthood, see ibid., 541.

6. Ibid., x, 13, 35, 61–64, 129–30, 459; on inversion as the basis of the sabbat, see Robin Briggs, *Witches and Neighbors* (New York: Viking, 1996), 38. For an application of the same sort of dynamic to the twelfth century, see R. I. Moore, *The Formation of a Persecuting Society: Power and Deviance in Western Europe, 950–1250* (Oxford: Oxford University Press, 1987), who in turn is indebted to Mary Douglas, *Purity and Danger* (London: Routledge & Kegan Paul, 1966).

7. Once the notion of the demonic pact was widespread, popular complaints about witches could become intense, and authorities may have had little choice but to respond to them. Additionally, witches were creative individuals who could inculpate themselves even further than their interrogators demanded. On witchcraft, popular protest, and prosecution, see Gustav Henningsen, *The Witches' Advocate* (Reno: University of Nevada Press, 1980), Chapters 2 and 4; Lyndal Roper, *Oedipus and the Devil* (London: Routledge, 1994), Chapter 9. On the role of local authorities, see Robin Briggs, " 'Many Reasons Why': Witchcraft and the Problem of Multiple Explanation," in *Witchcraft in Early Modern Europe: Studies in Culture and Belief,* ed. Jonathan Barry, Marianne Hester, and Gareth Roberts, Past and Present Publications

(Cambridge: Cambridge University Press, 1996), 49–63; and H. C. Erik Midelfort, "Witch Hunting and the Domino Theory," in *Religion and the People 800–1700,* ed. James Obelkevich (Chapel Hill: University of North Carolina Press, 1979), 277–88. For the witch's inventiveness in the face of her accusers, see Roper, ibid., Chapter 10; and Briggs, *Witches and Neighbors,* 39. Also see n. 8 below.

8. Clark, *Thinking with Demons,* 508. Also see ibid., 475: "[The concept of superstition] was a form of proscription in terms of which many of the apparently routine actions and utterances of ordinary people, together with the categories and beliefs that shaped their experience, were denounced as valueless." Clark links this process of classification to the notion of "acculturation," although he also states that witchcraft literature, and presumably inquisitorial records, disguise possible uniformity and exchange between majority and minority cultures (508–12).

9. The vision of witchcraft as social control—or as having a function in European society—is indebted to earlier anthropological studies by E. Evans-Pritchard and Mary Douglas. Numerous scholars have recently discarded the functionalist model because it either cannot encompass dysfunctional instances of witch-hunting, or because it proposes a significance for witchcraft that may have nothing to do with the meaning ascribed to it by the historical actors themselves. On demonology's connections to other European literatures, see Clark, *Thinking with Demons,* viii–ix.

10. For Scottish witchcraft, see the various studies by the late Christine Larner, especially *Enemies of God: The Witch-Hunt in Scotland* (Baltimore: Johns Hopkins University Press, 1981); for the English variety, the classic works by Alan Macfarlane, *Witchcraft in Tudor and Stuart England: A Regional and Comparative Study* (New York: Harper & Row, 1970), and Keith Thomas, *Religion and the Decline of Magic* (London: Charles Scribner, 1971). Also consult Jonathan Barry, "Keith Thomas and the Problem of Witchcraft," in *Witchcraft in Early Modern Europe,* 1–48.

11. Wolfgang Behringer, "Witchcraft Studies in Austria, Germany, and Switzerland," and Brian Levack, "State-Building and Witch Hunting in Early Modern Europe," in *Witchcraft in Early Modern Europe,* 77 and 96–118, respectively. The fact that larger and more centralized bureaucracies might stop witch panics instead of pursuing them corrects the notion that witch-hunting and state-building were entwined operations. But on treating elites as inevitably or naturally more enlightened than the masses, see Midelfort, "Witch Hunting and the Domino Theory."

12. Ruth Martin, *Witchcraft and the Inquisition in Venice, 1550–1650* (London: Basil Blackwell, 1989); Briggs, *Witches and Neighbors,* 38–59; Henningsen, *The Witches' Advocate,* 78–79, 89–91

13. On the risks of imposing a uniform typology on the witches' sabbat, for example, see Briggs, *Witches and Neighbors,* 38, 51, 58–59.

14. Most historiography on Spanish witchcraft focuses on the Basque country: Marcelino Menéndez y Pelayo, *Historia de los heterodoxos españoles,* ed. Enrique Sánchez Reyes, 2nd ed., 4 vols. (Madrid: CSIC, 1963), 4:374–92; Henry Charles Lea, *History of the Inquisition of Spain,* 4 vols. (New York: American Scholar Publications,

1966), 4:217–46. For the Basque region, which was positively notorious for witchcraft, see selected chapters in Iñaki Reguera, *La inquisición española en el país vasco (el tribunal de Calahorra, 1513–1570)* (Pamplona: Editorial Txertoa, 1984), and Monter, *Frontiers of Heresy*, as well as my review essay on Spanish witchcraft, "The Inquisitor and the Witch," forthcoming in a volume on the European historiography of witchcraft from the Arbeitskreis Interdisziplinäre Hexenförschung, Stüttgart.

15. These specific details from Spain came from trials conducted by the Logroño tribunal between 1609 and 1610, in the famous Zugarramurdi case studied by Henningsen, *The Witches' Advocate*. The confessions of the Zugarramurdi witches were destroyed during the Napoleonic wars; details of their activities come from official sentences against them, instead of their confessions per se.

16. Reguera, *La inquisición española en el país vasco,* 213; the priest also wrote the same formula on the child's stomach. The entire ritual presupposes correspondences between the sick youngster and Jesus on the cross, as well as absolutely permeable barriers between the spoken and the written word, and the body.

17. Inés's spell, recorded during her trial in 1524, is transcribed in Sebastián Cirac Estopañán, *Los procesos de hechicerías en la Inquisición de Castilla la Nueva* (Madrid: CSIC, 1942), 115–16.

18. "Con san Pedro y san Pablo / y el apóstol Santiago / y con el bienaventurado san Cebrián / suertes echastéis en la mar / muertas las echastéis / vivas las sacáis / así me saquéis vivas y verdaderas estas suertes / si *fulano* ha de venir / salga en camino." Ibid., 50.

19. The distinction between Northern and Mediterranean witchcraft comes from Julio Caro Baroja's work in particular, especially *The World of the Witches* (Chicago: University of Chicago Press, 1964, 1965, 1968), originally published in Spanish in 1961, with subsequent Spanish editions in 1966, 1968, 1970, and 1973.

20. Crucial proponents of this notion include Henry Charles Lea, Caro Baroja, and most historians of the Spanish Inquisition.

21. For the best explanation of the Inquisition's moderation vis-à-vis witches, consult Monter, *Frontiers of Heresy*, 270–72.

22. Caro Baroja, *The World of the Witches,* 155; Nalle, *God in La Mancha,* 180–81. For criticisms of a dichotomy between folk magic and learned demonology, see below.

23. Monter, *Frontiers of Heresy*, 273, 274 n. 43.

24. The most famous account of Spanish witchcraft—which contains all the elements enumerated here—concerns Inquisitor Alonso Salazar y Frías and the Zugarramurdi cases. The fullest account in English is in Henningsen, *The Witches' Advocate;* for objections to that narrative, see Homza, "The Inquisitor and the Witch."

25. On the bruja in Castile, Cirac Estopañán, *Los procesos de hechicerías,* 187–201. Reguera, *La Inquisición española en el país vasco,* 211, 212 n. 63, 213, admits that divination, treasure hunting, and healing, carried out by individuals, occurred in Navarre.

26. Such is the case with Inquisitor Salazar, who disputed the reality of the witches' flight in Zugarramurdi. See Lea, *The History of the Inquisition of Spain,* 4:211, 237, 239, 240, 246, in which he tied doubt over the reality of the sabbat to rational inquiry; Caro Baroja, *World of the Witches,* 184, 188; idem, *Inquisición, brujería, y cryptojudaismo* (Barcelona: Editorial Ariel, 1970), 194–97; Henningsen, *The Witches' Advocate,* 390.

27. The connection between lies and the Devil is borne out in the Toledo Inquisition tribunal's prosecutions from the sixteenth century, when the notaries collated cases of trickery with ones on sorcery. See, for instance, the trial of Francisco Díaz in 1549, AHN, Inqu., Leg. 85, exp. 6, ff. 3r–4r; Díaz was accused of healing through false and superstitious means.

28. This conclusion is clear from the deliberations that took place in 1526, when Inquisitor General Manrique called experts to Granada to review recent witchcraft cases and to help define the Inquisition's attitude toward them. The consultants, who included such prominent intellectuals as Luís Coronel, found that the Inquisition must proceed against persons suspected of witchcraft because the crime pertained to infidelity toward God. AHN, Inqu., Lib. 1231, f. 635v; the deliberations as a whole extend from ff. 634r to 637v.

29. Martin, *Witchcraft and the Inquisition in Venice,* 57–62, outlines some factors that could prompt the inquisitors to act leniently.

30. For objections to a simplistic vision of acculturation by elites, see Briggs, " 'Many Reasons Why,' " 52–53; on the role of clerics in the excommunication of locusts, see Christian, *Local Religion in Sixteenth-Century Spain,* 29–31.

31. "Aliqui tamen eorum querunt ab ipsa imagine dicentes: 'Sante Petre, succurre nobis in hac necessitate positis, ut impetres nobis a Deo pluviam, etc.' Hoc secundo, hoc tertio. Et cum ad singula nihil respondeat, clamant dicentes: 'Submergatur beatissimi Petri imago, si nobis apud Deum omnipotentem gratiam expostulatam pro imminente necessitate non impetraverit.' " This example comes from Martín Andosilla y Arles, *De superstitionibus* (Lyon, 1510), ed. José Goñi Gaztambide, "El tratado 'De superstitionibus' de Martín de Andosilla," *Cuadernos de etnología y etnografía Navarra* 3 (1971): 249–322, specifically p. 272.

32. With its elements of coercion and degradation, the ritual in Usún may have a medieval analogue in the formal monastic humiliation of the saints, which was preserved in liturgical manuscripts from the tenth until the thirteenth centuries, and practiced in Cluniac monasteries; see Patrick Geary, *Living with the Dead in the Middle Ages* (Ithaca, N.Y.: Cornell University Press, 1994), 95–115.

33. For the extrapolation of Christian symbols and texts into magical rites in Germany, see Roper, *Oedipus and the Devil,* 182–83; for the presence of Christian signs and rites in Italian sorcery, as well as clerical participation in the same, see Martin, *Witchcraft and the Inquisition in Venice,* Chapter 3.

34. For Castañega's biographical data, and the most recent edition of his treatise, which I have employed here, see *Fray Martín de Castañega, Tratado de las supersticiones y*

hechicerías, y de la posibilidad y remedio dellas, ed. Juan Robert Muro Abad (Logroño: Instituto de estudios riojanos, 1994), henceforth denoted as Castañega, *Tratado.*

35. I have used the most recent edition of Ciruelo's *Reprobación* for my citations: *Reprovación de las supersticiones y hechizerias,* ed. Alva V. Ebersole (Valencia: Albatros hispanofila, 1978), although Ebersole's version of the text omits the marginalia that highlight Ciruelo's references. For an edition with the marginalia, see the *Reprobación de las supersticiones y hechicerías,* ed. Francisco Tolsada, facsimile edition of Salamanca 1538 (Madrid: Colección joyas bibliográficas, 1952). When I refer to Ciruelo's references, I am relying on Tolsada's edition. On the difficulties of dating the *Reprobación's* first edition, see n. 104 below. For the sake of consistency, I have altered Ebersole's *v* to a *b* in my citations of her edition, although I have preserved her spelling in the bibliography.

36. David Darst, "Witchcraft in Spain: The Testimony of Martín de Castañega's Treatise on Superstition and Sorcery (1529)," *Proceedings of the American Philosophical Society* 123 (1979): 298–322; as well as the edition by Muro Abad. For Ciruelo's *Reprobación,* besides Ebersole, see the translation by Eugene A. Maio and Dorsay W. Pearson, *Pedro Ciruelo's A Treatise Reproving All Superstitions and Forms of Witchcraft* (Akron, Ohio: Fairleigh Dickenson University Press, 1977). For references to the two Spaniards in a recent study, see Clark, *Thinking with Demons,* 84, 98, 166, 191, 247, 487, 516, 665 (Castañega); and 170, 245, 292, 440, 469, 478, 482, 488, 498, 503, 564, and 632 (Ciruelo). Clark uses the Maio and Pearson translation of Ciruelo's *Reprobación,* and Maio and Pearon translated a very late redaction of the treatise, from 1628; it was glossed by a Barcelona lawyer named Pedro Jofreu.

37. For references to the *Tratado* by contemporaries, see the Introduction to the edition by Muro Abad, xxxix–xl.

38. Díaz de Lugo, *Aviso de curas,* f. 75r.; Juan de Quiñones, *Tratado de las langostas* (Madrid, 1620), f. 38r–v; Gaspar Navarro, *Tribunal de superstición ladina* (Huesca, 1631), ff. 45v, 75r, 78v, 89v, 90v–95r, 102r–v, 105r–107v.

39. Pettas, *A Sixteenth-Century Spanish Bookstore,* 142, 170.

40. "Pues desseando alumbrar a los christianos simples con la pequeña lumbre que Christo me quiso comunicar, y servir en ello a Vuestra Illustre Señoria, ordené y compusé este Tratado de las Supersticiones y Hechizerias [sic] en lengua castellana, para que los visitadores y curas, y aun todos los clerigos deste su muy honrrado y grande obispado, lo tengan entre manos, por ser la material peregrina y que no se halla por los dotores assi recolegida, particularizada, ni declarada, ni a los casos que acaecen aplicada. El qual, (a mi ver) no solo provechará a los simples para apartarlos de sus errores y engaños diabolicos, mas aun es necessario para quitar muchas ignorancias de muchos que, presumiendo de letrados, niegan las maneras de las supersticiones e hechizerias que aqui se ponen." *Tratado,* 5.

41. For Castañega's and Castillo's remarks about their readership, see *Tratado,* 9, 13.

42. Ciruelo, *Reprobación*, 25. The remark about prelates and judges could have been inserted by Pedro de Castro, who printed the 1538 edition of the work.

43. Darst, "Witchcraft in Spain," 298, 300; Muro Abad, ed., *Fray Martín de Castañega, Tratado*, xx, xxix, xxxiii.

44. Maio and Pearson, trans., *Pedro Ciruelo's Treatise*, 17; Ebersole, ed., *Reprobación*, 10.

45. *Reprobación*, ed. Ebersole, 10.

46. For cogent objections to referentiality, and arguments that witchcraft texts had their own inherent logic, see Clark, *Thinking with Demons*, Preface.

47. "Destos yo conocí y ví algunos quemar e reconciliar en que uno dixo que le hizo el demonio renegar de dios e de su fe, mas nunca pudo acabar con él que renegasse de nuestra señora; y era un hombre viejo y pequeño, y reconcilióse, y conoció su pecado." *Tratado*, 18.

48. Pedro Jofreu, the glossator of the *Reprobación* in 1628, claimed Ciruelo had acted as an inquisitor in Zaragoza for thirty years, but that declaration had more to do with presenting Ciruelo as a seasoned authority than with any experience we can verify. Maio and Pearson, trans., *Pedro Ciruelo's Treatise*, 21.

49. Cohn, *Europe's Inner Demons*, attributes the more outrageous attributes of witches to monastic fantasies.

50. Clark, *Thinking with Demons*, passim. For his endorsement of Jean Delumeau's theory of christianization, see 526–30, although Clark also points out weaknesses in the Delumeau thesis.

51. Castañega wrote that baptism signaled Christian allegiance to God, that infidelity was the most serious sin, and that the Devil attracted followers and gained their reverence by promising them worldly possessions; *Tratado*, 12–14. Ciruelo believed the Devil was God's enemy; he enumerated the bonds among treason, idolatry, and the demonic; and referred to the baptismal vow, pronounced by parents and godparents, to renounce Satan and all his works; *Reprobación*, 32–33, 52.

52. For Castañega, see the *Tratado*, 12–13, 20–23, on witches and transvection; the same topics in the same order are located on pp. 48–50 of the *Reprobación*.

53. "Con palabras claras e formales, renegando de la fe, hazen nueva profesion al demonio en su presencia, que les aparece en la forma e figura que él quiere tomar, dándole entera obediencia y ofreciéndole su anima y cuerpo." Castañega, *Tratado*, 18.

54. "Las bruxas o xorguinas, hombres o mugeres, que tienen hecho pacto con el diablo: que untándose con ciertos ungentos y diziendo ciertas palabras, van de noche por los ayres y caminan a lexos tierras a hazer ciertos maleficios." Ciruelo, *Reprobación*, 49. For Castañega on unguents, *maleficia*, and nightflight, see the *Tratado*, 15–16, 22–23.

55. For a translation of the *Canon episcopi*, see Alan C. Kors and Edward Peters, eds., *Witchcraft in Europe, 1100–1700: A Documentary History* (Philadelphia: University of Pennsylvania Press, 1972), 28–31.

56. "Assi como leemos y hallamos que el demonio y qualquier angel bueno o malo, por su virtud y poder natural, puede llevar a qualquier hombre que para ello estuviese obediente, permitiéndolo dios, por los ayres, aguas, y mares, assi leemos que pueden estar arrebatados los sentidos fuera de si, que llaman los dotores extasi, y que alli tuviesen revelaciones de grandes secretos y cosas que passan en partes remotas, y que pensassen que están o han estado en ellas." *Tratado*, 23.

57. "El demonio puede turbar los sentidos humano, como en muy pesado e grave sueño, de tal suerte que le haga parecer que está en aquel lugar que el demonio le representa." Ibid.

58. *Reprobación*, 49.

59. Gerson worked with similar notions: the Devil "tries now openly, now secretly, for the observance of his particular practices" ("intendit nunc aperte, nunc occulte ad observandum quaedam instituta sua"). *De erroribus*, 10:80.

60. For highly authoritative arguments about the implicit pact, see Augustine, *De civitate Dei, Opera*, Corpus christianorum, Latin Series 47, Part 14:1 (Turnholti: Brepols, 1955), Book 7, Chapter 35; Book 8, Chapter 19; Book 10, Chapters 8–9. Aquinas, *Summa contra Gentiles* (Notre Dame, Ind.: University of Notre Dame Press, 1975) Book 3, Part 2, Chapter 105, 94–97. Gerson, who was as powerful an authority on witchcraft as he was on penance, phrased the idea most cogently: a ritual for the working of some effect, which could not be rationally expected either from divine miracles or from natural causes, must be held among Christians as superstitious and suspect of a secret pact with demons. *De erroribus*, 10:79.

61. "Porque las vanidades son mentiras y las mentiras placen al diablo, manifiesto es que el hombre que hace las obras vanas sirve al diablo y peca muy gravemente contra su Dios." *Reprobación*, 42. Castañega invoked the notion of the implicit demonic pact when he railed against false exorcists and spurious healing spells; nevertheless, his explanation of that pact was not grounded in the authorities he cited. See the *Tratado*, 19, and below.

62. Thus "classic devil-worshipping witchcraft was quite often overshadowed by its (apparently) beneficient or 'white' counterpart. . . . The literature attacking the agents of *maleficium* thus blended imperceptibly into a more general campaign against those who provided both the immediate antidotes and many other arts and techniques on which ordinary lay people relied for their material and psychological welfare." Clark, *Thinking with Demons*, 463.

63. Castañega, *Tratado*, 38–40; Ciruelo, *Reprobación*, 80–83, 85–93.

64. Castañega, *Tratado*, 40–42, 57–61; Ciruelo, *Reprobación*, 94–96, 108–23.

65. "No nos oye Dios o no responde a nuestra peticion tan presto como desseamos, por provar y declarar nuestra virtud e paciencia, porque si permite males para provar y manifestar la bondad e virtud de la persona virtuosa como fue en Job, mucho mejor nos negara los bienes que le pedimos por la mesma razon; y assi muchas vezes no otorga los bienes que le piden quando selos piden, porque se funden más en la humildad y más claro parezca [sic] su virtud e paciencia." *Tratado*, 55.

66. "Para mayor claridad y mejor informacion de los buenos christianos, quiero aqui poner algunas reglas cerca de las nóminas y ensalmos. Y serán tan verdaderas y catholicas que ningun buen letrado las podrá negar. Es razon que los otros hombres y mugeres simples, sin letras, passen por ellas, porque en el pueblo de Dios la fe de los menores y baxos se a de regir por la de los mayores prelados y letrados." *Reprobación,* 87.

67. Ibid., 103, 119.

68. "E para librarse de los lazos y engaños del demonio, con la ayuda de Dios, trabajen de oyr en todos los dias de fiesta la missa mayor devotamente; y todas las vezes que pudieren, con mucha atencion oyan los sermones; confiessense con buenos confessores, a lo menos quando la yglesia lo manda . . . y sean siempre obedientes a los mandamientos de la yglesia; y tengan temor de incurrir en alguna descomunion, y más de estar por algunos dias descomulgados. Nunca crean liviandades ni otras cosas que en la yglesia no se enseñan; no rezen oraciones ni digan palabras, aunque parezcan devotas, que en la yglesia no se usan; y quando alguna duda tuvieren, luego lo pregunten a su cura o confessor." *Tratado,* 72.

69. "Y siempre bivan con recelo y temor de yr contra la fe de la santa madre yglesia y sus mandamientos." Ibid., 72–73.

70. *Reprobación,* 34, 51, 83.

71. For such dichotomies as nearly inescapable features of witchcraft texts, see Clark, *Thinking with Demons,* 31–42, 94–103, 110–17, 509–15.

72. Castañega, *Tratado,* 39.

73. "No es malo usar del agua del lavatorio del caliz o donde algunas reliquias se han lavado, para bever o derramar sobre algunos ganados enfermos, porque sin supersticion alguna, por su devocion, los hombres alguna vez piden del azeyte de la lampara que arde delante de la ymagen de tal santo o del sacratissimo sacramento, y el lavatorio de las llagas de la ymagen de sant Francisco, no para usar mal dello, salvo para recebirlo e usar dello con mucha devocion, desseando remediar sus passiones y enfermedades o de sus ganados." Ibid., 40.

74. "La primera es que busque luego todos los remedios que son possibles por via natural del saber humano para salir y se librar de aquel trabajo. La segunda es encomendar a dios y a sus sanctos con devocion su persona y familia y hazienda: y suplicarle que en aquel trabajo socorra con ayuda celestial en lo que no alcanzan las fuerzas naturales ni saber de los hombres." *Reprobación,* 79.

75. "Digo que deve el hombre hazer en aquel caso lo que él por su saber alcanzare, o tomar el consejo de los que más saben, o maestros, o amigos, o ancianos esperimentados." Ibid.

76. Ibid., 121. The idea was that vibrations from the artillery would dispel the clouds.

77. "Y libre aquella su familia y los terminos de aquel lugar del daño que podrá hazer aquella tempestad." Ibid., 121–22. Note Ciruelo's stress on the community's collective safety.

78. On cures for locusts, ibid., 126–28; on Job, ibid., 123. Ciruelo also cited the Book of Job as proof of the Devil's existence, ibid., 35.

79. "Clerigos, o frayles cobdiciosos, y necios." Ibid., 134. In this instance, Ciruelo repeated the content of his confessors' manual.

80. Ibid., 125; Christian, *Local Religion in Sixteenth-Century Spain*, 29–31.

81. *Reprobación*, 118–23. Castañega provided more details about cloud-conjurers in his *Tratado*, 57–59.

82. *Reprobación*, 109.

83. "Por lo qual los semejantes, en especial los ecclesiasticos que en estas cosas se entremeten, merecen ser muy reziamente castigados por sus obispos y perlados." *Tratado*, 54.

84. Castañega's only remark was that "sometimes the conjurers [exorcists] are participants in these tricks." Ibid., 69.

85. "Esta sesta [sic] regla de las nóminas vale tambien para las reliquias de los santos que algunos traen consigo. Porque de cierto sería cosa más devota y más provechosa para ellos, que pusiessen las reliquias en las yglesias o en lugares honestos; y ellos tomassen devocion de rezar cada dia algunas devociones a aquellos sanctos y santas cuyas reliquias dizen que son; y esto digo por tres razones. La una es porque ya en este tiempo ay mucha duda y poca certidumbre de las reliquias de los santos: que muchas dellas no son verdaderas; y contece algunas vezes lo que dizen de la raja o palo de la barca." *Reprobación*, 90.

86. Ciruelo's comment about the "splinter or timber of the boat" may echo Erasmus's colloquy, *A Pilgrimage for Religion's Sake;* it also could reflect the Inquisition's 1525 edict against the alumbrados. The latter decree quoted the following items among the charges: "A certain person, preaching, said that the cross does not have to be adored, stating that it was a piece of wood; that they [should] adore Jesus Christ crucified"; and "That a preacher reprimanded those who prayed to the saints and adored their images. And [he asked] why they adored the cross, which was a piece of wood that they could burn." Márquez, *Los Alumbrados*, Appendix I, props. 18 and 24.

87. *Reprobación*, 122–23.

88. Ibid., 123.

89. "Muchos tienen duda de la virtud y gracia que los saludadores tienen y por experiencia muestran contra los perros rabiosos e la ponzoña dellos. Para esto es de notar que las virtudes naturales son tan ocultas en la vida presente a los entendimientos humanos, que muchas vezes vemos . . . obras maravillosas y no sabemos dar la razon dellas, salvo que es tal la propiedad de las cosas naturales y que a nosotros es oculta." *Tratado*, 28–29.

90. "Todos los prelados y juezes que permiten en sus diocesis que anden estos publicos saludadores saludando, pecan mortalmente si no los castigan y echan de la tierra como supersticiosos y engañadores de la simple gente, que les roban sus haziendas y les infiernan las almas." Ciruelo would admit—at the very end of the relevant

chapter—that simple, good men might possess a special spiritual grace to cure. But he generally doubted that possibility. *Reprobación,* 103–4.

91. For the pseudo-Solomonic writings and other works on the conjuring of spirits, which appeared in Western Europe by the twelfth century, see Martin, *Witchcraft and the Inquisition in Venice,* 44–47, 86–101; S. M. I. Mathers, *The Key of Solomon the King (Clavicula Salomonis)* (New York: Samuel Weiser, 1974); D. P. Walker, *Spiritual and Demonic Magic from Ficino to Campanella* (Notre Dame, Ind.: University of Notre Dame Press, 1975).

92. *Reprobación,* 83, 122.

93. "Y aun digo que en la audiencia secreta de los confessores, se deve hazer diferencia entre los que an entrado en la superstición de ensalmos y nóminas; porque a las personas sin letras la inorancia [sic] las escusa, o aliviana el pecado. Esto es verdad antes que ellos sean avisados y corregidos por los sabios theologos y prelados; porque despues de ser avisados, si aun porfian en querer usar de ensalmos y nóminas, no los escusara la inorancia." *Reprobación,* 91.

94. *Tratado,* 13–15.

95. "Por el contrario, los execramentos diabolicos son en cosas que en la vida y conversacion humana no se hallan, como son unguentos y polvos hechos de cosas exquisitas, de animales y aves que con mucha difficultad se hallan, y con palabras oscuras y rithmadas." Ibid., 15–16.

96. Ibid., 19–20.

97. "Lo quarto porque son mas parleras que los hombres, e no guardan tanto secreto, e assi se enseñan unas a otras, lo que no hazen tanto los hombres." Ibid., 20.

98. "Primeramente, es de notar y examinar con mucha vigilencia, que espiritus sean aquellos de que dizen que la persona es atormentada, porque por experiencia se ha visto que algunas personas, en especial mugeres, por su propia malicia, como alguna vez fingen que están ligadas, maleficiadas o hechizadas, assi fingen que están espiritadas o endemoniadas, por algunos descontentos que tienen de sus esposos o maridos, o por grandes amores carnales que tienen con alguno, o por terribles tentaciones de la carne que el demonio enciende en ellas." Ibid., 68–69. For the rest of these points on women, see ibid., 20–21, 59–61, 66–71.

99. "Porque la muger que a ello se determina, ligeramente haze gestos espantosos y más que el demonio le da favor para ello." Ibid., 69.

100. "A more equivocal etiology of possession also produced more explanations, and more benign ones, for various manifestations of female spirituality." Alison Weber, "Between Ecstasy and Exorcism: Religious Negotiation in Sixteenth-Century Spain," *Journal of Medieval and Renaissance Studies* 23, no. 2 (1993): 230–31, 233.

101. For complementary points about women's frailty in the face of the Devil, this time in Protestant thought, see Roper, *Oedipus and the Devil,* 191–92.

102. "Vanidad y aun falta de fe parece, y cosa de judería o superstición, usar de los nombres hebraicos antiguos en las invocaciones christianas y catolicas, como si los

nombres viejos valiessen más que los nuevos. En especial son peligrosos para los ignorantes que poco saben, porque aquellos nombres hebraicos e griegos no sean ocasion de poner y dezir con ellos, otros incognitos e diabolicos." *Tratado*, 64, for this quote; for other anti-Jewish material, ibid., 15, 59.

103. Ibid., 65–66. Castañega's injection of Hebrew into his treatise recalls Andosilla y Arles's technique as well, for both invoked that language as a prominent part of nóminas, and pinpointed likely partners of the Devil as conversos as well as Jews. See Andosilla, *De superstitionibus*, ed. Goñi Gaztambide, 293.

104. Ciruelo also noted in the same prologue that he wrote the *Reprobación* many years after his confessors' manual (1514), and thought of it as an elaboration of something he had treated earlier: *Reprobación*, 25–26. For a 1530 date for this text, with additional references, see Francisco Tolosada's introduction to his edition of the *Reprobación*, xxxi–xxxvi. We have no evidence that the *Reprobación* appeared before 1530.

105. By duplicating Castañega's topics, Ciruelo ended up mimicking the *Malleus maleficarum* as well.

106. Compare the *Tratado*, 59–60, to the *Reprobación*, 110, 114.

107. Compare the *Tratado*, 11, to the *Reprobación*, 31–32.

108. "Y los fariseos, encegados de embidia, negavan de Jesu Christo la primera manera, que es la autoridad, virtud, y poder que tenía con que hechava los demonios, y acusavanle con la segunda manera, diziendo que como mago y nigromantico, por la familiaridad que con Beelzebuth tenía, le obedecían los demonios; y assi dezían en virtud o poder de Beelzebuth, principe de los demonios . . . lanza a los demonios menores o de menos poder y tambien ellos mesmos le obedecen, por la familiaridad y pacto que tiene con ellos. Ni más desto querían dezir quando otras vezes le dezían que tenía demonio." *Tratado*, 67.

109. Castañega contended that the first sort of exorcism treated the Devil as a subject and a prisoner; the second, as a servant; and the third occurred with people who truly were possessed and tormented by the Devil. His first and third categories involved the same type of demonic possession that Jesus cured. Ibid., 66–67.

110. "Quando nuestro señor Jesu christo curó un endemoniado mudo, y por fuerza, con su virtud divina, echó de alli al diablo, aunque él no quería y contra su voluntad [sic]. Y los fariseos maliciosos dixeron que en belcebub [sic] lo hazía; querían dezir que lo hazía como nigromantico por pacto secreto que tenía con el belzebub [sic], que es el diablo. Y aunque nuestro señor no negó que oviese algunos sacadores de spiritus por aquella manera mala, mas próboles . . . que él no sacava los demonios por pacto de amistad con el diablo." *Reprobación*, 111.

111. *Tratado*, 19.

112. "Si alguno para sanar a otro del dolor de la cabeza, o de la fiebre, le atasse a la pierna un poco de papel blanco o de lienzo sin otra cosa alguna; o le midiesse la cinta a palmos, o lo passase por un sarmiento hendido; claro es que sería una liviandad y cosa vana; porque ni el papel ni el lienzo de si no tienen virtud natural para echar fuera de la

cabeza o del cuerpo el mal humor que causa aquel dolor. . . . Mas porque el diablo es amigo de los que hazen obras vanas, contece muchas vezes que con aquel papel blanco o lienzo el paciente sana, y esto házelo el diablo por ciertas maneras secretas que él sabe. . . . Y haze lo para engañar a los simples." *Reprobación*, 42.

113. Ibid., 145.

114. *Tratado*, 62–63; *Reprobación*, 120, 122.

115. Julio Caro Baroja proposed this split in "Witchcraft and Catholic Theology," in *Early Modern European Witchcraft: Centres and Peripheries*, ed. Bengt Ankarloo and Gustav Henningsen (Oxford: Clarendon, 1993), 19–43. Clark, *Thinking with Demons*, 538–39, is willing to posit the same division for medieval demonologists, but not for their early modern successors.

116. This difficulty is particularly true for Ciruelo's *Reprobación*, because he listed his authorities in the prologue to his work, and never referred to them in the body of the text. The best way to glean his sources is to use his own introduction to the *Reprobación*, and then the 1952 facsimile edition by Tolsada, which preserves the marginalia of the 1538 printing. In the meantime, Castañega could cite authorities and then decline to use them: such was the case with his reference to Gerson and his exposition of the implicit demonic pact.

117. *Tratado*, 5–6.

118. Ibid., 6–7; he reiterated his point about a "rhetorical and persuasive style" on p. 10. Notably, the authors of the *Malleus* revealed a similarly polemical view about their topic. For witchcraft treatises as rhetorical exercises, see Peters, *The Witch and the Law*.

119. *Tratado*, 26. Immediately afterward, Castañega identified native oblations in the New World with Old Testament sacrifices, a maneuver that was supposed to heighten the barbarity of Judaism.

120. "La muerte figurado en el cuchillo de sant Pedro, que no mató sino que cortó la oreja, (esto es) que notifica y denuncia a los oydos del excomulgado y de los otros fieles la muerte espiritual del que es desobediente y rebelde a la yglesia y a los perlados della." Ibid., 49.

121. Matthew 26:52 and Luke 22:50 do not identify the aggressor as Peter; John 18:10–11 does. Only in Mark 14:47–48 did Jesus not rebuke the offender.

122. *The Malleus maleficarum of Heinrich Kramer and James Sprenger*, trans. Montague Summers (New York: Dover, 1971).

123. Castañega's predecessor, Andosilla y Arles, also devoted a short paragraph to "why more women than men were found to be superstitious" in his *De superstitionibus*. Explicitly following Johannes Nider and Gerson, Andosilla concluded that women were more credulous and more talkative, and possessed more changeable complexions, all of which rendered them more vulnerable to the Devil's influence. Castañega's sources on women could have included Andosilla as well as Krämer and Sprenger, but the sheer extent of his remarks echoes his German counterparts instead of his Spanish peer.

124. Andosilla too mentioned incubi, as well as maleficia that entailed snatching infants away from their mothers' breasts, and then roasting and eating them ("et alia nephanda agere, puta parvulos a lacte matris avellere, assare et comedere"). *De supersti-tionibus*, 29. But he treated incubi with much greater attention to concupiscence, and placed maleficia under the topic of transvection and the *Canon episcopi*. He concep-tualized these topics very differently than Castañega.

125. Part 2, qu. 2, ch. 6–8 of the *Malleus* enumerated, in order, lawful and ille-gitimate exorcisms, remedies against hailstorms and animals that were bewitched— namely, locusts—and "remedies prescribed against those dark and horrid harms with which Devils may afflict men." Castañega's sequence moved from the wicked conjur-ing of locusts, storms, and energumens, to orthodox strategies toward the same phenomena; he treated illegitimate and then legitimate measures in separate chapters, whereas his German counterparts handled both simultaneously.

126. Unlike Castañega's *Tratado,* the *Malleus* explicitly referred to idolatry and Exodus 22:18 as justification for the witch's persecution: Part II, qu. 2, ch. 8, p. 193.

127. Clark, *Thinking with Demons,* 508.

128. "Capitulo primero declara la grande eccelencia [sic] y dignidad del primero de los diez mandamientos de dios; para mostrar quan grandes pecados son los de las supersticiones que van contra este mandamiento." *Reprobación,* 29.

129. "De la virtud dize, amarás a tu dios de todo tu corazon, y de toda tu anima, y al señor tu dios adorarás, y a él solo servirás. Del vicio dize, no tendrás dioses agenos delante de mi, no los adorarás ni servirás a ellos ni a sus estatuas, o figuras. Del castigo dize, yo soy un dios muy celoso de mi honrra, y a quien me tocare en ella, yo lo castigaré a él y a todos sus descendientes, hijos y nietos, hasta la tercera y quarta generacion. Del premio de la virtud dize, yo soy muy misericordioso a los que me quieren bien y me sirven lealmente; y haré muchas mercedes a ellos y a sus de-scendientes hasta más de mil generaciones." *Reprobación,* 33.

130. "Tabula librorum bibliotecae collegii Sancti Ildefonsi," AHN, Sección de Universidades, Libro 1091-F, *Inventario del Archivo y Biblioteca de San Ildefonso* (1523), f. 8v. Clark, *Thinking with Demons,* 112–17, would argue that Ciruelo's relative neglect of women was not unusual, and that scholars too frequently interpret the *Malleus's* misogyny as the norm. I agree that academics too often treat the *Malleus* in isolation and as an archetype; still, Ciruelo's disregard for inversion and women becomes noteworthy when his Spanish peers—Castañega and Andosilla y Arles—favored such clichés.

131. For the interpretative angle that follows, I am indebted to H. C. Erik Mid-elfort, "Social History and Biblical Exegesis: Community, Family, and Witchcraft in Sixteenth-Century Germany," in *The Bible in the Sixteenth Century,* ed. David C. Steinmetz (Durham, N.C.: Duke University Press, 1990), 7–20, especially pp. 12–15. In this article Midelfort illustrates a similar intellectual independence among German Protestants, who did not uniformly endorse Luther's elevation of Lyra's reading.

132. *Targum Neofiti 1: Exodus, and Targum Pseudo-Jonathan: Exodus,* trans. Robert

Hayward and Michael Maher, *The Aramaic Bible,* vol. 2 (Collegeville, Minn.: The Liturgical Press, 1994), 226.

133. Hailperin, *Rashi and the Christian Scholars,* 76. Rashi urged a genderless reading of Leviticus 20:27, a verse that details virtually the same topic as Exodus 22:18.

134. *Vetus testamentum graecum, juxta septuaginta interpretes, cum latina translatione,* trans. J. N. Jaeger (Paris: Editore Ambrosio Firmin-Didot, 1878), 114.

135. "De esta arte en diversas tierras ay diversos libros y de diversas maneras que unas no conciertan con otras; pues salomon no las hizo todas ellas." *Reprobación,* 73.

136. In what probably was another swipe at Castañega, Ciruelo explained Old Testament sacrifices as temporary and adduced a psychological reason for them: God allowed the Jews to submit material offerings to Him because He wished to remove the chance of their "going after" (*de yr tras*) the false gods of the Gentiles. Ibid., 30.

137. *Manuale pampilonense* (Estella, 1561) adopted Ciruelo's instructions on demonic possession, ff. 124v–126r. So far as I know, every Spanish source that cited the *Reprobación* could be classified as a pastoral one. Ciruelo's example thus supports Clark's argument that pastoral authors in the sixteenth century frequently addressed demonology.

Epilogue

1. Kagan, "Prescott's Paradigm: American Historical Scholarship and the Decline of Spain," *American Historical Review* 101 (1996): 423–46.

2. For example, independence among Spanish intellectuals is still apparent as late as the 1570s. The Inquisition trial of Martín Martínez de Cantalapiedra—one of the three "Salamanca Hebraists," who included Luís de Leon—is rife with clues about the relative scholarly freedom that professors and students enjoyed at the University of Salamanca. Cantalapiedra held the chair of Hebrew and had large numbers of students, many of whom disagreed with his exegetical remarks and none of whom denounced him before his arrest. The historiography has treated Cantalapiedra's and his colleagues' ordeals in ways equivalent to the prosecution of Juan de Vergara, and with similar interpretive weaknesses. Miguel de la Pinta Llorente, O.S.A., *Proceso criminal contra el hebraísta salmantino Martín Martínez de Cantalapiedra* (Madrid-Barcelona: Instituto Arias Montano, 1946). Also see Fernández Marcos and Fernández Tejero, "Censura y exegesis: Las *Hypotyposeis* de Martín Martínez de Cantalapiedra," *Biblia y humanismo,* 27–33. The latter authors intend to prove that the Inquisition stifled scriptural hermeneutics by banning and expurgating Cantalapiedra's treatise on biblical interpretation in the Indices of 1583–84, but the same work went through two editions and escaped the censor at least once: see ibid., 30.

Bibliography

Primary Sources

Andosilla y Arles, Martín. *De superstitionibus* (Lyon, 1510). Ed. José Goñi Gaztambide. "El tratado 'De superstitionibus' de Martín de Andosilla." *Cuadernos de etnología y etnografía Navarra* 3 (1971): 249–322.

Anonymous Hieronymite. *Arte para bien confesar.* Toledo, 1524.

Antoninus of Florence. *Summa de confession, llamada Defecerunt de Fray Antonino, Arzobispo de Florencia.* Toledo, 1526.

Augustine. *De civitate Dei. Opera.* Corpus christianorum, Latin Series 47, Part 14:1. Turnholti: Brepols, 1955.

Avila, Juan de. *Escritos sacerdotales.* Ed. Juan Bifet Esquerda. Madrid: Biblioteca de autores cristianos, 1969.

——. *Obras completas del santo maestro Juan de Avila.* Ed. Luís Sala Balust and Francisco Martín Hernández. 6 vols. Madrid: Editorial católica, 1970–71.

Bautista, Juan de. *Doctrina de sacerdotes.* Seville, 1535.

Beinart, Haim. *Records of the Trials of the Spanish Inquisition in Ciudad Real.* 4 vols. Jerusalem: Israel Academy of Sciences and Humanities, 1974–85.

Beltrán de Heredia, Vicente. *Cartulario de la universidad de Salamanca: La universidad en el siglo de oro.* 6 vols. Salamanca: Universidad de Salamanca, 1972. Vol. 6.

Biblia complutense. 6 vols. Alcalá, 1514–17.

Biblia Latina cum glossa ordinaria. Ed. Karlfried Forehlich and Margaret T. Gibson. Facsimile reprint of the *editio princeps Adolf Rusch of Strassburg* (1480–81). 4 vols. Turnholti: Brepols, 1992.

Blanco Sánchez, Antonio. "Inventario de Juan de Ayala, gran impresor toledano (1556)." *Boletín de la Real Academia Española* 67 (1987): 207–50.

Bruni, Leonardo. "On the Correct Way to Translate." In *The Humanism of Leonardo Bruni: Selected Texts.* Trans. Gordon Griffiths, James Hankins, and David Thompson. Medieval and Renaissance Texts and Studies, no. 46. Binghamton, N.Y.: MRTS, 1987. Pp. 217–29.

Carranza, Bartolomé de. *Controversia de necessaria residentia personali episcoporum et aliorum inferiorum pastorum (Venice, 1547)*. Trans. and ed. José Ignacio Tellechea Idígoras. Facsimile edition with Spanish translation. Madrid: Fundación Universitaria Española & Universidad Pontificia de Salamanca, 1993.

——. *Speculum pastorum. Hierarchia ecclesiastica in qua describuntur officia ministrorum ecclesiae militantis (1551–52)*. Ed. José Ignacio Tellechea Idígoras. Salamanca: Universidad Pontificia de Salamanca, 1992.

Carranza de Miranda, Sancho. *Opusculum in quasdam Erasmi Roterodami annotationes*. Rome, 1522.

Castañega, Martín de, Fray. *Tratado de las supersticiones y hechicerías, y de la posibilidad y remedio dellas*. Ed. Juan Robert Muro Abad. Logroño: Instituto de Estudios Riojanos, 1994.

Cazalla, María de. *Proceso de la inquisición contra María de Cazalla*. Ed. Milagros Ortega-Costa. Madrid: FUE, 1978.

Ciruelo, Pedro. *Arte de bien confesar*. Valladolid, 1534.

——. *Contemplaciones sobre la passion del nuestro señor Jesu Christo*. Alcalá, 1547.

——. *Hexameron teologal sobre el regimento medicinal contra la pestilencia*. Alcalá, 1519.

——. *Libri septem, Job, Psalter, Proverbs, Ecclesiastes, Cantica salomenis, Esther, et Ruth*. 1537. Manuscript 590. Library of the University of Salamanca.

——. *Libro de la teología mística*. Alcalá, 1547.

——. *Paradoxae quaestiones numero decem*. Salamanca, 1538.

——. *Pedro Ciruelo's A Treatise Reproving All Superstitions and Forms of Witchcraft*. Trans. Eugene A. Maio and Dorsay W. Pearson. Akron, Ohio: Fairleigh Dickenson University Press, 1977.

——. *Penthateuci Mosayci veridicam interpretationem ad verbum*. 1536. Manuscript 589. Library of the University of Salamanca.

——. *Reprobación de las supersticiones y hechicerías* (Salamanca, 1538). Ed. Alva V. Ebersole. Valencia: Albatros hispanofila, 1978.

——. *Reprobación de las supersticiones y hechicerías* (Salamanca, 1538). Ed. Francisco Tolsada. Facsimile edition. Madrid: Colección joyas bibliográficas, 1952.

——. *Versiones tres Penthateuci*. 1533. Manuscript #B-411, Inventory 123. Cathedral Archive, Segovia.

Ciruelo, Pedro, and Alfonso de Zamora. *Interpretatio latina sacrae scripturae Veteris Testamenti ad verbum*. 1526. Manuscript G-1-4. Library, Monastery of El Escorial.

Covarrubias, Pedro. *Memorial de pecados*. Seville, 1521.

Darst, David. "Witchcraft in Spain: The Testimony of Martín de Castañega's Treatise on Superstition and Sorcery (1529)." *Proceedings of the American Philosophical Society* 123 (1979): 298–322.

Díaz de Luco, Juan Bernal. *Aviso de curas*. Alcalá, 1551.

——. *Carta desde Trento. Soliloquio y Carta desde Trento*. Ed. Tomás Marín Martínez. Barcelona: Juan Flors, 1962.

——. *Catalogus sanctorum episcoporum*. Tomás Marín Martínez, *"El Catalogus sanctorum episcoporum del Obispo Bernal Díaz de Luco." Miscelánea conmemorativa del Concilio de Trento (1563–1963): Estudios y documentos.* Madrid: Instituto Enrique Flórez, CSIC, 1963. Pp. 373–459, specifically pp. 406–58.

———. *Instrucción de perlados* [sic]. Alcalá, 1530.

———. *Prologue, Historiae sanctorum episcoporum.* Tomás Marín Martínez, "El Catalogus sanctorum episcoporum del Obispo Bernal Díaz de Luco." *Miscelánea conmemorativa del Concilio de Trento (1563–1963): Estudios y documentos.* Madrid: Instituto Enrique Flórez, CSIC, 1963. Pp. 373–459, specifically pp. 378–81.

Dueñas, Juan de. *Remedio de pecadores.* Valladolid, 1545.

Erasmus, Desiderius. *Annotations on the New Testament: Acts, Romans, I and II Corinthians.* Ed. Anne Reeve and M. A. Screech. Facsimile of the final Latin text with all earlier variants. Studies in the History of Christian Thought, no. 42. Leiden: Brill, 1990.

———. *Annotations on the New Testament: The Gospels.* Ed. Anne Reeve. Facsimile of the final Latin text with all earlier variants. London: Gerald Duckworth, 1986.

———. *Apologia de tribus locis quos ut recte taxatos a Stunica defenderat Sanctius Caranza theologus. Opera omnia.* Ed. Jean Le Clerc. 10 vols. Leiden: P. Van der aa, 1703–6. 9:401–28.

———. *Apologia qua respondet duabus invectis Edwardi Lei. Erasmi opuscula: A Supplement to the Opera omnia.* Ed. Wallace K. Ferguson. The Hague: Martinus Nijhoff, 1933. Pp. 225–303.

———. *Apologia respondens ad ea quae Iacobus Lopis Stunica taxaverat in prima dumtaxat novi testamenti aeditione.* Ed. H. J. de Jonge. *Opera omnia.* Vol. 9, Part 2. Amsterdam: North Holland, 1983.

———. *Explanatio Symboli Apostolorum.* Ed. J. N. Bakhuizen van den Brink. *Opera omnia.* Vol. 5, Part 1. Amsterdam: North Holland, 1977.

———. *Modus orandi Deum.* Ed. J. N. Bakhuizen van den Brink. *Opera omnia.* Vol. 5, Part 1. Amsterdam: North Holland, 1977.

———. *Opus epistolarum Desiderii Erasmi Roterodami.* Ed. P. S. Allen, H. M. Allen, and H. W. Garrod. 12 vols. Oxford: Oxford University Press, 1906–58. Vols. 6 and 7.

———. *Praise of Folly.* Trans. Betty Radice. *Collected Works of Erasmus: Literary and Educational Writings.* Vol. 27. Toronto: University of Toronto Press, 1986.

———. *The Shipwreck. Ten Colloquies.* Ed. Craig Thompson. New York: Liberal Arts Press, 1957.

Fernández de Madrid, Alonso. *Prologue. Erasmo: El enchiridion, o manual del Caballero Cristiano.* Ed. Dámaso Alonso. Anejos of the *RFE,* no. 16. Madrid: S. Augirre, 1932.

Frías, Martín de. *El Tratado del modo y estilo que en la visitacion ordinaria se a de tener.* In idem, *Tractatus perutilis.* Burgos, 1528.

Gerson, Jean. *L'A.B.C. des simples gens. Opera omnia.* Ed. Msgr. Pierre Glorieux. 10 vols. Paris: Desclée, 1960. 7:408–9.

———. *De arte audiendi confessiones.* 8:10–17.

———. *Examen de conscience selon les péchés capitaux.* 7:393–400.

———. *Le miroir de l'âme.* 7:193–206.

———. *Modus brevis confitendi.* 9:84–86.

Kors, Alan C., and Edward Peters, eds. *Witchcraft in Europe, 1100–1700: A Documentary History.* Philadelphia: University of Pennsylvania Press, 1972.

Kramer, Heinrich, and Jacob Sprenger. *The Malleus maleficarum.* Trans. Rev. Montague Summers. New York: Dover, 1971.

Manuale pampilonense. Estella, 1561.

Mazzolini da Prierio, Silvestro. *Summa summarum quae Sylvestrina dicitur.* Strasburg, 1518.

McNeill, John T., and Helen Gamer. *Medieval Handbooks of Penance.* New York: Columbia University Press, 1938.

Medrano, Antonio de. *Proceso inquisitorial contra el bachiller Antonio de Medrano (Logroño, 1526–Calahorra, 1527).* Ed. Javier Pérez Escohotado. Logroño: Instituto de Estudios Riojanos, 1988.

Navarro, Gaspar. *Tribunal de superstición ladina.* Huesca, 1631.

Nebrija, Antonio de. "Epistola del Maestro de Nebrija a Cardenal." Trans. Roque Chabás. *RABM* 8 (1903): 493–96.

Paz y Mélia, Antonio, and Manuel Serrano y Sanz. "Actas originales de las congregaciones celebradas en 1527." *RABM* 6 (1902): 60–73.

Pedraza, Juan de, O.P. *Summa de casos de conciencia.* Alcalá, 1568.

Pérez de Ayala, Martín. *Breve compendio para bien examinar la consciencia en el juyzio de la confession sacramental.* Valencia, 1567.

Peters, Edward, ed. *Heresy and Authority in Medieval Europe.* Philadelphia: University of Pennsylvania Press, 1980.

Petrarca, Francesco. *Letters on Familiar Matters.* Trans. Aldo S. Bernardo. 3 vols. Baltimore: Johns Hopkins University Press, 1985.

Pinta Llorente, Miguel de la, O.S.A., and Jose María Palacio y de Palacio, eds. *Procesos inquisitoriales contra la familia judía de Juan Luís Vives, 1: Proceso contra Blanquina March, madre del humanista.* Madrid: Instituto Arias Montano, 1964.

Plessis d'Argentré, Charles du. *Collectio judiciorum de novis erroribus qui ab initio duodecimi saeculi . . . usque ad annum 1735 in ecclesia proscripti sunt et notati . . . .* 3 vols. Paris: A. Cailleau, 1725–36. Reprinted Brussels: Culture et Civilisation, 1963. Vol. 2, Part 1:53–77.

Quiñones, Juan de. *Tratado de las langostas.* Madrid, 1620.

Raymund of Penyafort. *Summa textu sacrorum canorum.* Paris, 1720.

Ruiz de Virués, Alonso. *Philippicae disputationes XX adversus Lutherana dogmata per Philippum Melanchthonem defensa.* Antwerp, 1541.

Stunica. (Diego López de Zuñiga.) *Annotationes contra Erasmum Roterodamum in defensionem tralationis* [sic] *Novi Testamenti.* Alcalá, 1520.

———. *Erasmi Roterodami blasphemiae et impietates.* Rome, 1522.

"Tabula librorum bibliotecae collegii Sancti Ildefonsi." *Inventario del archivo y biblioteca de San Ildefonso.* 1523. Libro 1091-F. AHN, Sección de Universidades.

Talavera, Hernando de. *Breve forma de confesar.* Ed. Miguel Mir. Nueva Biblioteca de Autores Españoles, vol. 1. Madrid: Casa Editorial Bailly, 1911.

Targum Neofiti 1: Exodus, and Targum Pseudo-Jonathan: Exodus. Trans. Robert Hayward and Michael Maher. *The Aramaic Bible,* vol. 2. Collegeville, Minn.: The Liturgical Press, 1987.

Thomas Aquinas. *Summa contra Gentiles.* Notre Dame, Ind.: University of Notre Dame Press, 1975.

———. *Summa theologica.* Trans. Fathers of the English Dominican Province. New York: Benziger Brothers, 1947–48.

Thomas of Chobham. *Summa confessorum.* Ed. F. Broomfield. Analecta mediaevalia Namurcensia, no. 25. Louvain: Éditions Nauwelaerts, 1960.

Vallejo, Juan de. *Memorial de la vida de fray Francisco Jiménez de Cisneros.* Ed. Antonio de la Torre y del Cerro. Madrid: Impr. Baily-Balliere, 1913.

Valtanás, Domingo de. *Apología sobre ciertas materias morales y Apología de la comunión frecuente.* Ed. Alvaro Huerga and Pedro Saínz Rodríguez. Barcelona: Juan Flors, 1963.

———. *Confessionario.* Burgos, 1555.

———. "De la residencia de los obispos." *Apologia y declaracion sobre ciertas materias morales en que hay opinion.* Seville, 1556.

Vergara, Juan. *Proceso* of the Inquisition tribunal at Toledo. Manuscript. AHN, Sección de la Inquisición de Toledo, Legajo 223, número 7.

Vetus testamentum graecum, juxta septuaginta interpretes, cum latina translatione. Trans. J. N. Jaeger. Paris: Editore Ambrosio Firmin-Didot, 1878.

Vio, Tomasso de (Cajetan). *Summula Caietani.* Lyon, 1581.

Secondary Sources

Ahlgren, Gillian T. W. "Francisca de los Apostoles: A Visionary Voice for Reform in Sixteenth-Century Toledo." In *Women in the Inquisition.* Ed. Mary E. Giles. Baltimore: Johns Hopkins University Press, 1998. Pp. 118–33.

Alberigo, Giuseppe. *I vescovi italiani al Concilio di Trento.* Florence: G. C. Sansoni, 1959.

Alcina, Juan F., and Francisco Rico. "Temas y problemas del renacimiento español." In *Siglos de oro: Renacimiento, primer suplemento.* Ed. Francisco López Estrada. *Historia y crítica de la literatura española, 2/1.* Ed. Francisco Rico. Barcelona: Editorial crítica, 1991. Pp. 5–25.

Antonio, Nicolas. *Bibliotheca hispana nova.* 2 vols. Madrid: J. de Ibarra, 1788.

Arce, Rafael. *San Juan de Avila y la Reforma de la Iglesia en España.* Madrid: Ediciones Rialp, 1970.

Asensio, Eugenio. "Cipriano de la Huerga, maestro de Fray Luis de León." In *Home-*

naje a Pedro Saínz Rodríguez, vol. 3: *Estudios historicos*. Madrid: Fundación Universitaria Española, 1986. Pp. 57–72.

———. "El erasmismo y las corrientes espirituales afines." *Revista de filología española* 36 (1952): 31–99.

———. "El Maestro Pedro de Orellana, minorita luterano: Versos y procesos." In *La Inquisición Española: Nueva visión, nuevos horizontes*. Ed. Joaquin Pérez. Madrid: Siglo Veintiuno Editores, 1978. Pp. 785–95.

———. "Tendencias y momentos en el humanismo español." In *Siglos de oro: Renacimiento, primer suplemento*. Ed. Francisco López Estrada. *Historia y crítica de la literatura española 2 / 1*. Ed. Francisco Rico. Barcelona: Edicion Crítica, 1991. Pp. 26–35.

Asso, Cecilia. *La teologia e la grammatica: La controversia tra Erasmo ed Edward Lee*. Florence: Olschki, 1993.

Avilés, Miguel. *Erasmo y la Inquisición (El libelo de Valladolid y la Apología de Erasmo contra los frailes españoles)*. Madrid: FUE, 1980.

———. "Erasmo y los teólogos españoles." In *El erasmismo en España*. Ed. Manuel Revuelta Sañudo and Ciriaco Morón Arroyo. Santander: Sociedad Menéndez y Pelayo, 1986. Pp. 175–94.

Barry, Jonathan. "Keith Thomas and the Problem of Witchcraft." In *Witchcraft in Early Modern Europe: Studies in Culture and Belief*. Ed. Jonathan Barry, Marianne Hester, and Gareth Roberts. Past and Present Publications. Cambridge: Cambridge University Press, 1996. Pp. 1–48.

Bataillon, Marcel. *Érasme et l'Espagne: Nouvelle édition en trois volumes*. Ed. Daniel Devoto and Charles Amiel. Travaux d'Humanisme et Renaissance, no. 250. 3 vols. Geneva: Librairie Droz S.A., 1991.

———. *Les Portugais contre Érasme à l'Assemblée Théologique de Valladolid (1527)*. Miscelânea de Estudos em honra de D. Carolina Michaëlis de Vasconcellos. Coimbra: Imprensa da Universidade, 1930.

Behringer, Wolfgang. "Witchcraft Studies in Austria, Germany, and Switzerland." In *Witchcraft in Early Modern Europe: Studies in Culture and Belief*. Ed. Jonathan Barry, Marianne Hester, and Gareth Roberts. Past and Present Publications. Cambridge: Cambridge University Press, 1996. Pp. 64–95.

Beinart, Haim. *Conversos on Trial: The Inquisition in Ciudad Real*. Hispania Judaica, vol. 3. Jerusalem: Magnes Press, Hebrew University, 1981.

Beltrán de Heredia, Vicente, O.P. *Historia de la reforma de la Provincia de España (1450–1550)*. Rome: ad S. Sabinae, 1939.

Bentley, Jerry. *Humanists and Holy Writ*. Princeton, N.J.: Princeton University Press, 1983.

———. "New Light on the Editing of the Complutensian New Testament." *Bibliothèque d'Humanisme et Renaissance* 42 (1980): 145–56.

———. "New Testament Scholarship at Louvain in the Early Sixteenth Century." *Studies in Medieval and Renaissance History*, n.s., 2 (1979): 51–79.

Bergin, Joseph. "Between Estate and Profession: The Catholic Parish Clergy of Early Modern Western Europe." In *Social Orders and Social Classes in Europe since 1500: Studies in Social Stratification.* Ed. M. L. Bush. London: Longman, 1992.

——. *The Making of the French Episcopate, 1589–1661.* New Haven, Conn.: Yale University Press, 1996.

Bilinkoff, Jodi. *The Avila of St. Teresa.* Ithaca, N.Y.: Cornell University Press, 1989.

——. "A Spanish Prophetess and Her Patrons: The Case of María de Santo Domingo." *Sixteenth Century Journal* 23 (1992): 21–35.

Bireley, Robert, S.J. "Two Works by Jean Delumeau." *Catholic Historical Review* 77 (1991): 78–88.

Bloomfield, Morton W. *The Seven Deadly Sins.* East Lansing: Michigan State University Press, 1967.

Bonilla y San Martín, Adolfo. "Erasmo y España (episódio de la historia del Renacimiento)." *Revue Hispanique* 17 (1907): 379–548.

——. *Juan Luís Vives y la Filosofía del Renacimiento.* Madrid: Imprenta del asilo de huérfanos de sagrado corazón de Jesús, 1903.

Bossy, John. *Christianity in the West, 1400–1700.* Oxford: Clarendon, 1985.

——. "The Counter-Reformation and the People of Catholic Europe." *Past and Present* 47 (1970): 51–70.

——. "Moral Arithmetic: Seven Sins into Ten Commandments." In *Conscience and Casuistry in Early Modern Europe.* Ed. Edmund Leites. Cambridge: Cambridge University Press, 1988. Pp. 214–31.

——. "The Social History of Confession in the Age of the Reformation." *Trans. Royal Historical Society,* 5th ser. 25 (1975): 21–38.

Boyle, Leonard E. *Pastoral Care, Clerical Education and Canon Law, 1200–1400.* London: Variorum Reprints, 1981.

——. "The Summa for Confessors as a Genre, and Its Religious Intent." In *The Pursuit of Holiness in Late Medieval and Renaissance Religion.* Ed. Charles Trinkaus with Heiko Oberman. Leiden: Brill, 1974.

Briggs, Robin. " 'Many Reasons Why': Witchcraft and the Problem of Multiple Explanation." In *Witchcraft in Early Modern Europe: Studies in Culture and Belief.* Ed. Jonathan Barry, Marianne Hester, and Gareth Roberts. Past and Present Publications. Cambridge: Cambridge University Press, 1996. Pp. 49–63.

——. *Witches and Neighbors.* New York: Viking, 1996.

Brown, R. E. *The "Sensus Plenior" of Sacred Scripture.* Baltimore: Johns Hopkins Press, 1955.

Bynum, Caroline Walker. *Holy Feast and Holy Fast: The Religious Significance of Food to Medieval Women.* Berkeley: University of California Press, 1987.

——. *The Resurrection of the Body in Western Christianity, 200–1330.* Lectures on the History of Religions, no. 15. New York: Columbia University Press, 1995.

Caballero, Fermín. *Alonso y Juan de Valdés. Conquenses illustres,* vol. 4. Madrid: Oficina tipográfica de hospicio, 1875.

Camporeale, Salvatore I. *Lorenzo Valla: umanesimo e teologia*. Florence: Instituto Nazionale di Studi sul Rinascimento, 1972.

Caro Baroja, Julio. "Witchcraft and Catholic Theology." In *Early Modern European Witchcraft: Centres and Peripheries*. Ed. Bengt Ankarloo and Gustav Henningsen. Oxford: Clarendon, 1990.

———. *The World of the Witches*. Chicago: University of Chicago Press, 1968.

Carruthers, Mary. *The Medieval Book of Memory*. Cambridge: Cambridge University Press, 1992.

Castillo, Ottavio di. "Humanism in Spain." In *Renaissance Humanism: Foundations, Forms, and Legacy*. Ed. Albert Rabil Jr. 3 vols. Philadelphia: University of Pennsylvania Press, 1988. 2:39–104.

———. *El humanismo castellano del siglo XV*. Valencia: Fernando Torres Editor, 1976.

Chomarat, Jacques. "Les *Annotationes* de Valla, celles d'Erasme et la grammaire." In *Histoire de l'exégèse au XVIe siècle*. Ed. Oliver Fatio and Pierre Fraenkel. Geneva: Librairie Droz S. A., 1978. Pp. 202–28.

Christian, William A., Jr. *Local Religion in Sixteenth-Century Spain*. Princeton, N.J.: Princeton University Press, 1981.

Cirac Estopañán, Sebastián. *Los procesos de hechicerías en la Inquisición de Castilla la Nueva*. Madrid: CSIC, 1942.

Clark, Stuart. *Thinking with Demons: The Idea of Witchcraft in Early Modern Europe*. Oxford: Oxford University Press, 1997.

Cochrane, Eric. "Counter Reformation or Tridentine Reformation? Italy in the Age of Carlo Borromeo." In *San Carlo Borromeo: Catholic Reform and Ecclesiastical Politics in the Second Half of the Sixteenth Century*. Ed. John M. Headley and John B. Tomaro. Washington, D.C.: Catholic University of America Press, 1988. Pp. 31–46.

———. *Italy 1530–1630*. Ed. Julius Kirshner. London: Longman, 1988.

Cohen, Jeremy. *The Friars and the Jews: The Evolution of Medieval Anti-Judaism*. Ithaca, N.Y.: Cornell University Press, 1982.

Cohn, Norman. *Europe's Inner Demons*. New York: Basic Books, 1975.

Coleman, Janet. *Ancient and Medieval Memories: Studies in the Reconstruction of the Past*. Cambridge: Cambridge University Press, 1992.

Contreni, John S. "Carolingian Biblical Studies." In *Carolingian Essays: Andrew W. Mellon Lectures in Early Christian Studies*. Ed. Uta-Renate Blumenthal. Washington, D.C.: Catholic University of America Press, 1983. Pp. 71–98.

Contreras, Jaime. *El Santo Oficio de la Inquisición en Galicia, 1560–1700*. Madrid: Akal, 1982.

Contreras, Jaime, and Gustav Henningsen. "Forty-Four Thousand Cases of the Spanish Inquisition (1540–1700): Analysis of a Historical Data Bank." In *The Inquisition in Early Modern Europe: Studies on Sources and Methods*. Ed. Gustav Henningsen and John Tedeschi. DeKalb: Northern Illinois University Press, 1986. Pp. 100–129.

Dedieu, Jean-Pierre. *L'Administration de la Foi: L'Inquisition de Tolède XVI–XVIII siècle*. Bibliothèque de la Casa de Velázquez, vol. 7. Madrid: Casa de Velázquez, 1989.

Delumeau, Jean. *Sin and Fear: The Emergence of a Western Guilt Culture, 13th–18th Centuries*. New York: St. Martin's, 1990.

Domínguez Ortíz, Antonio. *The Golden Age of Spain, 1516–1659*. Trans. James Casey. New York: Basic Books, 1971.

Douglas, Mary. *Purity and Danger*. London: Routledge & Kegan Paul, 1966.

Douglas, Richard M. *Jacopo Sadoleto, 1477–1547: Humanist and Reformer*. Cambridge, Mass.: Harvard University Press, 1959.

Dröge, Christoph. "Quia morem Hieronymi in transferendo cognovi . . . Les débuts de etudes hébraiques chez les humanistes italiens." In *L'Hebreu au temps de la Renaissance*. Ed. Ilana Zinguer. Leiden: Brill, 1992.

Duggan, Lawrence G. "Fear and Confession on the Eve of the Reformation." *Archiv für Reformationsgeschichte* 75 (1984): 153–75.

Edwards, John. *The Jews in Christian Europe 1400–1700*. Christianity and Society in the Modern World. London: Routledge, 1988.

Ehlers, Benjamin. "Christians and Muslims in Valencia: The Archbishop Juan de Ribera (1532–1611) and the Formation of a *Communitas Christiana*." Ph.D. Diss. Johns Hopkins University, 1999.

Eire, Carlos M. N. *From Madrid to Purgatory*. Cambridge: Cambridge University Press, 1995.

Elliott, J. H. *Imperial Spain 1469–1716*. Reprint. New York: New American Library, Meridian Books, 1977.

Evans, G. R. *The Language and Logic of the Bible: The Earlier Middle Ages*. Cambridge: Cambridge University Press, 1984.

———. *The Language and Logic of the Bible: The Road to Reformation*. Cambridge: Cambridge University Press, 1985.

Evenett, Henry Outram. *The Spirit of the Counter-Reformation*. Ed. John Bossy. Cambridge: Cambridge University Press, 1968.

Fernández-Armesto, Felipe. "Cardinal Cisneros as a Patron of Printing." In *God and Man in Medieval Spain: Essays in Honour of J. R. L. Highfield*. Ed. Derek W. Lomax and David MacKenzie. Warminster: Aris & Phillips, 1989. Pp. 149–68.

Fernández Marcos, Natalio, and Emilia Fernández Tejero. "Biblismo y erasmismo en la España del siglo xvi." In *Biblia y humanismo: Textos, talantes, y controversias del siglo XVI español*. Madrid: FUE, 1997. Pp. 15–26.

———. "Censura y exégesis: Las *Hypotyposeis* de Martín Martínez de Cantalapiedra." In *Biblia y humanismo: Textos, talantes, y controversias en el siglo XVI español*. Madrid: FUE, 1997. Pp. 27–33.

———. "El texto hebreo de la Biblia Poliglota Complutense." In *Biblia y humanismo: Textos, talantes, y controversias en el siglo XVI español*. Madrid: FUE, 1997. Pp. 209–18.

Fioravanti, Gianfranco. "L'apologetica anti-giudaica di Giannozzo Manetti." *Rinascimento* 23 (1983): 3–32.

Firpo, Massimo. *Tra alumbrados e "spirituali": Studi su Juan de Valdes e il valdesianesimo.* Studi e testi per la storia religiosa del Cinquecento, no. 3. Florence: Olschki, 1990.

Fox, Alistair, and John Guy, eds. *Reassessing the Henrician Age: Humanism, Politics and Reform, 1500–1550.* Oxford: Oxford University Press, 1986.

Fragnito, Gigliola. "Cultura umanistica e riforma religiosa: Il 'De officio boni viri ac probi episcopi' di Gasparo Contarini." *Studi veneziani* 11 (1969): 75–189.

Friedman, Jerome. *The Most Ancient Testimony: Sixteenth-Century Christian-Hebraica in the Age of Renaissance Nostalgia.* Athens: Ohio University Press, 1983.

Garin, Eugenio. *L'umanesimo italiano.* 6th ed. Bari: Laterza, 1975.

Geary, Patrick. *Living with the Dead in the Middle Ages.* Ithaca, N.Y.: Cornell University Press, 1994.

Giles, Mary E. "Francisca Hernández and the Sexuality of Religious Dissent." In *Women in the Inquisition.* Ed. Mary E. Giles. Baltimore: Johns Hopkins University Press, 1998. Pp. 75–97.

Gleason, Elisabeth. *Gasparo Contarini: Venice, Rome, and Reform.* Berkeley: University of California Press, 1993.

Grafton, Anthony. *Defenders of the Text.* Cambridge, Mass.: Harvard University Press, 1991.

Grafton, Anthony, and Ann Blair, eds. *The Transmission of Culture in Early Modern Europe.* Philadelphia: University of Pennsylvania Press, 1990.

Hailperin, Herman. *Rashi and the Christian Scholars.* Pittsburgh: Pittsburgh University Press, 1963.

Haliczer, Stephen. *Inquisition and Society in the Kingdom of Valencia, 1478–1834.* Berkeley: University of California Press, 1990.

———. *Sexuality in the Confessional: A Sacrament Profaned.* Studies in the History of Sexuality. Oxford: Oxford University Press, 1996.

Hallman, Barbara McClung. *Italian Cardinals, Reform, and the Church as Property.* Berkeley: University of California Press, 1985.

Hamilton, Alastair. *Heresy and Mysticism in Sixteenth-Century Spain: The Alumbrados.* Toronto: University of Toronto Press, 1992.

Henningsen, Gustav. *The Witches' Advocate.* Reno: University of Nevada Press, 1980.

Hobbs, R. Gerald. "Hebraica veritas and traditio apostolica: St. Paul and the Interpretation of the Psalms in the Sixteenth Century." In *The Bible in the Sixteenth Century.* Ed. David C. Steinmetz. Durham, N.C.: Duke University Press, 1990. Pp. 83–99.

Hoffmann, Manfred. *Rhetoric and Theology: The Hermeneutic of Erasmus.* Toronto: University of Toronto Press, 1994.

Homza, Lu Ann. "Erasmus as Hero, or Heretic? Spanish Humanism and the Valladolid Assembly of 1527." *Renaissance Quarterly* 50 (1997): 78–118.

Hudon, William V. *Marcello Cervini and Ecclesiastical Government in Tridentine Italy.* DeKalb: Northern Illinois University Press, 1992.

——."Religion and Society in Early Modern Italy: Old Questions, New Insights." *American Historical Review* 101 (1996): 783–804.

——, ed. *Theatine Spirituality: Selected Writings.* The Classics of Western Spirituality. New York: Paulist Press, 1996.

Jarrot, C. A. L. "Erasmus's *In principium erat Sermo:* A Controversial Translation." *Studies in Philology* 61 (1964): 35–40.

Jedin, Hubert. *A History of the Council of Trent.* 2 vols. St. Louis: Herder, 1961.

Jedin, Hubert, and Giuseppe Alberigo. *Il tipo ideale di vescovo secondo la riforma cattolica.* Brescia: Editrice Morcelliana, 1985.

Jones, G. Lloyd. *The Discovery of Hebrew in Tudor England: A Third Language.* Manchester: Manchester University Press, 1983.

de Jonge, H. J. "Erasmus and the comma Johanneum." *Ephemerides theologicae Lovanienses* 56 (1980): 381–89.

Kagan, Richard L. "Contando vecinos: El censo toledano de 1569." *Studia Historica / Historia Moderna* 12 (1994): 115–35.

——. *Lucrecia's Dreams: Politics and Prophecy in Sixteenth-Century Spain.* Berkeley: University of California Press, 1990.

——. "Prescott's Paradigm: American Historical Scholarship and the Decline of Spain." *American Historical Review* 101 (1996): 423–46.

——. *Students and Society in Early Modern Spain.* Baltimore: Johns Hopkins University Press, 1974.

Kamen, Henry. *The Phoenix and the Flame: Catalonia and the Counter-Reformation.* New Haven, Conn.: Yale University Press, 1993.

——. *The Spanish Inquisition: A Historical Revision.* New Haven, Conn.: Yale University Press, 1998.

Kaplan, Yosef, ed. *Jews and Conversos: Studies in Society and the Inquisition.* Eighth World Congress of Jewish Studies, 1981. Jerusalem: World Union of Jewish Studies, Magnes, 1985.

Kelley, Donald R. *Foundations of Modern Historical Scholarship.* New York: Columbia University Press, 1970.

Kettering, Sharon. *Patrons, Brokers, and Clients in Seventeenth-Century France.* Oxford: Oxford University Press, 1986.

Kristeller, Paul Oskar. *Renaissance Thought and Its Sources.* New York: Columbia University Press, 1979.

——. *Studies in Renaissance Thought and Letters.* 2 vols. Rome: Edizioni di Storia e Letteratura, 1985.

Kuehn, Thomas. "Reading Microhistory: The Example of Giovanni and Lusanna." *Journal of Modern History* 61 (1989): 512–34.

Larner, Christine. *Enemies of God: The Witch-Hunt in Scotland.* Baltimore: Johns Hopkins University Press, 1981.

Lásperas, Jean Michel. "La librería del doctor Juan de Vergara." *RABM* 79 (1976): 337–59.

Lea, Henry Charles. *History of the Inquisition of Spain.* 4 vols. New York: American Scholar Publications, 1966.

Levack, Brian. "State-Building and Witch Hunting in Early Modern Europe." In *Witchcraft in Early Modern Europe: Studies in Culture and Belief.* Ed. Jonathan Barry, Marianne Hester, and Gareth Roberts. Past and Present Publications. Cambridge: Cambridge University Press, 1996. Pp. 96–118.

———. *The Witch-Hunt in Early Modern Europe.* 2nd ed. New York: Longman, 1995.

Llamas, José. "Documental inédito de exegesis rabinica." *Sefarad* 6 (1946): 289–311.

———. "Los manuscritos hebreos de El Escorial." *Sefarad* 1 (1941): 7–43.

Llorca, Bernardino, S.J. *La inquisición española y los alumbrados (1509–1667).* Bibliotheca Salmanticensis, no. 32. Salamanca: Universidad Pontificia de Salamanca, 1980.

Longhurst, John E. "Alumbrados, erasmistas y luteranos en el proceso de Juan de Vergara." *CHE* 27 (1957): 99–163; 28 (1958): 102–65; 29–30 (1959): 266–92; 31–32 (1960): 322–56; 35–36 (1962): 337–53; 37–38 (1963): 356–71.

———. *Erasmus and the Spanish Inquisition, the Case of Juan de Valdés.* Albuquerque: University of New Mexico Press, 1950.

Lualdi, Katharine J. "Self and Society: Sacramental Confession and Parish Worship in Late Medieval and Reformation France." Ph.D. Diss. University of Pennsylvania, 1996.

Lubac, Henri du. *Exégèse médiévale: Les quatre sens de l'écriture.* 4 vols. Paris: Aubier, 1959–64.

Lynch, John. *Spain under the Habsburgs.* 2 vols. 2nd ed. Oxford: Basil Blackwell, 1981.

Macfarlane, Alan. *Witchcraft in Tudor and Stuart England: A Regional and Comparative Study.* New York: Harper & Row, 1970.

Mansfield, Mary C. *The Humiliation of Sinners: Public Penance in Thirteenth-Century France.* Ithaca, N.Y.: Cornell University Press, 1995.

Márquez, Antonio. *Los Alumbrados, Orígenes y Filosofía 1525–1559.* Madrid: Taurus, 1972.

Martín, Melquiades Andres. *La teología española en el siglo XVI.* 2 vols. Madrid: Editorial Católica, 1976.

Martin, Ruth. *Witchcraft and the Inquisition in Venice, 1550–1650.* London: Basil Blackwell, 1989.

Martínez Gil, Fernando. *La ciudad inquieta. Toledo comunera, 1520–1522.* Toledo: Diputación provincial de Toledo, 1993.

Mathers, S. M. I. *The Key of Solomon the King (Clavicula Salomonis).* New York: Samuel Weiser, 1974.

McConica, James. *Erasmus.* Past Masters. Oxford: Oxford University Press, 1991.

Menéndez y Pelayo, Marcelino. *Historia de los heterodoxos españoles.* Ed. Enrique Sánchez Reyes. 4 vols. 2nd ed. Madrid: CSIC, 1963.

Michaud-Quantin, Pierre. "A propos des premières *Summae confessorum.*" *Recherches de theologie ancienne et moderne* 26 (1959): 265–69.

Midelfort, H. C. Erik. "Social History and Biblical Exegesis: Community, Family, and Witchcraft in Sixteenth-Century Germany." In *The Bible in the Sixteenth Century*. Ed. David C. Steinmetz. Durham, N.C.: Duke University Press, 1990. Pp. 7–20.

——. "Witch Hunting and the Domino Theory." In *Religion and the People, 800–1700*. Ed. James Obelkevich. Chapel Hill: University of North Carolina Press, 1979. Pp. 277–88.

Molho, Anthony. "Cosimo de'Medici: Pater Patriae or Padrino?" *Stanford Italian Review* 1 (1979): 5–33.

Monter, E. William. *Frontiers of Heresy: The Spanish Inquisition from the Basque Lands to Sicily*. Cambridge: Cambridge University Press, 1990.

Moore, R. I. *The Formation of a Persecuting Society: Power and Deviance in Western Europe, 950–1250*. Oxford: Oxford University Press, 1987.

Morocho Gayo, Gaspar. "Humanismo y filología poligráfica en Cipriano de la Huerga. Su encuentro con fray Luis de León." *Ciudad de Dios* 204 (1991): 863–914.

Nalle, Sara T. *God in La Mancha*. Baltimore: Johns Hopkins University Press, 1992.

——. "Literacy and Culture in Early Modern Castile." *Past and Present* 125 (1989): 65–96.

Nauert, Charles G., Jr. "The Clash of Humanists and Scholastics: An Approach to Pre-Reformation Controversies." *Sixteenth Century Journal* 4 (1973): 1–18.

——. *Humanism and the Culture of Renaissance Europe*. Cambridge: Cambridge University Press, 1995.

——. "Humanism as Method: Roots of Conflict with the Scholastics." *Sixteenth Century Journal* 29, no. 2 (1998): 427–38.

Navarro Rodríguez, Hipólito. "Una obra inédita de Fray Luis de León: *Expositio in Genesim* (Codex 83, biblioteca de la Catedral de Pamplona)." *Scripta theologica* 16 (1984): 573–78.

Netanyahu, Benzion. *The Origins of the Inquisition in Fifteenth-Century Spain*. New York: Random House, 1995.

Olin, John C. "The Jesuits, Humanism, and History." In *Erasmus, Utopia and the Jesuits*. New York: Fordham University Press, 1994.

——. *Six Essays on Erasmus*. New York: Fordham University Press, 1979.

O'Malley, John W. "Was Ignatius Loyola a Church Reformer? How to Look at Early Modern Catholicism." *Catholic Historical Review* 77 (1991): 177–93.

O'Rourke, Marjorie Boyle. *Erasmus on Language and Method in Theology*. Toronto: University of Toronto Press, 1977.

Overfield, James H. *Humanism and Scholasticism in Late Medieval Germany*. Princeton, N.J.: Princeton University Press, 1984.

Ozment, Steven. *The Reformation in the Cities*. New Haven, Conn.: Yale University Press, 1975.

Payne, J. B. "Toward the Hermeneutics of Erasmus." In *Scrinium erasmianum*. Ed. J. Coppens. 2 vols. Leiden: Brill, 1969. 2:13–49.

Pérez, Joseph. *El siglo de fray Luis de León: Salamanca y el Renacimiento.* Salamanca: Universidad de Salamanca, 1991.

Peters, Edward. *The Magician, the Witch, and the Law.* Philadelphia: University of Pennsylvania Press, 1978.

———. *Torture.* Philadelphia: University of Pennsylvania Press, 1987.

Pettas, William. *A Sixteenth-Century Spanish Bookstore: The Inventory of Juan de Junta.* Transactions of the American Philosophical Society, Vol. 85, Part 1. Philadelphia: American Philosophical Society, 1995.

Pinta Llorente, Miguel de la, O.S.A. *El erasmismo del Dr. Juan de Vergara y otras interpretaciones.* Madrid: Sánchez, 1945.

———. *Proceso criminal contra el hebraísta salmantino Martín Martínez de Cantalapiedra.* Madrid: Instituto Arias Montano, 1946.

Poschmann, Bernhard. *Penance and the Anointing of the Sick.* Trans. F. Courtney. The Herder History of Dogma. London: Herder and Herder, 1968.

Prosperi, Adriano. *Tra evangelismo e controriforma: Gian Matteo Giberti (1495–1543).* Rome: Edizioni di Storia e Letteratura, 1969.

Rabil, Albert, Jr., ed. *Renaissance Humanism: Foundations, Forms, and Legacy.* 3 vols. Philadelphia: University of Pennsylvania Press, 1988.

Redondo, Augustín. "Luther et l'Espagne de 1520–1536." *Mélanges de la Casa de Velázquez* 1 (1965): 77–86.

Reeves, Marjorie. "The Bible and Literary Authorship in the Middle Ages." In *Reading the Text: Biblical Criticism and Literary Theory.* Ed. Stephen Prickett. Oxford: Basil Blackwell, 1991. Pp. 12–63.

Reguera, Iñaki. *La inquisición española en el país vasco (el tribunal de Calahorra, 1513–1570).* Pamplona: Editorial Txertoa, 1984.

Reinhard, Wolfgang. "Reformation, Counter-Reformation, and the Early Modern State: A Reassessment." *Catholic Historical Review* 75 (1989): 383–404.

Reynolds, L. D., and N. G. Wilson. *Scribes and Scholars: A Guide to the Transmission of Greek and Latin Literature.* 2nd ed. Oxford: Clarendon, 1974.

Rice, Eugene F., Jr. "John Colet and the Annihilation of the Natural." *Harvard Theological Review* 45 (1952): 141–63.

———. *St. Jerome in the Renaissance.* Baltimore: Johns Hopkins University Press, 1985.

Rico, Francisco. *Nebrija frente a los bárbaros.* Salamanca: Universidad de Salamanca, 1978.

———. *El sueño del humanismo, de Petrarca a Erasmo.* Madrid: Alianza Universal, 1993.

Rico, Mariano Revilla. *La Poliglota de Alcalá.* Madrid: Imprenta helénica, 1917.

Rojo Vega, Anastasio. "Un sondeo acerca de la capacidad de lectura y escritura en Valladolid, 1550–1575." *Signo. Revista de historia de la cultura escrita* 3 (1996): 25–40.

Roper, Lyndal. *Oedipus and the Devil.* London: Routledge, 1994.

Rotsaert, Marc. "Les premieres contacts de saint Ignace avec l'érasmisme espagnol." *Revue d'histoire de la spiritualité* 49 (1973): 443–64.

Rueda, Jose López. *Los helenístas españoles del siglo XVI.* Madrid: Instituto "Antonio de Nebrija," 1973.

Rummel, Erika. *Erasmus and His Catholic Critics.* 2 vols. Nieuwkoop: De Graaf, 1989.

——. *Erasmus's Annotations on the New Testament: From Philologist to Theologian.* Toronto: University of Toronto Press, 1986.

——. *The Humanist-Scholastic Debate in the Renaissance and Reformation.* Cambridge, Mass.: Harvard University Press, 1995.

Rusconi, Roberto. "Manuali Milanesi di confessione editi tra il 1474 ed il 1523." *Archivum Franciscanum Historicum* 65 (1972): 107–56.

Seidel Menchi, Silvana. *Erasmo in Italia 1520–1580.* Torino: Bollati Boringhieri, 1987.

Seigel, Jerrold E. *Rhetoric and Philosophy in Renaissance Humanism.* Princeton, N.J.: Princeton University Press, 1968.

Selke, Angela. "El caso del Bachiller Antonio de Medrano, iluminado epicúreo del siglo xvi." *BH* 58 (1956): 393–420.

——. *The Conversos of Majorca: Life and Death in a Crypto-Jewish Community in XVII Century Spain.* Hispania Judaica, vol. 5. Jerusalem: Magnes Press, Hebrew University, 1986.

——. *El Santo Oficio de la Inquisición: Proceso de Dr. Francisco Ortiz (1529–1532).* Madrid: Ediciones Guadarrama, 1968.

——. "Vida y muerte de Juan López de Celain." *BH* 62 (1960): 136–62.

Shuger, Debora Kuller. *The Renaissance Bible: Scholarship, Sacrifice, and Subjectivity.* Berkeley: University of California Press, 1994.

Sicroff, Albert A. *Les controverses des statuts de "pureté de sang" en Espagne du XV au XVII siècle.* Paris: Didier, 1960.

Skinner, Quentin. "Meaning and Understanding in the History of Ideas." *History and Theory* 7 (1969): 3–53.

Smalley, Beryl. *The Gospels in the Schools, 1100–1280.* London: Hambledon, 1985.

——. *The Study of the Bible in the Middle Ages.* Oxford: Basil Blackwell, 1952.

Spicq, Ceslas. *Esquisse d'une histoire de l'exégèse latine du moyen âge.* Paris: J. Vrin, 1944.

Stinger, Charles. *Humanism and the Church Fathers: Ambrogio Traversari (1386–1439) and Christian Antiquity in the Italian Renaissance.* Albany: State University of New York Press, 1977.

Teetaert, Amédée, O. Cap. "La 'Summa de poenitentia' de Saint Raymond de Penyafort." *Ephemerides theologicae Lovanienses* 5 (1928): 49–72.

Tentler, Thomas. *Sin and Confession on the Eve of the Reformation.* Princeton, N.J.: Princeton University Press, 1977.

Thomas, Keith. *Religion and the Decline of Magic.* London: Charles Scribner, 1971.

Thompson, Colin. *The Strife of Tongues: Fray Luis de León and the Golden Age of Spain.* Cambridge: Cambridge University Press, 1988.

Tracy, James D. "Erasmus and the Arians: Remarks on the *Consensus Ecclesiae.*" *Catholic Historical Review* 67 (1981): 1–10.

Villanueva, Joaquín Pérez, and Bartolomé Escandell Bonet. *Historia de la Inquisición en España y América*. 2 vols. Madrid: Biblioteca de Autores Españoles, 1984.

Vincent, Bernard. "Un espacio de exclusión: La cárcel inquisitorial en el siglo XVI." In *Minorías y marginados en la España del siglo XVI*. Granada: Diputación provincial de Granada, 1987.

Vogel, Cyrille. *Le pécheur et la pénitence dans l'eglise ancienne*. Paris: Les éditions du Cerf, 1966.

Walker, D. P. *Spiritual and Demonic Magic from Ficino to Campanella*. Notre Dame, Ind.: University of Notre Dame Press, 1975.

Walsh, Katherine, and Diane Wood, eds. *The Bible in the Medieval World*. Oxford: Basil Blackwell, 1985.

Weber, Alison. "Between Ecstasy and Exorcism: Religious Negotiation in Sixteenth-Century Spain." *Journal of Medieval and Renaissance Studies* 23 (1993): 221–34.

Weiss, Roberto. *The Renaissance Discovery of Classical Antiquity*. Oxford: Oxford University Press, 1969.

Whinnom, Keith. "The Problem of the 'Best-Seller' in Spanish Golden-Age Literature." *Bulletin of Hispanic Studies* 57 (1980): 189–98.

Index

Index